# Action
# Writing

# Action Writing

## Jack Kerouac's Wild Form

Michael Hrebeniak

Southern Illinois University Press / *Carbondale*

Library of Congress Cataloging-in-Publication Data
Hrebeniak, Michael, 1965–
Action writing : Jack Kerouac's wild form / Michael
Hrebeniak.
    p. cm.
Includes bibliographical references and index.
1. Kerouac, Jack, 1922–1969—Criticism and interpretation.
2. Literary form—History—20th century. 3. Modernism
(Literature)—United States. 4. Beat generation in literature.
I. Title.
PS3521.E735Z678  2006
813'.54—dc22
ISBN-13: 978-0-8093-2694-5 (cloth : alk. paper)
ISBN-10: 0-8093-2694-9 (cloth : alk. paper)        2005027798

Printed on recycled paper. ♻

To Eric Mottram
1924–95
ideal friend • poet • teacher
whose constellational energy seeded this book


to be wise    to restore the earth
against priests of science
psychologists of money
. . .
          let the boundary
between yourself and fire
disappear
. . .
hope is that all created life be rescued
from tyranny      decay sloughed for a share
in magnificence      hoof thunder      silence of
pines and birches across the taiga

—Eric Mottram, *Elegy 4: Against Tyranny* (1975)

# Contents

# Acknowledgments

From the first place of intimacy, I wish to thank—for inspiration, for suste-nance—my wife, Denise; our first son, Louis, who slept on my lap through the mornings of his first year as I began typing the manuscript; and our second son, Ambrose, who did likewise during its completion. I owe much to the work and presence of five members of the Dionysian Order: Fielding Dawson, Jack Micheline, Jeff Nuttall, John Stevens, and Val Wilmer, instigators of the drama across many forms, and all—bar Val, who continues to thrive—taken too soon. My gratitude also extends to Karl Kageff, Barb Martin, Carol Burns, Julie Bush, and their colleagues at Southern Illinois University Press: ever patient and supportive. I must acknowledge, too, the backing of my parents, Beryl and Paul, who encouraged me to seek an education denied to members of their generation's social standing. It's a lasting shame that recent British governments, possessed by Blake's demon pathology Urizen, and knowing only petty utility, have reverted to a situation where only the wealthy can encounter art's promise of fabulous life, an awakening that's properly the right of all. Here's to a more tender, spirited, and enlightened future . . .

# Abbreviations

The following abbreviations are used throughout for cited works by Jack Kerouac:

| | |
|---|---|
| *BB* | *Book of Blues* |
| *BD* | *Book of Dreams* |
| *BS* | *Big Sur* |
| *DA* | *Desolation Angels* |
| *DB* | *The Dharma Bums* |
| *DS* | *Doctor Sax* |
| *GB* | *Good Blonde & Others* |
| *LT* | *Lonesome Traveler* |
| *MC* | *Maggie Cassidy* |
| *MCB* | *Mexico City Blues* |
| *OAM* | *Old Angel Midnight* |
| *OTR* | *On the Road* |
| *SD* | *Some of the Dharma* |
| *SGE* | *The Scripture of the Golden Eternity* |
| *SIP* | *Satori in Paris* |
| *SL, I* | *Selected Letters, 1940–1956* |
| *SL, II* | *Selected Letters, 1957–1969* |
| *SP* | *Scattered Poems* |
| *SU* | *The Subterraneans* |
| *TS* | *Tristessa* |
| *VC* | *Visions of Cody* |
| *VD* | *Vanity of Duluoz* |
| *VG* | *Visions of Gerard* |

# Action
# Writing

# Introduction

wo proposals drive this book: that the arts associated with New York, San Francisco, and Black Mountain College—late, possibly final, centers of Bohemian community—spur the great postwar consciousness shift in America and that the work of Jack Kerouac embodies this "projective" gestalt, as named by Charles Olson, and shares its values.

It has long occurred to me that there is far more to this unevenly regarded writer than the commodification of his work into salable Beat style would have us believe. I would argue that at its most confident, Kerouac's fiction and verse—he joyously blurs distinctions between the two ("all my books are as it were poetry sheeted in narrative steel" [*SL, II* 17])—have a revolutionary social purpose at the deepest level of form in the context of the Cold War 1950s. As such they could be classed as countercultural, if that term were not an anathema; "culture" implies locale, habitat, nourishment, and growth, which, in practice, is aberrant and heterogeneous. As an insistently singular imposition, the State is perhaps the counterculture.

This is by no means an exhaustive study of Kerouac's fictions. A number of writers have been there before, and I honor the pioneering work of Ann Charters, Gerald Nicosia, Timothy Hunt, Regina Weinreich, James T. Jones, Ben Giamo, and others. As a consequence, the organization of narrative around chronological survey—Kerouac's swirling meditation on memory and the recirculation of events and the sizable gap between composition and publication render historicity problematic—makes way for a gathering of aesthetic themes grounded in the experience of his life-affirming writing. I've located these within a twentieth-century speculative continuum, across not only literature but also other fields such as music and painting, for too few bridges have been built between the arts. More than bare histories of genre, an insight into ideas simultaneously arising across forms that bear striking similarities to one another can call into consciousness the attitudes, tendencies, and meanings that shape a period. This is particularly vital when considering Kerouac's work, which is born of a transdisciplinary poetics. By giving space to Charlie Parker and Jackson Pollock as well as to Walt Whitman and William Carlos Williams, I have aimed to release the radicalism within texts that refuse to yield definitive meaning in traditional literary terms.

At the core of Kerouac's work is a romantic test of experience for the creative man against the narrowing horizons of public America, as its corporate power fattens across international markets. Kerouac launches his career at midcentury, and it accelerates through the time of J. Edgar Hoover's industry of lawless demonization; of Senator McCarthy's "One Communist Too Many!" harangue to the 1952 Republican Convention, marked by his compulsive giggling; of PR technician Edward Bernays's baleful use of mass psychology to "engineer the consent" of citizens to the higher truth that the interests of business and America were indivisible ("those who manipulate this unseen mechanism of society," he wrote honestly in *Propaganda* in 1928, "constitute an invisible government which is the true ruling power of our country" [3]); of the McCarran-Walter Act's political means test for any foreigner wishing to visit the country; and of Congressman Dondero's coupling of innovation to treason in his tirade to the House of Representatives in 1949 ("[Art] is a weapon in the hands of a soldier in the revolution against any form of government or system other than Communism").

More obviously there was the threat of imminent nuclear annihilation supported by a techno-logical positivism, disastrous wars in east Asia, and a stream of enemies to complement the Soviet and Islamic blocs, including Guatemala: subjected to a display invasion and the overthrow of its government on behalf of United Foods' banana division in 1954 (spin courtesy of Bernays). While corporations at the kernel of Washington's imperial seat—an order dubbed the "military-industrial complex" by Eisenhower—sponsored these foreign interventions, domestically they generated the profound change in mass self-definition that accompanied suburban ambitions for luxury and leisure. Whereas in 1925 President Coolidge declared, "The business of the American people is business," by the early 1950s, writes Noam Chomsky,

> twenty-million people a week were watching business-sponsored films. The entertainment industry was enlisted for the cause, portraying unions as the enemy, the outsider disrupting the "harmony" of "the American way of life" and otherwise helping to "indoctrinate citizens

with the capitalist story." . . . Every aspect of social life was targeted and permeated—schools and universities, churches, even recreational programs. By 1954, business propaganda in public schools reached half the amount spent on textbooks. (qtd. in Pilger 539)

The accompanying reinvigoration of belief in upward personal mobility would survive Seymour Martin Lipset and Reinhard Bendix's 1959 study, *Social Mobility in Industrial Society*, which portrayed a developing aristocracy of the rich and serfdom of the poor and the contaminations of State morality with finance typified by Howard Hughes's contracts with the Defense Department and dramatized by Arthur Miller in *All My Sons*. Indeed, Max Weber's argument that the Puritan ethic—industry, restraint, asceticism, guilt—lubricated the engines of capitalism would mark a bygone machine age by the 1950s. The new America demanded not thrift but profligacy, an ethic of consumption, not production. Long before William Burroughs diagnosed the parasitical basis of market economics in *The Naked Lunch*, Wall Street banker Paul Maser had recognized the need to "shift America from a 'needs' to a 'desires' culture. People must be trained to desire; to want new things even before the old has been entirely consumed. We must shape a new mentality in America. Man's desires must overshadow his needs" (qtd. in Ewen 142). Charles Olson discussed the effects of what would soon become a global condition in "Human Universe":

> The notion of fun comes to displace work as what we are here for. Spectatorism crowds out participation as the condition of the culture. And bonuses and prizes are the rewards of labor contrived by the monopolies of business and government to protect themselves from the advancement in position of able men or that old assertion of an inventive man, his own shop. All individual energy and ingenuity is bought off—at a suggestion box or the cinema. Passivity conquers all. Even war and peace die (to be displaced by world government?) and man reverts to only two of his components, inertia and gas.
>
> It is easy to phrase, too easy, and we have had enough of bright description. To say that in America the goods are as the fruits, and the people as the goods, all glistening but tasteless, accomplishes nothing in itself, for the overwhelming fact is, that the rest of the world wants nothing but to be the same. Value is perishing from the earth because no one cares to fight down to it beneath the glowing surfaces so attractive to all. (*Collected* 159–60)

Kerouac's work inevitably moves within these circumstances, which far transcend relegation to background. The term "Beat" would project an alternative America during the civil rights and Asian war years, a counter to philistinism and paranoia and part of an ongoing inquiry into the construction of nationhood. Like Mark Twain, Kerouac forges an empirical American history, from the Depression 1930s through a sequence of global military interventions to the surfacing of international youth protest movements and their assimilation into mass culture. Driven by the ecstatic model of bebop, the ensuing Duluoz Legend celebrates the principles of perpetual renewal upon which the Constitution was built, resisting that "One-Dimensional" America described by Herbert Marcuse, a nation wasteful of resources and possibilities and a bastion of counterrevolution far beyond its own hemisphere, which, in turn, becomes susceptible to Kerouac's transforming impulse. The growing realization that the production-consumption cycle linked affluent US society with the Soviet system and similarly failed to service human needs—"America vs. Russia is a war / between 2 kinds of lip-service," Kerouac notes in 1954 (*SD* 172)—underscores this desire to recover the cultural confidence defined by Ivan Illich as "conviviality":

> I choose the term "conviviality" to designate the opposite of industrial productivity. I intend it to mean autonomous and creative intercourse among persons, and the intercourse of persons with their environment: and this in contrast with the conditioned responses of persons to the demands made upon them by others, and by a man-made environment. I consider conviviality to be individual freedom realized in personal independence and, as such, an intrinsic ethical value. I believe that, in any society, as conviviality is reduced below a certain level, no amount of industrial productivity can effectively satisfy the needs it creates among society's members. (11)

Kerouac's search for conviviality means immersion in a generous field of experience, moving beyond the familiar in a multiplication of personality, both real and imagined. The rhetoric of these narratives is vigorously performative: an act of making that abandons patterns of "re-cognition" or any enforced correspondence with given "truths." How he attains and then loses this mastery forms the core inquiry of this book. For while much of his early to mid-period work preempts the loosening of codes and relations between classes, races, and genders that marked 1960s America, Kerouac would cut a tragic figure in his final decade. As Timothy Leary observed after failing to palm off psilocybin-induced instant enlightenment on him, "the Catholic carouser" and "old-style Bohemian without a hippie bone in his body . . . opened the neural doors to the future, looked ahead, and didn't see his place in it. Not for him the utopian pluralist optimism of the sixties" (206).

Having enjoyed "the wildest time of all time" from "all that ROAD noise" (*SL, II* 95) that accompanied the discharge of his most famous book into America in September 1957, Kerouac rapidly tires of the duplicitous whirl of attention ("my god every day, every night, no rest, no solitude, no reflection, no staring at the ceiling or clouds possible anymore" [*SL, II* 160]) and is demoralized by critical spite, the overarching theme of his later letters. "Daily the indictment grows," he complains in December of that year, warning Philip Whalen that "fame is a bad bit. . . . Watch out for yr future" (*SL, II* 93, 96).

The subsequent mortification gains potency through his agony as hero-victim, echoing Pollock's corrosive entrance into celebrity after a 1949 feature in *Life* mockingly asked, "Is he America's greatest Living Artist?" "I have to constantly drink to put up with nervous appointments with everybody in sight," Kerouac tells his agent,

> and vast nervous parties where everybody is staring at me and fulfilling their preconceptions of me as a drunken fool. And the mail! whether pro or con it has a frightening intensity that makes me wonder if they simply dont want somebody to crucify or tear apart limb from limb like some sacrificial hero in their own minds. (*SL, II* 180)

The pitching of a working-class conservative training against Bohemian euphoria resolves in a steady creative dip: a manifestation of personal insecurity within a culture of dragging decay. "ROAD was learned in my Springtime," Kerouac records in his journal,

> & prepared incredible work of summer (CODY, SAX, MAGGIE, SUBS, GERARD, ANGELS etc.)—Then came Autumn, to which BIG SUR belongs & all my present unhappy exhaustion of harvest time—For next 10 years I'll be harvesting & winnowing chaffs but with no great mindless purpose of summer— (*SL, II* 355)

By 1965 on his own admission, Kerouac had turned into "an orating drunken 'author'" (qtd. in C. Cassady 381). Having become the dancing bear of media sycophants who mold taste ("Wasn't there a time when American writers were left alone by personality mongers and publicity monsters?" [*SL, II* 93]), he retraces the narrative of demolition through discovery described in Hemingway's *A Movable Feast*, published in the year of Kerouac's Big Sur breakdown. Learning too late that "you kill yourself to get to the grave before you even die, and the name of that grave is 'success,' the name of that grave is hullaballoo boomboom horseshit" (*VD* 23), like Hemingway, whose death he repeatedly alludes to in *Desolation Angels*, he ends up "fat, dejected, ashamed, bored, pestered & shot. I must get a cabin or die" (*SL, II* 235). The author fades in 1969, as Seymour Krim notes, "lonely and isolated like a hunched old man at only [47] with a comicstrip beer belly and faded, gross, ex-good looks, full of slack-lipped mutterings about the New York Jewish literary Mafia" (*Views* 201).

And so, unlike John McNeil Whistler, his Lowell-born predecessor and Ezra Pound's "first great American," Kerouac never "won through," as his measured disintegration and "prodigal returns" to deep-seated conflicts testify. Nevertheless, the Duluoz Legend shares the same principle of risk opened by that progenitor, who "[t]ested and pried and worked in many fashions" with no "one style from birth, but tried and pried / And stretched and tampered with the media," bearing "the brunt of our America" and wrenching "her impulse into art" (Pound, *Personae* 235). As an Ishmael figure of outward who fears violence and dissipation if he stays home (Melville's intimations at the opening of *Moby Dick*), Kerouac's passages across the land take their place among the mythic geographies of America: Sherwood Anderson's Winesburg, Ohio; Thomas Wolfe's Asheville; William Saroyan's Fresno; Nathaniel Hawthorne's Salem; and the Long Island Sound at the conclusion of *The Great Gatsby*—that "fresh green breast of the new world" that "for the last time in history" had been commensurate to man's "capacity for wonder" (171).

The resulting novels situate language at an existential point of discovery, though far from Albert Camus and Jean-Paul Sartre's despair over the failure to fit the world to closed orders of logic and classification, which only enhance the dilemma of life itself. Like Olson, Kerouac insists on that need to return language to its place in experience—

> There are no hierarchies, no infinite, no such many as mass,
>     there are only
> eyes in all heads,
> to be looked out of
>
>                                         (Olson, *Maximus* 33)

—where the act of writing itself can become the method of evaluating and countering the State's megalomania and messianism derived from its origins. In a twenty-first-century environment defined by the grand bureaucracy of corporate power and its complement of theocratic death cults, Judeo-Christian as well as Islamic, this need is more pronounced than ever.

# The Beat Scene

Tradition has been broken, yet there is no new standard to
affirm.
—Paul Goodman, "Growing Up Absurd"

Everywhere the Beat Generation seems occupied with the
feverish production of answers—some of them frightening,
some of them foolish—to a single question: how are we to live?
—John Clellon Holmes, "The Philosophy of the
Beat Generation"

. . . a vision [of] crazy illuminated hipsters suddenly rising and
roaming America, serious, curious, bumming and hitchhiking
everywhere, ragged, beatific, beautiful in a graceful new way—
a vision gleaned from the way we had heard the word *beat*
spoken on street corners on Times Square and in the Village,
in other cities in downtown-city-night of postwar America—
*beat,* meaning down and out but full of intense conviction.
We'd even heard old 1910 Daddy Hipsters of the streets speak
the word that way, with a melancholy sneer. It never meant
juvenile delinquents; it meant characters of special spirituality
who didn't gang up but were solitary Bartlebies staring out the
dead wall window of our civilization.
—Jack Kerouac, "Aftermath: The Philosophy of the Beat
Generation"

n June 1949, between early drafts of *On the Road* and his first cross-na-
tion trips with Neal Cassady, Jack Kerouac sets down the Beat impetus
to Allen Ginsberg. The unpublished writer, not yet twenty-eight, had
arrived, and the inquiry is on:

I believe there will be a Judgment Day, but not for men . . . for *society*. Society is a mistake. . . . It is evil. It will fall. Men have to do what they want. It has all got out of hand—began when fools left the covered wagons in 1848 and rode madly to California for Gold, leaving their families behind. And of course, there ain't enough gold for all, even if gold were the thing. . . . Thoreau was right; Jesus was right. It's all wrong and I denounce it and it can all go to hell. I don't believe in this society; but I believe in man, like Mann. . . . I don't even believe in education any more. . . . "Culture" (anthropologically) is the rigama-role surrounding what poor men have to do to eat, anywhere. History is people doing what their leaders tell them; and not doing what their prophets tell them. Life is that which gives you desires, but no rights for the fulfillment of desires. It is all pretty mean—but you can still do what you want, and what you want is right, when you want honestly. Wanting money is wanting the dishonesty of wanting a servant. Money hates us, like a servant; because it is false. Henry Miller was right; Bur-roughs was right. Roll your own, I say. (SL, I 193–94)

Writing eight years before *On the Road* would galvanize public attention, Kerouac records the sacrificial locale of an American era, playing out the theme of disillusioned survival in the face of entrapment that previously resonated for Henry Miller, Jack London, John Dos Passos, and Ernest Hemingway, where "no man alone ain't got no bloody fucking chance" (*To Have* 165). Now the advent of Ike, McCarthyism, Korea, Madison Avenue, nuclear annihilation, and the defeat of Stevenson further "demoralized and discredited" the "academic and intellectual establishment," according to Kenneth Rexroth in a 1966 broadcast: "Young men by the thousands were re-turning from the Korean War to the colleges disillusioned and contemptuous of their elders." The movement between social withdrawal and re-immersion would drive Kerouac's work through the next two decades, a life-devouring force positioned against the decadent prerogatives of the Cold War State, as clarified by government strategist George Kennan in 1948:

We have 50 per cent of the world's wealth, but only 6.3 per cent of its population. In this situation, our real job in the coming period is to devise a pattern of relationships which permit us to maintain this posi-tion of disparity. To do so, we have to dispense with all sentimentality. . . . We should cease thinking about human rights, the raising of living standards and democratization. (qtd. in Pilger 59)

The ensuing challenge to what Norman O. Brown calls the "death in-stinct" of State fundamentalism and to assumptions of European supremacy in the arts gave rise to a dazzling renaissance: abstract expressionism, the gathering of American and European émigré artists and scientists at Black Mountain College in North Carolina, Beat literature, the music of John Cage's circle, and the new jazz of Charlie Parker, Miles Davis, John Coltrane, and Ornette Coleman affirming a uniquely American art. Recognizing Kerouac as "the peer of Céline, Destouches or Beckett, [one of] a small handful of bona fide high brow writers working today," Rexroth documented the radicalism of this emerging scene in his essay "Disengagement: The Art of the Beat Generation," which shared his basis in "disaffiliation" from the mainstream "convergence of interest—the business community, military imperialism, political reaction, the hysterical, tear and mud drenched guilt of the ex-Stalinist, ex-Trotskyite American intellectuals":

> After World War I, there was an official line for general consumption: "Back to Normalcy." . . . The measure of decay in thirty years is the degree of acceptance of the official myth today—from the most obscure hack on a provincial newspaper to the loftiest metaphysicians of the literary quarterlies. The line goes: "The generation of experimentation and revolt is over." . . . [I]n the arts nothing could be less true. (179–88)

While glossing over instances of suicide and heroin addiction, Lawrence Lipton's *Holy Barbarians* chronicled this wider context of Americans in a disturbed country, "holy in their search of self, barbarian in their total rejection of the so-called civilized standards of success, morality and neurosis," a people living in "a total resignation of the whole society, and that, in present-day America, means the business civilization" (7). The Venice district of Los Angeles is Lipton's "laboratory of dissent," where responses to the pressures of conformity are as diverse in alleviation and ruin, outrage and fashion, as conformity itself. Early Beat hero Dylan Thomas is cited as "part of a generation trying to find a way of life it could believe in, to find it and express it in music, in poetry, in prose, in painting and dance, as men have always groped their way to new values and to a new way of life through the arts" (24).

Whereas the effects of what Ed Sanders termed a "Total Assault on the Culture" were perceived by the established order only at "more materialistic levels, where it is called delinquency"—really, as Lipton pointed out, the quality of impatient adolescent capitalists (294)—Rexroth drew attention to the proliferation of young writers, readings, and small press publications and a responsive audience in San Francisco, utopian city of art, ecology, and religion (Buddhist, Indian Shamanic, theosophical), now augmented by Ruth Witt-Diamant's Poetry Center and KPFA, the listener-sponsored radio station founded in Berkeley in 1949. Comparing "heroes of the post-war generation" Charlie Parker and Dylan Thomas to "the pillars of Hercules, like two ruined

Titans guarding the entrance to one of Dante's circles," Rexroth added, "as an old war horse of the revolution of the word, things have never looked better from where I sit. The avant-garde has not only not ceased to exist. It's jumping all over the place. Something's happening, man" ("Disengagement" 180, 193).

The literary and political "world of the disaffiliated . . . anyone who by definition is divorced from society and cannot afford to believe even an iota of the social lie (Rexroth, "Disengagement" 186) coalescing in North Beach and Greenwich Village now broadened to embrace junkies, mystics, hoboes (Kerouac's "real wandering Taoist bums"), and sexual deviants: underground habitués whose refusal of bourgeois standards traditionally undertook a less visible course. The precedents for this scene are many and varied, part of the "rise, decline and future prospects" of a counterindustrial impulse originating in 1830s Paris, according to Ronald Sukenick (15). Taking root in mid-nineteenth-century America with the rural spread of utopian communes, this assumed an urban orientation with the New York painters' set depicted by Herman Melville in *Pierre,* grew with the Greenwich Village and Big Sur Bohemianism of the 1920s and 1930s and the populist strike of Bodenheim, Sandburg, O'Neill, and Jeffers, and shifted into the hipster challenge to smug, self-righteous masculinity as stereotyped by John Wayne from *Stagecoach* onward. And just as Rexroth and Lipton succeeded to the Chicago line of activism, Ed Sanders's uncovering of New York's Lower East Side as a hippie/yippie "Power Zone" in the 1960s was followed by the realization that

> it had been discovered over and over for two hundred years by the beaten-down, the broken, the anarcho-syndicalists, the suffragettes and feminists, the Trotskyites, and in our time by the bards and pot-heads, the jazz-hips, and those just passing through on the Gold-Paved Streets of the West. (iii)

Gary Snyder's recognition extended further still, to the

> outcropping . . . of the Great Subculture which runs underground all through history . . . the tradition that runs without break from Paleo-Siberian Shamanism and Magdalenian cave-painting; through megaliths and Mysteries, astronomers, ritualists, alchemists and Albigensians; gnostics and vagantes, right down to Golden Gate Park. (*Earth* 115)

Kerouac acknowledged this, too, in a late interview:

> We are just the older ones. You see I'm forty-six years old, these kids are just eighteen. It's the same movement which is apparently some kind

of Dionysian movement in late civilization, which I didn't intend any more than Dionysus did. It's just a movement which is supposed to be licentious but it isn't really. The hippies are good kids, better than the beats. Ginsberg and I, we started this, now we are in our forties and the kids have taken it up. (Buckley)

The publication of Jay Landesman's *Neurotica* in St. Louis in 1948 and the appearance of *Liberation and Dissent* renewed leftist positions from the previous decade and gave voice to those without a stake in consumerism. A 1948 editorial from George Leite's Berkeley magazine, *Circle*, advertised for a new group:

### WRITERS

There is a struggle going on for the minds of the American people. Every form of expression is subject to the attack of reaction. This attack comes in the shape of silence, persecution, and censorship: three names for fear. In the face of this fear, the writer can speak. We believe in the possibility of a culture which fights for its freedom, which protects the economic interests of its workers in all fields including the arts, and which can create for itself new forms and new voices, against reaction and the threat of war.

Building on an IWW and anarcho-pacifist legacy thriving in the Northwest from Jack London's era, the shift from industrial models of class struggle was emphasized in a 1947 editorial of James Harmon's *Ark*, which, like *Circle*, also came from Rexroth's milieu:

[I]n direct opposition to the debasement of human values made flauntingly evident by the war, there is rising among writers in America, as elsewhere, a social consciousness which recognizes the integrity of the personality as the most substantial and considerable of values. . . . Today, at this catastrophic point in time, the validity if not the future of the anarchist position is more than ever established. It has become a polished mirror in which the falsehoods of political modes stand naked. (qtd. in Charters, *Penguin* 299)

The staging of the "Six Poets at the Six Gallery" reading in October 1955—"a great night, a historic night . . . the birth of the San Francisco Poetry Renaissance" (*DB* 13)—and the first interaction of East and West Coast Beats confirmed durable transitions in American civilization, resisting efforts by *Time* and Henry Luce to emasculate its radicalism into fashionable exotica. Michael McClure described the atmosphere of that night:

We were locked in the Cold War and the Asian debacle—the Korean War. . . . We hated the war and the inhumanity and the coldness. The country had the feeling of martial law. An undeclared military state had leaped out of Daddy Warbucks' tanks and sprawled over the landscape. As artists we were oppressed and indeed the people of the nation were oppressed. . . . We knew we were poets and we had to speak out as poets. We saw that the art of poetry was essentially dead—killed by war, by academies, by neglect, by lack of love, and by disinterest. We knew we could bring it back to life. We could see what Pound had done—and Whitman, and Artaud, and D. H. Lawrence in his monumental poetry and prose. . . . We wanted to make it new and we wanted to invent it and the process of it as we went into it. We wanted voice and we wanted vision. (qtd. in Charters, *Penguin* xvii)

Active in the city since the late 1920s and promoting a many-sided lineage embracing Kokinshu, Tu Fu, Boehme, Kropotkin, and Goldman as well as Blake, Lawrence, and Yeats, Rexroth credited the participants for their "change of medium—poetry as voice not as printing," placing the event above book publication as "the climacteric . . . of twenty years of the oral presentation of poetry in San Francisco" (qtd. in Charters, *Penguin* 230). Responding to Ginsberg's premiere of *Howl,* McClure also realized that everyone in the audience of 150 knew

at the deepest level that a barrier had been broken, that a human voice and body had been hurled against the harsh wall of America and its supporting armies and navies and academies and institutions and ownership systems and power-support bases. (qtd. in Charters, *Penguin* xxviii)

The surging renaissance, celebrated in the June 1957 issue of *Evergreen Review,* not only cemented a mutual awareness of poets' fraternity in the city, sharing Lawrence Ferlinghetti's sense of "a quest for direct, interpersonal communication . . . speech from one human to another" (notes for *Poetry*), but also expanded a community of ideas onto a national, and eventually international, matrix.

This is the milieu that propels Kerouac's fiction, which modulates over twenty years to sound the call for energizing change, answered most feverishly in his dramatizations of Neal Cassady, who stands for Dionysian risk and difference against the life of enclosure. Taking on Whitman's sense of "traveler," with implications beyond the geographical, Kerouac updates an American tradition of civil disobedience established by Thoreau and

Emerson in the face of an authority that expects its citizens "to become a soldier or worker or consumer at the next command" (Mottram, *Blood* 37). By 1952, as Ginsberg corroborates, both Kerouac and Cassady

> were at their wits' ends with the world and America—the "Beat Generation" was about that time formulated, the Korean War just about to be continued American bodied (as 'twas already funded American dollar'd via opium pushing France and French-Corsican Intelligence agencies). . . . Taken for eternal Midcentury America was all along camp, shallow camp upheld onstage with a million dollar production number trying to pass itself off as old and traditional as the Pyramid imitated on the Dollar Bill; just a bunch of inflated Bucks in USA. 1920–50. An era that had to end, an era that died of its own shrunken-hearted wars. (*Deliberate* 355)

In common with those performers at the Six Gallery's inaugural moment, the term "Beat" under Kerouac's hand denotes revelation: a full-blooded participation in life, "submissive, to everything, open, listening" (*GB* 72), and the search for a "company in which to be nourished, a confidence to fill the void left by that state" (Mottram, "Preface" 60). The poets enjoyed a spirit of camaraderie rather than shared aesthetic beliefs—Michael Davidson notes that the Six Gallery reading alone brought together every poetic style associated with the period, from vatic confessionalism and imagist precision to satirical self-projection, surrealism, and personalist meditation (4)—but their work collectively stands for resistance of habit, for experiment in notation, and for discovery without safety net. This in turn becomes an invitation to transform an identity that is ideologically conferred, through the insecurity of creativity and the denial of limits, which at once takes on wider ramifications.

For Kerouac, existential regeneration is initially sought in Céline's *Journey to the End of the Night*, where trench warfare and mass production are mutually informing technologies of apocalypse—the basis, too, of Henry Miller's confrontation with the self-legitimizing State; in the orgiastic alienation of Jean Genet ("really *the* most honest writer we've had" [qtd. in Berrigan 112]); in the heroic refusal of Gide's *Immoralist* to imitate social customs; in Saroyan's romantic image of the author as "spiritual anarchist . . . discontented with everything and everybody . . . a rebel who never stops" (*Reader* 7); and in the struggle of Dostoevsky's *Idiot* to withstand industrial coercion and maintain personal ethics. "Being beat goes back to my ancestors, to the rebellious, the hungry, the weird, and the mad," asserts Kerouac (qtd. in Wolf and Fancher 24), countering academic accusations over his lack of a legitimate literary past. Mottram ranges over further resources:

Sherlock Holmes and Moriarty, Hemingway, the swing bands at the Apollo in the 1940s ... *Citizen Kane* (which made Kerouac want to be "a genius of poetry in film"); Joyce ("to delineate all of Lowell as Joyce had done for Dublin"); Thoreau; the S.S. *Dorchester* ("trapped on a steel jail floating in icy oceans of the Arctic circle and a slave at last"); Gary Snyder's Buddhism and mountaineering; Billy Budd (remembered in the crow's nest of a ship in the Atlantic); Renoir's aristocratic De Boildieu in *La Grande Illusion* paired with and against his own Gabin figure of the "peasant soldier" life (part of the fellaheen material, the noble/peasant dream in *Book of Dreams*); Gide's *acte gratuite,* from *Les Caves du Vatican* and elsewhere, and his accounts of freedom ("To know how to free oneself is nothing; the arduous thing is to know what to do with one's freedom"); Rimbaud's voyant self-created from "a long, immense and reasoned derangement of all the senses," in whom "all forms of love, of suffering, of madness . . . all poisons" are consumed (Kerouac's poem "Rimbaud" delineates his version); Cocteau's *Le Sang d'un Poète* and many other instances of "the Dionysian overflow of the artistic morality." ("Preface" 57)

With the postwar State fostering a crude anti-intellectualism, the need for immersion in vigorous acts of mind—past and present, local and international—becomes a necessary expedient for change. How otherwise could Lowell's "wandering revolutionist," the man of overflowing boundaries ("I may not be a Party-liner . . . 'with nostrils sniffing for power'") on a "mission to present Beauty to the Collectivists," evade institutional attempts to frustrate virility? The "Leftist" ("I couldn't be otherwise") who declares that he "cannot live in a world of vested wealth, property, privilege and selfish greed" (*SL,* I 41–53) in his early letters to Sebastian Sampas must find an alternative to Bartleby's suicidal self-isolation in Wall Street and the Tombs or to Thoreau's "majority of one." Anticipating Hoover's identification of America's menaces as "Communists, beatniks and eggheads" at the 1960 Republican Convention, the two central figures in *On the Road* show a respect for mental acumen, which signals a need to recover potency in a nation where masculinity is assigned an expressly commercial orientation in warfare and sport.

Subtitled *An Adventurous Education 1935–46,* Kerouac's final confession, *Vanity of Duluoz,* calls on Henry Adams's exploration of the social through the personal to frame his vocation as a man of independence, given the liberty "to be a writer who didn't have to do other people's work" (*LT* 135). Inspired by Joyce's record of "silence, exile and cunning" as a relinquishment of religious training in *A Portrait of the Artist as a Young Man* and

Wolfe's tales of "escape and wandering"—"the initiation to the voyage this life will make . . . a prelude to exile [and] the blind groping of a soul toward freedom and isolation" (454)—Kerouac takes on a significant modernist tension between the desire to live inside an order and Whitman's declaration in "A Song of Joys" that "nothing exterior shall ever take command of me" (*Complete Poems* 212). The subsequent dialogue builds both creatively and destructively throughout. Reflecting the Daedalian quests undertaken in his novels, Kerouac struggles to sustain confidence in mobility in order to avoid, in Ginsberg's words, "the great betrayal of that manly America . . . made by the pseudo-heroic pseudo-responsible masculines of Army and Industry and Advertising and Construction and Transport and toilets and Wars" (*Deliberate* 357).

Born in 1922 into a Breton-Canadian working-class family and schooled under the Jesuits, Kerouac achieves local success as a football player, winning scholarships to Horace Mann and Columbia University before injury curtails his career. The realization that Olympian images of sport are rooted in the management of national ideology, bolstering the war machine through mass release, soon follows: the use made of Joe Louis's victory over Max Schmeling in 1937 to coerce African Americans into military service being a case in point. "That little winding dirt road going west to my lost dream of being a real American man" includes Sebastian Sampas and the Lowell-based football players on their "dusty bloody field," who would end up sacrificed in World War II or "eviscerated of 1930s innocent ambition" (*VD* 46). "[Columbia coach] Lou Little didn't put me in," Kerouac tells the *New York Post*:

> But the reason I quit was deeper than that. I was just sitting in my room and it was snowing, and it was time to go to scrimmage, time to go out in the snow and the mud and bang yourself around. And then, suddenly, on the radio it started—Beethoven. I said, "I'm going to be an artist. I'm not going to be a football player." That's the night I didn't go to scrimmage. And I never went back, see? (qtd. in Aronowitz, "Beat")

That "was the most important decision in my life so far," he adds in *Vanity of Duluoz*. "What I was doing was telling everybody to go jump in the big fat ocean of their own folly. I was also telling myself to go jump in the big fat ocean of my own folly. What a bath! It was delightful. I was washed clean" (68).

Kerouac moves on through a variety of orthodox roles, including navy enlistment in 1943, where he earned an honorable discharge for announcing he would never kill and for possessing a "schizoid personality [with] angel tendencies," a stint in the Merchant Marine problematized by his refusal to accept the "regimented life I hated so much" (*BD* 45), and a further assignment as an armed guard at a shipyard construction workers' barracks in 1947: a failed initiation into authoritarianism that replicated his naval experiences from the reverse side. Kerouac fictionalizes this episode in *On the Road*, where he describes being surrounded by "men with cop-souls" who "wanted to make arrests and get compliments from the chief of police in town. . . . They were always sitting around on their asses; they were proud of their jobs. They handled their guns and talked about them. They were itching to shoot somebody." The narrator goes on to depict the addictive violence possessing an ex-Alcatraz guard, "retired but unable to keep away from the atmospheres that nourished his dry soul all his life. . . . I told him I wasn't cut out to be a cop" (63–65).

Dismissing the claim of "cool" to worldly knowing, Kerouac plays Olson's raw "Figure of Outward" ("means way out way out / *there:* the / 'World' . . . opposite to a / personality which so completely does (did) / stay at home? And so to *forward* a / motion I / make him" [qtd. in Butterick 3]). "If I retain vision in myself by removing my own single identity in experience—" he explains to Sampas in 1943,

> that is to say, distil myself off until only the artist stands—and observe everything with an unbiased, studious, and discriminate eye, I do more good, as far as creation goes that the Byronic youth . . . who identifies himself with the meaning of the world or if not that places himself in the center of its orbit and professes to know all about humanity when he has only taken pains to study himself. That's sheer adolescence! (*SL, I* 51)

Kerouac then retransmits Eugene Gant's "foiled quest of himself . . . possessed of that obscure and passionate hunger that has woven its shuttle across the seas. . . . And now for the voyage out" (Wolfe 237); Huckleberry Finn's "light[ing] out for the Territory" (Twain 260); hobo Jack Black's setting "off for the train—and the world" (2); and Sherwood Anderson's "young man going out of his town to meet the adventure of life. . . . [His] mind was carried away by his journey passion dreams" (41). The experience is the American need to clear out of claustrophobic small-town settlement (Blake's "Expect poison from the standing water" [149]) and seek "adventurous education" on the road. In *Book of Dreams,* Kerouac tells of a downtown errand on behalf of his Canuck landlord:

> [T]hey begin dreary Lowellstreet instructions—for the prodigal returner—I experience momentary despair and bleakness of being back and subject to "laws of Lowell" again . . . bleak wintry city streets of Lowell Canada—not a happy or even interesting dream. (120)

To write "all the talk of the world . . . with roars of me / all brain—all world / roaring—vibrating" (SP 11) means to "dig" the world: the term bellowed by Melville's Azore Sailor in *Moby Dick*: "Rig it, dig it, stig it, quig it, bellboy!" (151) and celebrated by Snyder as denoting "to penetrate, to absorb and enjoy" (Place 9). *On the Road* seizes the appeal of the "fellaheen streets" for Dionysian immersion in activity, subsuming the "abstract morality" of parental and social parameters and rejecting a Christian-capitalist inheritance. "Buddhism is a Fellaheen thing," he writes in *Some of the Dharma*: "Fellaheen is Antifaust Unanglosaxon Original World Apocalypse. Fellaheen is an Indian Thing, like the earth. Jean-Louis the Fellaheen Seer of New North America.—The Unfaust, the Antichrist . . . Unsquare, Ungothic" (114). In the sequence of core novels that starts with *On the Road* and ends with *Vanity of Duluoz,* Kerouac joined fraternal resources such as Cassady (Dean Moriarty/Cody Pomeroy), Ginsberg (Carlo Marx/Irwin Garden/Alvah Goldbook), Snyder (Japhy Ryder/Jarry Wagner), and William Burroughs (Old Bull Lee/Bull Hubbard) in an optimistic bid for a manhood that might escape degradation from corrupted sports, high finance, alienated labor, and military violence, "refusing life-leakage and the dispersal of energy into sterility" (Mottram, "Preface" 57).

In Kerouac's first published novel, *The Town and the City,* Francis Martin's friend Wilfred Engels emerges as the precursor to these heroic initiators:

> What was most important to Francis was that for the first time in his life he heard spoken—and spoken in the articulate fluent language of "contemporary thought"—all the misty indistinct feelings that he had been carrying around with him for the last few years in Galloway. . . . He was amazed to think that a whole coherent language had sprung into being around this restless, intelligent, determined trend, this gentle, invisible revolt in America. (115)

The desire for excitement and revelation subsequently opens every experiential area, including those covert desires of inner life—Kerouac's "unspeakable visions of the individual"—to coverage without embarrassment. From mythic to historical, from present into past and future, his subject matter reconciles the learned with the commonplace to encompass suppressed esoteric forms such as daosim, tantrism, and peyotism alongside fascinations with the unselfconscious workingman and criminal transgressor, as seeded by friendships with jailbirds Cassady and Gregory Corso, Village hipster Stanley Gould, and Times Square raconteur Herbert Huncke.

The texts play on these pressures between public and private extremes of experience, an indifference to imported sectarianisms of high/low, aristocratic/plebian, and sacred/vulgar upon which the "midcult" ideology, as named by Dwight MacDonald, trades. "What difference is there between shit and gold?" asks Kerouac in *Some of the Dharma,* calling on Buddhist Sutra. "Shit on gold—shit is gold—goldshit—shit. . . . And honor Mind" (26). This is a thrust traveling far beyond T. S. Eliot's flat citations of working-class speech in *The Waste Land* to the deepest plane of form. Reflecting Olson's quotation of Heraclitus ("Man is estranged from that with which he is most familiar" [*Special* 25]) as a direction for exploring Gloucester, Kerouac's nonstop interior participation in the American present takes Emerson ("I explore and sit at the feet of the familiar, the low" [102]), Williams ("work which bridges the gap between the rigidities of vulgar experience and the imagination is rare. It is new, immediate" [*Imaginations* 134]), and Whitman ("All current nourishments to literature serve" to find glory in "the meal in the firkin; the milk in the pan; the ballad in the street" [*Complete Poems* 765]) as points of departure. As the latter has it:

> Poets here, literats here, are to rest on organic different bases from other countries; not a class set apart, circling only in the circle of themselves, modest and pretty, desperately scratching for rhymes, pallid with white paper, shut off, aware of the old pictures and traditions of the race, but unaware of the actual race around them—not breeding in and in among each other till they have the scrofula. Lands of ensemble, bards of ensemble! (769–70)

As Kerouac notes of *Visions of Cody*'s hero, "There were no images springing up in the brain of Cody Pomeroy that were repugnant to him at their outset. They were all beautiful"(355)—a principle of nonselectivity behind his dramatization of the infant's growth among the Denver poor:

> Older heroes of other generations had darkened the walls of the poolhalls long before Cody got there; memorable eccentrics, great poolsharks, even killers, jazz musicians, traveling salesmen, anonymous frozen bums who came in on winter nights to sit an hour by the heat never to be seen again. (67)

Kerouac works as archivist of the marginal, the unfashionable, the self-doomed, against the general tenor of literary convention controlled by and for the benefit of academics, critics, and editors. "With sympathy," D. H. Lawrence writes of Whitman's "glad recognition of the soul" and his "exultant message of American Democracy": "Stay in the dark limbs of Negroes. Stay in the body of the prostitute. Stay in the sick flesh of the syphilitic. Stay in the marsh where the calamus grows" (*Studies* 180–87). Kerouac copies this passage into his ninth notebook and draws on it throughout. His "MODEL FOR DUST JACKET OF 'THE DHARMA BUMS'"" is exemplary:

> Through these pages pass hoboes, blondes, truckdrivers, poets, hunters, Negro preachers, Mexicans, librarians, hound dogs, children, janitors, forest rangers, loggers, cowboys and Zen thinkers in a bewildering and delightful variety as the story races true to life to its conclusion. (*SL, II* 138)

Echoing Lautréamont—"everyone is an artist, naturally" (*SL, II* 16)—the Beat recovery of the outcast and the unknown within America's endless flux not only subverts normative binaries of success and failure but also performs a visionary slippage between worlds. As Robert Duncan notes, "Plagiarism, fraud, perversion by pun, by reversal of values & displacement of content, of above into below, of male into female, left into right, before into after—all these Freud saw as operations of the unconscious" ("Rites" 76). And as Maria Damon remarks:

> Who could contest "Howl's" attempts to capture for literary posterity the lives of junkies and queers of the American underworld? Or "Kaddish's" status as a love letter to an otherwise anonymous Jewish immigrant woman whose traumas of displacement and class mobility American-style finally caught up to her? Or *On the Road*'s mythologizing of innumerable small towns and of a flophouse orphan as Dionysian Adonis? Beat culture, whose jazz-inspired name epitomizes its oxymoronic embrace of sacralized fatigue, rock-bottom soul-poverty and mystic joy (much as the word "shaman" descends from a sanskrit root, "to exhaust or fatigue"), derived its energy from all explosive marriages of heaven and hell. (qtd. in Phillips 142)

Having declared that his "first serious writing took place" after reading "about Jack London at the age of 17" (*GB* 17), Kerouac's incursion into an American underclass seizes the hobo's sense of the United States as a disintegrating yet mobile society, built upon an accessible frontier. Whereas the economic crash of 1873 hurled three million into vagrancy and converted the tramp into a burden and threat, by the Depression, 1930s labor organizers pounding the rails between city picket lines rendered this latent political power explicit. Distinguishing between down-and-out transients and migratory hoboes in works such as "How I Became a Socialist," "The Tramp," and *The Road*, London depicts isolated struggles inside a hostile wilderness through IWW agitation, boxcar hopping, and riding the rods with bindle stiffs as a teenager in 1894, a heroic contest that half a century later Kerouac translates into a cross-continental antidote to consumer-belt stasis. In *White Fang,* London writes of two fellows and their team of dogs transporting the coffin of a man whom the

> wild had conquered and beaten down until he would never move nor struggle again. . . . Most ferociously and terribly of all does the Wild harry and crush into submission man—man, who is the most restless of life, ever in revolt against the dictum that all movement must in the end come to the cessation of movement. (170)

This is an act of survivalism, of "men penetrating the land of desolation and mockery and silence, puny adventurers bent on colossal adventure, pitting themselves against the might of a world as remote and alien and pulseless as the abysses of space" (170). Finding its echo in Céline's *Journey to the End of the Night*—"Death comes chasing after you, you've got to get a move on, and you have to find something to eat too, while you're searching, and dodge war as well" (61)—this is the Beat position, as Mottram explains:

> mobility, labor for food, dodging the predatory world you never made, "the Thomas Wolfe darkness" . . . , trying to find that instance which might bring about the "rupture" with the world of induced anxiety and conflict, through a "qualitative leap" (Marcuse). This involves "a radical transformation of the needs and aspirations themselves, cultural as well as material; of consciousness and sensibility; in the work process as well as leisure. . . ." Moral and aesthetic needs become basic, vital needs and drive toward new relationships between the sexes. . . . Freedom is understood as rooted in the fulfillment of these needs, which are sensuous, ethical and rational in one. ("Preface" 57)

Setting out to avoid ideological baptism and Herbert Marcuse's "enlarged universe of exploitation . . . a totality of machines—human, economic, political, military, education" (21), Kerouac experiments by living under different social and religious systems—a legacy of the 1893 Congress of World Religions in Chicago, where a number of heretical movements were introduced into the United States. This reinforced the impact of the Indian Vedic tradition that nurtured the Transcendentalists and seeded an interest in Chinese T'ang dynasty haiku that informed early modernism, the two major strands of Eastern influence on the nation's writing. Their cultural associations sponsor a major inquiry into generative forces in Beat America, which embraces the use of pot and LSD as both isolated and collective experiences; Reich's advocacy of "bion energy," updating eighteenth-century fascinations with ether; and occult dalliances and exhumations of primitive rites, among them Daisetz T. Suzuki's Zen Buddhism, Martin Buber's Hasidism, and Olson's Mayan hieroglyphs.

Kerouac's search for "ecstasy of mind all the time" (*SL, II* 46) would also take in jazz, restless sexuality, intense discussion, exhaustive mobility, and the reinvention of writing: what Robert Creeley describes as "the intimate, familiar, localizing, detailing, speculative, emotional, unending talking that has given my life a way of thinking of itself in the very fact and feeling of existence. God knows one wants no end to that ever" (*Prose* 8). Refuting the "Sunday writer" jibes that plague him throughout, Kerouac cycles rhythmically between such acts of euphoria and disciplined work inside the matriarchal home—the source of a binding moral, financial, and less than psychologically healthy commitment, as he moves his mother fretfully around the country for ten years. The ensuing ebb and flow of nerve is reflected in the degree of risk applied to his "Spontaneous Prose," which peaks through the 1950s with the encyclopedic ambition of *Visions of Cody,* the experimental prose poems *Old Angel Midnight* and "October in the Railroad Earth," and the *Blues* series. The overflowing vitality of such work implicitly blasts through boundaries held rigid by a market ideology that collapses together the terms "capitalism," "democracy," and "freedom" and responds to Henry Miller's rallying cry: "To go forward into death! Not backward into the womb. Out of the quicksands, out of the stagnant flux! This is the winter of our life, and our drama is to secure a foothold so that life may go forward once again" (*Wisdom* 9–12).

How Kerouac generates, sustains, and then partially surrenders such vigor in the face of a contrary training threatening reassertion is the concern of what follows.

# 2

# Dionysus Descends: The Shape of Energy

I am part of the American temper, the American temperament,
the American tempo.
—Jack Kerouac, *Atop an Underwood*

JESUS HOW I HATE THE MIDDLE COURSE!
—Michael McClure, "Love Lion Blues"

aving been affected by Thomas Wolfe like "a torrent of American heaven and hell" that "opened my eyes to an America as a subject in itself" (qtd. in Berrigan 117), Kerouac plans a "giant epic," tracing a generational mosaic of observation. Calling on Wolfe's four-volume portrayal of modern America's infancy, which in turn draws on Honoré de Balzac's assemblage *The Human Comedy,* and being equally inspired by the memory structure of Marcel Proust's *A la recherche du temps perdu,* he created the "endless Duluoz Legend (Duluoz is the curious Breton name I use for Kerouac)" (*SL, I* 536)—a literary weave of cyclical time that converges on loss and exile:

> My work comprises one vast book like Proust's except that my remembrances are written on the run instead of afterwards in a sick bed. Because of the objections of my early publishers I was not allowed to use the same personae names in each work. *On the Road, The Subterraneans, The Dharma Bums, Doctor Sax, Maggie Cassidy, Tristessa, Desolation Angels, Visions of Cody* and the others including . . . *Big Sur* are just chapters in the whole work which I call *The Duluoz Legend.* In my old age I intend to collect all my work and re-insert my pantheon of uniform names, leave the whole long shelf full of books there, and die

happy. The whole thing forms one enormous comedy, seen through
the eyes of poor Ti Jean (me). (*BS* 2)

However, unlike the work of Balzac and Wolfe, Kerouac's sequence trades
linear organization for a more adventurous principle of fictive overlay. Recurring events are superimposed to build a series of themes and variations
neutralizing a single career narrative: a hypertext of many narratives and
selves with each book a ratio within the whole. In the case of *Visions of Cody,*
this principle is internalized within a single novel:

> The final scope of the Legend will be simply a completely written
> lifetime with all its hundreds of characters and events and levels in-
> terswirling and reappearing and becoming complete, somewhat *a la*
> Balzac and Proust. But each section, that is, each novel, has to stand
> by itself as an individual story with a flavor of its own and a pivot of its
> own. Nevertheless, they must all fit together on one shelf as a continu-
> ous tale. (qtd. in "Books News")

As an initial statement of intent, Kerouac employs the bildungsroman
model in *The Town and the City* to work through the traditional entry to
manhood in Lowell. Huge Wolfean paragraphs convey the Martin family's
cyclical growth and collapse in nineteenth-century naturalist prose, labored
under his pen and later dismissed as fraudulent:

> I spent three years writing the *The Town and the City.* That was my first
> book, a novel-type novel, with all traditional characters and develop-
> ment and everything like that. . . . The *Town and the City* was mostly
> fiction. Fiction is nothing but idle day-dreams. Bah! The way to write
> is with real things and real people. The way to write is to get excited
> in telling a real story. Just like a story-teller, just like Homer probably
> did, or Shakespeare. (qtd. in Aronowitz, "Beat")

Kerouac reconfigures his elegy for Depression America's loss of potential
in *Doctor Sax,* a typical feat of improvisation on old material published long
after it was written. *On the Road* surfaces in 1957, soundly "regularized"
into punctuated and paginated form to satisfy his editor, Malcolm Cowley,
seven years after Kerouac's celebrated three-week burst and a contrast to the
tortuous nature of *The Town*'s composition.

In itself a rewrite of Kerouac's earliest version, begun around 1948 after
his marital breakdown and departure from the navy, the book emerges from
a prolonged single performance with a raw, unrevised scroll as its relic.
Bearing out Thomas Parkinson's conjecture that Beat authors are "perfectly

happy to place themselves in a tradition of experimental writing" and are "alert to the existence of writers they can claim as ancestors" (288–89), *On the Road* consolidates and extends the century's line of speculative fiction, moving into alignment with *Finnegans Wake* and Molly Bloom's soliloquy at the close of *Ulysses* in defiance of standard conventions. The upshot is a new phenomenology, as Ginsberg explains:

> *On the Road* was written around 1950, in the space of a few weeks, mostly on benny, an extraordinary project, sort of a flash of inspiration on a new approach to prose, an attempt to tell completely, all at once, everything on his mind in relation to the hero Dean Moriarty, spill it all out at once and follow the convolutions of the active mind for direction as to the "structure of the confession." And discover the rhythm of the mind at work at high speed in prose. An attempt to trap the prose of truth mind by means of a highly scientific attack on new prose method. The result was a magnificent single paragraph several blocks long, rolling, like the Road itself, the length of an entire onion-skin teletype roll. The sadness that this was never published in its most exciting form—its original discovery—but hacked and punctuated and broken—the rhythms and swing of it broken—by presumptuous literary critics in publishing houses. . . . The long lines of *Howl* are piddling compared to the sustained imagic rhythms of that magnificent endless paragraph. (*Deliberate* 342)

As will be seen, the transition from *The Town and the City* to *On the Road* and beyond yields a rhetorical trajectory that sheds re-presentation or imitation for the performative act: a discovery of form and the world in the process of writing. Taking on Charles Altieri's term "immanence," Michael Davidson identifies the performative impulse as common to all the diverse voices of the San Francisco Renaissance, one in which the prevailing academic definition of poetics as synthesis of opposition into transcendent singularity gives way to "*Negative Capability*," the governing principle of John Keats's work, defined in 1817 as the desire to remain "in uncertainties, Mysteries, doubts, without any irritable reaching after fact & reason" (*Letters* 43).

Having studied Keats's *Letters* in 1949, Kerouac reactivates the romantic complexity of attitude entering American poetry through Whitman—"Do I contradict myself? / Very well, then I contradict myself, / (I am large, I contain multitudes)" (*Complete Poems* 123)—to affirm a world of immanent value urged by Wordsworth in his preface to *Lyrical Ballads*. The forging of a literary model that "enacts in its own realm forces (whether psychological or physiological) that structure the natural world" and "engages the reader as a collective whole or tribe" by foregrounding oral and muscular stimuli (Davidson 18–20) would become a vital aesthetic and political intervention in the face of the reactionary push of the New Critics and a Cold War logical positivism bordering on pathology.

Kerouac's decision to forsake the traditional prose form used for *The Town and the City* is inextricably linked to the entrance of Neal Cassady into his life. As he later declares:

> I got the idea for the spontaneous style of *On the Road* from seeing how good old Neal Cassady wrote his letters to me, all first person, fast, mad, confessional, completely serious, all detailed, with real names in his case. . . . [Cassady] has written better than I have. . . . [H]e's the most intelligent man I've ever met in my life. (qtd. in Berrigan 111)

The switch of mentors and media from the "rolling style" of author (Wolfe) to the speed of action-talker (Cassady), from print to orality, is crucial to the text and career as a whole.[1] As Ginsberg testifies, the ongoing conversational style of Kerouac's prose is tested and refined in letters to Cassady and comprises

> the long confessional of two buddies telling each other everything that happened, every detail, every cunt-hair in the grass included, every tiny eyeball flick of orange neon flashed past in Chicago by the bus station; all the back of the brain imagery. This required sentences that did not necessarily follow exact classic-type syntactical order, but which allowed for interruption with dashes, allowed for the sentences to break in half, take another direction (with parentheses that might go on for paragraphs). It allowed for individual sentences that might not come to their period except after several pages of self reminiscence, of interruption and the piling on of detail, so that what you arrived at was a sort of stream of consciousness visioned around a specific subject (the tale of the road) and a specific view point (two buddies late at night meeting and recognizing each other like Dostoyevsky characters and telling each other the tale of their childhood). (*Allen* 45–46)

With the first drafts of *On the Road,* Kerouac begins to reconfigure Cassady's excitement into a virile fictional model. Following truck driver Joe Martin's restless retreat from exterior controls in *The Town and the City,* Cassady's oral blasts complement his feral movements across the continent: a prototype for Kerouac's translation of the mobility of the car driver and bop musician into literary style. "Move" and "mad to live" intersect throughout with the adjective "tremendous" as key refrains, actively probing Freud's conservative relegation of free motion into "repetition compulsion" in *Beyond the Pleasure Principle* and generating the required intensity for discovery of, and capitulation to, "IT": "the root, the soul" (*OTR* 137) of the book's occult quest.

Under the name of Dean Moriarty, Cassady's raw intellect stands as the narrator's gateway to innumerable rebirths, a shamanic agency of the masculine, offsetting the boyhood grounding in Catholic guilt, which they additionally share. In Dean, Sal Paradise sees "a kind of holy lightning . . . flashing from his excitement and his vision" (*OTR* 8), and he is canonized accordingly as the "Holy GOOF," "the Saint of the lot" with an "enormous series of sins": "his bony mad face covered with sweat and throbbing veins, saying 'Yes, yes, yes,' as though tremendous revelations were pouring into him all the time now, and I'm convinced they were" (198).

Kerouac thus employs Cassady to dramatize an ancient fascination with ecstatic release from conformity into overwhelming pleasure, an ambivalence at the heart of Freud's and Reich's work and personified in the Renaissance figure of Faust. Such desires are earthed in the anarchic executive drives of Dionysus, associated with trance rituals of fertilizing change and a primary source for Satan, horned cipher of heroic disobedience in Christian mythology. Part of a triple order alongside Apollo and Eros, Dionysus in his complexity gives a multiple eminence as man-woman-beast (Euripides' "magician . . . with perfumes wafted from his flaxen locks / and Aphrodite's wine-flushed graces in his eyes" [199]), bringer of spring depicted in foliage, force of perpetual renewal refusing urban enclosure, god of ivy and inventor of the vine, and technologizer of agriculture and the corn.

As emissary of sympathetic magic, the rites of Dionysus ensure constant transformation through growth and decay, death and resurrection. Descending through a Mediterranean line of Hermes, Thoth, Pan, Mercury, Bacchus, Zagrias, and Prometheus—half-god, half-man assured of transcendence—the geographical breadth of the cult, from Babylon, Syria, and India to Phrygia, Egypt, and the Aegean, and its progress from the agrarianism of Thrace to the metal and war industries of the Athenian state suggest a universal within the mind concerning the position of man within society and ecology alike.[2] The social function of Dionysian ritual was "essentially cathartic, in the psychological sense," writes E. R. Dodds:

> It purged the individual of those irrational impulses which, when dammed up, gave rise, as they have always done in other cultures, to outbreaks of dancing mania and similar manifestations of collective hysteria; it relieved them by providing them with a ritual outlet. (45)

In *The Bacchae,* the agency of the god marks orgiastic nonlegislation, exploiting primal tensions between the psychic need for discharge and the State's nervousness toward mind-body expression. The amoral shaman is invoked to restrain Pentheus, symbol of pathological rule within the over-organized Theban polis. The suppressed weight of the counterurge is unleashed: parameters of authority and self-possessive identity shatter, displacing desire beyond the semicontrolled release of art and sex into violence. For Whitman, this archaic force of transgressive eroticism surges through his evolving nation and bestows only vitality: "Always America will be agitated and turbulent . . . with such vast proportions of parts! As for me, I love screaming, wrestling, boiling hot days" (*Complete Poems* 772). Cast, too, in cyclical terms by William Carlos Williams in *Spring and All* as "progress since / destruction and creation / are simultaneous" (*Collected* 115), such energies remain forever in productive play, "guarantee[ing] nothing but *energia,* and certainly not Satan" (Mottram, "Preface" 55)—the Christian demonization of his pressures into dualistic paralysis.

These poles underpin Kerouac's Legend at every point, converging on art and identity as a challenge to rational goal and stasis. The ensuing release from limitation renders turmoil and uncertainty productive: the experience of all mankind, according to R. D. Laing, "of the primal man, of Adam and perhaps even [a journey] further into the beings of animals, vegetables and minerals" (13). However, as he concludes at the end of the 1950s, no age had moved so far from "ego-loss" as this, the crucial healing quality of communal re-orientation that Norman O. Brown also attributes to the god of flux:

> Dionysus . . . breaks down the boundaries; releases the prisoners; abolishes the *principium individuationis,* substituting for it the unity of man and the unity of man with nature. In this age of schizophrenia, with the atom, the individual self, the boundaries disintegrating, there is, for those who would save our souls, the ego-psychologists, "the problem of identity." But the breakdown is to be made into a break-through. (*Love's Body* 161)

Likewise Robert Duncan applies the cult to the contemporary scene in *Bending the Bow* and calls on the god to intervene in the secular State, "possessed" by the demonic ideology suggested by Dostoevsky's 1872 novel of that name and re-embodied in

> Eisenhower's idiot grin, Nixon's
> black jaw, the sly glare in Goldwater's eye, or
> the look of Stevenson lying in the U.N. that our
> Nation save face

> . . . in the assassin's mind
> the world is filld with enemies,      the truth
> itself is enemy and quickens   action to override
>      subversive thought.
>
> . . .
>
>      Dionysos, Zeus's Second Self,
>
>         Director of the Drama,
>         needed.
>
> (43, 130–31)

Cassady's presence in Kerouac's fiction corresponds to this role, a virtuoso of revolt against Cold War America that, as Duncan suggests, is itself a reversed Dionysus with control manias, assimilating exhilaration for its own purposes. Embodying the counterforces of metamorphosis, Cassady is positioned in the midst of this as a true Dionysian, whose liberatory productions of lawlessness, art, and unrestricted sex disrupt the State's limitation of the human as a product of power. As such he stands polarized to Blake's figure of abstract rationalism, Urizen, and to Burroughs's Lobotomy Kid in *The Naked Lunch*: the model of voluntary subjection, devoted to molding the all-American de-anxietized man from viscous jelly and a black centipede.

Cassady's assumption of the mad god symbol edges into the schematized latent brutality outlined in Oswald Spengler's *Decline of the West,* a primary source for Beat and high modernist writing alike. A passage from volume 2 stands not only as a European progenitor for America's obsession with youth and rebel innovation but also as a spur for the generational marker itself:

> What makes the man of the world-cities incapable of living on any but this artificial footing is that cosmic beat in his being is ever decreasing, while the tensions of his waking-consciousness become more and more dangerous. . . . Beat and tension, blood and intellect, Destiny and Causality are to one another as the countryside in bloom is to the city of stone. . . . Intelligence is only the capacity for understanding at high tension, and in every Culture these heads are the types of its final men—one has only to compare them with the peasant heads, when such happen to emerge in the swirl of the great city's street-life . . . the sensed beat of life—through the city-spirit to the cosmopolitan intelligence. . . . Tension, when it has become intellectual, knows no form of recreation but that which is specific to the world-city—namely, *detente,* relaxation, distraction. Genuine play, joie de vivre, pleasure, inebriation, are products of the cosmic beat. (250)

Distributed by Burroughs among his mid-1940s New York circle, the book seeds Kerouac's prejudicial sense of "immense historical forces" (*SL, II* 63) widely shared since the First World War[3] and incubates his sense of the "pulse-beat of our becoming . . . the long prophesied . . . new kind of American saint" who will sweep across *On the Road*'s "plane without limit" (11, 34). "The profound ignorance of the modern world is Horrible," Kerouac writes in 1954. "'The Horror' is why I'll have to take refuge in the Apocalypse of the Fellaheen" (*SL, I* 453). Beat means "a kind of Second Religiousness (that Spengler spoke)," he adds three years later,

> which *always* takes place in late Civilization stage, i.e., as corresponding examples, Dionysianism and Pythagoras-ism coming in late stages of Graeco-Roman civilization, and Tao coming in late stages of Chinese civilization, and Buddhism in late stages of Indian civ. etc.—The 2nd Relig. is sublime, it takes place during the coldhearted days of big city skepsis but it is indifferent to that because it is a reappearance of the early springtime forms of the culture and as such well-rooted— (*SL, II* 59–60)

As Dean Moriarty, Cassady is historicized, as the god of desire has always been, as an agent of affirmative regeneration. Posited as a model of Fellaheen and Faustian man, he complements the book's other "aboriginal" descendants: Mexican laborers, jazz improvisers, addicts, and hoboes, often unnamed frontiersman of refreshment living on the ruins of the polis and prone to savagery. In a nation built upon genocide, land-grab, and slavery, these men symbolize "the Independence of the Old Real America" (*BD* 35) and offer the displaced newcomer a way to "originate" himself in America, redressing Sal's inner restlessness. Theirs is the peasant ethos of survival, informed by suspicion toward the bourgeois narrative of "progress," where the consolidation of capital through increased productivity does not reduce scarcity, where dissemination of knowledge fails to advance democracy, where the advent of leisure brings not personal fulfillment but mass manipulation, and where economic and military unification generates not peace but permanent war.

Dean's amoral ecstasy evokes the Spenglerian source of barbarian revolution that precludes democracy, a force rising in the occultism of Yeats's "Second Coming" and "Leda and the Swan" and in the Marxian belief in an uncultivated proletariat. "Without exception, the cultural treasures [the historian] surveys have an origin which he cannot contemplate without horror," writes Walter Benjamin. "There is no document of civilization which is not at the same time a document of barbarism" (254–56). Brown shares this vision of violent change in *Closing Time*:

> Indeed, only barbarians are capable of rejuvenating a world
> laboring under the death throes of unnerved civilization . . .
> Man is maniac
> the Dionysian origin of civilization
> enthusiasm . . .
> the fortunate fall

(62, 74)

As Euripides discovered two millennia previously and Richard Schechner affirmed in his New York production *Dionysus in 69,* the revolutionary leader may qualify as a psychopath. Alan Harrington confers this status upon Cassady, guaranteed by a career summary that includes exhaustive transience, a succession of jobs, prison sentences, refusal of property for his family, and illegal possession of 500 cars, a description reiterated by Old Bull Lee in *On the Road*: "He seems to me to be headed for his ideal fate, which is compulsive psychosis dashed with a jigger of psychopathic irresponsibility and violence" (102).

The violation of self and others indeed formed a pattern across the Beat scene. Emerging at the end of a decade that included jailing, sectioning, overdoses, suicides, and Lucien Carr's act of manslaughter, the Beat scene is compared by Allan Temko to Dostoevsky's "*Possessed.* Terribly destructive people. . . . The level of violence was very high, and Kerouac liked that, and Ginsberg liked it" (qtd. in Gifford and Lee 62). This recurs through the agitated lives recorded in Ginsberg's *Howl,* steeped in biblical traditions of apocalypse and in the stage attitude of "Underground Man" struck by Lenny Bruce: a "ruthlessly appetitive and amoral being," according to his biographer, "who achieved heroic intensities through the violence of [his] rebellion against middle-class norms" (Goldman 4).

Though consistent with Spengler's mysticism, Kerouac's work diverges from this current in its relentless pursuit of a life founded creatively in the particularities of person and place. Cassady's role in the Legend is akin to that designated to the "[a]ngelic Dylan singing across the nation" by Ginsberg in "Witchita Vortex Sutra," a release of divine energy in Americans doomed by "war reflexes" and "black magic language" ("Ike who knelt to take / the magic wafer in his mouth / from Dulles' hand"), germinated by the actions of a Kansas temperance fanatic:

> Carry Nation began the war on Vietnam here
> with an angry smashing axe
> attacking Wine—
> Here fifty years ago, by her violence

began a vortex of hatred that defoliated the Mekong Delta—
Proud Wichita! vain Wichita
cast the first stone!—
That murdered my mother
who died of the communist anticommunist psychosis
in the madhouse one decade long ago
(*Planet* 131–32)

Whereas the pathology of the State enforces panic and limit, Cassady's charismatic appeal demands movement and dismantling of authority, a thrust pivotal to the deregimented self within Kerouac's autobiographical "I." In keeping with his mythological precursor, Cassady wreaks havoc and revitalizes but leaves humans to organize themselves after a vision of ecstasy and liberation. As such he qualifies as a true revolutionary, transgressing the hypocrisy, restraint, and muteness integral to bourgeois norms through direct and shameless activity. Operating outside the economy of libidinal denial, Cassady's vivacity calls into question our subordination to the mass superego and reverses the two-thousand-year western denigration of the energy god.[4] As Brown observes:

> The whole evolution from Trickster to Devil and on into the pseudos-ecular demonic of capitalism shows the progressive triumph of the death instinct. . . . The withdrawal of Eros hands over culture to the death instinct; and the inhuman, abstract, impersonal world which the death instinct creates progressively eliminates all possibility of the life of sublimated Eros, which we nostalgically so admire in ancient Greeks. . . . This problem is bound up with the larger one of power—and of possession. (*Life* 302–5)

This feeds into the role of the outlaw in America, a sociopath of necessary mutation who, in Mottram's words,

> embodies an historical ambivalence of energy in a culture whose development has long been impregnated with an accelerated inflow of technology and access to personal power. The barbarian in Whitman's and Melville's writings . . . works for a self-fulfillment which preaches *laissez-faire* and then attempts to pressurize the agent of enterprise into the conformities of the genteel, the legalistic, and those nuclear forces of family, state, and labor, all of which limit a man's freedom to be reborn. (*Blood* 197)

The destiny figure is similarly realized by Norman Mailer as "the de-structive, the liberating, the creative nihilism of the Hip, the frantic search for potent Change" that "may break into the open with all its violence, its confusion, its ugliness and horror," the erotic charge of "universal rebellion in the air" countering the "collective murders of society" and failing energy of the two ebbing super States (Mailer, *Advertisements* 325). A cynic without ideology, the hipster resists impotence as a new American manifestation of the contradictory force, a marriage of opposites running through Blake's "Tension of the Contraries" and Paul Gauguin's "Civilisation is sickness, barbarianism rejuvenation":

> Hip, which would return us to ourselves, at no matter what price in individual violence, is the affirmation of the barbarian, for it requires a primitive passion about human nature to believe that individual acts of violence are always to be preferred to the collective violence of the State; it takes literal faith in the creative possibilities of the human be-ing to envisage acts of violence as the catharsis which prepares growth. (Mailer, *Advertisements* 319)

Immersed in this nonrational way of knowing, Cassady enters Kerouac's Legend in the form of a youth unalloyed to conventional ethics and newly freed from imprisonment, a clear psychological metaphor:

> "Whooee!" yelled Dean. "Here we go!" And he hunched over the wheel and gunned her; he was back in his element. . . . We were all delighted, we all realized we were leaving confusion and nonsense behind and performing our one and noble function of the time, *move*. And we moved! (*OTR* 127)

The ensuing drama orbits a maniac who, like Mailer's Hipster, instigates simultaneous destruction and creation and holds, according to Robin Blaser, "within himself all the contradictions, the change and process of the world as it is known, and the terror that goes with that process" (qtd. in Allen and Tall-man 242). The primary motif of this seminal text, reiterated in *The Dharma Bums* and *Lonesome Traveler*, is the open road, location of "the great home of the soul," as maintained by D. H. Lawrence in his endorsement of Whit-man: "Not Heaven, not paradise. Not 'above.' Not even 'within.' The soul is neither 'above' nor 'within.' It is a wayfarer down the Open Road" (*Studies* 181). Kerouac patterns his narrative upon fitful continental switches, initi-ated by the westward pull away from New York and an unspecified "serious illness" that "had something to do with the miserably weary split-up [with my wife] and my feeling that everything was dead" (*OTR* 7).

The talismanic call of the rejuvenating frontier immediately counters the "Great Divide" at the center of a declined America: "In the month of July

1947, having saved fifty dollars from old veteran benefits, I was ready to go to the West Coast" (14). With Moriarty at the wheel, the "permissible dream" (*MCB* 51) of the mythic nation can be temporarily restored for exploration in simultaneous release from the limitations of finished identity. Citing Nietzsche on his opening page, prior to attending a production of *Fidelio* in a western ghost town, Kerouac takes on the imperatives of *Beyond Good and Evil*, a transgression of the moral orders of power as a means of reinvigorating existence. As such the text consciously travels along a romantic axis ("At the age of 24, I was groomed for the Western idealistic concept of letters from reading Goethe's *Dichtung und Wahrheit*" [*GB* 92]), stretching back via Rousseau and Schiller to the Faustian myths of fifteenth-century Germany and interpreted anew by the New England Transcendentalists.

Placing himself in the care of this energizer and assisted by techniques of consciousness alteration, the narrator moves in the role of the initiate, exercising the resurgent desire for revelation and return that recurs throughout American literature. Moriarty plays off the ancient trickster presence, "the exuberant rejuvenating Hermes thief" [Mottram, "Preface" 58], guiding Paradise away from the nexus of war, football, and church to forfeit conscious control, an envoy of the ones who

> are mad to live, mad to talk, mad to be saved, desirous of everything at the same time, the ones who never yawn or say a commonplace thing, but burn, burn, burn like fabulous yellow roman candles exploding like spiders across the stars and in the middle you see the blue centrelight pop and everybody goes "Awww!" (*OTR* 11)

As such Dean becomes a representative universal who incorporates the etymological overlap between the words "knowing," "cunning," and "conning." Like Billy the Kid and Jesse James, underground hero robbers of the banking and railroad elite (and perpetrators of acts of squalid sadism), Moriarty takes on the traditional role of dissenting rogue-exemplar, spawning an ambivalent response. Poised between heroic and mock-heroic, the "Holy Goof" synchronizes Conan Doyle's trickster villain genius with shaman and buffoon, echoing the likening of Paradise's friends to W. C. Fields and Groucho Marx (and in *Desolation Angels*, "Charley Chaplin"): Dostoevskian "idiots" or balancers of vulnerability and superiority, pitching improvised routines within a survivalist environment.

Given "the face of a great hero—a face to remind you that the infant springs from the great Assyrian bush of a man, not from an eye, an ear or a forehead—the face of a Simón Bolívar, Robert E. Lee, young Whitman, young Melville, a statue in the park, rough and free" (*OTR* 68), Dean's disposition

within a "Great Man" creation lineage of the Americas allows the transposi-
tion of a range of international figures onto a symbolic proletarian. These
include Satan in Milton's *Paradise Lost,* dissenting energy source opposed
to a tyrannical God ("Poor, poor Dean—the devil himself had never fallen
farther" [178]); Judas, celebrated in Mexico for his function of focusing aggression; Melville's *Confidence Man,* a fluid identity swindling the *Fidele*'s
passengers with panaceas and charity schemes for redemption; Hercules,
the personification of physical strength; Oedipus (Carlo Marx initially
refers to Dean as "Oedipus Eddie," who "bore his torment in his agonized
priapus" [12]); Samson, emasculated by the female; and Ulysses, who seeks
the recovery of home embodied by his father.

Firmly in line with the book's location in national myth, with Cassady
renamed accordingly in *Visions of Cody,* Dean's delinquency is represented
as "a wild yea-saying overburst of American joy; it was Western, the west
wind, an ode from the Plains" (3). Moving in from the Colorado mountains
to fertilize the urban East, he is configured as pre-Fall man, source of the
natural: "His dirty workclothes clung to him so gracefully, as though you
couldn't buy a better fit from a custom tailor but only earn it from the Natural
Tailor of Natural Joy, as Dean had, in his stresses . . . eager for bread and
love" (13–14).

Kerouac's search for an original local energy thus takes on a task started
in the 1920s by Williams, whose *In the American Grain* attempted to unearth
an authentic spirit of place before

> the great catastrophe to our letters—the appearance of T. S. Eliot's *The
> Waste Land.* There was heat in us, a core and a drive that was gather-
> ing headway upon the discovery of a primary impetus, the elementary
> principle of all art, in the local conditions. Our work staggered to a halt
> for a moment under the blast of Eliot's genius which gave the poem back
> to the academics (*Autobiography* 146)

and by Lawrence, who in celebrating the intercultural condition of the United
States situated American identity in "the aboriginal life of the continent"
and insisted on a set of propositions that reflected its boundary-breaking
nature (*Studies* 11). (Olson called Lawrence the "prospective" poet in terms
of form, ecology of the imagination, criticism of the West, and respect for
Native American cultures.) Noting that the nation's history was one of
"Americanization," of "continuity" between "the murdered Red America
and the seething White America," Lawrence recognized that the retrieval of a
primitive discourse of "masterless . . . living, organic, *believing* community"
was mandatory at a time when "[a]ll America is now going one hundred per

cent American" (*Studies* 12). Lawrence's words from "The Spirit of Place" provide the scaffolding for Kerouac's portrayals of Cassady, even prefiguring the typography used for the signifier of discharge from an encroaching State consciousness:

> If one wants to be free, one has to give up the illusion of doing what one likes, and seek what IT wishes done. But before you can do what IT likes, you must first break the spell of the old mastery, the old IT. . . . Liberty in America has meant so far the breaking away from *all* dominion. The true liberty will only begin when Americans discover IT, and proceed possibly to fulfill IT. IT being the deepest *whole* self of man, the self in its wholeness, not idealistic halfness. That's why the Pilgrim Fathers came to America, then; and that's why we come. Driven by IT. We cannot see that invisible winds carry us. . . . IT chooses for us. (*Studies* 13)

Embodying Rousseau's post-Enlightenment intuition that civilization has much to learn from the primitive and Williams's observation that "[t]he primitives are not back in some remote age—they are not BEHIND experience" (*Imaginations* 134), Dean obeys from within to break the bond of servility or Lawrence's "European spirit" ("Europe is precisely what I'm trying to get away from—To find the primitive, find the natural" [*SD* 100]) and is idealized as having "four little ones and not a cent, and was all troubles and ecstasy and speed as ever" (*OTR* 233). The "mythological present" of Claude Lévi-Strauss's *Savage Mind* is his habitat, devoid of concern for the goals of the State and its regulation of the past and characterized by an ongoing orality rather than an accumulated library. "Such people live vastly in the present," contends Gary Snyder.

> Their daily reality is a fabric of friends and family, the *field of feeling and energy that one's own body is,* the earth they stand on and the wind that wraps around it; and the various areas of consciousness [that grants] closer subjective knowledge of one's own physical properties than is usually available to men living . . . impotently and inadequately in "history." (*Earth* 117–18)

Moving south out of the neurotic American center ("frosty fagtown New York"), Dean announces,

> "[W]e all must admit that everything is fine and there's no need in the world to worry, and in fact we should realize what it would mean to us to UNDERSTAND that we're not REALLY worried about ANYTHING. Am I right?" We all agreed. (*OTR* 127)

As Mottram points out, Dean has "no apparent anxiety, and that is his attraction. The fears of ennui, endemic to the modern, were apparently vanquished by the automobile, wine, pot, de-anxietized sensuality, ebullient speech" ("Preface" 58). Following Ginsberg's "Green Automobile," Kerouac invests Cassady's movements through American space with a psycho-geographic significance. These mythicized depictions are balanced by his subject's flawed, though genuine, attempts to hold down a railroad job, raise a family, and relaunch himself as an autodidact and writer: a refusal to relapse into the pure exigencies of survival. "I went to Hector's," reports the narrator of *Visions of Cody,* "the glorious cafeteria of Cody's first New York vision when he arrived in late 1946 all excited with his first wife; it made me sad to realize" (25). The subsequent accumulation of detail emerges not sentimentally but as vision, the very "Life of Prose": a mapping of man's presence in the world and a set of tangible markers given importance beyond economic expediency. "I got that from Neal Cassady," explains Kerouac.

> He once wrote me a great 40,000 word masterpiece, just telling me about whatever happened one time in Denver, at a football game, and he had every detail. It was just like Dostoevski. And the way he wrote it was just to sit down and write—you don't stop, you just keep going. (qtd. in Aronowitz, "Beat")

To Kerouac this approach offers a method of writing into re-existence an American landscape that had already disappeared, chafing against the geographical "overwriting" that erases a path back or forward—ironically the pattern of the nation's settlement. This is the sense of "habits and haunts" given by Olson to Gloucester as he "digs in" to *Maximus,* and an analogous sense of loss, witnessed by the poet's description of "THE GULF OF MAINE," where the simulacra life of tourism colonizes a shore hitherto marked by the unselfconscious work of the locale. Both writers share the compulsion to enter into and set down the ecological orders and consequences of place before it is emptied of sacred resonance: a nonconformist gesture that finds the prospect of a future manipulated by the Amnesia State intolerable.

Kerouac thus assigns particular urgency to reenacting the traceless early movements of Cassady, whose displaced Depression childhood is given further light in his autobiography, *The First Third.* Trained at an early age out of the conventional sense of the family as an area of security with only a hobo father for protection, Cassady leads a "motherless, feverish life across America and back numberless times, an undone bird" (*VC* 178). Without past or predictable future, he embodies both an American Adam of the new and the rootless disquiet of the United States, the anguished death-in-life previously dramatized by Kerouac's master-exemplar:

[Eugene Gant] felt suddenly the devastating impermanence of the nation. Only the earth endured—the gigantic American earth, bearing upon its awful breast a world of flimsy rickets . . . this broad terrific earth that had no ghosts to haunt it. Stogged in the desert, half-broken and overthrown, among the columns of lost temples strewn, there was no ruined image of Menkaura, there was no alabaster head of Akhnaton. Nothing had been done in stone. Only this earth endured, upon whose lonely breast he read Euripides. Within its hills he had been held a prisoner; upon its plain he walked, alone, a stranger. . . . And the old hunger returned—the terrible and obscure hunger that haunts and hurts Americans, and that makes us exiles at home and strangers wherever we go. (Wolfe 370–71)

Eugene's loss of himself into the "great camp of vagrant floaters" (452) is repeated in *Visions of Cody,* where the hero is depicted as an anonymous child roaming the Denver pool halls, "not to be remembered by anyone because there was no one there to keep a love check on the majority of the boys as they swarmed among themselves year by year with only casual but sometimes haunted recognition of faces" (67). Unable to accrue an identity beyond reform school, Pomeroy moves into a pattern of repetitive crime and prison. Venturing out of wrecked domesticity, he personifies the existential dropout, trapped in an endless cycle of present "moments." Hence his choral phrase, "we know time," recalling Mailer's "White Negro," a figure for whom "now" is too dangerously immediate to allow reflection on past or future and the cold necessities of survival too pressing for anxiety.

Within such a compulsion lies the sexual and intellectual need to prevent knowledge, friendship, and lovers—the orders of manhood energy—ebbing away into the waste of poverty and alienation that informs his early adolescence: "It was dawn; he lay on the hard reformatory bed and decided to start reading books in the library so he would never be a bum, no matter what he worked at to make a living, which was the decision of a great idealist" (*VC* 77). In *Cody,* the hero separates from his background with a dream vision, the axis of the book. "Forever rushing," he wakes repulsed from a nightmare of his derelict father in search of wine money, "stumbling up the street with a convulsive erection in his baggy pants, howling hoarsely 'Hey Cody, Cody, did you sell the mattress yet?'" (104). Mottram pans over his ensuing adventurous education:

The urgent search for signs hidden in life follows. Life has to be discovered as a wonder, a mystery of experience. Car-stealing is given as "adventures in auto-eroticism" (like the erotic theft in Genet's *Thief's Journal*)—"tho' undeniably stupid," mythicized into a fantasy of "this mythological super race driver," "a true fanatic—Under no circumstances would he allow *anyone* to pass him." To be released from Denver meant to live by style (in the sense of Mailer's "hipster" of 1957), becoming a driver beyond fears, and learning, existing in a state of "not knowing" and an illusion of indestructibility, "the Charmed One," an absolute of fantasy, immorality and luck: "his car never seemed controlled." A woman is subsumed into the car fantasy, or "driven." ("Preface" 56)

The barbarian peasant image is maintained in an American act of self-reinvention—Schopenhauer, history, encyclopedias, *Lives of the Saints,* an intense desire that endows his carnivalesque movements with an underlying melancholy. His relationship with Kerouac and Ginsberg promises mutual benefit in an effort to shape a career that will nevertheless end as it began, in alienated labor and asocial sexuality. As Mottram notes, rather than generating any sense of permanent shift within the class hierarchy, Kerouac records his hero "breaking into whatever society presents and . . . nervously attempting to charm and appropriate it for his own needs and security." This is in keeping with a Dionysian energy "which counters social enslavement with amoral commitment to the self-possessive accumulation of experience from others in order to dominate them" ("Preface" 53).

In the more self-conscious prose of John Clellon Holmes's *Go!,* Cassady surfaces as Kennedy, catalyzing the hip 1940s New York intelligentsia through frantic attentions to the present, "digging everything" with romanticized confidence: "Everything happens perfectly for me because I know it's going to! . . . [E]verything is kicks. . . . *[E]verything's* really true on its own level" (44). As in *On the Road,* his deceptions are embedded in exhilarated stimuli, but the pathos that darkens Kerouac's spirit guide is missing. As Sal discerns:

> He was simply a youth tremendously excited with life, and though he was a con-man, he was only conning because he wanted so much to live and to get involved with people who would otherwise pay no attention to him . . . the holy con-man with the shining mind. (78)

Deciding in 1949 to organize his second novel as a quest—"a tremendous journey through post-Whitman America to FIND that America and to FIND the inherent goodness in American man" (*SL, II* 289)—Kerouac again deploys a generic matrix but this time overhauls its conventions. Not only does the Nietzschean aura break from the basis of the quest tradition in Christian authority, but the book also recalls forerunners such as Malory's *Le Morte d'Arthur* and Cervantes' *Don Quixote* ("probably most sublime work of any man ever lived" [*SL, II* 87]), only to violate the rationale of their form (Weinreich 25–28).

As a consequence, the plot mechanics, which turn within a "classical picaresque ring" (*SL, I* 597), are markedly subverted; the episodic adventures are not morally incremental, as Kerouac withholds the necessary signs for revelation of final meaning. That strangers drift in and out of the text like the inconsequential shadows populating *Le Morte d'Arthur,* regardless of Sal and Dean's desperate attempts to hail their magical significance, only adds to this. The non-causal arrangement of events suggests that selectivity, the value basis of dénouement, is subsumed into inclusive experience. As with the more radical form of *Visions of Cody,* the textual body as a whole becomes the dramatic focus.

Furthermore, unlike the traditional questing hero, neither the narrator nor his mentor accumulates a terminal identity by the book's conclusion. Even after they arrive in Mexico, having laid behind them "the whole of America and everything Dean and I had previously known about life, and life on the road" (*OTR* 260), Sal's joy at "finally [finding] the magic land at the end of the road and we never dreamed the extent of the magic" is comically undermined by Moriarty's abandonment of him to dysentery. And although Paradise frames "my goal" in conventional terms—

> All these years I was looking for the woman I wanted to marry. I couldn't meet a girl without saying to myself, What kind of wife would she make? . . . "I want to marry a girl," I told [Dean and Marylou], "so I can rest my soul with her till we both get old" (111)

—and achieves nominal fulfillment through union with Laura ("the girl with the pure and innocent dear eyes that I had always searched for and for so long"), this is dealt with in cursory fashion: "We agreed to love each other madly" (288).

Additionally, Sal's "so-longed-for" West, where the baggage of personal station and "European spirit" can be laid to rest—as in "October in the Railroad Earth"'s "clarity of Cal" where "nobody knew or far from cared who I was all my life three thousand five hundred miles from birth—O opened up and at last belonged to me in Great America" (*LT* 44)—is perpetually invoked only to be consciously undermined. Whereas to Thoreau the West is "but another name for the Wild. . . . [I]n Wildness is the preservation of the World. . . . In literature it is only the wild that attracts us. Dullness is but another name for tameness" (*Excursions* 534), by the 1940s this American Orient had been oversatiated by the thousands of pulp narratives that Kerouac avidly consumed as a child and had been delimited by the fact of the frontier's closure for half a century. As Paradise quickly learns, its "proud tradition" of survivalism had long since degenerated into the Southern Californian prototype of suburban sprawl molded by the automobile and the simulated experience first offered by Buffalo Bill Cody in 1877, selling a version of the world he had helped destroy with defeated Native peoples reenacting Custer's murder the previous year:

> "Hell's bells, it's Wild West Week," said Slim. Big crowds of business-men, fat businessmen in boots and ten-gallon hats, with their hefty wives in cowgirl attire bustled and whooped on the wooden sidewalks of old Cheyenne. . . . Blank guns went off. . . . I felt it was ridiculous: in my first shot at the West I was seeing to what absurd devices it had fallen. (*OTR* 34)

As R. J. Ellis observes, these obsolete ciphers subsist only in a thematic ter-rain saturated by what Jean Baudrillard calls the "commodity code" (42). This is understood by Sal, who is "more interested in some old rotting cov-ered wagons and pool tables sitting in the Nevada desert near a Coca-Cola stand" (*OTR* 29).

The traditional associations of the quest with either territory, the entry into manhood or a girl, thus remain incidental to the book's primary inquiry for continuously available techniques of regeneration: the sustained heights of "meaning-excitement" registered as "IT." Within the text, "IT" marks the point at which a particular dynamism finds its pure incarnation through jazz, mobility, male fraternity, or sexual union—"It's my contention that a man who can sweat fantastically for the flesh is also capable of sweating fantastically for the spirit," Kerouac later comments; "Dean had God sweating out of his forehead" (*SL, II* 288–89)—and rises to its highest intensity in a provisional, and typically American, release from history. "For just a moment," reports Sal, "I had reached the point of ecstasy that I always wanted to reach, which was the complete step across chronological time into timeless shadows" (*OTR* 164). "The blank tranced end of all innumerable riotous angelic particulars that had been lurking in our souls all our lives" and "the morning world" of *Visions of Cody* (307) promise to dissolve the ennui of Cold War deadlock to fulfill dream expectations of the nation.

Found at a juncture of erotic excitement and religious fervor embedded in the flux of perception, "IT" similarly evokes the romantic gnosis ("'Excess is the pathway to wisdom' is Goethe's here-applicable axiom" [*SD* 287]) and is capitalized to designate occult potency, echoing the status assigned to "Con-trol" in Burroughs's *Naked Lunch* and "Zone" and "System" in Pynchon's

*V* ("IT" also appears in *Gravity's Rainbow*). This nontangible presence signals the arrival of Dionysian energy, sparking a necessary adjustment of consciousness for connection with sources outside personality, a resonance bolstered by Kerouac's allusion to "Reichianalyzed ecstasy" (*OTR* 200), the "vibratory atmospheric atoms of life principle" of Old Bull's orgone accumulator (152), and his later reference to Alan Watts's intuition of "'[a] security and certainty, beyond any imagining.' . . . He calls it 'IT'—'Give Up'—'Plop into nothing'" in *Some of the Dharma* (409). As a transient, multiple sensation to be assimilated and released, "IT" wards off the fatalism of the book's generic coding, both energies nonetheless remaining omnipresent and surfacing at points in the Legend.

For Sal and Dean, the perfect circuits of "IT" never extend beyond a flash, the temporal and conceptual boundaries of the State being an entropic trashbin of outworn conformities that refuse to perish and continually reassert themselves. For instance, having blasted and "blow[n] at the peak" to achieve "*it*," the be-hatted tenorman immediately defuses the crowd's "rocking and roaring" furor with the ballad "Close Your Eyes" and confirms that "[l]ife's too sad to be ballin all the time" (*OTR* 196–99). The antitheses of ecstasy and desolation are rendered simultaneous, corroborating the twofold nature of the "Beat" signifier as "played out" and "beatific." Inhabiting another breakthrough point of synchronicity where "[e]verything happened," Sal describes his new model intellectual, the "wild ecstatic Rollo Greb," who

> didn't give a damn about anything . . . a great scholar who goes reeling down the New York waterfront with original seventeenth century musical manuscripts under his arm, shouting. . . . His excitement blew out of his eyes in stabs of fiendish light. He rolled his neck in spastic ecstasy. He lisped, he writhed, he flopped, he moaned, he howled, he fell back in despair. He could hardly get a word out, he was so excited with life. Dean stood before him with head bowed, repeating over and over again, "Yes . . . Yes . . . Yes." He took me into a corner. "That Rollo Greb is the greatest. . . . [T]hat's what I want to be. . . . He's never hung-up, he goes every direction, he lets it all out, he knows time. . . . You see, if you go like him all the time you'll finally get it."
>
> "Get what?"
>
> "IT! IT! I'll tell you—now no time, we have no time now." (121–22)

Dean is again entranced as he "stood bowed and jumping before the big phonograph, listening to a wild bop record called 'The Hunt,' with Dexter Gordon and Wardell Gray blowing their tops before a screaming audience that gave the record fantastic frenzied volume" (108). He shares his primitivist investment with esoteric celebrants such as Slim Gaillard ("Now Dean approached him, he approached his God; he thought Slim was God; he shuffled and bowed in front of him" [167]), Lester Young ("Lester blows all Kansas City to ecstasy and now Americans from coast to coast go mad, and fall by, and everybody's picking up. . . . Lester sneers at [Cody] from the bandstand; this is the mark of the hip generation, 'I'm hip, man, I'm hip'" [*VC* 457]), and the English pianist George Shearing ("Old God") (*OTR* 122). Writing at the time of bebop's ascendancy, Kerouac renders "IT" analogous to a soloist's technique: a means of configuring the relations between language, perception, and memory. The altoman in *On the Road*

> starts the first chorus, then lines up his ideas. . . . All of a sudden somewhere in the middle of the chorus he *gets it*. . . . Time stops. He's filling empty space with the substance of our lives, confessions of his bellybottom strain, remembrance of ideas, rehashes of old blowing. He has to blow across bridges and come back to do it with such infinite feeling soul-exploratory for the tune of the moment that everybody knows it's not the tune that counts but IT. (194)

In *Cody,* the transforming "IT" also appears as "GO," the word screamed by the audience at the Gordon/Gray jam session,

> which has the same blind unconscious quality as the orgasm, everything is happening to all their souls—this is the GO—the summation pinnacle possible in human relationships—lasts a second—the vibratory message is on—yet it's not so mystic either, it's love and sympathy in a flash. Similarly, we who make the mad night all the way (four-way sex orgies, three-day conversations, uninterrupted transcontinental drives) have that momentary glumness that advertises the need for sleep—reminds us it is possible to stop all this. (31)

In life, Cassady's supraconscious desire never stopped, prolonged beyond Beat times at the wheel of Ken Kesey's Magic Bus until his drug-sodden collapse by a Mexican railroad. In *On the Road,* Dean deploys his skills as a vehicle parker and driver, going beyond McLuhan's contention that people do not use cars but put them on, to wearing them out completely. Of the Hudson Dean drives to move Sal's brother's furniture, the narrator states: "It was a brand-new car bought five days ago, and already it was broken" (111). Regarding Cassady's domestic behavior, his wife, Carolyn, corroborates in *Off the Road* "that Neal had gone through eighteen cars in less than two years" (376). Technology and destruction fuse with ownership. As de Tocqueville noted in 1835, to be American implies a purchase on unlimited individual power, a central tension between the Constitution's egalitarian promise and its theological dispensation for a privileged elect.

Inheriting the cowboy mystique of self-reliance, the car under Dean's control becomes an instrument of extreme defense against the anonymity and powerlessness of urban mass society and a symptom of "the main myth of masculinity" that insists on survival "in a competitive free-for-all . . . in which the main lethal combination is alcohol, a car, and a gun, in various arrangements" (Mottram, *Blood* 4).[5] Williams's peculiarly American sense of driving as "a formal game . . . moderately dangerous" involving "duels with the other guy," which "are a test of skill. . . . No cowboy on the range could be happier in the chances he takes" (*Autobiography* 307), not only locates Cassady's obsession but also underwrites Kerouac's attempt to transmit his momentum by seeding new vocabularies. Concepts of freedom and masculinity become interchangeable throughout the text: the words "blow," "swing," and "ball" transfer freely between the realms of sex, jazz, and automobile, as in the description of the

> taut little Negro with a great big Cadillac . . . hunched over the wheel . . . [who] blew the car clear across Frisco without stopping once, seventy miles an hour. . . . Dean was in ecstasies. "Dig this guy, man! dig the way he sits there and don't move a bone and just balls the jack." (*OTR* 189)

Conversely, law means limitation, family, and quietude. Danger arises when the technologies of mobility are undermined, when the "sharptongued" female (61), emblem of domestic settlement, governs use of the car. Significantly, an auto with "no pick-up and no real power" requisitioned for a hitched ride is christened a "fag Plymouth"—'Effeminate car!' whispered Dean in my ear" (194). The "purity of the road" (127) is similarly debased by the "psychological warfare" of the Washington police, another source of inertia, who "inquire about everything, and can make crimes if the crimes don't exist to its satisfaction. 'Nine lines of crime, one of boredom,' said Louis-Ferdinand Céline" (130).

Dean's fascination with the epic insurgence of wild transit thus replays the Italian futurist celebration of masculine speed, noise, and death and takes on Marinetti's description of his sharklike poet's car, "more beautiful than the *Victory of Samothrace*," as it plunges through the electric Italian night (qtd. in Rothenberg and Joris, *Two* 362). In each case this inevitably ends in a sadomasochistic drive for extinction, rendered explicit in the intersections of machine technology and totalitarian power in the paintings of Balla, Boccioni, and Carrà. Indeed Marinetti's 1909 *Manifesto of Futurism* could double as a prospectus for Kerouac's Dionysian star, promising regeneration in devouring ecstasy and singing of "the love of danger, the habit of energy" and "feverish insomnia":

> We want to hymn the man at the wheel, who hurls the lance of his spirit across the Earth, along the circle of its orbit. . . . We stand on the last promontory of the centuries! . . . Why should we look back, when what we want is to break down the mysterious doors of the impossible? Time and Space died yesterday. We already live in the absolute, because we have created eternal, omnipresent speed. (qtd. in Rothenberg and Joris, *One* 197–98)

The narrator's admiration for Dean's lawless thrust and supersexual stamina certainly evokes European antidemocratic stances descending from futurism in the 1930s, trading on connections between athleticism, seminudity, and speed.[6] This extends beyond Christopher Isherwood's and W. H. Auden's palate of vaguely homosexual power-types to the heroic scale of endeavor extolled in the novels of A. K. Chesterton, Wyndham Lewis, and Henry Williamson (embodied in his fascist leader Birkin, wrongly named after Lawrence's hero in *Women in Love*) and Hitler's Aryan cult of brutish violence. Citing Dean in the dehistoricized present ("What do they call such young people in Goethe's Germany?" [*OTR* 11]), Kerouac compares his fleshy, masterful friend to the god Apollo, posing statuesquely against the sky to dupe passing holidaymakers, a middlebrow race in the presence of a natural aristocrat:

> Blue distances opened up in the sky. We got out of the car to examine an old Indian ruin. Dean did so stark naked. Marylou and I put on our overcoats. We wandered among the old stones, hooting and howling. Certain tourists caught sight of Dean naked in the plain but they could not believe their eyes and wobbled on. (153)

"One morning he stood naked," Sal later reports, "looking at all San Francisco out the window as the sun came up. He looked like someday he'd be the pagan mayor of San Francisco. But his energies ran out" (166). Gazing again at his Olympian deity, Sal notes that "[e]verything swirled around [Dean] like a cloud" (190). The narrative angle recalls the neoclassical iconography of Riefenstahl's *Triumph of the Will* and *Olympia,* with long-panning shots taken from beneath epic giants. Kerouac's depiction of his "western kinsman of the sun" (14) integrates these bases within the twentieth-century adulation of industrial design for consumption that impregnates the American myth of infinite personal freedom. By the late 1940s, the chromed images of streamlined speed would translate into the domestic machine future of fridges, radios, and pencil sharpeners and would fire the nation's recurrent fascination with cybernetics, entropy, and revenge against technology (Kerouac in 1943: "[W]e must admit that there is a certain element of virility in ruining cars" [*SL, I* 38]). Whereas New York's Chrysler Building, the manmade edifice nearest to the sky at the time of its completion in 1927, had its Inca temple steps dressed with the corporate apparel of solar discs in the form of vast steel hubcaps, Henry Adams coupled discoveries of new sources of energy with the human inability to control them:

> Power leaped from every atom, and enough of it to supply the stellar universe showed itself running to waste at every pore of matter. Man could no longer hold it off. Forces grabbed his wrists and flung him about as though he had hold of a live wire or a runaway automobile. . . . So long as the rates of progress held good, these bombs would double in number and force every ten years. (404)

Accordingly, Dean plugs into his technology and integrates with the landscape that he blasts through. Warned of his motorized "coming" to Denver, Sal conjures a Yeatsian vision of a "rough beast":

> a burning shuddering frightful Angel, palpitating towards me across the road, approaching like a cloud, with enormous speed, pursuing me like the Shrouded Traveler on the plain, bearing down on me. I saw his huge face over the plains with the mad, bony purpose and the gleaming eyes; I saw his wings; I saw his old jalopy chariot with thousands of sparking flames shooting out from it; I saw the path it burned over the road; it even made its own road and went over the corn, through cities, destroying bridges, drying rivers. It came like wrath to the West. I knew Dean had gone mad again. . . . Behind him charred ruins smoked. He rushed westward over the groaning and awful continent again, and soon he would arrive. . . . It was like the imminent arrival of Gargantua; preparations had to be made to widen the gutters of Denver and foreshorten certain laws to fit his suffering bulk and bursting ecstasies. (*OTR* 244)

The search for identity, and more precisely the definition of "an archetypal American man," as Kerouac calls Cassady in his original preface to *Visions of Cody,* is framed by the ebb and flow of the narrator's relationship with Moriarty. Sal's vulnerability, which will be passed onto the remote, "unselfconfident man" (Leo Percepied) who tells the story of *The Subterraneans,* and his need for those "threads of manly friendship" situate him astride the poles of hipster and pedestrian as he vacillates between Dean, "side-burned hero of the snowy West" (48), and the city intellectual Carlo Marx, "sorrowful poetic con-man with the dark mind" (28). This need for simultaneous participation and detachment, "shambling" after "the mad ones," is, as Davidson notes, Kerouac's characteristic position, allowing him

> both a narrative and an existential distance from his own story: he may act as first and third person, subject and observer . . . even while the ostensible focus is the wild, spontaneous life of others. For a novelist who set such stock in the uses of immediacy, his own narrative strategy is curiously Jamesian. (68)

This throws light on Sal's coy response to his shaman's demand for unconditional surrender to the moment, a product of his reflexive location in the text, which, as Ellis notes, allows Kerouac to undermine his persona. This is seen, for example, in his desire for agrarian return, picking cotton in the West with his Mexican girl, Terry, and her son Johnny:

> We bent down and began picking cotton. It was beautiful. . . . Terry sat mending clothes. I was a man of the earth, precisely as I had dreamed I would be, in Paterson. . . . I carried a big stick . . . in case [the Okies] got the idea we Mexicans were fouling up their trailer camp. They thought I was Mexican, of course; and in a way I am. (*OTR* 92, 94)

This is, of course, ironically charged; Paradise is less competent than either of them: "What kind of old man was I that I couldn't support [Johnny's] own ass, let alone theirs?" (93).

On returning to the camp, Paradise "sighs" with indolent contentment "like an old Negro cotton-picker" (94). Later in the narrative he wishes he

> were a Negro, feeling that the best the white world had offered was not enough ecstasy for me, not enough life, joy, kicks, darkness, music, not enough night. . . . I wished I were a Denver Mexican, or even a poor overworked Jap, anything but what I was so drearily, a "white man disillusioned."

But this is at once countered by the memory of his training: "All my life I'd had white ambitions; that was why I'd abandoned a good woman like Terry" (169–70). Significantly, Paradise forgets his identity papers on the way to Denver, which aids the adoption of new personae as he drifts freely between social groups (Ellis 44–46). Here and elsewhere Kerouac may sentimentalize working-class destitution ("Everything belongs to me because I am poor" [*VC* 33]), but in the end his narrator can usually "feel the pull of my own life calling me back [I was through with my chores in the cottonfield]" and rely on some "rich girl I knew," who in the morning could pull "a hundred-dollar bill out of her silk stocking. . . . So all my problems were solved" (*OTR* 94, 171). The quest for "IT" and the freedom of self-reinvention is thus underwritten by a latent class consciousness—the "French Canadian Iroquois American aristocrat Breton Cornish democrat" of *Desolation Angels* (331)—that will increasingly manifest itself in subsequent fictions as he gropes for fixed moorings.

Underpinning the quest of *On the Road* as both end in itself and axis of formal design, "IT" recalls Joyce's mode of "epiphany" and Wordsworth's "spots of time" in "The Prelude," that "with distinct preeminence retain / A renovating Virtue, whence / . . . our minds / Are nourished and invisibly repaired; . . . [S]uch moments / Are scattered everywhere, taking their date / From our first childhood" (737). As an alternative time structure, "IT" casts the linearity of Dean and Sal's continental charge into tension with the belief that "everything was about to arrive—the moment when you know all and everything is decided forever" (*OTR* 211). Upon emergence, these "moments" are isolated from the inconstant conjunctions of perception and memory, descriptions fashioned from a nodal point that lies simultaneously in and out of time.

As Warren Tallman notes, Kerouac's sense of "Jewel Center," his term for the ring of consciousness outlined in "Essentials of Spontaneous Prose," is inextricably linked to a barely articulable "hip talk," a "language art in which spontaneity is everything. The words are compact, mostly monosyl-labic, athletic . . . sensitive to the nuances and possibilities . . . of the always threatened moment" (156). In both *On the Road* and *Visions of Cody*, "IT" surfaces in passages where Cassady's speech rhythms are internalized within the narrator's own thought patterns, through immersion in the memory of "knowing time" or the moment, or through intensely physical descriptions of jazz. Of the "little alto" player in *Cody*, blowing "two hundred" choruses "completely cool in the shower of frenzies that poured from his lungs and fingers," Pomeroy asks:

> "[D]ig him? see his kind? [he] learned to blow and go continually and
> cast off the negatives and completely relaxed, though not hung, in, or
> behind, bumkicks of any kind . . . but listen to *him*, listen to *him*. *It*,
> remember? *It! It!* He's got *it*, see? That's what *it*—means. . . . Yes!" as
> little alto rose with the band that sat behind him—three pieces, piano,
> drums, bass—working the hound dog to death, rattle-ty-boom, crash,
> the drummer was all power and muscles, his huge muscular neck held
> and rocked, his foot boomed in the bass, old intervals, blump, be whom,

blump, boom; the piano rapping his outspread fingers in chordal offbeat drive clank, beautiful colors emanating from the tone of his crashing-guitar chords; blues; and the bass like a machine slapping in through the chugedychug of time with its big African world beat that comes from sitting before fires in the crickety night with nothing to do but beat out the time by the great wall of vines, a tuck a tee, a tuck a teek a tuck a teek, and make your moan, go moan for man, the disaster of the world, evil souls and innocent mountain stones . . . all realize they've got *it, IT,* they're in time and alive together and everything's alright, don't worry about nothin, I *love you,* whooee— (409)

Such diction orbits the sphere of the hipster, core subterranean in Kerouac's opus, who rises as an antidote to *Life* magazine's GI Joe, the no-bullshit insubordinate (within limits) at the service of imperial power, and the complacent suburbanism personified by Thomas R. Rath, hero of Sloan Wilson's novel *The Man in the Gray Flannel Suit,* who proclaims, "We might as well admit that what we want is a big house and a new car and trips to Florida in the winter, and plenty of life insurance" (10). Taken up as a proletarian resource, Cassady joins criminal habitués Huncke (Elmo Hassel/Huck/Junky) and Corso (Yuri Gligoric/Raphael Urso) in confronting the new Beat literati with existential alternatives to an official rationality sunk in cynicism or nostalgia. Literary fascination shifts from the Hollywood detective or reporter who acts as hangman to a new symbol of transgressive hoodlum, for whom Hegel's aphorism "the State is the reality of the moral idea" is an inconceivable abstraction. Whereas the courage of the former serves an impersonal cause, to those of Baudelaire's "floating existence" it is pure. Currency lies with the individual, not the citizen; friendship is a passion and the police a mafia.

Doubling as Virgilian guides to the lower depths, these urban frontiersmen have assimilated the geographical and psychic extremes of the western edge and carry the promise of menace and transformation announced by Hart Crane in *The Bridge.* The rhythm and content of their parlance run close to the "high-spirited belligerent" black jive, popularized in 1931 by Cab Calloway in "Minnie the Moocher" and defined by hipster-clarinetist Mezz Mezzrow in *Really the Blues* as "not only a strange linguistic mixture of dream and deed [but] a whole new attitude towards life" (Mezzrow and Wolfe 220). "Blacks supplied the argot," writes Richard Pell of Mailer's alliance between black archetypes, Beat Bohemianism, and criminality, "the worship of 'abstract states of feeling' (nourished by marijuana), and the knowledge of what it meant to live with perpetual danger. Insofar as the hipster had absorbed 'the existential synapses' of the blacks, he was in effect a white Negro" (209).

The potency of this speech is given complete expression in the esoteric and ritualistic character of jazz, reinforced by the knowledge of its signs and codes of behavior, and embodied in tenor icon Lester Young, "great hero of the beat generation and now enshrined" (*LT* 111). Holmes quotes Kerouac in his essay "This Is the Beat Generation":

> [Beat is] a sort of furtiveness . . . like we were a generation of furtives . . . with an inner knowledge there's no use flaunting on that level, the level of the "public," a kind of beatness . . . and a weariness with all the forms, all the conventions of the world. . . . So I guess you might say we're a *beat* generation. (qtd. in Nicosia 252)

That language can be orgiastic, with its etymological connotations of secret rites practiced only by initiates, and remain sacred is, as Lipton contends, intolerable to "the official culture . . . especially in a predominantly Protestant society" (167), with the exemption, of course, of its permitted sublimations of university and business fraternities. The impact of this elaborate jive talk of "bubbling energy and unshackled invention" as it ripples across Beat poetics, the New Left, and eventually the discourses of the mainstream cannot be overstated. Whereas for Ginsberg, "*Really the Blues,* read at the counter of the Columbia U Bookstore in the mid-Forties," was "the first signal into white culture of the underground black, hip culture that pre-existed before my own generation," for Henry Miller this "quite superb, perfectly marvelous book conveys a powerful, vital message of unadulterated joy. I should like millions of people to read this book and receive the message it contains. It is a great book. . . . Hallelujah!" (qtd. in K. Williamson 32–33). In the opening of the "Frisco: the Tape" section of *Visions of Cody,* Pomeroy alludes to his discussion with Burroughs over the merits of the text, with implications for Kerouac's own orality as it moves onto the level of form. As Mezzrow suggests:

> It's *the language of action* . . . which comes from the bars, the dance-halls, the prisons, honky-tonks, ginmills, etc., wherever people are busy living, loving, fighting, working or conniving to get the better of one another. . . . This lingo has to be *heard,* not seen, because its free-flowing rhythms and intonations and easy elisions, all following a kind of instinctive musical pattern just like Bessie Smith's mangling of the English language, can only hit the ear, not the eye. . . . This jive is a private affair, a secret inner-circle cooked up partly to mystify the outsiders. . . . Their language could hardly keep up with their restless, roving activities. It was the poetic expression of an immobilized people who, at last, see the day coming when all the action in the world will

be open to them, and all things will become possible. (Mezzrow and Wolfe 220–23)

Kerouac's fascination with the confidence of Cassady's speech emerges from this furious need to talk, described by Mezzrow as an "excited rush" swelling to "a torrent" of an attentive though "*beaten* people,"

> keyed-up with the effort to see and hear everything all at once, because that's how bottomdogs got to be unless they want to get lost in the shuffle. . . . You can't get by in the hard American scuffle just by shaking your weary old head and pulling your scraggy whiskers. You got to *talk*, man . . . twice as fast as anybody else. . . . Their sophistication didn't come out of moldy books and dicty colleges. It came from opening their eyes wide and gunning the world hard. . . . [Their hipness] bubbled up out of the brute scramble and sweat of living. . . . Spawned in a social vacuum and hung up in mid-air, they were beginning to build their own culture. Their language was a declaration of independence. (Mezzrow and Wolfe 223–25)

Mezzrow's words anticipate the opening characterization of "con-man" Moriarty upon his release from prison, to the extent of a thorough assimilation. "Dean's intelligence was every bit as shining and complete but without the tedious intellectualness," notes Paradise.

> And his criminality was not something that sulked and sneered; . . . Besides, all my New York friends were in the negative, nightmare position of putting down society and giving their tired bookish or political or psychoanalytical reasons, but Dean just raced in society. (*OTR* 13–14)

Kerouac takes on the hipster's ability to maintain an acute awareness within situations charged with speed and fervor, where conversely time slows. In *Cody*, Cassady's linguistic mobility and potential for metamorphosis will present the key to Kerouac's search for "wild form": a prolongation of ecstasy to counteract the enervation of sanctioned narratives and the Square's patronage of the outsider as "a poor sociological cripple who is doomed and damned and goes down to his inevitable defeat" (Mailer, *Advertisements* 381). However, overlaying the bildungsroman pattern of *Road*, Cassady's presence cannot save the current quest from entropy. As Ellis notes, for the time being neither geographical myth nor the ownership of consumer technology fulfills the desire for refreshment (47). The prairie girl whom Paradise meets in the ecologically barren western theme park of Cheyenne, for instance, responds gloomily to his advances:

"[L]isten, we'll take a nice walk in the prairie flowers."

"There ain't no flowers there," she said. "I want to go to New York. I'm sick and tired of this. Ain't no place to go but Cheyenne, and ain't nothin in Cheyenne."

"Ain't nothin in New York."

"Hell there ain't," she said. (*OTR* 31)

For Sal too, from California, New York seems "brown and holy" (88) as he faces east and resolves "to make my trip a circular one" (66–67). In the second journey across America, his confidence in the quest yields a spectacle of "the whole country like an oyster for us to open; and the pearl was there" (114). On the return westward, however, his disillusion amplifies: "What I accomplished by coming to Frisco I don't know" (168). Echoing his Times Square experience of standing in the "subway doorway," trying to get enough nerve to pick up a 'beautiful long butt'" (102), Paradise is again "out of my mind with hunger and bitterness. . . . I walked around, picking butts from the street" (162–63).

However, the East only seems "holy" to him from afar: "that's what I thought then." Having "traveled eight thousand miles around the American continent," he arrives "back on Times Square; and right in the middle of a rush hour, too." The "absolute madness and fantastic hoorair" of the city with its "millions hustling forever for a buck among themselves, the mad dream—grabbing, taking, giving, sighing, dying, just so they can be buried in those awful cemetery cities beyond Long Island City" becomes a transcontinental phenomenon, with New York, "the place where Paper America is born" (102), its genesis.

The traditional polarity between the "East of my youth and the West of my future" that Sal gleans at "the one distinct time in my life . . . when I didn't know who I was—I was far away from home, haunted and tired with travel . . . halfway across America, at the dividing line" (16), breaks down into barren homogeneity, robbed of symbolic promise. Space is compressed into a pure point—"With frantic Dean I was rushing through the world without a chance to see it" (205)—as the limits of their goal-driven discharge of energy are progressively felt on a structural plane. "I realized I was beginning to cross and recross towns in America as though I were a traveling salesman—" Sal discloses, "raggedy travelings, bad stock, rotten beans in the bottom of my bag of tricks, nobody buying" (231).

This is borne out by his meeting with the Ghost of the Susquehanna, an old hobo made crazy by aimless wandering and a presage of what Paradise and Moriarty may become. The bad portents escalate with Sal's apprehension of the Shrouded Traveler,

a strange Arabian figure that was pursuing me across the desert; that I
tried to avoid; that finally overtook me just before I reached the Protec-
tive City. . . . Something, someone, some spirit was pursuing all of us
across the desert of life and was bound to catch us before we reached
heaven. (118)

Undeterred, Sal strives to preserve his quest by cultivating a pan-American
foundation myth bridging multiple histories:

[T]here is a wilderness in the East, it's the same wilderness Ben Frank-
lin plodded in the oxcart days when he was postmaster, the same as it
was when George Washington was a wild-buck Indian-fighter, when
Daniel Boone told stories by Pennsylvania lamps and promised to find
the Gap, when Bradford built his road and men whooped her up in
log cabins. (101)

The envisioning of great men as commoners, a reiteration of Whitman's
celebration of Lincoln as fenceman and his own image of America in *Book of
Dreams,* springs from an impulse both Christian and democratic in its vision
of man's place under law. However, the promise is undermined by a growing
awareness of the nation's betrayal of individual potential, consistent with the
tone of the book and the Legend as a whole:

There were not great Arizona spaces for the little man, just the bushy
wilderness of eastern Pennsylvania, Maryland and Virginia, the back-
roads, the black-tar roads that curve among the mournful rivers like
Susquehanna, Monongahela, Old Potomac and Monocacy. (101)

With the object of the path increasingly inseparable from the headlong
rush, descriptions of the four circular journeys starting from New York become progressively less detailed in their revelation of mythic purpose (Ellis
40–42). Analogous to the enlightened exploration of writing, the sense of
linear destination collapses to be replaced by the author's steady realization
of pleasure in process: a thematic principle of discovery through the act of
composition itself. Direction first arises as a motif in part 1, in Sal's admission that "[i]t was my dream that screwed up, the stupid hearthside idea that
it would be wonderful to follow one great red line across America instead
of trying various roads and routes" (*OTR* 16), and resonates throughout.
Within a few pages a "tall lanky fellow," another nomad but with a carnival
occupation, "came over to us" and asked:

"You boys going to get somewhere, or just going?" We didn't understand his question, and it was a damned good question.

. . . I said, "I don't know, I'm going as fast as I can and I don't think I have the time." (24–25)

Carlo similarly inquires of their design in part 2:

"I have an announcement to make."
"Yes? yes?"
"What is the meaning of this voyage . . . I mean, man, whither goest thou? Whither goest thou, America, in thy shiny car in the night?"

Again Paradise and Moriarty are unable to answer: "'Whither goest thou?' echoed Dean with his mouth open. We sat and didn't know what to say; there was nothing to talk about anymore. The only thing to do was go" (114).

Sal later admits that the projection of "thirty hours for a thousand miles north and south" was similarly without motive: "It was a completely meaningless set of circumstances that made Dean come, and similarly I went off with him for no reason" (123). "Everything was falling apart," he declares as his first stay in San Francisco draws to a close. "How disastrous all this was compared to what I'd written [Remi Boncoeur] from Paterson, planning my red line Route 6 across America. Here I was at the end of America—no more land—and now there was nowhere to go but back" (75). "This can't go on all the time," he tells Moriarty and Marylou, "all this franticness and jumping around. We've got to go someplace, find something" (111). Within ten pages, Old Bull Lee interrogates them twice more, again without eliciting a satisfactory response:

"Now, Dean, I want you to sit quiet a minute and tell me what you're doing crossing the country like this."
Dean could only blush and say, "Ah well, you know how it is."
"Sal, what are you going to the coast for?"
"Only for a few days . . ." (138)

Indefinite prolongation of movement within the narrative becomes as neurotic and addictive as goal-orientation. Lawrence's insights stand as commentary on Moriarty's wanderlust as it degenerates into the Dantean dread of interminable restlessness:

We have pushed a process into a goal. The aim of any process is not the perpetuation of that process, but the completion thereof. . . . The process should work to a completion, not to some horror of intensification and extremity wherein the soul and body ultimately perish. (*Aaron's Rod* 200–201)

Connected thematically, a Godot-healer, conjured periodically as one of many invested with symbolic promise, fails to appear and deliver redemption:

> In the whole eastern dark wall of the Divide this night there was silence and the whisper of the wind, except in the ravine where we roared ... mad drunken Americans in the mighty land. We were on the roof of America and all we could do was yell, I guess—across the night, eastward over the Plains, where somewhere an old man with white hair was probably walking towards us with the Word, and would arrive any minute and make us silent. (*OTR* 54)

By the book's conclusion, the persistent linear scramble reduces Moriarty to an idiot of ravaged body and mind, stammering "yes, yes, yes," and rendered inert. With "his balloon thumb stuck up in the night," Moriarty's tumult "came to a whirling stop in the middle of the road, looking everywhere above him for the signs" (191). Having applied the jazzman's dedication to immediacy across the spheres of sex, friendship, driving, and discussion, the hitchhiker's sign of energized displacement is mutilated for shattering bourgeois injunctions to sexual silence and terminal domesticity. The destructions, resurrections, and initiations of the body of Kerouac's Dionysus are complete: the supercharged hobo diminished to skid row bum. Whereas in 1923 Williams records how "the pure products of America / go crazy" through

> promiscuity between
> devil-may-care men who have taken
> to railroading
> out of sheer lust of adventure
>
> (*Shorter* 123),

Snyder notes that Cassady

> was like so many Americans who had inherited the taste for the limitless [but] when the sheer physical space disappears you go crazy. Which is like the story of America. . . . Initially you are moving very slowly in a totally wide area. . . . What you end up doing is going very fast in a densely populated area. Space becomes translated into speed . . . the energy of the archetypal West, the energy of the frontier . . . the cowboy crashing. (qtd. in Charters, *Kerouac* 287)

Having posed vertical dynamic ecstasy against the mythology of the State, Dean cannot transcend the constraints of the Cold War era, the generative completion of act, and thus metamorphosis is rendered impossible. Whereas in life Cassady's allegiance to narcotics and Edgar Cayce—"a blank new insistent religiosity, 'like Billy Sunday in a suit,' epistled Jack" (Ginsberg, *Deliberate* 338)—eventually ends in waste, *Road*'s "Western kinsman of the sun" (14) is defeated by the burnout that follows such manic translations of space into time. Recrossing the vast expanse of the United States in near total indifference, the intervals that traditionally separate the traveler from his objectives are canceled. Distance ceases, along with the fundamental qualities of time-space: duration, extension, and horizon—the modes against which man measures himself. Dean's breaking down of all resistance, all dependence on locality and scale, thus wears down the opposition of time, "not only with regard to the terrestrial horizon but also to the circumterrestrial altitude of our natural satellite" (Virilio 119). Realizing the ultimate purpose of communications technology, he grows into Paul Virilio's

> [c]onqueror of the length that drags, the passenger of the communications vehicle [who] eliminate[s] one by one the obstacles that nonetheless allowed him to exist here and now in motion. From that moment he not only pollutes nature but also its grandeur, its life-size magnitude. (120)

Desiring only endless speed, he is reduced to sudden immobility, his "know[ledge of] time" locked within Zeno's paradox of nonmotion in space. The journey is effectively freed from a referential axis of native earth as Dean enforces a separate space trajectory, dispensing with the concrete bearings of local geography that comprise memory and therefore the depth of the past itself. The "hotrock capable of everything at the same time" with "unlimited energy" (*OTR* 128) becomes the self-destructive manifestation of Pound's Vortex:

> the highly energized statement . . . that has not yet SPENT itself. . . . All experience rushes into this vortex. All the energized past, all the past that is living and worthy to live. ALL MOMENTUM . . . is pregnant in the vortex, NOW. Hedonism is the vacant place of a vortex, without force, deprived of past and of future. (Lewis 153)

Dean's subsequent degeneration confirms the psychic center of the outlaw as madness and isolation, bonding derangement to dissent. While Henry Miller's citation of Lawrence resonates strongly against him ("He who gets nearer the sun, is leader, the aristocrat of aristocrats. . . . But the most powerful being, is that which moves towards the as-yet-unknown blossom!" [*Wisdom* 2]), the spontaneous transfiguration promised by this "mad Ahab at the wheel" proves unsustainable (*OTR* 221). *On the Road* may reveal, in

Timothy Hunt's words, "the split between the unity of a culture as it exists symbolically and the individual's actual fragmentary and contradictory experience of that culture" (241), but the internal threat to the propaganda of frontier America is imprisoned within the East-West pivot of a linear narrative that neither characters nor text can eclipse (Ellis 45–46).

Dean's own behavior lapses into repetitiousness, being confined to its own mythological system or cycle of conditioned action. Habitualized mobility becomes another manifestation of "the junk world" where, according to Burroughs, "NOTHING ever happens," or, more accurately, "only one thing ever happened. Junkies lived in a universe endlessly imploding upon a single event: the fix. Junk time was thus cyclical time, and cyclical time is, by definition, ritual time" (qtd. in Maynard 95). The ritual "IT" within such a frame reproduces only itself, not freedom; the "know[ing of] time" exists inside memory as history, mapped within national enclosure, rather than *entheos*—filled with the god, "enthused" like the dervish at the apex of concentration.

This played-out fabric inevitably falls short of Louis Zukofsky's ideal in *All*, where "the poet's form is never an imposition of history, but the desirability of making order out of history as it is felt and conceived" (5). Kerouac will achieve that in a future novel. For now, configuring death when Paradise "looks back on it" (*OTR* 118), the pursuing Shrouded Traveler embodies this irreconcilable dualism by signaling the decay of ecstatic time and looming re-entry into State chronology. Anxiety expands into the meaning of America itself, an ongoing crisis that is also met by the heroine of Pynchon's *Crying of Lot 49*:

> Another mode of meaning behind the obvious, or none. Either Oedipa in the orbiting ecstasy of a true paranoia, or a real Tristero. For there either was some Tristero beyond the appearance of legacy America, or there was just America and if there was just America then it seemed the only way she could continue, and manage to be at all relevant to it, was as an alien, unfurrowed, assumed full circle into some paranoia. (186)

While Sal intuits no Tristero (an occult organization beyond the jurisdiction of official power), his stance and desire for something beyond "just America" is similar. The intimation that there may not be "another mode of meaning behind the obvious" is intolerable and recurrent in American literature, and it possesses Sal as it did the Puritans and the Transcendentalists before him. The frontier charge ebbs into fatigue, anticipating the protagonist's "total disgust" in *Desolation Angels* when, in the middle of the ocean, Jack Duluoz suddenly understands that he no longer has anywhere to go and experiences "a repulsion in every sense of the word" (259).

The imminent decline into alcoholism and disenchantment is prophesied in the downbeat final journey of *Road*, where the narrator is left with dysentery in Mexico, the ironically appointed place of regeneration, and reduced to cadging money from a rich woman to reach Moriarty. Having earlier "reminded [Paradise] of some long lost brother" (10), Dean now replays Gerard Kerouac's personification of loss at an instinctual level. The Faustian Doctor Sax's apocryphal words—"[Y]ou'll never be as happy as you are now in your quiltish innocent book-devouring boyhood immortal night" (176)—melt into further mythic transmutations of Cassady's memory ("Cody is the brother I lost" [*VC* 368]), confirmation of regressive tendencies that will eventually overtake Kerouac's protagonists. From *On the Road*:

> The one thing that we yearn for in our living days, that makes us sigh and groan and undergo sweet nauseas of all kinds, is the remembrance of some lost bliss that was probably experienced in the womb and can only be reproduced (though we hate to admit it) in death. (124)

Mottram interprets this need to discover "a lost brother with whom to share vivacity and conviviality" as an essential "counter to anxieties incipient from a Jesuit brothers rearing: namely that 'human beings lived in a guilt machine'" ("Preface" 51). Fending off dread for a while through exuberance, Cassady is arrayed against the "quivering meat conception" that surfaces in *Mexico City Blues* (211) and resurges through the final fictions as desire shrivels into jaundice. "I feel as though everything *used* to be alright," contends the narrator of *Cody*, "and now everything is automatically—bad" (300). Whereas in *Road*, Sal admits, "I accept lostness forever" (201), in *Cody* the narrator's melancholy endows the act of writing itself, invoking a fatalism that jars with the book's celebration of inventive autonomy:

> I'm writing this book because we're all going to die—in the loneliness of my life, my father dead, my brother dead, my mother faraway, my sister and my wife far away, nothing here but my own tragic hands that once were guarded by a world, a sweet attention, that now are left to guide and disappear their own way into the common dark of all our death, sleeping in me raw bed, alone and stupid: with just this one pride and consolation; my heart broke in the general despair and opened up inwards to the Lord, I made a supplication in this dream. (427)

*The Subterraneans*, too, concludes with the lines "And I go home having lost her love. And write this book" (111). The future will be governed by the need to dam leakage. As the dream of America fragments and the nation seeks imperial perpetuation, the conclusions of *On the Road* and *Visions of Cody* present a eulogy that throws each text back onto itself: a promise unlikely to be fulfilled and probably doomed to waste. Having exposed the hucksterism of the State, guaranteed by "[g]reat displays of war . . . that looked murderous" (128), the narrator's re-entry into organized society during the finale of *Road* is marked by a conspicuously different final trip: in the back of a chauffeur-driven Cadillac with tickets for a Duke Ellington concert at the Metropolitan Opera—another incongruity. The clash between the anarchist dedication to "pure activity," transmitted by Miller in *Tropic of Cancer,* and the accountability of the bildungsroman hero to the erotic and financial controls of bourgeois society compel Paradise to draw back and reluctantly let "Old Dean" go:

> Dean, ragged in motheaten overcoat he brought specially for the freez-ing temperatures of the East, walked off alone, and the last I saw of him he rounded the corner of Seventh Avenue, eyes on the street ahead, and bent to it again. . . . Old Dean's gone, I thought . . . and all the time I was thinking of Dean and how he got back on the train and rode over three thousand miles over that awful land and never knew why he had come anyway, except to see me. (290–91)

Whereas Kerouac's life would soon head into a downward trajectory, a solution to the incompatibilities inside his most famous text and to Cold War ennui would emerge from another direction. The "Word" that Paradise longs to hear in fact resonates from the East, not in the Old World form of an ancient guru or secret historically embedded in the landscape but in what Mottram terms the "traditional American transcendental call . . . the old invitation taken up from Confucius, Thoreau and Pound, 'Make it New'" (qtd. in *SGE* 18–19). This would be augmented by direct study of the Bud-dhist path ("What's really influenced my work is the Mahayana Buddhism, the original Buddhism of Guatama Śàkyamuni, the Buddha himself, of the India of old" [qtd. in Berrigan 117]) and applying de Crèvecoeur's existential definition of the American as "the new man who acts on new principles: he must therefore entertain new ideas and form new opinions" (160).

## 3

# "The Too Huge World": Visions of Form

> I need more than one string for a fabric. I am trying to get a
> bracket for one kind of ideas, I mean that will hold a whole set
> of ideas and keep them apart from another set.
> —Ezra Pound, *Guide to Kulchur*

> A multiphasic experience sought a multiphasic form . . .
> cultivating the metaphysical ground in life.
> —Robert Duncan, "Ideas of the Meaning of Form"

The language and title of *On the Road*—written at the time Kerouac was devising his theory of poetics—indicate a significant
shift in Kerouac's career to an examination of potential form.
As he suggests in *Black Mountain Review,* "Modern bizarre
structures . . . arise from language being dead, 'different' themes give illusion
of 'new' life" (*GB* 70). From this, Kerouac's great serial vision of America
broaches core motifs of the nation's construction. In *On the Road* he writes
of excitedly planning his trip, "poring over maps of the United States" for
months, and "even reading books about the pioneers and savoring names
like Platte and Cimarron and so on" (15).

However, having set out in 1947 to forge "a huge study of the face of
America itself" within "the ruling thought in the American temperament . .
. a purposeful energetic search after useful knowledge," Kerouac finds that
the deployment of a linear model serves only to frustrate the possibilities
of individual heroism and trailblazing vitality—"the 'livelihood of man' in
America instead of the vague and prosy 'brotherhood of man' of Europe"
(*SL, I* 107)—that vibrated for Thoreau, Emerson, and Whitman.

In mass America, the Sublime cannot be realized geographically through the solitary transversal of vast, savage space by speed. "I saw that it was an arbitrary conception to say 'infinite'—even to say 'space'—that it was size-less & distanceless," Kerouac writes in *Some of the Dharma*. "You could travel forever in the arbitrary conception of 'distance' of the universe before you'd learn it was just a void" (85). As Olson proposes in *Call Me Ishmael*, time itself must be changed into space through an alchemical act, one that in Michael McClure's words may allow man to "move in it and step outside of the disaster that we have wreaked upon the environment and upon our phylogenetic selves" (*Scratching* 21). Kerouac's "subject of America" in all its physical grandeur and geomantic complexity demands a new mode of personal disaffiliation, an act of mind to release the visionary experience beneath the flux of observational detail in a rebirth of language.

As Regina Weinreich contends, the paradigm of "IT" presents a possible metanarrational solution for the problem of design in *On the Road*, a built-in distinction between classical plot progression (horizontal themes in unified time) and a series of nodal points (vertical moments of excitement) that intersect within a field (40–55). Causality breaks up into smaller cells open to analysis as tropes of "exhaustion and building," or tension and release, evident in Sal's oddly melancholic response to *Fidelio* ("What gloom"), the breakdown of his relationship with Terry, the prolonged drunkenness and sexual frustration surrounding Dean's theft of a car in Denver, and the "be-hatted tenorman's" juxtaposition of crashing "[u]proars of music" with a ballad from "this sad brown world" (*OTR* 197). These shifts from the nu-minous to the temporal world are carried by the choral refrain "Everything was collapsing," as if to convey the corrective limitations of extreme psy-chological and spiritual states—a major Beat concern, according to Michael Davidson—and interiorized within a "sharp-necessitating 'ending,'" where "language shortens in race to wire of time-race of work, following laws of Deep Form, to conclusion, last words, last trickle—" (*GB* 70).

However, empirically this stops short of fulfillment. "All carefully planned out yet falling far from what is dearly meant," Kerouac writes on the dedicatory screed to Robert Giroux. Constrained by the demands of publishers and his own lack of confidence, the various drafts of *On the Road* stand as preparatory works from his "middle style (1951) between *Town & City* and *Doctor Sax*," "soften[ing] the public for the real business in hand" (*SL, II* 97, 48), and in the case of the final version, a postlude for the great fictional experiment yet to appear in print. In a 1952 letter to John Clellon Holmes, dispatched in the midst of writing *Doctor Sax*, Kerouac asserts that he has begun to discover now . . . something beyond the novel and beyond the arbitrary confines of the story . . . into the realms of revealed picture . . . revealed whatever . . . revelated prose . . . *wild form*, man, *wild form*. Wild form's the only form holds what I have to say—my mind is exploding to say something about every image and every memory in—I have now an irrational lust to set down everything I know—in narrowing circles around the core of my last writing, very last writing, when I am an old man or ready to die, will be calm like the center of whirlpools and Beethoven's quartets—I love the world, and especially do I love the external eye and the shining heart of pure heart-to-heart mornings in a sane eternity, with love and security, but at this time in my life I'm making myself sick to find the wild form that can grow with my wild heart. (*SL, I* 371)

After Kerouac works through realist styles, *Visions of Cody,* published in part in 1960 and then posthumously as a whole in 1972, is the consummation of his search ("O my best prose there" [*SL, II* 189]). A compendium of spatial forms in the encyclopedic tradition of *Moby Dick, Cody* comprises a synthesis of Kerouac's most far-reaching ideas over two decades of experimentation and, as such, is the key to understanding the radicalism of the Duluoz Legend. Here the temporal progression into closure is transformed, eclipsing the paradoxes of Kerouac's role as storyteller of the limitless speed and multiplicity of Cassady's "hurricane of energy" (*OTR* 165). Along with jazz, his hero is again invoked in *Cody,* but this time on the level of form: a model of narrative organization unavailable in the literary past. Written at the same time and documenting the same period in the Legend, *Cody* expands *Road*'s linear elegy of deprivation into a generative metafiction that approximates Henri Bergson's idea of "duration," a conception of memory dependent on intensity of experience and creative participation rather than on chronological ordering. Immersed in the actions of Cassady, the retelling of his story reincarnates the actuality of his presence: the vehicle of myth in a new life and the true purpose of the liminal text. "Bear with me, wise readers," begs Kerouac in *Some of the Dharma,* as he explains a strategy that applies equally to *Cody,*

in that I've chosen no form for the Book of Mind Because everything has no form, and when you've finished reading this book you will have had a glimpse of everything, presented in the way that everything comes: in piecemeal bombardments, continuously, rat tat tatting the pure pictureless liquid of Mind essence. (147)

Realizing the potential of Stephané Mallarmé's "integrity of the book," the text breaks with received novelistic craft by approaching language plastically, for shaping a personal imprint and record of kinetic tension produced at every design stage. When traditional syntax is adequate to convey his observations, Kerouac works comfortably within it. But when it is incapable of yielding precise meaning, he reconfigures it projectively, risking disconnectedness to suit the requirements of the work in progress. It is this perpetual movement between poles of recognition and experiment that gives the book its unique energy.

The channeling of desire of two lives held in tension—as text, as myth—breaks the novel into five discrete sections. These are written and rewritten in multiple styles over a number of separate sittings, a new form to satisfy complexity of act and a divergence from the circumstances of *On the Road*'s composition. What emerges is a work that cannot be subsumed into a single interpretative position or philosophy. Rather than assert an authoritative realist reading of the past, Kerouac reflects the jazz musician's use of cross-references traced in memory to generate ever-new effects as measures of fervor or point signs, offering a variety of directions beyond causality.

Surpassing even Kerouac's description of his technique—"I began sketching everything in sight," he tells Ginsberg in 1952, implying that *Cody* is the earlier, untrammeled version of *Road*, "so that *On the Road* took its turn from conventional narrative survey of road trips etc. into a big multi-dimensional conscious and subconscious invocation of Neal in his whirlwinds" (*SL, I* 356)[1]—the novel does not revolve around a subject axis but dynamically balances events within its heterogeneity of times, methods, and speeds. The motive is not to contain Cassady but to understand and register his energies inside an open field without compromise—the indomitable motive marking the transition between the two books. As Henry James puts it: "There is a the story of one's hero, and then, thanks to the intimate connexion of things, the story of one's story itself" (qtd. in Tanner 34). With confessional remembrances of both author and hero continually dismantled and reassembled, the book of Cassady outstrips private chronicle to become an invitation to mobility and risk, an exploration of poetic form as vessel for wildness, and a visual design emerging from materials in transformation.

Reshaping his given syntax through principles of improvisation and overlay, Kerouac designates a number of alternative paths that his configuration of Cassady as Cody Pomeroy may take. Precisely because his reminiscences proceed from personal associations with an originating experience replayed variously throughout the Legend, questions of historical accuracy are superseded by the structure of the work. To remember is to create and vice versa—the Sufi process of invoking the divinity residing in all forms—with the text its own end, regardless of external style to which it may point, inadvertently or otherwise. Drawing on Gilles Deleuze's idea of leaping "transversals," Mottram names Kerouac's impetus as the avoidance of reducing multiplicity "to a dominant One, of refusing to fuse affirmation and criticism into a circular pattern" ("Preface" 55). Instead, *Cody* advances a fast current, a field of action where an effective reading does not position a static image of Cassady as central icon but rather seeks to experience flashes of intensity, of great moments followed by minor moments, none of which are necessarily privileged over another.

So, unlike the exhaustion of *On the Road,* or the later surrenders to sacrificial succession in *Vanity of Duluoz* and self-conscious irony in *Satori in Paris,* the conclusion of *Cody* releases not certainties but a permanent "ETC," to call on Alfred Korzybski's abbreviation for the extending, inexhaustible character of non-Aristotelian forms. This underpins Kerouac's sense of American rhythm and energy that runs through the book, a shift from centripetal linearity as suggested by the image of

> thousands of young men of Denver hurrying from their homes with arrogant clack and tie-adjustments towards the brilliant center in an invasion haunted by sorrow because no guy whether he was a big drinker, big fighter or big cocksman could ever find the center of Saturday night in America. (*VC* 78)

Instead of cataloging dead elements, Kerouac narrates the rhizomic complexity of twentieth-century understanding at full tilt, a would-be historian who enters, as Henry Adams did some four decades earlier, "a far vaster universe, where all the old roads ran about in every direction, overrunning, dividing, subdividing, stopping abruptly, vanishing slowly, with side-paths that led nowhere, and sequences that could not be proved" (400). As the narrator of *Big Sur* later suggests, "Obvious at this time now, by the way and parenthetically, that there's so much to tell about the fateful following three weeks it's hardly possible to find anyplace to begin. Like life actually—And how multiple it all is!" (47–48). Recalling Leo Frobenius's use of the term "Paideuma" to signify "the tangle or complex of the inrooted ideas of any period," Pound's assertions in *Guide to Kulchur* further illuminate *Cody*'s treatment of time and experience:

> The history of a culture is the history of ideas going into action. . . . We do NOT know the past in chronological sequence. It may be convenient to lay it out anaesthetized on the table with dates pasted on here and there, but what we know we know by ripples and spirals eddying out from us and our own time. (43, 57)

Holding up Pound's works as "[t]he foundation of 20th Century American letters" (*SL, I* 389) and having read the *Cantos* prior to embarking on his *Blues* series, Kerouac emulates Pound's inventory of techniques within a library of his time. Occasions are witnessed and collected in *Cody* over an indeterminate period and organized by composition, whence arise the new momentary understandings of self described by Williams in *Paterson*:

> For the beginning is assuredly
> the end—since we know nothing, pure
> and simple, beyond
> our own complexities.
>
> (3)

Accordingly, Kerouac turns history into personal discovery or "proprioception," Olson's term for the "introceptive" imagination that demands "movement at any cost. Kinaesthesia: beat (nik) . . . the data of depth sensibility / the 'body' of us as object which spontaneously or of its own order produces experience of 'depth'" (*Collected* 181). Kerouac's text buds forth as an expansive vessel for cultural materials and posits a Poundian model of nonacademic knowing that is immediate, relational, and "in the air" (*Guide* 48).

Apprehending the nation through industrial images and technologized day and night locations, part 1's tableau of "bottom of the world" America evokes Edward Hopper's intense revelations of solitude within public spaces associated with dense crowds. Indeed, loneliness and the void haunt Kerouac's novels, and as Davidson notes, "many of his best moments" occur when evoking "the solitude of bus stops, of wind in the trees, of winos on the skids, of a jazz saxophonist wailing in the night, of foghorns over the bay, of empty space itself" (69). The collagist nature of these prose chains, which continue into part 2, is thrown into relief by their previous incarnation within the altered sequence of "Manhattan Sketches" in LeRoi Jones's collection *The Moderns*. Kerouac implicitly sets up a multidirectional form without fixed reading order, an indeterminate field of prose-poems that mirrors the procedures employed by Karlheinz Stockhausen in the nineteen fragments of *Klavierstuck XI*. In both works, performance is not determined by chronology alone. *Cody*'s urban scenes are observed and notated in all their disjunctive plurality, the closure of each reflective passage signaled by confident abandonment.

The third section consists of "Frisco: the Tape," an impression of recorded conversations between Cody and the narrator made at the turn of the 1950s. This ditches the fictional conventions sedimented in literary language and is bereft of the editorial comment conventionally used to colonize reader sympathy and guide elucidation. Here the transition from what Kerouac describes as "just a horizontal study of travels on the road" to the nomadic principles of his "vertical, metaphysical study" of Cassady (*SL, I* 327) is inextricably linked to technologies of memory retrieval. "We also did so much fast talking between the two of us, on tape recorders, way back in 1952," reports Kerouac, "and listened to them so much, we both got the secret of LINGO in telling a tale and figured that was the only way to express the speed and tension and ecstatic tomfoolery of the age" (qtd. in Berrigan 103). The result covers, in Ginsberg's words,

> a set of nights on newly discovered Grass, wherein these souls explored the mind blanks impressions that tea creates: that's the subject, unaltered and unadorned—halts, switches, emptiness, quixotic chatters, summary piths, exactly reproduced . . . transcribing *first* thoughts of true mind in American speech . . . the God-worship in the present conversation, no matter what. Thus the tape may be read not as hung-up which it sometimes is to the stranger, but as a spontaneous Ritual performed once and never repeated, in full consciousness that every yawn & syllable uttered would be eternal. . . . Kerouac's style of transcription is . . . impeccably accurate in syntax punctuation—separation of elements for clarity . . . labeling of voices, parenthesizing of interruptions. A model to study. (*Deliberate* 351–52)

Tape machines thus complement Kerouac's use of nonaddictive narcotics to break linguistic habit and extend what J. D. Bernal defines as "the human sensory motor arrangement" (11). As Walter J. Ong notes in *Orality and Literacy:*

> Many of the features we have taken for granted in thought and expression in literature, philosophy and science, and even in oral discourse among literates, are not directly native to human existence as such but have come into being because of the resources which the technology of writing makes available to human consciousness. We have to revise our understanding of human identity. (5)

Kerouac's devotion to radio as recorded in *Doctor Sax* testifies to his awareness of speech-body transactions from an early age. Encouraged by Cassady and Holmes, he purchases a portable machine in 1951, and novelistic form is reevaluated accordingly. *Cody*'s shift to orality gears the narrative into a condensed sense of time that Olson calls "listening vertically," bearing out Ong's contention that the "electronic age" builds on writing and print while still remaining "an age of 'secondary orality,' the orality of the telephone, radio and television, which depends on writing and print for its existence" (9).

Moving far beyond *Road*'s exchanges between colloquial American hip and approximated dictation, *Cody*'s mapping of the two voices exceeds transcription and prepares Kerouac for his delineation of the nonhuman sound world of *Big Sur*. Cassady's speech, frequently edging into mania, dramatically challenges the rhetoric of print technology that ironically controls language, the ensuing dialogue doubling as an unscrambling device, analogous to Burroughs's attempts to decode or "cut up" the linguistic enclosure of the State. "We are governed by words," corroborates Pound with regard to the refreshment of *Ulysses;* "the laws are graven in words, and literature is the sole means of keeping those words living and accurate" (*Literary Essays* 409).

Kerouac then emphatically defies the platitudinous illustrations of the spoken word that have preoccupied literary criticism since Leavis's attack on Joyce in *Scrutiny* in 1933, which implicitly precluded a creative dynamic. His built-in analysis of the vernacular that continues into the *Blues* series flags up a departure from what characters would "really say," a consensus that, in referring to an individual version, is always ideological. Kerouac contests the proclivities of a language that seek to restrict and finalize experience, one that estranges man from "being"—Heidegger's term for the divinity of existence that only speech can reveal. As such he assumes a comparable position to Olson (via Gertrude Stein) in Olson's essay "Human Universe":

> We have lived long in a generalizing time, at least since 450 B.C. And it has had its effects on the best of men, on the best of things. Logos, or discourse, for example, has, in that time, so worked its abstractions into our concept and use of language that language's other function, speech, seems so in need of restoration that several of us go back to hieroglyphics or to ideograms to right the balance. (*Collected* 155–56)

Kerouac's interrogation of the limits of language traces the same postwar surge in American poetics from modernism to postmodernism. While the perceiving self coheres the disparate episodes of his early novels, by *Visions of Cody* it has been superseded thematically by the process of language itself and by the commandeering and reconstruction of materials, utterances, and texts emerging elsewhere in the Legend. Kerouac introduces a spoken hermeneutics: a tape of talking about talking about writing and a set of constant self-subversions and diversions grounded in the linguistic play of predecessors such as Stein, Khlebnikov, and Schwitters.

Having ascribed to Cassady the book's annals of their friendship as "a muscular rush of your own narrative style and excitement. . . . [I]t hides nothing;

the material is painfully necessary" (*SL, I* 247), Kerouac utilizes his mentor's existential energy to make compositional decisions. "I see now the whole Cathedral of Form," he declares to Malcolm Cowley in September 1955,

> and am so glad that I self-taught myself (with some help from Messrs. Joyce & Faulkner) to write SPONTANEOUS PROSE . . . and at the same time what rejoices me most: RHYTHMIC—It's prose answering the requirements mentioned by W. C. Williams, for natural-speech rhythms and words— (*SL, I* 515)

As John Tytell suggests, the resulting novel is "the grand register of how Cassady affected the Beats with the kinesis of being and an appreciation of the cataclysmic import of the here and now." Yet Tytell's contention that Cassady was "the model of the common urge to communicate ordinary experience in a natural, unpretentious voice" (175) overlooks not only Kerouac's declaration of his status in the text as fabulator but also Cody's attention to the phrase and "get[ting] it down." For here, as Davidson notes, Duluoz is both interlocutor and editor, self-consciously constructing his hero by shaping the tone and context of the conversation through stage directions (CODY. [*laughs*] That tea'll overcome anything. [*pause*] . . . Why don't you let me read John's letter? [*playing whiny little boy*] [*VC* 155]) (74). The metadiscourse extends into Cody's concern with Duluoz's parenthetical description of his "*demurely downward look*" in the previous transcript, which recounts details of his visit to Old Bull Lee:

> And, so—that's what I say when I say "I can't get it down," and then . . . "two minutes"—but you picked up on that, of all the different things I was sayin, and so you said, "But you don't *have* to get it down," you know, that's what you said . . . and so the demure downward look . . . was simply in the same tone and the same fashion . . . as my reaction and feeling was when I said the words "but you can't get it down" you know. (165)

Such mediations also inform the *Book of Dreams,* supposedly written "nonstop so that the subconscious could speak for itself in its own form, that is, uninterruptedly flowing & rippling—Being half awake I hardly knew what I was doing let alone writing" (4):

> I'm dashing down this street, cloppity clip, just left Cody and Evelyn at a San Francisco spectral restaurant or cafeteria table at Market and Third where we talked eagerly plans for a trip <u>East</u> it was (as if!) (as if there could be East or West in that waving old compass of the sack, base set on the pillow, foolish people and crazy people dream, the

world wont be saved at this rate, these are the scravenings of a—lost—
sheep)—the Evelyn of these dreams is an amenable—Cody is—(cold
and jealous)—something—dont know—dont care—Just that after I
talk to them—Good God it's taken me all this time to say, I'm riding
down the hill— (7–8)

The rhythm of Cassady's speech thus qualifies as an apprenticeship in
the phenomenology of writing. "Consider, too," Kerouac tells him in 1955,
"that our friendship and brotherhood has really been a literary association,
djever think that?" (*SL, I* 474). *Cody*'s eponymous hero serves as a catalyst
for exploration or as a set of phonetic symbols in the surface of the reading
that need not refer to a fixed presence. As Kerouac explains, "VISION [means]
full-length prose works concentrating on character of one individual, with
no other form than that, including verse and any thing, even pictures" (*SD*
342). Cassady's body of work as a published writer, *The First Third* and a few
surviving letters, is small and largely unexceptional—"There is something
in me that wants to come out," he discloses to Kerouac in 1947, "something
of my own that must be said. Yet, perhaps, words are not the way for me"
(qtd. in C. Cassady 49)—but the "speaking man" fully materializes upon
Kerouac's shaping of his vibrancy into *Cody*'s text. In line with the narrative,
Pomeroy shifts and changes to invoke the improvised moment, a past that is
alternately erased and remade anew. This theme is announced at the beginning of the "Frisco: the Tape" section, where Kerouac quotes Lee ("[H]e
said 'I'm an artist!'"), and is amplified throughout with references to literary
predecessors and experimental writing techniques:

> CODY. . . . I've just spent the last minute thinking and I had a complete
> block.
> JACK. Well speaking of that, look at this sentence (*flute*). Now. Concern-
> ing . . . THE TAPE RECORDER IS TURNING, THE TYPEWRITER IS WAITING,
> AND I SIT HERE WITH A FLUTE IN MY MOUTH. And so you're just sittin
> there thinking while it's playing (*plays flitty flute*)
> CODY. That's just what I've been doin but I couldn't think of the thought.
> And I guess the reason I can't think of it and why I'm blocked is because
> I didn't formalize it or I didn't think about it long enough, soon as the
> thought hit me, why, I didn't think it out, because I was gonna blurt it
> out. Damn, if I'd have just spoken—(*Cody running water at sink, flute
> blowing, watery flute*) Your coffee's gettin cold. *I'll* bring it over but I
> don't know which one it is (*really meant, he says, he didn't know whether
> I wanted cream or sugar or what*). (*VC* 187–88)

Kerouac admits the outside world into his performance, which synchronizes with dialogue to lend the impression of thinking, feeling, and writing at once. This metanarrational gesture corresponds to Jean-Luc Godard's decision to leave the sound of the camera rolling in *Vivre sa vie* and to John Cage's pleasure at environmental interference during concerts of his music, a refusal to cover up the act of making that imbues the open form work. Here is Cody quoted in part 3:

> Used to not feel couple of years ago hardly worth it to complete the sentence and then it got so try as I might I couldn't and it developed into something that way, see, so now in place of that I just complete the thought whatever I've learned. . . . [I]nstead of trying to make myself hurry back to where I should be . . . I go on talking *about* these things, thinking about things, and memory, 'cause we're both concerned about, ah, memory, and just relax like Proust and everything. So I talk on about that as the mind and remembers and thinks. . . (179)

The claims of causality slip away into the layered expanse of the book as the act of talking spurs the multidirectional language through which the postwar Beat experience can be remembered. Again, Henry Miller may be cited as a precursor, particularly in his configuration of Katsimbalis in *The Colossus of Maroussi*, observed here by the narrator while asleep:

> Once I approached close to him and bending over I explored the silent cavity [of his mouth] with a photographic eye. What an astounding thing is the voice! By what miracle is the hot magma of the earth transformed into that which we call speech? If out of clay such an abstract medium as words can be shaped, what is to hinder us from leaving our bodies at will and taking up our abode on other planets or between the planets? What is to prevent us from rearranging all life, atomic, molecular, corporeal, stellar, divine? Why should we stop at words, or at planets, or at divinity? Who or what is powerful enough to eradicate this miraculous heaven which we bear within us like a seed and which, after we have embraced in our mind all the universe, is nothing more than a seed—since to say universe is as easy as to say seed, and we have yet to say greater things, things beyond saying, things limitless and inconceivable, things which no trick of language can encompass. *You* lying there, I was saying to myself, where has that voice gone? Into what inky crevices are you crawling with your ganglionic feelers? Who are you, *what* are you now in drugged silence? Are you fish? Are you spongy root? Are you *you*? (77)

Moving within a global warfare scenario, Miller's germ of speech morphology yields a glimpse of pulsating, egoless new life that renders binary adjustment useless. The numinous aspect of existence is there to be discovered through a performative language that defies limit. With both Miller and Kerouac, fiction and world alike are decisively opened to the full range of demotic and hieratic discourses, opposing their official damnation to the margins and fulfilling Whitman's 1860 prophecy of a poetry that, like "the Real Dictionary" he also envisioned, would incorporate "all words that exist in use . . . [a] range of treasure-houses . . . full of ease, definiteness and power—full of sustenance" (qtd. in Rothenberg and Joris, *Two* 6).

Through the decade of *Visions of Cody, Doctor Sax,* and "October in the Railroad Earth," a pattern develops whereby Kerouac's written idiolect moves closer to spoken forms, pitched uniquely between literary and sonic composition. Outlining his intention in a 1950 journal entry to create an "American Times series to be narrated in the voices of the Americans themselves," Kerouac admits to Cassady that "[f]or a long time [my voice] sounded false":

> I labored on several other variations . . . one an outright voice for "the boys" . . . and a [LITERARY] voice for the critics. . . . My important recent discovery and revelation is that the voice is all. Can you tell me Shakespeare's voice per se? . . . What I'm going to do is let the voices speak for themselves. I'm going to write one book in nigger dialect, another in bum dialect, another in hip-musician dialect, another in French-Canadian-English dialect, another in American-Mexican dialect, another in Indian dialect, another in cool dialect, and I might one day write a slim little volume narrated by an effeminate queer. (*SL, I* 230–33)

That "enormous rushing noise of a great voice muted in the silence of books" (*SL, I* 232) will arise from an act of cultural "negative capability." In *Tristessa,* for example, the delineation of voices crosses race, class, and national boundaries, with a Mexican prostitute junkie appointed as speech catalyst. Kerouac omits articles, prepositions, and connectives to notate the rhythms of her broken English: "I breeng you back the moa-ny" (43). As is the case with Mardou in *The Subterraneans,* Kerouac synchronizes asides and thoughts eddying above the level of consciousness via urban measures in both monologue and conversation (Weinreich 115). Ever attentive to the need for analytical prowess, Kerouac's double relationship to mystic surrender in these books extends the supreme sense of shaping that is a feature of *Road.* As Mottram suggests, "The seeker after IT in *On the Road,* the laughing religious, the artist, the American dionysiac of the historical underground always poised himself between spontaneity and discipline, a lesson he learned from jazz and Thomas Wolfe" ("Preface" 51).

Kerouac's reflexive position in *Cody* thus resolves the dilemma of how to transform dialogue (the "first-happening") into prose without sloppy retreat into linear maxim or single voice. Duluoz and Pomeroy's compulsion to arrest the elusive quality of spontaneity in their metatalk is clear. Prompted by his study of the transcript of the previous night's tape, which has become "a telling" and therefore a narrative, Cody remarks:

> [W]hat it actually was, was a recalling right now on my part. . . . [A]ll I did now was re-go back to that memory and bring up a little rehash . . . in little structure line, a skeletonized thing of the—what I thought earlier, and that's what one does you know, you know when you go back and remember about a thing that you clearly thought out and went around before, you know what I'm sayin the second or third or fourth time you tell about it or say anything like that why it comes out different. . . . [T]he effort to go back and remember in detail all those things that I've thought about earlier, is such a task, and unworthy. (178)

This is, of course, thematic. The Legend's leitmotif of permanent loss, both personal and national, is locked into the memory of Cassady, impelling Kerouac to retrieve by language the "orgiastic future that year by year recedes before us;" Fitzgerald's words from *The Great Gatsby* (171) are like a subtext inside *Visions of Cody*. Recurrent parings of "night" and "time" alongside "rainy," "gloomy," "sad," and "tragic" amplify the struggle to regain the early equilibrium of exhilaration and dissipation. To Mottram, the book's form emerges from this

> urgent desire to counter imminent loss of vitality—that the Dionysian form of Cody will leave, as the gods used to leave men in ancient Mediterranean societies, and as Shakespeare says the gods left Antony. But the gain is language which produces a text to recover both the presence of energy and its absence. Kerouac is here a master of those urgent gestures to recover what escapes all too easily into the unconscious, to regain by techniques of memory at the transmission point of language in discourse. ("Preface" 50)

The textual surface then does not advocate nostalgia; rather it observes, eschewing re-presentation in favor of a leap into the risk of ceaseless new form. Charged with hermeneutic pressure, *Cody* is an envisioned world that moves ahead of given orders and overlays them. Minute decisions made within the confessional dialogue echo the jazz improviser's split-second interactions with an ensemble. Olson's call for a poetics of "embodiment" and a "Projective Verse," wherein "ONE PERCEPTION MUST IMMEDIATELY AND DIRECTLY LEAD TO A FURTHER PERCEPTION," is a primer here:

[A]t *all* points (even, I should say, of our management of daily reality as of the daily work) get on with it, keep moving, keep in, speed, the nerves, their speed, the perceptions, theirs, the acts, the split second acts, the whole business, keep it moving as fast as you can citizen. . . . USE USE USE the process at all points, in any given poem always, always one perception must must must MOVE, INSTANTER, ON ANOTHER! (*Collected* 240)

With Kerouac, the road as structural device for advancement through time is modified into an expansive platform, marked by a prose tone speeding erratically between confidence and despair. Moments collapse into one another "instanter" without break or explanation, forging the mobile self. From *Cody*: "[T]he moment is ungraspable, is already gone and if we sleep we can call it up again mixing it with unlimited other beautiful combinations—shuffle the old file cards of the soul in demented hallucinated sleep" (31).

Consciousness is embodied by constant "occurrence," to utilize Robert Creeley's term: an attention to "now," which in *Cody* turns on reconfigured speech (often one word) or bop improvisation and precludes both chronometric frame and mythology (the fulfillment of the previous). This test of perception extends into the fourth section of the book, the "Imitation of the Tape in Heaven," an imagined recreation of a recorded dialogue or Duluoz's "movie house of mine in the dream" (289). Deliberately redolent of *Finnegans Wake,* the interior monologue of merging personalities and voices offers a world trajectory transmitted through a solitary speaker. Again the text assumes an analytical stance toward language, as demonstrated by the dissertation on composition and memory by "Lady Godiva":

> Let us ascertain, in the morning, if there is a way of abstracting the interesting paragraphs of material in all this running consciousness stream that can be used as the progressing lightning chapters of a great essay about the wonders of the world as it continually flashes up in retrospect. (291)

Godiva's sentence stands as a commentary on Kerouac's fictive processes, the reworking of past experience being the foundation of the Legend. Before closing with continuing "imitations" and a re-creation of *Road*'s adventures, Kerouac introduces "Joan Rawshanks in the Fog," an observation of the film *Sudden Fear,* made in the streets of San Francisco. This "American scene" joins disparate frames in cinematic montage, a writing technique he calls "MOVIE" ("Bookmovies, or Mindmovies, prose concentration camera-eye visions of a definite movie of the mind with fade-ins, pans, close-ups, and fade-outs" [*SD* 342]) that gives a panoramic mode removed from *Road*'s unitary perspective. As Ellis points out, the symbolic meaning and position of the passage within the text forms a telling contrast to the Detroit Cinema episode in the earlier book, where Paradise is constrained by the mythic patterning of the plot (53):

> The people who were in that all-night movie were the end. . . . [I]f you sifted all Detroit . . . the beater solid core of dregs couldn't be better gathered. The picture was Singing Cowboy Eddie Dean and his gallant white horse Bloop, that was number one; number two . . . was George Raft, Sidney Greenstreet, and Peter Lorre in a picture about Istanbul. We saw both of these things six times each during the night. We saw them waking, we heard them sleeping, we sensed them dreaming, we were permeated completely with the strange Grey Myth of the West and the weird dark Myth of the East when morning came. All my actions since then have been dictated automatically to my subconscious by this horrible osmotic experience. (230)

Here Kerouac dramatizes through its Hollywood simulation the supremacist western myth of boundless expansion and exploitation that renders the spirit of place incidental. This is also the concern of Burroughs's novel *The Place of Dead Roads*, which starts by citing a newspaper headline that participates in its own reproduction: "September: Shoot-out in Boulder, September 17th 1889. What appeared to be an old western shoot-out took place yesterday afternoon at the Boulder cemetery" (3). Set in a period of decline for the territory, a series of signifiers follows: guns, Dodge City stores, and heroes like the original Cody, Buffalo Bill, which are constantly dredged up and played back for re-use. Kerouac's critique of the myth suggests a similar entrapment of human needs within obsessive ideologies. In *Road* this code prescribes a constant reversion to the culture of "rubbish America," within which the narrator's desire for freedom is given, to paraphrase Baudrillard, endless, timeless, discursive replication (Ellis 49). Paradise awakes to the stench of trash collected by the cinema's attendants before "they almost swept me away too":

> Had they taken me with it, Dean . . . would have had to roam the entire United States and look in every garbage pail from coast to coast before he found me embryonically convoluted among the rubbishes of my life, his life and the life of everybody concerned. (*OTR* 230)

Whereas *Road*'s narrator twice compares his authoritarian dumbshow as a reluctant uniformed guard to "a Western Movie" (62), in *Cody* he follows his own advice in "Belief & Technique for Modern Prose" to become

"Writer-Director of Earthly movies, Sponsored & Angeled in Heaven" (*GB* 73). From within the text, and no doubt drawing on his role at this time as a synopsis writer for 20th Century Fox, Kerouac recognizes the hypnotic design of commercial media, which for those contained within the "narrow milieu" of the city creates "a pseudo-world beyond, and a pseudo-world within themselves as well"—C. Wright Mills's observation from 1956 (321). Unlike Paradise in Detroit, Duluoz is a producer, not a passive consumer of meaning—"In the movies but not at all At them," as Fitzgerald has it (*Tender* 101)—as consistent with the change in his own narrative bearings with regard to Cassady.

Using the cinematic plasticity of light thematically in "Rawshanks," Kerouac recoils from complicity in the proletarian rhetoric of the production called "America," a commodification that Guy Debord defines as an "immense accumulation of *spectacles*" replacing "all that was directly lived" with "mere representation" (12). Distanced from Hollywood's confounding of illusion, news, and history in the service of power, he fastens instead on a narrative principle of inclusiveness—voices, moods, speeds, points of view, modes of lighting—to confront the problem of presentation. Containment and rank, one thing placed inside another as explanation, shift into collage, an architectural method whereby the events of perception are flush with language. What Williams describes as "rotating the object" in *Spring and All* takes *Cody*'s text out of the nineteenth-century classical sense of space and into quantum multiplicity, the density and rapidity of Kerouac's writing in this section being part of the process:

> Joan Rawshanks stands alone in the fog. Her name is Joan Rawshanks and she knows it, just as anybody knows his name, and she knows who she is, same way, Joan Rawshanks stands alone in the fog and a thousand eyes are fixed on her in all kinds of ways. . . . [T]he angry technicians muster and make gestures in the blowing fog that rushes past kleig lights and ordinary lights in infinitesimal cold showers, to make everything seem miserable and storm-hounded, as though we were all on a mountain top saving the brave skiers in the howl of the elements, but also just like the lights and the way the night mist blows by them at the scene of great airplane disasters or train wrecks or even just construction jobs that have reached such a crucial point that there's overtime in muddy midnight Alaskan conditions; Joan Rawshanks, wearing a mink coat, is trying to adjust herself to the act of crying but has a thousand eyes of local Russian Hill spectators who've been hearing about the Hollywood crew filming for the last hour, ever since

dinner's end, and are arriving on the scene here despite the fog (move over from my microphone wire, there) in driblets . . . (*VC* 318)

The metatheme of visual depiction is introduced in part 1, where the city sketches integrate references to the film industry. The second textual block opens with a description of the run-down "capricio B-movie," its broken marquee lighting and misplaced lettering "spelled out by crazy dumb kids who earn eighteen dollars a week," symbolizing the broken fabric of representational illusion and the implied questioning of complicit consumption. Surrounded by the detritus of "banana peels," "old splashmarks of puke," "broken milk-bottles," and "an old beat gas station—diner on the other corner—right next to movie is a hotdog-Coke-magazine establishment with a big scarred Coca-Cola sign at base of an open counter topped by a marble now so old that it has turned gray and chipped," this, realizes the narrator, "is the bottom of the world" (18). The mythic commercial signs no longer invigorate the story incessantly rehearsed by Hollywood (Ellis 51), which, in Marshall McLuhan's words, saturates "the childish mental processes of those locked in the mass dream" by advancing the "trek toward the voluntary annihilation of our individual humanity" (*Mechanical* 230). Even the word "America" corrodes into a signifier of degradation, recalling the cheated nation commemorated in Ginsberg's poem of that name:

America is being wanted by the police, pursued across Kentucky and Ohio, sleeping with the stockyard rats and howling tin shingles of gloomy hideaway silos, is the picture of an axe in *True Detective Magazine,* is the impersonal nighttime at crossings and junctions where everybody looks both ways, four ways, nobody cares—America is where you're not even allowed to cry for yourself. . . . America is what's laid on Cody Pomeroy's soul the onus and the stigma—that in the form of a big plainclothesman beat the shit out of him in a backroom till he talked about something which isn't even important anymore—America (TEENAGE DOPE SEX CAR RING!!) is also the red neon and the thighs in the cheap motel—it's where at night the staggering drunks began to appear like cockroaches when the bars close—It is where people, people, people are weeping and chewing their lips in bars as well as lone beds and masturbating in a million ways in every hiding hole you can find in the dark—It has evil roads behind gas tanks where murderous dogs snarl from behind wire fences and cruisers suddenly leap out like getaway cars but from a crime more secret, more baneful than words can tell—It is where Cody Pomeroy learned that people aren't good, they want to be bad—where he learned they want to cringe and beat, and snarl is the name of their lovemaking—America made bones of a young boy's face and took dark paints and made hollows around his eyes, and made his cheeks sink in pallid paste and grew furrows on a marble front and transformed the eager wishfulness into the thicklipped silent wisdom of saying nothing, not even to yourself in the middle of the goddamn night—the click of coffee saucers in the poor poor night—Someone's gurgling work at a lunchcart dishpan (in bleakhowl Colorado voids for nothing)—Ah and nobody cares but the heart in the middle of US that will reappear when the salesmen all die. America's a lonely crockashit. (*VC* 118)

The interrogation continues in the "Rawshanks" passage, which stresses the affectation behind "the general materialism of Hollywood": the manipulation of the "surrounded," "cooped up" onlookers; the tears concocted to order; and the director's "cruel" manipulation of Joan's head in a "scarf noose." The actress "stands alone" in a variation on the B-movie stunt hero who evokes suspicion in part 1 and who "wouldn't act like that in real unreality" (68). The fluid masks endemic to her profession seed new meanings and identities, as the name "Joan Rawshanks" resonates through the circular structure of the prose as "jewel center," to use Kerouac's key term from his manifesto. The passage winds down into broken syllables of alliterative sound freed from literal analogy ("as a bouy in the bay goes b-o, as a buoy in the bag goes b-o, bab-o, as a buoy in the bag goes bab-o" [319]), taking with it the vitality of the myth that her performance supposedly conveys.

Having modified Wolfe's phrase "unreal-reality," through which Gant's suggestibility is indicated (80), Kerouac gives himself license to relinquish the compromise of vision and reproduction of the official stories of America that limited the possibilities of *On the Road* ("our B-movie again" [202]). The realization that "little raggedy Codys dream, as rich men plan" follows, along with the exposure of Hollywood's pressure to homogenize experience into a simulacrum of "all the movies we've ever been in" (116; Ellis 53). As he notes in *Some of the Dharma,* "Hollywood Movies are the modern version of the violence and murder of the Roman Circus. You can tell by the continual plot-line of murder, greed, hatred, lust, unsympathy—" (220). "Wise repose" and "independence from all false education, propaganda, and organized entertainment" (111) therefore start with refusing the consumer instruction of shock and sentiment:

This movie house of mine in the dream has got a golden light to it though it is deeply shaded brown, or misty gray too inside, with thousands not hundreds but all squeezed together children in three diggin the perfect cowboy B-movie which is not shown in Technicolor but dream golden . . . (*VC* 289)

Moreover, the emphasis on the Rawshanks film as something made, a series of retakes leading to a final "TAKE," which in itself may not be authoritative, suggests a further meta-analogy with Kerouac's strategies. The meanings of *Cody* accrue through comparing its events with those in *Road*, hence Ginsberg's sense of *Cody* as both an "in-depth" version of the other book and a "historical sequel" (*Deliberate* 353). The emphasis on self-referentiality informs the novel's closing sections, where the speaker cranks himself up with a mock entreaty to muse and patron that characterizes the traditional medieval quest and launches into a further rewrite of his great travel narrative of 1940s America:

> The thing to do is put the quietus on the road—give it the final furbishoos and finishes, or is that diddling? Kind King and Sir, my Lord, God, please direct me in this—The telling of the voyages again, for the very beginning; that is, immediately after this. The Voyages are told each in one breath, as is your own, to foreshadow that or this rearshadows *that, one!*
>
> I first met Cody in 1947 but I didn't travel on the road with him till 1948. (*VC* 391)

The sense of time regained and lost in *Road* now allies personal and mythic planes and is articulated through a phantasmagoria of re-evocation and revision, blurring life and dream. Embodying Carlyle's belief that history is a text that we must continually read and write and in which we, too, are written, Duluoz becomes a cipher in his own book and recomposes the beginning of Cody's story. This includes the story of his own story, seemingly infinite and circular, the ramifications of the central tale being dizzyingly redoubled into digressing tales with no attempt made to gradate their levels of reality. Laboring now to perpetuate Cody's image by setting down each experience to the present instant, the life of "a great rememberer redeeming life from darkness" inevitably hits the juncture of composition, and the hero must be released:

> Goodbye Cody—your lips in your moments of self-possessed thought and new found responsible goodness are as silent, make at least a noise, and mystify with sense in nature, like the light of an automobile reflecting from the shiny silverpath of a sidewalk tank this very instant, as silent and all this, as a bird crossing the dawn in search of the mountain cross and the sea beyond the city at the end of the land.

Adios, you who watched the sun go down, at the rail, by my side, smiling—

Adios, King. (462–63)

# 4

## Fabulous Artifice

Bizarre that we can so live in the imagination of our "world"
and yet so bitterly contest any sense that it is not the actual
one, or perhaps more aptly, the right one. I wonder that my
own generation, having come of age in the cataclysmic "image"
of order which was World War II, finds such difficulty in
considering any alternative, in recognizing that it indeed
might be otherwise, that the possible devastation of all worlds
might be in the mind awry and not simply a fact of nature. Or
if it is such a fact, if our convulsion and self-immolation are
"organic," then how do we think ourselves to be, and for what
conceivable reason? Have all such questions been answered?
Or do they continue to matter?
— Robert Creeley, introduction to *Collected Prose*, by
Charles Olson

My business is not to write like in the 1920's but to make a new
literature, which I've done.
— Jack Kerouac, letter to Tom Guinzburg, January 1962

Kerouac's "saga," his term for recording the processes of "my
mind, wrapped in wild observation of everything" (*SL, I* 231),
is consistent with the great displacement in twentieth-century
fiction from authorial control to linguistic plasticity. As *Visions
of Cody* shows, Kerouac's texts frequently refer to their own construction,
using techniques introduced into the novel by Sterne, Diderot, and Flaubert
("[I envisage] a book about nothing . . . without external attachments . . .
stand[ing] by itself through the internal forces of its style as the earth stands
without being supported, a book with hardly any subject, or at least with

an almost invisible subject" [203]) and advanced across high modernism, OuLiPo, and the *nouveau roman* alike. These include metacommentaries; abrupt switches of subject, dialect, and tone; movements between narrative logic and sound structure; and incursions of nonverbal forms, effectively turning page into canvas and drawing attention to the book's materiality.

In *Vanity of Duluoz*, Kerouac names Joyce and his experimental epic *Ulysses* as a resource for his writing apprenticeship. Early notebook imitations are inserted accordingly ("That's how writers begin, by imitating the masters" [107]), as his forerunner had done in *Look Homeward, Angel*. But whereas Wolfe's stream of consciousness prose fails to transcend pastiche, Kerouac actively celebrates the "fabulous artificer," Daedalus, in *Visions of Cody* by turning the creative process into an artifact. Punning allusions to *Ulysses* abound in the exchanges between the two protagonists: "Bloom let the soap melt in his back-pocket he was so hot"; "JACK. Yes—fit for desert nights, I'd say it was fit for rugs in loverooms / CODY. Blooms, blooms—but we'll turn off this tape" (364).[1]

As opposed to recording the quantifiable aspects of society—more properly the realm of reportage—Kerouac plies a new set of fictional skills in the face of the eroded positivist basis of realism. The time frame of the Duluoz Legend unfolds around the procedures of perception and memory, the "appearing, disappearing and reappearing characters" who surround "the 'I' of Kerouac . . . from book to book" (*SL, II* 393), having no life apart from the narrator's observations; when they leave the stage they cease to exist. As with Miller, Nin, Proust, Céline, and Wolfe, the subject of Kerouac's books is the author's own life in retrospect, and yet the concentration on the phenomenology of writing confers an independence upon the texts, something that consistently eludes his biographers.[2]

Following Joyce, Kerouac spends a lifetime writing each book in a different way, influenced by Joyce's contention that "[o]ne great part of every human existence is passed in a state which cannot be rendered sensible by the use of wideawake language, cutanddry grammar and goahead plot" (qtd. in Ellmann, *Joyce* 412). Countering notions of propriety deriving from the stylization of language into established rhetoric, Kerouac's fictions imply that the artist's role is to choose between forms acquired experientially, apparently arbitrary models being as legitimate a skin for the creative act as any other. "*Doctor Sax* was written high on tea without pausing to think," he informs Ginsberg in 1952. "[S]ometimes Bill Garver would come into the room and so the chapter ended there" (*SL, I* 349). And as Ronald Sukenick suggests:

> Rather than serving as a mirror or redoubling on itself, fiction adds itself
> to the world, creating a meaningful "reality" that did not previously

exist. Fiction is artifice but not artificial. It seems as pointless to call the creative powers of the mind "fraudulent" as it would to call the procreative powers of the body such. (qtd. in Federman, *Surfiction* 24)

As Kerouac realizes, having worked through the "novel-type novel" of *The Town and the City,* immersion within systematized form and symbol, in this case the Wolfean naturalism that "anticipat[es] the organic confusion and variety of life with a strict iron-clad 'concept'" (*SL, I* 162), may in itself be a kind of repression. "The novel's dead," he tells Alfred G. Aronowitz. "I broke loose from all that and wrote picaresque narratives. That's what my books are" (qtd. in "Beat").

Straining against the entrenched conservatism of the publishing industry ("Giroux isn't fond of my idea, he insists on 'narrative' and 'narrative styles,' but the list at Harcourt isn't exactly going to make history" [*SL, I* 449]), the ensuing books work free from a logic of imitation into a series of forms composed of their own integrity. In line with the relegation of causality in twentieth-century physics, the Legend sheds the mundane literalism upon which social realist writers habitually rely: a consensus grounded in the chronological pattern of expectation and delayed resolution (thematic metamorphosis), totality of coverage, omniscient narration, full-bodied characterization, and fixed denouement from the laying bare of relationships and motives.

Endorsed by the State on both sides of the Cold War, such an apparatus is naturalized as a given, guaranteeing sovereign judgment and stable subjectivity legislated by "common sense," finished identity, universal truth, and patriarchal justice.[3] The upshot is an audience trained to insist on "accessible" meaning, which is singular or obvious, and thus an instrument of power (*author-ity*). Such representational designs are not only addictive, as Burroughs and Brion Gysin note in *Minutes to Go,* but murderous, as scores of writers at midcentury could testify. "To make the meaning subtle is a political act," corroborates Roland Barthes, "just as it always is, to seek to shred . . . to disrupt . . . to break down this mania for meaning. This is not without its dangers" (*Writing* 57).

A work such as *Visions of Cody* responds by suspending ideological reinforcement, drawing attention to the word as a performative presence, away from what McLuhan calls its "[m]acadamized surface." "Freedom, like taste," he writes in *The Mechanical Bride,* "is an activity of perception and judgment based on a great range of particular acts and experiences. Whatever fosters mere passivity and submission is the enemy of this vital activity" (22). Kerouac vigorously deploys the principles of ellipsis and multiplicity identified by Sartre in *What Is Literature* and by Alain Robbe-

Grillet in *For a New Novel* as directions for the postmodern text, *Cody*'s sheer malleability emphasizing the gaps between talk, writing, and memory as a way of separating the act of enunciation and what is enounced. The book's constant reminder of the transactions between speech and language, body and typography, is developed by Ginsberg:

> [Kerouac] actually writes about writing, just as the subject of [*Visions of Cody*] is Visions of mind, just as the hero is real, just as the scene is an actual tape of the hero talking about his memories & visions, just as the actual hero-author-tape-transcribed becomes a living scene of an art worked book in progress prosed; so part of that scene is author & hero explaining their speech to each other, so introduced here also . . . is the book-writer writing a sentence of his book, in the scene of the book he's writing—that's one scene itself. (*Mystery* 15)

The novel thus clears the realist pretense of objective transparency, which presupposes unmediated authority. *Cody* discovers as it moves and as such discourages direct transportation between the minds of writer and reader, bolstering Raymond Federman's insistence that to create fiction is "to abolish reality, and . . . the notion that reality is truth" (*Surfiction* 8). As Kerouac himself asks in *Book of Dreams*: "Who objective? Who subjective? Who real? What real? All liquid phantomry in my mind essence dreaming, like life—Ha!" (155). Dismissing the "demand that everyone comply with the rules set down as to how to think and what to do"—Kerouac's words from an unpublished 1950 philosophy paper—his work encourages active participation in the ordering of syntax and meaning. This effectively gives an integral critique of the genre's schematized norms, its "cool medium" demanding neither the recollection nor anticipation of the kind required to elucidate a conventional narrative. Recovering the hermeneutic built into the Latin verb *interpretor,* which suggests the more subtle "to put a construction upon" and "to negotiate" as well as "to explain," the reader of *Cody* encounters, to quote Mottram,

> a writing which does not require passive-consumption and acts of writing recognition. At the moment we read reminiscences of style, the text subverts. One of Kerouac's strategies is to make us find out how to read at different points of entry. . . . Nor are we invited to interpret the text into *a priori* meaning at every point, the fallacious basis of academic literary criticism. *Visions of Cody* draws us to an experience of language in itself and to speculations on the foundations of material presences rather than to poke around for prior subject. ("Preface" 50)

Starting from the prospect of language as an existential act, such narratives fuel Federman's contention that to write "is to *produce* meaning, and not to *reproduce* a pre-existing meaning. To write is to progress, and not *remain* subjected (by habit or reflexes) to the meaning that supposedly precedes the words." His term for this is "Surfiction," the revelation of life as fiction:

> The experience of life gains meaning only in its recounted form, in its verbalized version, or, as Céline said . . . in answer to those who claimed that his novels were merely autobiographical: "Life, also, is fiction . . . and a biography is something one invents afterwards." [The purpose of fiction is] to unmask its own fictionality, to expose the metaphor of its own fraudulence, and not to pretend any longer to pass for reality, for truth, or for beauty. Consequently, fiction will no longer be regarded as a mirror of life, as a pseudorealistic document that informs us about life, nor will it be judged on the basis of its social, moral, psychological, metaphysical, commercial value, or whatever, but on the basis of what it is and what it does as an autonomous art form in its own right. (*Surfiction* 7–8)

Having at first bypassed an awareness of how meaning is produced in *The Town and the City*, Kerouac writes himself and his reader into liberation, realizing, like Olson in *Maximus*, that "I have been an ability—a machine—up to / now. An act of 'history'" (495). The Legend adds to this drive to reinstate artisanal potency, described by Williams as the "transition [from] worn-out conceptions of the late nineteenth century" to the "active invention" of modernity:

> We have, above all, for our own Occidental thought, Shakespeare's, "To hold the mirror up to nature"—as vicious a piece of bad advice as the budding artist ever gazed upon. It is tricky, thoughtless, wrong. It is NOT to hold the mirror up to nature that the artist performs his work. It is to make, out of the imagination, something not at all a copy of nature, but something quite different, a new thing, unlike any thing else in nature, a thing advanced and apart from it. To imitate nature [as spoken of in Aristotle's *Poetics*] involves the verb to do. To copy is merely to reflect something already there, inertly. . . . But by imitation we enlarge nature itself, we become nature or we discover in ourselves nature's active part. [This] enlarges the concept of art, dignifies it to a place not yet fully realized. (*Autobiography* 240–41)

This is further delineated by Robert Duncan as "The Truth and Life of Myth":

All the events, things and beings, of our life move then with the intent of a story revealing itself. . . . [N]ot only are dreams the stuff life is made of, but life is the stuff dreams are made of. And in the psychopathology of daily life, the still more real world of the actual begins to be a text of meanings, actions that reveal ritual intention, symbolic functions, words and appearances that are not what they seem. . . . But whatever realm of reality we seek out, we find it is woven of fictions. (*Fictive* 2–10)

*Visions of Cody* takes on these propositions, allowing the reader to engage in creative construction rather than to hunt for evidence of validation by reducing materials to skeleton paraphrase or theory. Interpretation is increasingly problematized as the Legend unfolds. Beginning with *On the Road*, Kerouac abandons the mechanics of the well-made plot and the emulation of journalism as literary mode in order to distance himself from a narrative position that is relentless and direct in its assertions. As Barthes affirms, "Another expression of fragility is, paradoxically, the close and insistent gaze of the artist. Power, because it is violent, never gazes. If it were to do so, to look a moment longer, a moment too long, it would lose its power" (*Writing* 57).

By *Cody,* the textual focus has swerved completely from the instrumentality of final meaning onto a vision that opens outward, an attitude of uncertainty underpinning the author's interrogation of memory and event. Fluctuating patterns and recesses between nonnarrative sections encourage agility in the act of reading, an unprejudiced adventure, as opposed to a failure of communication. As Eliot observed with regard to St. John Perse's *Anabasis,* any "obscurity" that results from the disconnected cluster of meanings is attributable

> to the suppression of "links in the chain," of explanatory and connecting matter, and not to incoherence, or to the love of cryptogram. . . .
> Such selection of a sequence of images and ideas has nothing chaotic about it. There is a logic of the imagination as well as a logic of concepts. (*Prose* 77)

Conceived as a series of fragments to be visited at will and recalling both *Finnegans Wake* and Mallarmé's "The Book: A Spiritual Instrument"—"Let us have no more of those successive, incessant, back and forth motions of our eyes," Mallarmé writes in 1895,

> traveling from one line to the next and beginning all over again. Otherwise we will miss that ecstasy in which we become immortal for a brief hour, free of all reality, and raise our obsessions to the level of creation.

... [For] each of us has within him that lightning-like initiative which
can link the scattered notes together (82–83)

—one is free to dip into and "actively create" the novel of Cassady at any
point without loss of impact. *Cody*'s spatial field supersedes linearity, makes
no reference to given scheme, and confers no prescriptive connection between signs. "Then I began to think," Kerouac tells Cassady of his own
revolution of the word: "who's laid down the laws of 'literary' form? Who
says that a work must be chronological; that the reader wants to know what
happened anyhow? . . . Let's tear time up. Let's rip the guts out of reality"
(*SL, I* 274). Leaving *The Town and the City* far behind, established denota-
tions are constantly adapted for fresh purpose, exposing the relationships
between syntax, fiction, and the process of understanding, which remain
open to challenge.

This is, of course, thematic. Immersed within the locale of Cassady,
Kerouac advances a polymorphism that illustrates Robert Jay Lifton's idea
of "Protean Man," a Dionysian figure without permanent shape or identity.
Activating previous experience in perpetual variation, terms such as character, role, and narrator receive evolving definitions, reinforcing Lifton's
sense of a "continuous psychic recreation of self as the person's symbol of
his own organism," which "takes place in the social constellation" (xi–xii).
Accordingly, Kerouac's book moves in and out of events, comprehended as
directions inside a larger territory without permanent walls, while continually criticizing, disintegrating, and reshaping itself. The memory of Cassady
recurs as a generative core, or "meadow" to call on Duncan's sense of the
creative act ("a given property of the mind / that certain bounds hold against
chaos, / that is a place of first permission" [*Opening* 7]), and his image arises
as a many-layered "fictive certainty" contrary to fact.

Kerouac's preference for an economy of speculation over the traditional
notion of the novel as closed circuit surfaces as early as 1947, in a letter comparing Ginsberg's religious allegiance ("Allen does not doubt enough") to
Cassady's "perfection of doubt":

> We don't doubt enough, we form too many convictions, like idiots
> we live by them. It were far better that, instead of perfecting our at-
> tributes, or perfecting our position in the world even, we would spend
> time perfecting doubt—develop a perfection of doubt, become saints,
> saints. (*SL, I* 118)

Just as Cassady fuels Kerouac's desire for irreducible risk and multiplicity
in life, his speech patterns defy termination in fictional form. In *Cody,* the first
person narrative dissolves into tape-scripts and their imitations and third

person modulations. The speech act cancels the distance between observer and observed, author and subject, extinguishing what Barthes describes as the "smooth" narrative plane (*Writing* 45). Such inconsistencies suggest not undisciplined rambling but a rhizome operating between the lines of theme and voice, a relative of Burroughs's cinematic jump-cuts in *Naked Lunch*, edited by Kerouac and Ginsberg at the time of *Cody*'s composition.

The "cut-up" analogy extends to the novel's disjunctive domain, which aids Kerouac's recovery of the value of observational detail from its reduction to plot expedient or suffocation amid prefabricated classification. Pursuing his own recommendations in "Belief & Technique for Modern Prose"— "Don't think of words when you stop but to see the picture better. . . . Details are the Life of Prose" (*GB* 72)—Kerouac learns from Blake's call to

> Labor well the Minute Particulars, attend to the Little-ones . . .
> He who would do good to another must do it in Minute
>     Particulars:
> General Good is the plea of the scoundrel hypocrite &
>     flatterer,
> For Art & Science cannot exist but in minutely organized
>     Particulars
>
> (548)

and Williams's desire in *Paterson*

> To make a start,
> out of particulars
> and make them general, rolling
> up the sum.
>
> (3)

The hero's early life in Denver is dramatized through an inexhaustible litany of urban minutiae, connecting mimesis and catalog via the rough interjection of metacommentary:

> [H]aunted by the sooty girders and worn old black planks of railroad bridges behind warehouses, by cinder yards where great concentrations of cardboard crates that were a nuisance to foremen of factories became the sly opportunity of bums—the backplaces of what we call downtown, the nameless tunnels, alleys, sidings, platforms, ramps, ash heaps, miniature dumps, unofficial parking lots fit for murders, the filthy covered-with-rags plazas that you see at the foot of great redbrick chimneys—the same chimney that had bemused Cody on many a dreaming afternoon when he looked at it toppling forward

as clouds upswept the air in readiness for the big disaster—it was as though these things had been the—(and of course many more, why list any further, and besides we shall come back on other levels and more exhaustively)—these things had been the necessary parts of his first universe, its furniture. (*VC* 103)

Although guided by Joyce's panoramic inclusiveness, Kerouac's prose does not turn on "epiphany," that single revelation within the ordinary clutter of circumstance that gels the narrative. In *Cody* the continuous intensities of theme and perception interact and are distributed in a succession of "plateaus," to borrow Gregory Bateson's term for the libidinal economy of Balinese culture, as distinct from the West's orgasmic orientation. Mirroring the Legend's overall design, the novel gathers resonance through the cumulative impact of a series of scenes within a field, none of which are necessarily assigned superior importance. Hence the meticulous detail, the whole imminent in its parts.

The descriptions of interiors in part 1 are a further case in point. Redolent of *Howl*'s liturgical mode, "Hector's Cafeteria" is depicted cinematically in sensuous, radiant language that, in turn, recalls the medieval heavenly realm of the alliterative "Pearl" poet. In a complex sonic and visual structure, Kerouac exalts the "*shiny*" diner food as "huge," "immense," "enormous," "vast," "big," "mountainous," and "great," "illuminat[ed]" on a "glittering counter" surrounded by "decorative walls" and a "noble old ceiling of ancient decorated in fact almost baroque (Louis XV?) plaster now browned a smoky rich tan color—where chandeliers hung (obviously was an old restaurant) now electric bulbs with metal casings or shades." Aided by mirrors, the cubist juxtaposition of surfaces is invested with a transcendental aura: "But most of all it's that shining glazed sweet counter—showering like heaven—an all-out promise of joy in the great city of kicks." Connotations of religious "splendor" are reinforced by the "rose-tint walls decorated with images, engraved," and the cathedral light on religious iconography that followed "cold fish . . . great loaves of rye bread sliced" (25). Kerouac's mythic heightening owes much to Wolfe, in particular the passage in *Look Homeward, Angel* where Gant confronts the new American technological plane at the 1904 World Exposition:

Once in a huge building roaring with sound, he was rooted before a mighty locomotive, the greatest monster he had ever seen, whose wheels spun terrifically in grooves, whose blazing furnaces, raining red hot coals into the pit beneath, were fed incessantly by two grimed fire-painted stokers. The scene burned in his brain like some huge splendor out of Hell: he was appalled and fascinated by it.

Again, he stood at the edge of the slow, terrific orbit of the Ferris Wheel, reeled down the blaring confusion of the midway, felt his staggering mind converge helplessly into all the mad phantasmagoria of the carnival. . . . [Once Daisy] took him with her through the insane horrors of the scenic railway; they plunged bottomlessly from light into roaring blackness, and as his first yell ceased with a slackening of the car, rolled gently into a monstrous lighted gloom peopled with huge painted grotesques, the red maws of fiendish heads, the cunning appearances of death, nightmare and madness. (60–61)

The story of Cassady progresses through another carnival of lunch counters, body parts, journeys, and the transitory privileging of various signs no longer ranked by their proximity to a supreme signified. As previously indicated, this is a major Beat principle. "The bum's as holy as the seraphim! the madman is holy as you my soul are holy!" claims Ginsberg in "Footnote to Howl." "Everything is holy! everybody's holy! everywhere is holy! everyday is in eternity! Everyman's an angel!" (*Howl* 27). Such an assault on authoritative notions of taste does not simply ennoble a "low" object over a "high" one, by reversing sovereignties within a new metaphysics (*Tropic of Cancer*'s turd in a bidet). In the sixth paragraph of *Cody*, "masturbation" does not replace "immaculate conception" (22); the fall of one elevated system is neither stabilized nor succeeded by another, a fact ironically noted by John Hollander who in the *Partisan Review* complained of *Howl*'s "utter lack of decorum of any kind."

The forbidden territories of the self are instead laid bare to suggest an American rhetoric of unrestricted potential, undermining referential frames and symbols without junking them altogether. This is especially marked in *Visions of Gerard,* where a theistic Chain of Being is subjected to Buddhist overlay, restoring the wider meaning of the term "catholic":

Hearken, amigos, to the olden message: it's neither what you think it is, nor what you think it isn't, but an elder matter, uncompounded and clear—Pigs may rut in field, come running to the Soo-Call, full of sow-y glee; people may count themselves higher than pigs, and walk proudly down country roads; geniuses may look out of windows and count themselves higher than louts; tics in the pine needles may be inferior to the swan; but whether any of these and the stone know it, it's still the same truth: none of it is even there, it's a mind movie, *believe* this if you will and you'll be saved in the solvent solution of salvation and Gerard knew it well in his dying bed in his way, in his way—And who handed us down the knowledge here of the Diamond Light? Messengers unnumberable from the Ethereal Awakened Diamond Light. (71)

By implication, cultural values undergo redefinition in an ecocentric reading of past and present, which Duncan speaks of as "a symposium of the whole," opening the literary work into a dialogue between all modes of speech and occasion. In such a new "totality," he writes,

> all the old excluded orders must be included. The female, the proletariat, the foreign; the animal and vegetative; the unconscious and the unknown; the criminal and failure—all that has been outcast and vagabond must return to be admitted in the creation of what we consider we are. ("Rites" 24)

*Cody*'s opening pileup obliges with an inventory of commonplace images lacking thematic center or development. Everything remains marginal: a pageant of unending life with each part afforded its own distinct being, not a repository of people, creatures, and objects to be pressed into the author's service. Kerouac makes no attempt to efface difference or hinder the capacity for future rearrangement, a principle shared with Blake's *Marriage of Heaven and Hell,* which he read alongside Whitman's *Specimen Days & Collect* and Perse's *Anabasis* (which he also translated) in preparation for writing *Cody.*

The Beat disengagement from adjustment to "natural aristocracy" and the "truth" of original sin, espoused in the postwar sophistry of Russell Kirk, Reinhold Niebuhr, and Leo Strauss, therefore starts at the deepest level of form. This is amplified in *Desolation Angels,* where Kerouac's meditations on Hozomeen provoke a series of rhetorical questions and oppositions ("bitter" or "sweet") before a Taoist settlement on the futility of choice, since each contains its opposite anyway: "And still the Void is still and'll never move" (30–32). The binaries of either/or give way to an inclusive field of disseminated objects in his cabin, which are listed in a single breath and are irreducible to any sort of unity.

This is not to imply that Kerouac's role is reduced to passively mirroring undifferentiated activity, in the vein of Warhol's exercises in nonintervention. A schism exists in Kerouac's thought between the celebration of the heterogeneous—animality, inconsequential detail, bodily function—and the drive to explain and justify: an interpenetration of chaos and reason. Moreover, description of an object as it is "set before the mind" as "jewel center of interest . . . at *moment* of writing" (*GB* 69–70) demands an ecstatic focus or reverie if Spontaneous Prose is to fulfill its numinous potential.

The vital memory of "IT" in jazz performance through *On the Road* and *Visions of Cody* thus stands out from recounted events in the writer's consciousness to demonstrate the significance of linguistic decision, rhythm, and arrangement without conferring a still-point of referential authority upon the work. Kerouac's careful notation of the mind's movement creates its own rationale, holding discontinuous occasions together within a constantly evolving process. This imperative shares little ground with the eventless banality of films such as Warhol's *Sleep* and *The Chelsea Girls,* commodifications of total surveillance and progenitors of reality TV, where boredom and vulgarity are cast as erotic display.

Instead, elements of Kerouac's ironic self-defamation as "jolly story-teller" intersect in *Cody* with a transcursive, rather than discursive, path: a plasticity of writing that ceaselessly composes and decomposes his confessions into forms no longer signifying extranarrative symbols. It is evident from his letters that this scale of ambition is already in place at the beginning of his career but consistently undermined by editorial interference, *The Dharma Bums* manuscript alone being subjected to almost 4,000 corrections in order to meet Viking's house style. His overarching "vast Divine Comedy of my own" written in "free prose" suggests the heterogeneous rhetoric of *Cody* in macrocosm, changeable and genealogically complex in its interior relationships. From a linear point of view, the fragmentation in single text and grand sequence alike is incomprehensible, with events continually working loose from historical order into chance and mobility. However, Kerouac endorses Sartre's break with the classical insistence on consecutive logic and emerges within collage, the great revolution of twentieth-century form, datable to Planck's definition of quantum physics as an arrangement of discontinuous matter in 1900 and Freud's removal of chronology from descriptions of consciousness in *The Interpretation of Dreams* the same year.

Kerouac then innovates within what McLuhan terms the "multilocational" trajectory of cubism, the modernist sense of space that fractures the unified, continuous volumes of Euclidean geometry into planes and loses the causal relations derived from the Renaissance cosmologies of Copernicus, Alberti, and Newton. Taken into the literary field by Stein, Apollinaire, and Reverdy and adapted further by Tzara and Schwitters, *Cody* reflects the work of these predecessors in permitting neither dominant overview of shape nor coherence of a single point perspective converging on the reader. The novel thereby joins other precedents across the American arts for projects of accumulation that celebrate disjunction as an organizing principle. These include Joseph Cornell's compartmentalized boxes, which invite ambiguous communications between coexisting elements, and Charles Ives's polytonally layered Fourth Symphony, which synthesizes portions of his earlier work with hymns and popular songs.

Juxtaposition initiates these works and Kerouac's exploration of writing, prompted by shifting veneers of free-association and recollection. Inspired by *Finnegans Wake,* Kerouac freely selects his materials from what André Malraux calls a "Museum without Walls": an available and usable past without personal, geographical, or historical restriction. Through individual text and opus as a whole, tensions are exploited and diversity celebrated: a playful disunity of style as excitement production. In such light, Ann Charters's conjecture that Kerouac tried but failed to discover a means of binding his work within a chronological frame appears reductive:

> He couldn't come up with any literary technique to help him fit all the volumes of the Duluoz Legend into one continuous tale. All he could think of was to change the names in the various books back to their original forms, hoping that this single stroke would give sufficient unity to the disparate books, magically making them fit more smoothly into their larger context as the Duluoz Legend. . . . [H]e wanted the books reissued in a uniform edition to make the larger design unmistakable. (*Kerouac* 359)

Was this Kerouac's motive? The harmonization of proper names would indeed do little to alleviate unevenness within the series, serving mainly to disqualify a number of works from inclusion on a thematic basis alone. For instance, while *The Town and the City* was later dismissed by Kerouac as "satisf[ying] all the demands of Thirties Fiction" (*SL, II* 298) and was partially reworked as *Doctor Sax* and *Vanity of Duluoz,* much of the former reconstitutes old "Shadow" stories and childhood fantasies. And whereas the titular hero of *Pic* is, uniquely to his work, entirely fictional, several biographers have pointed out that *Visions of Gerard* was essentially composed by Kerouac's mother, with his contribution restricted to complementary dialogue. On the basis of recursive memoir alone, the Legend would consist of *Maggie Cassidy, Vanity of Duluoz, On the Road, Visions of Cody, The Subterraneans* (disregarding its switched location), *The Dharma Bums, Tristessa, Desolation Angels, Lonesome Traveler, Big Sur,* and *Satori in Paris.* Where this leaves *Old Angel Midnight, Book of Dreams, Some of the Dharma,* and the *Blues* volumes is open to question.

It is more appropriate, perhaps, to view the Legend as deliberately paratactic, a rejection of final form and homogenized schedule that previously vibrated for Williams in *Spring and All,* with its misnumbered titles and nonlinear combinations of poetry and prose. Kerouac steers his chronicle into theme and variation to assume a projective shape, as if to prevent early experiments solidifying into style; like Eliot's use of vegetation myths in *The Waste Land* and Joyce's platform in Homer's *Odyssey* in *Ulysses,* old materials are deployed to forge new practices of writing and reading.

Taking up the multiplicity of twentieth-century experience, as Mallarmé, Joyce, and McLuhan had with the newspaper format, Kerouac maps out its divergence and dispersion into fragments. He finds in collage what Jacques Derrida describes as "the domain of empirical discovery" (284), a syntax to conserve and reformulate recollections and previous recording techniques. Deploying traditional procedures only to confuse them, *Cody* assumes a similar orientation to the "Combines" of Kerouac's contemporary, Robert Rauschenberg. Late 1950s works like *Odalisque, Monogram,* and *Canyon* convene pieces of junk and mythic American symbols on a plane without unity of style, giving an implied critique of received connotations and narrative organicism. Resisting tidy limitation, outcomes are never certain. Every gesture remains provisional with personal energy existentially pitted against impersonal order—a primary Beat concern. Here, Lévi-Strauss's definition of "bricolage" in *The Savage Mind* illuminates the actions of both artists, a retrieval of "waste" that includes its sacrificial connotations:

> The "bricoleur" is adept at performing a large number of diverse tasks; but unlike the engineer, he does not subordinate each of them to the availability of raw materials and tools conceived and procured for the purpose of the project. His universe of instruments is closed and the rules of his game are always to "make do with whatever is at hand," that is to say with a set of tools and materials which is always finite and is also heterogeneous because what it contains bears no relation to the current project, or indeed to any particular project, but is the contingent result of all the occasions there have been to renew or enrich the stock or to maintain it with the remains of previous constructions or destructions. (17)

Selection and transformation, as opposed to originality, become the criteria of creativity: a "liberation," to coin William C. Seitz's description of Mallarmé's use of the page and Picasso, Braque, and Schwitters's treatment of the canvas (13). Every assemblage becomes a reassemblage, with inspiration recast as intuition of potential form. Kerouac learns from past masters of bop and poetics—as the admiring allusions to musicians and writers peppering his correspondence testify—and enriches borrowed materials through active provocation, distancing himself from the Oedipal competitiveness of Harold Bloom's "Anxiety of Influence" that sterilizes under patriarchal tradition. Kerouac thus makes of *Cody* a generative performance, drawing upon a vast anthology of information from self and others without claim for encyclopedic coherence. As Mottram observes:

> [Kerouac] learned from Joyce the effects of language as discourse—the interplay of words in syntax, linguistic combinations in both the im-

mediate reading and the "architexture" (a term Mary Ann Caws puts into circulation through a *Metapoetic of the Passage*—"both construction and material texture," origin and building process in interplay in a text, and the situating of the text in the world of other texts). ("Preface" 50)

Composed of labyrinthian tales within tales with different points of genesis, completion, and abandonment, *Cody* circulates references within the Legend's continual re-creation of events. Kerouac thereby invokes the recognition common to all accomplished improvisers: namely, that other modes of experience—and versions of history—are possible. Removing his observations from the unfolding fate narrative of realism, writing becomes a commentary for both techniques and subject matter. As with Laurence Sterne's great metafiction, the authorial voice is seldom stable, being liable to continuous and random self-scrutiny: a comparable orientation to the bop soloist, who jettisons linear development and adopts a critically reflexive stance toward performance.

In *Vanity of Duluoz,* the return to a more standardized syntax is fractured by an intrusive marriage of digression, aphorism, French dialogue, musings over disparate threads of the past, and exhortations to the audience (Weinreich 153). In reminiscing over Lowell, for instance, Kerouac's protagonist stops to comment: "This is the story of the techniques of suffering in the working world, which includes football and war" (76). And in an extract documenting his time at Columbia, he interrupts a passage of literary criticism to pay tribute to Wolfe, who "made me want to prowl, and roam, and see the real America that was there and that 'had never been uttered'" (56).

Cross-referencing becomes thematic to the novel and the Legend alike, a declaration of the presence and jurisdiction of the creator in the fable. While Kerouac charges through the Midwest, for example, the manuscript of *On the Road* is evoked from within the text by the roar of the wind, which "made the plains unfold like a roll of paper" (142). "Mind is shapely, art is shapely," comments Ginsberg with reference to Kerouac's sense of pleasure in form: "Art lies in the consciousness of doing the thing, in the attention to the happening, in the sacramentalization of everyday reality" (*Deliberate* 351). Consistent with the etymology of the word "poet" (from the Greek *poiein,* "to make"), *Visions of Cody* in particular qualifies as a work of "fabulation" within Robert Scholes's definition, which confers freedom upon fiction as its paramount condition and pronounces orthodoxy a bore:

With its wheels within wheels, rhythms and counterpoints, this shape is partly to be admired for its own sake. . . . Delight in design, and its concurrent emphasis on the art of the designer, will serve in part to distinguish the art of the fabulator from the work of the novelist or the satirist. Of all narrative forms, fabulation puts the highest premium on art and joy. (2–3)

Kerouac's position in his hypertext undermines any claim to mediate the past with impartiality, tacitly negating the authoritarian mania for historical absolutes, ends, and beginnings bound within guarantees of the unchanging nature of power. Kerouac persistently "re-embodies" his images, to call on Joyce's term, suggesting the continuities and blurred edges of mobiles, the name given by Alexander Calder to his kinetic sculptures poised within air currents. The same nonlinear thrusts, associations, interruptions, and reversals that characterize the hero drive our navigations through the book of Cassady and echo Melville's manner of telling in *Moby Dick*: "There is no staying in any one place; for at one and the same time everything has to be done everywhere. It is much the same with him who endeavors the description of the scene. We must now retrace our way a little" (270).

Recalling, too, the circularity of *Finnegans Wake*, the novel's final unnumbered and untitled section doubles as a preamble to "Visions of Cody." Reconfiguring *On the Road*'s adventures, the section even invokes the traditional beginning of an American quest narrative, Duluoz setting "out West to find" his alter ego "in the Summer of 1949" (338). Again, at another point Kerouac asserts, "It began in Denver" (436). With the nation cast into radical disturbance through internal and external warfare, the message is that the novel genre must cease to represent security.

Kerouac's celebration of the dynamics of fabulation within collage again parallels Rauschenberg's work in admitting quotations and parodies from exterior sources that, in the instance of *Cody*, may be sonic or filmic as well as literary. Following the "Rawshanks" episode, Kerouac plants a metafictional homage to a previous *bricoleur* into the textual body, complete with bibliographic protocols, to supply an exegesis on his own prose: "'Obviously an image which is immediately and unintentionally ridiculous is merely a fancy.'—T. S. Eliot, *Selected Essays, 1917–1932*, Harcourt, Brace and Company, 383 Madison Avenue, New York 17, New York, Fifth Printing, June 1942" (355). Such switches of time, space, style, and memory give the intense experience of transition that Maurice Blanchot writes of in *L'entretien infini*, with regard to a narrative of literary fragments whose sole relationship is difference. Glad invention itself becomes the only authoritative binding, a notion that sits happily alongside Buckminster Fuller's sense of "organism" in *I Seem to Be a Verb* to elucidate further Kerouac's approach:

Man is a complex of patterns, or processes. We speak of our circulatory system, our respiratory system, our digestive system, and so it goes.

Man is not weight. He isn't the vegetables he eats, for example, because he'll eat seven tons of vegetables in his life. He is the result of his own pattern integrity. (Fuller, Agel, and Fiore 4)

Kerouac makes no attempt to diminish the "pattern integrity" of *Cody's* organism to harmonious paths on a linear grid. The novel's occasions do not neutralize each other but remain potent and heterogeneous: an open series that is never the expression of a system in final equilibrium but one of unlimited experiences through which the writer passes and simultaneously remakes. The effect is redolent of Gilles Deleuze and Félix Guattari's "Nomad thought," "mov[ing] freely through . . . exteriority" and "rid[ing] difference" rather than "repos[ing] on identity" within "the edifice of an ordered interiority." Formal gaps in the book's information suggest a "machine" designed as a "system of interruptions or breaks," made of mobile units of "continual detachments . . . valuable in and of themselves [which] must not be filled in" (*Anti-Oedipus* 36–39).

The "nomadic" interior of Kerouac's metanovel reflects the exterior shell of the Legend itself, with past events continually reproduced from each other. Fissures in the narrative process are themselves productive, sharing a quality of Cage's music where subjects traverse each other and supersede any dominant chain of development to meet within "a state of multiplicity of centers in interpenetration and non-obstruction" (Mottram, "Notes on Poetics" 32) and Jackson Pollock's biomorphic presentation of paint as total periphery on "all-over" canvases such as *Number One* and *Lavender Mist.* Kerouac's writing is similarly immersed in a continuous "becoming" where, to quote Deleuze and Guattari, the "vocation of the sign is to produce desire, engineering it in every direction" (*Anti-Oedipus* 39).

The traditional mode of storytelling thus gives way to the division of prose into cells, passed from one style to another. "So huge and timeless," Kerouac writes of his mental maps in *Book of Dreams,* "the events strung out from some intenser center and forming vague distant points only to be found again when centers and universes shall shift in other dreams—" (52). A kaleidoscopic sense of variation emerges as one dimension transforms the other. Each line or chorus of a poem, paragraph within a novel, or composition inside the Legend builds from what preceded without need for procedural links or superstructure, a correspondence with the "serial movie" sequence of prewar Saturday afternoon picture shows that fascinated Kerouac as a child. "After my brother died when I was four," he writes in *The New American Poetry,* "they tell me I began to sit motionlessly in the parlor, pale and thin, and after a few months of sorrow began to play the old Victrola and act out movies to the music. Some of these movies developed onto long serial sagas, 'continued next week'" (*GB* 92).

This is most striking in *Mexico City Blues,* where the poem's body flexes
to accommodate a variety of concise details placed untidily side by side. As
McClure suggests, the unique character of each chorus resonates haiku-like
in each line as "a complete, and whole, independent image" (*Scratching* 71).
The "230th Chorus" is exemplary:

> Love's multitudinous boneyard
> > of decay
> The spilled milk of heroes,
> Destruction of silk kerchiefs
> > by dust storm,
> Caress of heroes blindfolded to posts,
> Murder victims admitted to this life,
> Skeletons bartering fingers and joints . . .

Such a self-referential gathering of images functions as part of something
greater, melting into Kerouac's definition of each book as "a chapter in the
whole story" (*SL, II* 270) and Duncan's sense of the "world poem" ("Rites"
25). "Like uproar of FINNEGANS WAKE," explains Kerouac, "[it] has no beginning and no end—so that in the end the WRITTEN Duluoz Legend is only
a tiny fragment of the huge ignorance of consciousness in the Tathagata's
Womb" (*SL, I* 516–17). Like Duncan, Kerouac can boast of being "a derivative poet," the inference being not of direct allusion, as with Eliot, but of a
material flux of language across time and voice as an integrated activity. The
result is a wild order, a diversity of presence at an assembly, admitting, in
Paul Carroll's words, any "object which stands in an existential skin without moral or aesthetic significance or as one which helps to point a moral or
adorn a tale" (163). The notion of biography within the Legend's inclusive
fabric undergoes a profound overhaul, its oeuvre now "carnivalesque," to use
Mikhail Bakhtin's intuition of life as ongoing performance, or what Deleuze
characterizes as "direct participation in the logos":

> [O]bservers, friends, philosophers, talkers, homosexuals *a la grecque,*
> intellectuals . . . are with varying qualifications the characters of a
> single universal dialectic: the dialectic as Conversation among friends,
> in which all faculties are exercised voluntarily and collaborate under
> the leadership of the Intelligence, in order to unite the observation of
> Things, the discovery of Laws, the formation of Words, the analysis
> of Ideas, and to weave that perpetual web linking Part to Whole and
> Whole to Part. . . . Is this not . . . the totalizing impulse we variously
> recognize in the conversation of friends, in the analytic and rational
> truth of philosophers, in the methods of scientists and scholars, in the

concerted work of art of *littérateurs,* in the conventional symbolism of words themselves? (*Proust* 31)

Kerouac's relationships to friends, lovers, jazzmen, and literary predecessors are thus reworked through multiphasic storytelling, a national definition according to Olson in *The Maximus Poems*:

> There is no strict personal order
> for my inheritance
> . . . An American
> is a complex of occasions,
> themselves a geometry
> of spatial nature.
>
> (184–85)

Kerouac parallels Olson's concern with sustaining expansive forms over time and contributes to an American tradition of the serial work that stems from Whitman's *Leaves of Grass,* one profoundly opposed to the quick instigation and discharge of the pop paradigm. This principle enters painting with Marsden Hartley's four canvases, *The German Officer* (1914), which emulates Eadweard Muybridge's sequential photographs of athletes and animals in a single print, and extends via Stuart Davis's *Egg Beater* abstracts (1927–1928) into Mark Rothko's environmental groups, Adolph Gottlieb's tiers of discrete symbols, and Louise Nevelson's vertically piled boxes of cast-off objects swathed in monochrome, all of which emerge in the 1950s. These are joined by Dos Passos's *U.S.A.* triptych; Jack Spicer's *Heads of the Town Up to the Aether;* Duncan's *Structures of Rime;* Williams's *Paterson;* Pollock's numbered "drip" sequence; Willem de Kooning's *Women;* Robert Motherwell's *Elegies to the Spanish Republic;* Jasper Johns's numbers, targets, and flags; Rauschenberg's mixed-media *Quartermile or Two-Furlong Piece;* the thematic fragments of Duke Ellington and Billy Strayhorn's "Jazz Suites"; and extended performances by Ornette Coleman and John Coltrane.

In common with all these, the Legend offers an elastic framework for experiment that pursues no realization of final scheme beyond liberatory process. Taking on Alfred North Whitehead's example—"[H]ow shallow, puny and imperfect are efforts to sound the depths in the nature of things. In philosophical discussion, the merest hint of dogmatic certainty as to finality of statement is an exhibition of folly" (vi)—Kerouac participates in a postwar avant-garde that insists, in Jerome Rothenberg's words, that "the work deny itself the last word, because the consequences of closure & closed mind have been & continue to be horrendous in the world we know" (*Pre-faces* 4). As Lewis Mumford corroborates:

Scientific truth achieved the status of an absolute, and the incessant pursuit and expansion of knowledge became the only recognized categorical imperative. Now, if the history of the human race teaches any plain lessons, this is one of them: *Man cannot be trusted with absolutes.* (*Pentagon* 13)

Under Kerouac's hand, the writer's role becomes an ongoing apprehension of the world, the reverse of which he warns Ginsberg away from in 1947: "[a] search for pure fact, or . . . the reality you wish *embodied* in yourself. . . . You saw the dualism, and you don't like dualisms, you're after fact, which does not exist anyway, except for a moment, and then time changes it" (*SL, I* 120). The last clause stands as source for *Visions of Cody,* where lively points of departure and nonfinite plateaus replace statements of petrified truth.

The early mapping of America within the social realist matrix of *The Town and the City* thus rapidly fragments into an imprint of overlay and superimposition, itself a resolutely American idiom. Set against the US government's use of media to propagate its image as extensional conscience of the people and promote a mass culture that supposedly originates in collective desire, the Legend's convergence of fictive techniques implicitly exposes a "national crisis of legitimation" (Ellis 57) underwriting the WASP story: a singularity that blocks the forms, vocabularies, and narratives essential to generating America's multiple histories and topographies. Kerouac's role as fabulator in the text and his refusal to conform to the discourses bundled within an official commercial culture locate him firmly within a twentieth-century continuum of investigative composition. To redirect Henri Corbin's response to Hegel's claim that philosophy consists of "turning the world inside out," the work of the active imagination shows that it is this world, here and now, that is inside out (*Spiritual* xiii). Kerouac's visionary fictions are part of a continuing desire to put it right-side out once more.

# Beatitude and Sacrifice

> [With] roots anchored in the current of life [man] will float
> on the surface like a lotus and he will blossom and give forth
> fruit. . . . The life that's in him will manifest itself in growth,
> and growth is an endless, eternal process. The process is
> everything.
> —Henry Miller, *Sexus*

> Every man is born as many men and dies as a single one.
> —Martin Heidegger

A century prior to Beat upheavals, Walt Whitman, "American lost bearded idealistic" agency of liberation (*SU* 22), identified the impulse to stay new rather than settle into patterns of repetition and eventual parody: "I, for my poems—What have I? . . . I have all to make" (*Complete Poems* 764). Throughout the Duluoz Legend, Jack Kerouac echoes the same autobiographical momentum that feels no obligation to self-propagandize via the rhetoric of imitation. His desire to master, as opposed merely to report, experience and to translate it at speed into poetic syntax without loss of intensity hurls each given scenario into an inspired improvisation. The bold prose motifs of relaxation into self-dispersal that result, however, remain in perpetual conflict with regressive drives for stability: the lionizing of patriarchy and industrialized man straining against the free flux of perception. This is made explicit in both *The Scripture of the Golden Eternity* ("All these selfnesses have already vanished" [33]) and *Visions of Cody*:

> Now events of this moment are *so mad* that of course I can't keep up but
> worse they're as though they were fond memories that from my peace-
> ful hacienda or Proust-bed I was trying to recall in toto but couldn't

because like the real world so vast, so delugingly vast, I wish God had made me vaster myself—I wish I had ten personalities, one hundred golden brains, far more ports than are ports, more energy than the river, but I must struggle to live it all, and *on foot,* and in these little crepesole shoes, ALL of it, or give up completely. (99)

The ensuing "big structure of Confession" empirically tells "the true story of the world in interior monolog" (*GB* 72) via a combination of fabulation and autobiography. From the elegiac attempt to arrest childhood happiness in *The Town and the City* to the air of embittered betrayal and spent eroticism in *Vanity of Duluoz,* Kerouac identifies self with fiction. "I am not 'I am' but just a spy in somebody's body," he writes in his final book (*VD* 15), aligning himself with Whitman's self-multiplicity in "Song of Myself," Arthur Rimbaud's "I is another," Henri Michaux's "provisional *ME is only a position in equilibrium* (One among a thousand others, continually possible and always at the ready)" (76–77), Duncan's sense of "not 'I' but words themselves speak to you" (*Opening* 18), and the satirical self-proliferations of Ginsberg in "America" and Ferlinghetti in "Autobiography," all of which reflect the nation's cast. "Don't think of me as a simple character—" advises the narrator of *Desolation Angels*:

[a] lecher, a ship-jumper, a loafer, a conner of older women, even of queers, an idiot, nay a drunken baby Indian when drinking. . . . In fact, I don't even know *what* I was—Some kind of fevered being different as a snowflake. . . . In any case, a wondrous mess of contradictions (good enough, said Whitman) but more fit for Holy Russia of 19th Century than for this modern America of crew cuts and sullen faces in Pontiacs. (189)

Writing in manifold styles and assuming a variety of masks or "personae," Kerouac's "I" is a complex, free, and rigorous performance in tension with "the perspective of a single, historical individual" (Davidson 74). Extending at its furthest point to the African American boy protagonist of *Pic,* Kerouac establishes this thematically from the beginning in *The Town and the City,* where the Ginsberg figure, Leon, cuts a hole in a newspaper through which he peers at New York subway riders to see how they react. True to the Blakean delineation of innocence, he finds that only a four-year-old boy is not afraid of him: "[Children] haven't had the time to burden themselves with character structure and personality armors and systems of moral prejudice and God knows what. Therefore they're free to live and laugh, and free to love" (189).

The term "personality" remains fluid within the Legend's emerging rhetoric of inclusion, leaving behind the fashionable auto-psychology of Lowell, Berryman, and Plath to meet Olson's demands for "getting rid of the lyrical interference of the individual as ego" as a producer of meaning (*Collected* 247). As he writes in "Maximus of Gloucester,"

> . . . It is not I,
> even if the life appeared
> biographical. The only interesting thing
> is if one can be
> an image
> of man
>
> (*Maximus* 473)

This is the same exploration of potential selves that underwrites Kerouac's reflexive transference between the "I" and the mimetic substitution of identity. "I could call the DULUOZ LEGEND:- 'Analyzed Visions of Myself,'" he writes in *Some of the Dharma* (315), long before telling Ted Berrigan in a fit of pique:

> I am so busy interviewing myself in these novels, and I have been so busy writing down these self-interviews, that I don't see why I should draw breath in pain every year of the last ten years to repeat and repeat to everybody who interviews me what I've already explained in the books themselves. It begs sense. And it's not that important. It's our work that counts, if anything at all. (128)

At the root of this is the impulse to abandon representation in both self and text, shared with John Cage's belief that art is not self expression but "self alteration," a means of becoming "more open" and increasing "one's enjoyment of life" (qtd. in Alan Miller), and Harold Rosenberg's conviction that abstract expressionism denotes

> self-creation or self-definition or self-transcendence; but this dissociates it from self-expression, which assumes the acceptance of the ego as it is. . . . Action Painting is not "personal," though its subject matter is the artist's individual possibilities. (Hess and Rosenberg 21)

Creativity must be loosened from the parameters of personality, offsetting the confusion of "authorship" with intellectual capital that drives the transgenerational *Cantos* of Pound—"There is no ownership in most of my statements and I can not interrupt every sentence or paragraph to attribute authorships to each pair of words, especially as there is seldom an a priori claim even to the phrase or the half phrase" (*Guide* 60)—to become the performative act of discovery defined by Gertrude Stein in *What Are Masterpieces*:

> The thing one gradually comes to find out is that one has no identity that is when one is in the act of doing anything. Identity is recognition, you know who you are because you and others remember anything

about yourself but essentially you are not that when you are doing anything. I am I because my little dog knows me but creatively speaking the
little dog knowing that you are you and your recognizing that he knows,
that is what destroys creation. That is what makes school. (84)

Kerouac is certainly assisted in this by the traditional submission to
drug-induced altered states, a practice revalidated in the modernist era by
William James, who observed from "nitrous oxide intoxication" that "our
normal waking consciousness, rational consciousness as we call it, is but
one special type of consciousness, whilst all about it, parted from it by the
flimsiest of screens, there lie potential forms of consciousness entirely different" (*Varieties* 387–88). "O boy that healthgiving mescal," attests Kerouac
to Ginsberg in 1959, several years after reading James's *Varieties of Religious
Experience*:

> [I]f everybody in the world took mescaline but once there would be
> eternal peace—I trembled, I shuddered, I saw the earth opening up
> with light flashes and then I saw the assembled dancers in Heaven and
> you way up there one of the highest of the saints. . . . Most miraculous
> of all was the sensational revelation that I've been on the right track
> with spontaneous never-touch-up poetry of immediate report, and Old
> Angel Midnight most especially, opening out a new world of connec-
> tion in literature with the endless spaces of Shakti Maya Kali Illusion.
> (*SL, II* 220–21)

However, while he may boast that "Poem 230 from *Mexico City Blues* [was]
written purely on morphine. Every line in this poem was written within an
hour of one another" (qtd. in Berrigan 124), ingestion never overrides the
primacy of linguistic play itself. *Wild form* is his means of courting the visionary potential that dances attendance on the depersonalized self, one that
"expands, unites and says yes," to quote James. "It brings its votary from the
chill periphery of things to the radiant core. It makes him for the moment,
one with truth" (*Varieties* 408). Praising his "quality of negative capability"—Kerouac himself proclaims in 1943 that his "malleable personality . . .
assumes the necessary shape when in contact with any other personality" (*SL,
I* 61)—Ginsberg draws attention to this ability to hold anomalous identities
in mind simultaneously in an ecstatic transcendence of ego:

> "I am Canuck, I am from Lowell, I am Jewish, I am Palestinian, I Am,
> I am the finger, I am the name." Kerouac was not heavily entangled
> in such fixed identity. . . . He could empathize with the all-American
> boy, football hero. He could be a sophisticated *littérateur* or an old

drunk, alternatively. He could be country bumpkin, he could be as Thomas Wolfe, or he could empathize with William Burroughs as a "non-Wolfian" European sophisticate. So in the end, his poetry and prose becomes a perfect manifestation of his mind. That was the whole point of the spontaneous prosody . . . true to the nature of mind as understood traditionally by Buddhist theories of spontaneous mind, how to achieve and how to use it. (*Deliberate* 370–71)

Like Ginsberg, Kerouac rigorously explores Buddhist Sutra in his poetry, most notably in *The Scripture of the Golden Eternity* and in the theological compendium of *Some of the Dharma,* and assimilates its reversal of the western emphasis on permanence, negating desires for authority expressed by Yeats in his essay "Magic," where "many minds can flow into one another, as it were, and create or reveal a single mind, a single energy" (98). Ginsberg quotes Kerouac's use of a passage from the *Diamond Sutra*: "All conceptions as to the existence of the self, as well as conceptions as to the existence of a supreme self, as well as all conceptions as to the non-existence of the supreme self, are equally arbitrary, being only conceptions" (*Deliberate* 368).

Ten years after composing the *Scripture,* Kerouac mockingly tells Ann Charters: "I was a Bodhi Sattva and had lived twelve million years in twelve million directions" (*Kerouac* 361). "The Victor is Not Self," he declares in the "129th Chorus" of *Mexico City Blues,* a sustained encounter with representations of identity, first raised in the "6th Chorus":

> Self depends on existence of other
> self, and so no Solo Universal Self
> exists—no self, no other self,
> no innumerable selves, no
> Universal self and no ideas
> relating to existence or non-
> existence thereof—

Whereas in the "122nd Chorus" Kerouac places the personal pronoun in quotation marks ("Don't break your tenderness / Is advice that comes to 'me'"), in the "125th Chorus" he advocates anonymity over any dominant One:

> and all I gotta say is,
> remove my name
>      from the list
>   And Buddha's too
> Buddha's me, in the list,
>      no-name.

Dispensing completely with the single point of view and its baggage of conventional understanding, he entreats, "O thou purifier, purify all / who are in bondage to self," in the "192nd Chorus," before a final release into ego extinction two verses later:

> Being in selfless one-ness
> With the such-ness
> That is Tathagatahood,
> So is everybody else
> Lost with you
> In that bright sea
> Of non-personality.

Catalyzed by Alan Watts, Episcopal priest turned Zen philosopher, and filtered through the San Francisco Beat scene by Kenneth Rexroth, Gary Snyder, and Philip Whalen—"urban Thoreaus" inspired by a "contemplative mystic and antimaterialistic as if existentialist . . . standpoint" (*SU* 15)—Buddhist practice is vigorously assimilated by Kerouac into narratives that accommodate its teaching vehicles of orality, improvisation, and contradiction. This includes the question and answer form known as *mondo,* which speeds up thought to facilitate an abrupt breakthrough into awareness, and the discontinuity and ellipsis of the *koan* riddle ("When you climb to the top of a mountain, keep climbing" [*SD* 498]), which contains the seeds of shock to release consciousness from the Aquinian state refuted in *Some of the Dharma*: "[I]n the reality and purity of Universal Mind there are no dualistic differentiations such as good and evil. . . . Catholic Dualism is behind the error of Western Civilization with its war of machines, each machine claiming the 'Good'—" (66). Writing in *Mexico City Blues* of an ideal condition in which one "is Free From Arbitrary Conceptions of Being or Non-Being," he adopts in *The Scripture of the Golden Eternity* the same symbol as Henry Miller for renouncing the decayed basis of Christianity: "A hummingbird can come into a house and a hawk will not: so rest and be assured. While looking for the light, you may suddenly be devoured by the darkness and find the true light" (32).

Composed after *Visions of Cody,* the *Scripture*'s use of aphorism extends the novel's fascination with non-explanatory structures. Aiming to reverse habitual patterns, these undermine their predecessors by enhancing the nonproduction of meaning:

> 5
> I am the golden eternity in mortal animate form.
> 6
> Strictly speaking, there is no me, because all is

emptiness. I am empty, I am non-existent.
All is bliss.

7
This truth law has no more reality than the world. (24–25)

Recalling the Tibetan Buddhist practice of "Tonglan" and Christ's instructions to his disciples in the Acts of St. John—"and if thou wouldst understand that which is me, know this: all that I have said I have uttered playfully—and I was by no means ashamed of it" (Pulver 180)—these become tools for nonconceptual enlightenment, or the term Kerouac favors, *satori*, a set of maxims turning in on themselves to disallow moral advocacy:

65
This is the first teaching from
the golden eternity.

66
The second teaching from the golden eternity
is that there never was a first teaching
from the golden eternity. So be sure. (61)

As with the nondialectical design of his Western Haikus or "Pops," contesting paths are set into motion without resolution. Such expansions in the gap between composition and interpretation give an understanding, in the face of Cold War sloganeering, that phenomena can never be fully apprehended. In line with Federman's demarcations for the "fiction of the future," Kerouac effectively abolishes

all distinctions between the real and the imaginary, between the conscious and the subconscious, between the past and the present, between truth and untruth. . . . All forms of duplicity will disappear. And above all, all forms of duality will be negated—especially duality: that double-headed monster which for centuries now, has subjected us to a system of values, an ethical and aesthetical system based on principles of good and bad, true and false, good and ugly. (*Surfiction* 12)

This is true of Kerouac's writing, which at its most confident breaks with a Jesuit training to assert an internally referential model of creativity, constantly remade by the mobile self. But this drive fails to stay the Legend's course. Drawing on his biographical trajectory, Ginsberg uses the *Scripture* to map an "ethical and philosophical dialectic" in Kerouac's work between "non-theistic Buddhist space-awareness or awareness practice, and theistic Catholicism's contemplation of or fixation on the cross of suffering" (*Deliber-*

*ate* 370). Whereas the "open and accommodating space" of *Cody* and *Mexico City Blues* embodies the principle of *Sunyata,* which is the release of thought and image from referentiality also found in Blake's:

> He who binds to himself a joy
> Does the winged life destroy
> But he who kisses the joy as it flies
> Lives in Eternity's sun rise.

> (184)

Kerouac's emancipation is over by the time of *Big Sur.* His "withdrawal" from the "outward" life, as announced to Ginsberg in the summer of 1958—

> I don't want no more frantic nights, associations with hepcats and queers and village types, far less mad trips to unholy frisco. . . . I'm retired from the world now. . . . I tired of outside influences. . . . Besides I'm only interested in Heaven . . . my own kind of Lowell boy life. (*SL, II* 142–43)

—accompanies his disengagement from Buddhism: "I've not been able to 'meditate' or make any Buddhist scene now for a long time and have actually started writing catholic poems" (*SL, II* 155). "The dharma is slipping away from my consciousness," Kerouac reports the following year (*SL, II* 206), displaced by the crucifixion iconography obsessively reproduced in paint but left undeveloped as a literary subject, other than as a symbol of his own mortification. As will be seen, the terminal reestablishment of monotheistic centers of sanctuary or condemnation has major consequences for both the writer and his fictions.

A significant aspect of Kerouac's recasting of identity during his Catholic and Buddhist incursions is his treatment of sexuality, a recurrent motif in the Legend and in the nation's literature as a whole. Celebrating America's erotic potentials as "avowed, empowered, unabashed," Whitman launches an early challenge to censorious orthodoxy promoting "neuter gender" and "shame," the embedded Puritanism that licensed J. Edgar Hoover's suspicions of the inner being as deviant or incriminating:

> Infidelism usurps most with foetid polite face; among the rest infidelism about sex. By silence or obedience the pens of savants, poets, historians, biographers, and the rest, have long connived at the filthy law, and books enslaved to it, that what makes the manhood of a man, that sex, womanhood, maternity, desires, lusty animations, organs, acts, are unmentionable and to be ashamed of, to be driven to skulk out of

literature with whatever belongs to them. This filthy law has to be re-
pealed—it stands in the way of great reforms. Of women just as much as
men, it is the interest that there should not be infidelism about sex, but
perfect faith. . . . Of bards for These States, if it come to a question, it is
whether they shall celebrate in poems the eternal decency of the ama-
tiveness of Nature, the motherhood of all, or whether they shall be the
bards of the fashionable delusion of the inherent nastiness of sex, and
of the feeble and querulous modesty of deprivation. This is important
in poems, because the whole of the other expressions of a nation are
but flanges out of its great poems. (*Complete Poems* 770–71)

Invigorated too by the inheritance of Dylan Thomas and D. H. Lawrence,
Kerouac and his contemporaries voice a pattern of continuing opposition to
the codifying of the body into uniform negatives, which includes the ethics
of Marx and Freud. While Freud understood, in spite of his conservatism,
that civilization had reached a point of untenable strain, the Beat flight from
inner colonization by the agencies of power—church, school, nuclear family,
nation, political party—also extends to the "behaviorist" style of analysis that
subordinates desire to duty as a normative value. As Parkinson corroborates,
"Freud in the 1920s meant sexual liberation, whereas psychoanalysis in Bohemia and suburbia in the 1950s was primarily a mode of keeping going . . .
so that they can continue their business and professional life" (278).

Subsequent revisions of Freud by Wilhelm Reich and Herbert Marcuse
into a discourse of insurgency identified a broader relationship to Marx's
conception of alienated labor, extending to disaffection, neurosis, envy, and
acquisitiveness. Having read Reich's *Function of the Orgasm* with enthusiasm
in 1953, Kerouac's fictions record a shift in the experience of desire into new
zones: a reverence toward sex and discharge from guilt inside an environment
of aspirational repression that remains dominant and inevitably feeds back
into his work. As such his 1950s texts anticipate the amalgam of revolutionary
and anti-repressive politics characterizing the next decade, a battle fought on
two fronts against social exploitation and psychic coercion.

Advocating the Nietzschean self-regulation invoked on the opening page
of *On the Road,* which links much Beat writing, Michel Foucault suggests
in *The History of Sexuality* that "we must . . . conceive of sex without the
law, and power without the king" (91). Most obviously, the dramatization of
Cassady's movements across society and continent radiates a sexual confidence that defies voluntary self-limitation through the rigid figurative roles
of wife or mother, homo- or heterosexual: the hegemonic definitions exposed
as fallacious in Alfred Kinsey's reports on sexual behavior, which drew on the
experiences of Burroughs, Ginsberg, and Huncke. Taking Foucault's location

of repression as the fundamental link between power, knowledge, and sexuality, Cassady's actions comprise "nothing less than a transgression of laws, a lifting of prohibitions, an irruption of speech, a reinstating of pleasure within reality, and a whole new mechanism of power" (Foucault 5).

These narratives burst forth from an America under the influence of Hoover's sado-paranoiac fantasy of unlimited power, channeled via sexual intimidation and manifested in a capricious terrorism that generated its own momentum. Whereas Aleister Crowley points out that sexuality is the greatest and most easily accessible form of magic, the experience of erotic curbs and mass violence in Nazi Germany and Maoist China demonstrate the capacity to confer or deny orgasm as a key investment of control. That Kerouac is conscious of the erotics of domination is made clear from his description of the uniformed barracks cop in *On the Road,* a figure straight out of Genet's *Chant d'Amour.* Sledge

> rigged himself out like a Texas Ranger of old. He wore a revolver down low, with ammunition belt, and carried a small quirt of some kind, and pieces of leather hanging everywhere, like a walking torture chamber: shiny shoes, low-hanging jacket, cocky hat, everything but boots. He was always showing me holds—reaching down under my crotch and lifting me up nimbly. (65)

Such observations threaten a male supremacy passed off as biological and permanent within the social-Darwinist construction of power. In postwar America, this means the sanctioning of an expanded white-collar class, newly converted into suburban homeowners with a stake in the consumer economy. Compensating for the enforced decline in female employment, metonymic shifts between "house" and "woman" give rise to the term "homemaker," technician of the domestic factory. While John Wayne was out taming the world and reinforcing *pax Americana* in a long succession of war films, a stream of vehicles for Doris Day sanctified patriarchal authority via glamorous opportunism; that Wayne, like his buddy Ronald Reagan, spent the entire 1940s on set in California escaped the attentions of an American public enthralled by wartime reminiscences that were little more than garbled movie synopses.

This severely restrictive image production, which includes its nominal reversal of the "chick," symbol of sexual potency without commitment and epitomized by the laconic blonde Dagmar, is the badge of a society edging nervously into a garrison State, one in which questions of sexual orientation, class, gender, and race are framed inside those of loyalty and national identity. Failure to adjust to such routine fantasies, which in 1953 contributed to the marriage of 50 percent of American women by the age of nineteen, served only to exacerbate middle-class anxieties, spurring mass dependency on anti-psychotic pharmaceuticals such as Thorazine and Mellaril.

Through his emphasis on "that amoral display of energies in sex and art we can still call Dionysian, the sources of generative or creative transformation" (Mottram, "Preface" 54), Kerouac implicitly challenges the need for patriarchal family and alienated labor: essential forms through which oppression and repression operate. Since, according to Reich,

> authoritarian society reproduces itself in the individual structures of the masses with the help of the authoritarian family, it follows that political reaction has to regard and defend the authoritarian family as *the* basis of the state, culture, and civilization. (104)

Such views echo Friedrich Engels's insights on the conflicts between the rights of women, sexuality, and the family, deriving in part from Lewis Henry Morgan's studies of the Iroquois Confederacy and reworked in America via the Anarcho-Snydicalists and the IWW. Significantly, Kerouac relocates himself in 1955 within the environment of San Francisco "poets and gurus" who had attended meetings of the "'Anarchist Circle'—old Italians and Finns—in the 1940s." These men and women "lived a kind of communalism," notes Gary Snyder, "with some lovely stories handed down of free love" in the face of its formalization by property, monogamy, patrilineage, and the legitimacy of heirs into the smallest model of intimacy in history. "Their slogan was more than just words: 'Forming the new society within the shell of the old.'" Among their concerns was the need for a "community style of life," with a tantric vision of "spiritual and physical love . . . opposed for very fundamental reasons to the Civilization Establishment," which panics at the release of "too much creative sexual energy . . . into channels which are 'unproductive'":

> It has taught that man's natural being is to be trusted and followed; that we need not look to a model or rule imposed from outside in searching for the center; and that in following the grain, one is being truly "moral." . . . All this is subversive to civilization: for civilization is built on hierarchy and specialization. A ruling class, to survive, must propose a law: a law to work must have a hook into the social psyche—and the most effective way to achieve this is to make people doubt their natural worth and instincts, especially sexual. To make "human nature" suspect is also to make Nature—the wilderness—the adversary. Hence the ecological crisis of today. (*Earth* 106–15)

The desire to rediscover agrarian tribal community is reflected in the honoring of oral traditions and the divinity of nature in San Francisco Renaissance poetry, which exalts the life-source of Lawrence's "savage pilgrimage" and Whitman's notion of sexual "discorruption" in "I Sing the Body Electric":

> Was it doubted that those who corrupt their own bodies conceal themselves?
>
> . . .
>
> The love of the body of man or woman balks account
> The body itself balks account
> That of the male is perfect, and that of the female is perfect
>
> . . .
>
> O I say now these are the soul!
>
> (Complete Poems 127–36)

This, in turn, moves through *On the Road*'s search for a sacramental vision of the body, rejecting its Judeo-Christian denigration into obscenity and the industrial abstractions of total styling afloat in the culture, as incarnated by the Radio City Music Hall Rockettes: an ordeal of lockstep-robotics by sixty-four grinning women of interchangeable height and shape with faces buttered pink that impressed Busby Berkeley and the Nuremberg rally choreographers alike.

The Rockettes' bleak display of mechanized pleasure and the general cultural obsession with talking about sexuality, the late Catholic secret index of character that informs the common currency of prurience, is displaced by the sexual act itself. "No fear or shame in the dignity of yr experience, language & knowledge," states Kerouac in "Belief & Technique for Modern Prose" (*GB* 73), an assertion of the mutuality of perception and sensual pleasure that echoes Ginsberg's proclamation, "The skin is holy! The nose is holy! The tongue and cock and hand and asshole holy!" in "Footnote to Howl" (*Howl* 27) and Georges Bataille's dismissal of the pineal gland as Cartesian seat of consciousness in "The Pineal Eye." This is not simply to reduce, in Bataille's words,

> myth and collective experience to the status of ideal mental (and academic) categories, but instead create an anthropology that will provide a living—and orgiastic—myth to overturn, through its experience on a collective level, "modern" sterile bourgeois society. (158)

McClure applies this to his analysis of 1960s student uprisings that, in his view, transcend the resistance of local bureaucratic power and assign "a challenge that allows new openings for glandular, organic, hormonic, intel-

lective energies," a surge against "biological ignominy," and the beginning
not only of "the long march through the institutions"—in Rudi Dutschke's
phrase—but of "a new relation with nature" ("Wolf" 166–72).

This recognition is in the foreground of Kerouac's work. Cassady's Dionysian naturalness profanes moral barriers of power that allow patriarchal
heterosexuality and limited homosexuality as their permitted erotic bases;
"the first Frantic exhilarated realization of social freedom *different* from rules
& regulations posited as eternal in American Presumption middleclass gram-
mar-school media propaganda" (Ginsberg, *Deliberate* 354). With an outlaw
virility that is distinctly American, he disrupts, to quote Mottram,

> an order which demands resignation, authority, control of the "vital
> instincts" [and which] is enforced by Fate, or the god, kings, wise
> men, or by conscience and guilt feeling, or it is "just there." . . . Cody
> is the action of anxiety and resistance within the controls of alienation
> and depression partly sketched in the opening paragraph of Marcuse's
> *Counterrevolution and Revolt.* ("Preface" 54)

The softening of gender norms in *On the Road, The Dharma Bums,* and
*Visions of Cody* declassifies the secrets of the male body and the nonmo-
nogamous presence in American life, following Whitman's call in *Democratic Vistas* for a registration of the "threads of manly friendship," which,
although "everywhere observed in The States," had "not the first breath of
it . . . observed in print":

> Intense and loving comradeship, the personal and passionate attach-
> ment of man to man—which, hard to define, underlies the lessons and
> ideals of the profound saviors of every land and age, and which seems
> to promise, when thoroughly develop'd, cultivated and recognized in
> manners and literature, the most substantial hope and safety of the
> future of these States, will then be fully express'd. It is to the develop-
> ment, identification, and general prevalence of that fervid comradeship
> (the adhesive love) . . . that I look for the counterbalance and offset of
> our materialistic and vulgar American democracy, and for the spiritu-
> alization thereof. (134)

While Kerouac's homosexual desires remained for the most part latent,
biographical studies and Ginsberg's testimonies have established Cassady's
bisexuality. "I'm completely your friend, your 'lover,'—he who loves you
and digs your greatness completely—haunted in the mind by you" (*VC* 39),
Duluoz tells Cody, before hearing his reciprocal declaration: "I love you,
man, you've got to dig that; boy, you've got to know" (381). Ginsberg's

"[s]ociability without genital sexuality between them, but adoration and love" (*Deliberate* 353), takes place in a society of prescriptive masculinity that demonizes such bonds as "queer," one that equates Whitman's sense of its "deepest relations to general politics" (*Democratic* 136) with the crime of treason advanced by the head of the American secret police who failed to come to terms with his own complement of homoerotic energy.

But as surely as Kerouac's work loosens sexuality from its degradation into sin, taboo, and voyeuristic decadence, the restrictions of working-class patriarchal capitalism are equally omnipresent. While his construction of gender is, to an extent, inevitably constrained by its contemporary representations, his directions, both liberatory and repressive, cannot be explained as mere passive mimesis. In *On the Road*, for example, the male messianism of Beat advances beyond the biblical signifier of the narrator, Sal Paradise, and recurrent image of the white-haired old man to the canonically named Dean Moriarty, whose "coming" on page 1 fuses the sexual and the religious in a promise of deliverance. What ensues is a retreat from the poisoned domesticity of marriage and entry into the free-ranging mobility of brotherhood. This is consistent with the "statements of new found principles" in John Clellon Holmes's 1954 letter to Ginsberg: "The social organization which is most true of itself to the artist is the boy gang," to which Ginsberg adds, "not society's perfum'd marriage" (*Journals* 80), a policy of non-engagement with women as naturalized.

In part 2 of *Road*, Kerouac echoes Burroughs's utopia of male transcendence—the viral image of the female parasite freed by labor-saving devices pervades his work—through Dean's

> dream that he was having a baby and his belly was all bloated up blue as he lay on the grass of a California hospital. Under the tree with a group of colored men, sat Slim Gaillard. Dean turned despairing eyes of a mother to him. Slim said, "There you go-orooni." (167)

"The time has come for every single one American male to go out and be a pimp," Kerouac writes in *Cody*, untroubled by notions of victim blame: "[T]he women have got up such an upper hand that there's no alternative to salvation. Let all the young women be whores, the old ladies . . . who like to do it still. Just like in France, like in Henry Miller's mad dreams" (305). The disturbing sense of gender relations intensifies during his ruminations on the historical decline of male mastery:

> The caveman had the right to kill his wife and child and move on to another woman; of course it also meant moving on to other men, to git the woman from. . . . [T]he question is, did they fight or had they just

an agreement, in order to protect their own interests as members of the organic race, otherwise men wouldn't have survived; yes, they must have arranged systems of shuffling and shuttlin wives, like through a master male agency, almost a union, where you waited in line and kept your eyes peeled on that Reindeer Man board with its buffalo signs for who's the next cunt coming to, and will she fit the bill. (306–7)

Given this summary and a constantly looming mother, "whose reality for Jack was so encompassing and devouring that all other women flittered across his consciousness like shadows"—the words of ex-girlfriend Joyce Johnson (624)—it is no surprise that Kerouac consistently fails to dramatize complementarity in sexual love. "We turned at a dozen paces," writes Sal in *Road* as he takes leave of his Mexican paramour, "for love is a duel" (101). As his career runs down, the assassinated eroticism of each protagonist hardens further. In *Big Sur,* for instance, he records an argument with his mistress, Jacky, over her assertion of the right to have another boyfriend: "He's much kinder to me than you'll ever be: at least he gives of himself." To this Kerouac replies, "But what's all this giving of ourselves, what's there to give that'll help anybody?" "You'll never know," she counters, "you're so wrapped up in yourself" (97). And yet elsewhere in the book, he laments the fact that "he can't move emotionally" and that all his lovers have been "betrayed or screwed in some way by me" and wonders: "Can it be I'm withholding from her something sacred just like [Jacky] says, or am I just a fool who'll never learn to have a decent eternally-minded deep-down relation with a woman and keep throwing that away for a song at the bottle?" (143).

In *Desolation Angels,* the narrator's reverie of sexually dominating the female, who takes pleasure in degradation, is reinforced by the phallic potential of the gun-toting Fellaheen:

I think of the marvelous sex fantasy of earlier in the day when I'm reading a cowboy story about the outlaw kidnapping the girl and having her all alone on the train (except for one old woman) who (the old woman now in my daydream sleeps on the bench while ole hard hombre me outlaw pushes the blonde into the men's compartment, at gun point, and she wont respond but scratch (natch) (she loves an honest killer and I'm old Erdaway Molière the murderous sneering Texan who slits bulls in El Paso and held up the stage to shoot holes in people only)—I get her on the seat and kneel and start to work, French postcard style, till I've got her eyes closed and mouth open until she cant stand it and loves this lovin outlaw so she by her own wild willin volition jumps to kneel and works, then when I'm ready turns while the old lady sleeps and the train rattles on—"Most delightful my dear" I'm saying to myself in Desolation Peak and as if to Bull Hubbard. (37–38)

Running against a sexual imperialism ("I am pleased that a man can always get laid in a Latin American country" [*BD* 110]) and misogyny that edges into the grotesque, any female liberatory potential in the Legend is arguably limited to reversing the bourgeois assumption of the woman as reward for earning power. But even this is denied by the debauching of the romance quest of *On the Road* amongst the "leech[ing]" whores of Mexican brothels into what Omar Swartz calls "a perverse spectacle of colonization and consumption. . . . [T]he more exotic the women, the more marginalized and impoverished, the better the sex" (79–80). The sybil, Galatea, with "long hair streaming to the floor, plying the fortune-telling cards," appraises male prerogatives from within the narrative: "You have absolutely no regard for anybody but yourself and your damned kicks. All you think about is what's hanging between your legs and how much money or fun you can get out of people and then you just throw them aside" (*OTR* 181–83).

Permanent male bonding proves equally unavailable. Dean's recognition of the potential for companionship at "the pivotal point" of his friendship with Sal, and the narrator's own sudden "concern for a man who was years younger than I, five years, and whose fate was wound with mine across the passage of the recent years," suffer an inverse relation to the backdrop of a Greek wedding in San Francisco: a mutual union among "ancient people . . . probably the thousandth in an unbroken dark generation of smiling in the sun" (179). Unalloyed to Eros, the life instinct generating sustainable change and kinship, Dean preys on personal energies. Fulfilling Galatea's prediction, he uses Sal as a convenience and ultimately deserts him in Mexico, penniless and dysenteric. Dean's refusal of sexual confinement to the single locus of the home and its utilitarian absorption into reproduction fails as his Dionysian release empties into hedonistic wastage. As Mottram notes:

> When Dionysus sheds Eros his energy turns negative. He becomes the Devil, and the Devil, as Norman O. Brown emphasizes in *Life Against Death*, is the form of excrement, waste, and "filthy lucre." The true Dionysus offers an opportunity to affirm the dialectical unity of male and female, destruction and creativity, men and the Earth. Dionysus deteriorated, as Nietzsche understood, gives us a "mixture of sensuality and cruelty," the sexuality of sado-masochistic power. Capitalism and any form of enforced control under ideology therefore gives sympathy to the Devil, where sympathy derives from *sun pathos*, feeling together, a source of revival or of malign ecstasy. (*Blood* 207)

As Weinreich observes, this strain is inextricably linked to Kerouac's tendency to designate liturgical status to the female, investing the whore and the alienated in general with the iconography of catholic ritual. While Maggie Cassidy "could have been the mother or the daughter of God" (*MC* 34), Roxanne, a hipster figure of "mystery" in *The Subterraneans*, is marked by "snaky hair, snaky walk, pale pale junky anemic face and we say junky when once Dostoevski would have said what? if not ascetic or saintly?" and wears a "Jesus Coat" as she moves through "Heavenly Lane" and "the jazz club with the cathedral 'high ceiling'" (13–17). And whereas the main focus of disaffiliation, the black heroin addict, Mardou, is likened to a "confessing" Madonna (33)—an analogue of Mailer's emulation of the African American in "The White Negro"—the eponymous heroine of *Tristessa* is introduced as "radiant and shining" with "the correct Cathedral Indian hairdo." Entitled "Trembling and Chaste," part 1 presents her as "the Virgin Mary of Mexico—Tristessa has a huge ikon in a corner of her bedroom. . . . I sit admiring that majestical mother of lovers," an image augmented by the mock-heroic description of her partner "El Indio," the "vendor of curios," who "prays devoutly when going out to get some junk" (11–12).

The by now characteristic fusion of sexual and theological discourses in these texts is amplified by the drugged condition of the two heroines. Kerouac's scenarios recall Keats's "La Belle Dame sans Merci," where passion drives a knight from the temporal plane into a revelation of what in *Tristessa* is described as "death's eternal ecstasy" (81). Provoked by erotic rapture, the narrators Leo Percepied and Jack Duluoz are permitted a glimpse of transcendental forces, with love and death placed in close proximity through the fact of their lovers' addictions. This encapsulates Kerouac's conception of womanhood: a conflict between idealism and sensuality, or what he calls "the dualism—the paradox—of trying to reconcile Jesus and the 'black cunt'" (*SL, I* 281), which is temporarily resolved in Catholic iconography. As only the image of mortality can match its intensity, physical consummation inevitably results in extinction.

The beatific Tristessa and "essential woman" Mardou, who Leo refers to as "Eve, the woman who by her beauty is able to make the man do anything" (*SU* 149), enslave the two males by an otherworldly love, giving life only to give death. Whereas the image of the junkie and Holy Mother facing each other in prayer in *The Subterraneans* suggests something "inexhaustible," sustained for "weeks on end, like Tibetan prayer-wheels" (12), enchantment descends into cartoon racism with Leo's dread of Mardou as "really a thief of some sort [who] therefore was out to steal my heart, my white man's heart, a Negress sneaking . . . the holy white men for sacrificial rituals" (49).

Behind these figures lurks a tradition of ambivalent archetypes encircling Morgan le Fay, Celtic fairy goddess and half-sister of Arthur, who is both source of evil and protector of heroes, instructing them in the arts of magic and prophecy, and Circe, Homer's sorceress who detains Odysseus on her island and turns his soldiers into swine. His characterizations also chime with Keats's idea of "demon Poesy," harnessing imagination only to watch it fade into oblivion. But whereas the transfiguration in Mardou's eyes is progressively revealed as mental degeneration, with Tristessa it is the "sick[ness]" of the morphine-"shooting," "staggering" addict, the ironically mortal configuration of Burroughs's "Algebra of Need."

The facet of addiction in both these heroines is thus vital, replaying La Belle Dame's beguiling of an innocent knight by feeding him relishes, only to leave him as she has left many others, unconscious with "starved lips," alone on a "withered," "cold hill's side" (Keats, *Complete* 336). And as with Kerouac's heroines, Keats's symbol of female inconstancy is problematic. Although La Belle Dame is a seductress and destroyer without mercy, she weeps and "sigh[s] full sore" at the prospect of sending the knight to his death (335). However, unlike Keats's knight, the yearning of Kerouac's protagonists for absorption into erotic love, however flawed and temporary, usually moves beyond any fear of self-annihilation. Even the "desperate hedonism" of Moriarty, "a prophet of the libido, of the instincts and appetites," is not, as Gregory Stephenson notes, merely "an end in itself but rather a means to an end" (155). The desire is always for transcendence, however twisted or unattainable, as Sal observes in *On the Road*:

> Boys and girls in America have such a sad time together; sophistication demands that they submit to sex immediately without proper preliminary talk. Not courting talk—real straight talk about souls, for life is holy and every moment is precious. (56)

The presence of the female may initially provoke male aggression, but once this is overcome at points of confidence, she serves as a potential agency for ecstatic dissolution of the self and time—that "unbeatable surge when you go into your beloved deep and the whole world goes with you" (*TS* 54)—in keeping with the spiritual charge of the Legend.

Whereas in *The Subterraneans*, Leo Percepied recalls his "shuddering" orgasm and his partner Mardou's remark, "'I was lost suddenly' and she was lost with me tho not coming herself but frantic in my franticness (Reich's beclouding of the senses) and how she loved it" (48), sex carries a reverse connotation in the purifying Zen journey of *The Dharma Bums*: "'Pretty girls make graves,' was my saying" (27). Both Cassady's "sexual sadism" (*SL, I* 434) and the rashly conscious orgy undertaken by the narrator at the beginning lie contrary to the novel's advocacy of strict ecological and Buddhist disciplines. Changeable to the end, Kerouac inverts this perspective in *Book of Dreams*—"Woke up realizing sex is life—sex & art—that or die" (61)—and in a later interview, where he denounces Buddhist controls over the libido as "just words. Wisdom is heartless. I quit Buddhism because Buddhism—or Mahayana Buddhism—preaches against entanglement with women. To me, the most important thing in life is sexual ecstasy" (Aronowitz, "Yen").

Once again orbiting a process of withdrawal followed by a crazed search for usable energies, *The Dharma Bums* intensifies Kerouac's preparation for abandoning the self to nonwestern techniques of rebirth, or

> Samadhi ecstasy, which is the state you reach when you stop everything and stop your mind and you actually with your eyes closed see a kind of eternal multiswarm of electrical Power of some kind ululating in place of just pitiful images and forms of objects, which are, after all, imaginary. (30)

Here the Beat imperative recalls Thoreau's wilderness confrontation in *Walden* and the thread of American anti-materialism running through his essay "Civil Disobedience." Relinquishing the social mainstream ("a system of lures") for ascetic self-reliance with a religious basis, the quest is for reconnection to the primordial ecological mind: "a great rucksack revolution," independent of the self-perpetuating State. The book's hub, Japhy Ryder (Gary Snyder), foresees

> a world full of rucksack wanderers, Dharma Bums refusing to subscribe to the general demand that they consume production and therefore have to work for the privilege of consuming, all that stuff they really don't want anyway such as refrigerators, TV sets, cars, at least new fancy cars, certain hair oils and deodorants and general junk you always see a week later in the junk anyway, all of them imprisoned in a system of work, produce consume, work, produce, consume . . . (97)

This is a timely intervention. In the United States, the appearance of *The Dharma Bums* coincided with official figures showing a settlement rate that accounted for over 90 percent of the nation's forests, while abroad the US Air Force geared up for the systematic spraying of Monsanto's Agent Orange over a million acres of Vietnamese woodland. As the 1960s wore on, land despoliation would be seen not merely as a centralized economic pressure, stemming from the Puritan injunction to put wilderness to work, but as an ideological elimination of counterindustrial subversion. Inspired by ancient Asian and Native American civilizations, Snyder in life offers a cultural etiquette acutely opposed to the laissez-faire exploitation of labor and ecology in profligate conquest, the basis of which he defines at the 1965 Berkeley Poetry Conference as "the fertility of the soil, the magic of animals, the power of vision in solitude, the terrifying initiation and rebirth, the love and ecstasy of the dance, the common work of the tribe" (*Real* 3).

Befittingly within the book, Kerouac's mentor-hero is once more aligned with a nonorthodox indigenous resource, Japhy's fusion of Wobbly anarchism and frontier agrarianism having been forged in a Pacific Northwest lumbering community: "His voice was deep and resonant and somehow brave, like the voice of oldtime American heroes and orators. Something earnest and strong and humanly hopeful" (16). Diametrically opposed to Dean's immersion in supra-social speed ghosted by imminent atomic catastrophe, Japhy recognizes the need for stillness or equilibrium within mobility: a solution to the tropes of ecstasy and collapse that extends into the novel's sequel. "The void is not disturbed by any kind of ups and downs," contends the narrator of *Desolation Angels*, "[b]ut I will be the Void, moving without having moved" (30–32).

As with *The Dharma Bums* and *Mexico City Blues*, *Desolation Angels* marks a preoccupation with the nature of consciousness, envisioned by Kerouac in 1955 as "many selves divided into many living beings or many selves united into one Universal self" (*SL, I* 457), and its transient relations. This is self-referentially echoed in the novel's circular narrative that, contrary to Kerouac's boast of its "(deliberate) formlessness" (*SL, II* 12), is repeated internally via its numbered subdivisions and "passing through" chapter headings. As before, the "man of contemplations" can only sustain himself through disaffiliation from the Business State and "this Western 'work' idea [which] is essentially . . . Faustian Totalitarianism (read both Capitalism and Communism, Tit and Tat.) Buddha is Antifaust but not Antichrist" (*SL, I* 446):

> And now, after the experience on top of the mountain where I was alone for two months without being questioned or looked at by any single human being I began a complete turnabout in my feelings about life. . . . I knew now that my life was a search for peace as an artist, but not only as an artist—As a man of contemplations . . . I was searching for a peaceful kind of life dedicated to contemplation and the delicacy of that, for the sake of my art (in my case prose, tales) (narrative rundowns of what I saw and how I saw) but I also searched for this as my way of life, that is, to see the world from the viewpoint of solitude and to meditate upon the world without being imbroglio'd in its actions. (247–48)

Unlike the situations in *Road, Cody,* or *Dharma Bums,* the narrator's own isolated consciousness rather than the mentor persona is the catalyst for discovery of reflexive relationships between experience, perception, and writing through which the self mobilizes. However, as he admits in *Some of the Dharma,* the artist's doubt over the monastic path never wholly recedes:

> After all these years and all this art and all this Buddhist Learning I still don't know what to do, what course to follow, or whether to follow no course. The constant flow of "creative" imagination in my brain prevents me from appreciating the crystal emptiness (the "artistic impoverishment") of the Eightfold Path . . . a path so arid to behold, so juicy to experience, yet so arid to behold, constantly thinking about it with the thinking-mind. (282)

Having chosen "lonely bored solitude" (*DA* 64) atop Desolation Peak in response to "all this contemptuousness, cold drollery, viciousness, hypocrisy, and derangement [that] convinces me man must leave society and learn to live by himself purely in a solitary out-of-the-way hut . . . and enter the Pure Room of Mind . . . pretty soon I won't write anything" (*SD* 124, 147), Kerouac at first recognizes the futility of permanent disavowal:

> I sit wondering if my own travels down the Coast to Frisco and Mexico wont be just as sad and mad—but by bejesus j Christ it'll be bettern hangin around *this* rock. . . . At night, Fall hints in the Cascade Summer . . . and that's when hairflying me'll be stomping down the trail for the last time, rucksack and all, singing to the snows and jackpines, en route for further adventures, further yearnings for adventures— (*DA* 59)

And then, more troublingly, self-loathing from social-sensual depravation:

> I learned that I hate myself because by myself I am only myself and not even that and how monotonous it is to be monostonos. . . . I learned to disappreciate things themselves and hanshan man mad me mop I don't want it—I learned learn learned no learning nothing—A I K—I go mad one afternoon thinking like this. . . . I want to come down RIGHT AWAY because the smell of onions on my hand as I bring blueberries to my lips on the mountainside suddenly reminds me of the smell of hamburgers and raw onions and coffee and dishwater in lunchcarts of the World to which I want to return at once. . . . [L]et there be rain on redbrick walls and I got a place to go and poems to write about hearts not just rocks— (88–89)

Japhy's meditational path, which in lifting the dualistic boundaries between self and world meets Kerouac's observational aim of "dreaming upon object before you" in "tranced fixation" (*GB* 72), proves only temporarily viable. Sixty-three reclusive days within the landscape of the sublime conclude in disconnection, a "sunk[en]," "unexcited" nihilism ("It's all over") that leaves the speaker's mind "in rags" with no greater ambition than "a peaceful sorrow at home [as] the best I'll ever be able to offer the world" (379–96). Kerouac's vacillating attitude toward the pathetic fallacy, that romantic hunger for mutual participation of consciousness in landscape, in effect stands as a barometer of confidence throughout his career. For example, driving excitedly into the intense heat of Mexico, *On the Road*'s narrator claims that

> [f]or the first time in my life the weather was not something that touched me, that caressed me, froze or sweated me, but became me. The atmosphere and I became the same. . . . The dead bugs mingled with my blood; the live mosquitoes exchanged further portions; I began to tingle all over and to smell of the rank, hot, and rotten jungle, all over from hair and face to feet and toes. (277)

The sea also appears throughout the Legend as a metaphor for the continuity between the narrator and the impersonal elemental forces outside the conscious mind: those "abysses of time" that resonated for Woolf in *The Waves*. While Kerouac had written and hand-printed a novel, *The Sea Is My Brother*, in December 1942—"a dreary attempt at Naturalism with a sea background" (*BD* 48)—two decades later the sea returns as both a thematic model for symbolist techniques of dislocation and a "signpost . . . of something wrong" in *Big Sur* (36), Kerouac's account of nervous collapse, and in its meditative verse appendix, "Sea: Sounds of the Pacific Ocean at Big Sur."

Written in advance of the preceding text, the coda's evocation of "We the sea" via free-flowing particles initially suggests the positive fluid associations within William James's definition of consciousness as a "succession of states, waves, or fields of knowledge, feeling, desire, deliberation—that pass and repass to constitute inner life" (*Principles* 26). Kerouac cites *Ulysses* ("Ju see the Irish sea? / Green winds on tamarack vines— / Joyce—James—Shhish") as Basho, Telemachus, Neptune, Napoleon, Atlas, Cornwall, Ariel, Shelley, Pluto, Tennyson, Coyote, various unnamed women, "the men with a thousand / arms!" "The frog who / never moves & thunders, sharsh," and

> The dog
> with the light on his nose,
> supine, with shoulders so
> enormous they reach back to
> rain crack

and the author himself glide into the multiple perspective of "Buddhalands & Buddhaseas!"

> . . . A billion
> years ain't nothing—
> O the Cities here below!

(BS 169–88)

However, in the main narrative the "voices of the creek amusing me so much at first" metamorphose into "the later horror of that madness night becoming the babble and rave of evil angels in my head" (20). A "huge deep Yogic breath . . . of iodine" taken by the shore yields the "horror of an eternal condition of sick mortality in me—" leaving him

> completely nude of all poor protective devices like thoughts about life or meditations under trees and the "ultimate" and all that shit, in fact the other pitiful devices of making supper or saying "What I do now next?" . . . I see myself as doomed, pitiful—An awful realization that I have been fooling myself all my life thinking there was a next thing to do to keep the show going and actually I'm just a sick clown and so is everybody else. . . . The sea seems to yell to me GO TO YOUR DESIRE DONT HANG AROUND HERE— (37–38)

The hopelessly self-absorbed narrator then projects an anthropomorphic "[g]argantuan leprous face" onto the "insane shivering canyon" with "broad nostrils and huge bags under its eyes and a mouth big enough to swallow five thousand jeepster stationwagons and ten thousand Dave Wains and Cody Pomeroys without a sigh of reminiscence or regret" (72). The loss of euphoric independence that had taken hold on Desolation Peak four years earlier is now permanent.

Casting off from his skid-row awareness of "hit[ting] the end of the trail" (4) in the summer of 1960, Kerouac records in fragmentary measures the "turning from a youthful brave sense of adventure to a complete nausea concerning experience in the world at large" (*DA* 300). Whereas in 1957 Henry Miller had celebrated the isolated cleft as a symbol of liberation from organized society in *Big Sur and the Oranges of Hieronymus Bosch,* for Jack Duluoz, it triggers paranoia: "its Blakean groaning roughrock Creation throes, those vistas when you drive the coast highway on a sunny day opening up the eye for miles of horrible washing sawing" (*BS* 17). This panic-reaction is prophesied in *On the Road,* where Sal's trust in the boundaryless West is undermined ("'What in the hell is this?' I cried out") when confronted by "long flat wastelands of sand and sagebrush" (29). In an agoraphobic reversal he greets the socially circumscribed "rangeland" as a means of reasserting conceptual-control (Ellis 39). In *Big Sur* the wish to restore stability through enclosure is even more pronounced:

> [T]here's an awful roar of surf but it isn't coming from the right place, like you'd expect it to come from "over there" but it's coming from "under there." . . . "What in the hell is this?" . . . The sea roar is bad enough except it keeps bashing and barking at me like a dog in the fog down there, sometimes it booms the earth but my God where is the earth and how can the sea be underground! . . . [T]his roaring high horror of darkness . . . the closer I get to the Creek . . . the louder it roars, I begin to think I'll fall right into it before I can notice it—It's screaming like a raging flooded river right below me—Besides it's even *darker* down there than anywhere! There are glades down there, ferns of horror and slippery logs, mosses, dangerous plashings, humid mists rise coldly like the breath of death, big dangerous trees are beginning to bend over my head and brush my pack . . . (12–16)

In the appendix, too, Duluoz is finally defeated by the equation of the "machinegun sea" with extinction:

> The sea'll
>   only drown me—. . .
> But these waves scare me—
> I am going to die
>    in full despair . . .
>     For me, for us, the Sea,
>    the murdering of time by eating
>     lusty cracks of lip feed wave
>      at aeons of sandy artistry
>       till nothing's left but old age . . .
> Farewell, Sur—
>
>                        (181–88)

Tensions between the writer's boyhood training in guilt and atonement and the exuberant scenes he documents intensify as venomous attacks on his work and personality spiral into an anti-Beat industry. Life and fiction move into terminal crisis, chafing against the years of accomplishment. "What comes now, after [the work of Kerouac the Younger], is that of Kerouac the Elder," he warns a student of his work in 1960. "It will be quite different, harsher, bitter at times. . . . I'm changing. I'm middle aged now and no longer an enthusiastic college boy lyrically feeling America" (*SL, II* 274–75).

Devotion to "the joyous mysterious essence of Arrangement" (*SGE* 60) and the "life of non-interference" that Dean proposes to Sal as a "Tao decision" ("let them all win out" [qtd. in C. Cassady 189]) ebbs away into *Big Sur*'s lament that "[n]othing, nothing, nothing O but *nothing* could interest me any more for one god damned minute in anything in the *world*" (140) and the poisonous urge for conquest, dogma, and hierarchy scarring *Satori in Paris*—"the first book I wrote with drink at my side" (qtd. in Berrigan 103). Raised within an impositional order ("My earliest childhood reading was Catechism in French" [*GB* 93]), Kerouac's fictions break away, in line with Jefferson's ancestry of renewal, but make constant returns, playing out the theme of the abandoned parent that haunts American culture. As Deleuze and Guattari observe:

> Strange Anglo-American literature . . . from D. H. Lawrence to Malcolm Lowry, from Henry Miller to Allen Ginsberg and Jack Kerouac, men who know how to leave, to scramble the codes, to cause flows to circulate, to traverse the desert of the body without organs. They overcome a limit, they shatter a wall, the capitalist barrier. And of course they fail to complete the process, they never cease failing to do so. The neurotic impasse again closes—the daddy-mommy of oedipalization, America, the return to the native land—or else the perversion of the exotic territorialities, then drugs, alcohol—or worse still an old fascist dream. Never has delirium oscillated more between its two poles. (*Anti-Oedipus* 132–33)

Fascinations with the Fellaheen and succession across his work take on a clarified shape as he becomes an advocate for authoritarianism, echoing the anti-liberal urge for permanence voiced by William Faulkner three decades earlier and the signing of pro–Vietnam War petitions by Ralph Ellison, James T. Farrell, and John Dos Passos. Pressurized against an omnipresent vulnerability and self-questioning in the narrative voice, excitement drains away as Kerouac retreats into sour irony and Catholic certainties ("each cup of strong drink is a draught of Dualism" [*SD* 79]). Whereas in *The Scripture of the Golden Eternity* he could propose that "[r]oaring dreams take place in a perfectly silent / mind. Now that we know this, throw the raft away" (35), and "[t]here / are no warnings whatever issuing from the / golden eternity: do what you want. . . . When you've understood this scripture, throw it / away. If you can't understand this scripture, / throw it away. I insist on your freedom" (44–46), by the time of *Vanity of Duluoz,* the dream of perpetual mobility shifts into a Dantean horror of endless agitation, his "restless mental searching" no longer regulated by feral reflex. Self and art veer toward the ideologies of identity and belief in order to tackle experiences of personal and social collapse, a preoccupation with death and revelation announced through the sanctification of his brother in *Visions of Gerard*—

Gerard Duluoz was born in 1917 a sickly little kid with a rheumatic heart and many other complications that made him ill for the most part of his life which ended in July 1926, when he was 9, and the nuns of St. Louis de France Parochial School were at his bedside to take down his dying words because they'd heard his astonishing revelations of heaven delivered in catechism class on no more encouragement than that it was his turn to speak—Saintly Gerard, his pure and mournful face. . . . For the first four years of my life, while he lived, I was not Ti Jean Duluoz, I was Gerard . . . (7)

—and the assumption of guilt for his death "and my father's as well": "I was the knower of [Gerard's] death. It has been ever since then that I feel like the knower of every man's death, every man I knew that has died. Always they die on me . . . and only when I die myself will this guilt go away" (*SL, I* 272–73).

The image of heroic sacrifice gains currency, a yearning for security and lost order reinforced by his interpretation of the First Noble Truth of Buddhism: "All life is suffering." "Love, Suffer, and Work is the motto of my family (Lebris de Keroack)," he declares in *Desolation Angels,* "but it seems I suffer more than the rest" (396). Having defined the human condition in *Visions of Gerard* as "a mass of sin, a veritable barrel of it, you swish and swash in it like molasses—You ooze mistakes thru your frail crevasses. . . . Sin is sin and there's no erasing it" (41–42), Kerouac's mysticism morphs into a desire to be overwhelmed by a colossal hermetic structure. A 1958 interview confirms:

What I believe is that nothing is happening. . . . [W]e're made out of atoms, electrons. We're actually empty. We're an empty vision . . . is one mind. . . . We can give it any name. We can call it tangerine . . . god. . . . But I do know we are empty phantoms, sitting here thinking we are human beings and worrying about civilization. . . . And yet, all is well. . . . We're all in Heaven now, really.
    *You don't sound happy.*
Oh, I'm tremendously sad. I'm in great despair. . . . It's a great burden to be alive. . . . I wish I were safe in Heaven, dead. (Wallace)

This concern is there from the start, dramatized in his debut novel through the Martin family's martyrdom in the face of economic defeat and the deteriorating "tender Nation." After the collapse of their father's printing press, the brothers Peter and Mickey attend church to see Christ "suffering and heroic . . . dear great sacrificial Jesus the hero and the lamb":

[T]he mighty drama of life's meaning was marching all around them, these were the "soreheads" of the earth indifferently turning away from immortality and heroism, abysmal, empty, and unamazed. That was not for Peter, not for Mickey. They had to be heroes or nothing. (*Town* 121)

Setting a precedent for the following fictions, the personal ambitions for adventure and immersions in football, horse racing, and Thanksgiving dinners described in the book's first part, decline to tragic pathos by the close. This is echoed in the "everything is collapsing" leitmotif of *On the Road,* which articulates Kerouac's ambivalence toward mythic America, a sequence of optimism and defeat that eventually settles on withdrawal:

Isn't it true that you start your life a sweet child believing in everything under your father's roof? Then comes the day of the Laodiceans, when you know that you are wretched and miserable and poor and blind and naked, and with the visage of a gruesome grieving ghost you go shuddering through nightmare life. (23)

Fittingly, the book's quest for "sweet, swinging bliss" is pitched within the passivity of Catholic and Buddhist transfiguration:

A wonderment in the bleakness of the mortal realm, and the sensation of death kicking at my heels to move on, with a phantom dogging its own heels, and myself hurrying to a plank where all the angels dove off and flew into the holy void of uncreated emptiness, the potent and inconceivable radiances shining in bright Mind Essence, innumerable lotus-lands falling open in the magic mothswarm of heaven. . . . I realized that I had died and been reborn numberless times but just didn't remember especially because the transitions from life to death and back to life are so ghostly easy, a magical action for naught, like falling asleep and waking up a million times, the utter casualness and deep ignorance of it. (164)

Connected to his metabolic decline, Kerouac starts to mythologize the outsider status of Beat with priestly definitions, a further recurrence of the Creationist discourse dogging America since the Puritan settlement:

The Lost Generation from what I can tell from the books, was based on an ironic, romantic negation. "Beat" generation is sweating for affirmation, and yet here is an irony, almost a cynicism, involved, a kind of lip-service about the "greatness" of life. And, of course, Romanticism is dead. In its place, the search for gnosticism, absolute belief in a Divinity of Rapture. I believe God is Ecstasy in His Natural Immanence. (qtd. in "On the Road Back")

The alibi of what Conrad called "special righteousness"—"I'm not a beatnik, I'm a Catholic. . . . But yeah, as you get older you get more genealogical" (Kerouac qtd. in McLintock)—fuses with a macho-American orientation, played out through currents of blue-collar anti-Bohemianism and elevations of American workers to an iconic status redolent of Lewis Hine's WPA photographs. The superficial disavowal of a high vocation surfaces: the New England Puritan suspicion toward the professional artist merging with Jesuit guilt,[1] which he strains to consolidate in the image of the artist as "adept," proficient in manual skills including ecstatic transfiguration:

> In 1954, I went to Lowell, Massachusetts, where I had lived as a kid. I got a room in skid row near the depot and walked 20 miles around Lowell every day. Went to my old church where I got my first confirmation—all alone, all alone in church, and the great silence of the church. And I suddenly realized that beat means beatitude. Beatific. (qtd. in Aronowitz, "Beat")

Circuits also close on a formal level. Having told Robert Giroux in 1962 that his next book would "mark the end of my 'experimental' period of 'spontaneous prose.' . . . I'm going back to the careful writing of Town & City only this time with more experience about how to make non-spontaneous prose look spontaneous" (*SL, II* 345), he thereafter reports to Ted Berrigan that *Vanity of Duluoz* was done "in a more moderate style, so that, having been so esoteric all these years, some earlier readers would come back and see what ten years had done to my life and thinking" (366).

As is also the case with Proust, these later works contain little dialogue, a facet linked to his most inventive interrogations of memory and observation. The prose of *Big Sur* no longer suggests the "adventurous education" of an American optimist but conscious self-justification:

> Any drinker knows how the process works: the first day you get drunk is okay, the morning after means a big head but so you can kill that easy with a few more drinks and a meal, but if you pass up the meal and go on to another night's drunk, and wake up to keep the toot going, and continue on to the fourth day, there'll come one day when the drinks wont take effect because you're chemically overloaded and you'll have to sleep it off but cant sleep any more because it was alcohol itself that made you sleep those last five nights, so delirium sets in—Sleeplessness, sweat, trembling, a groaning feeling of weakness where your arms are

numb and useless, nightmares, (nightmares of death) . . . well, there's more of that up later. (61)

The characteristic American need for a double security of existential independence and "real" inheritance is reconciled by fixing upon an Old World ancestry of "wildness"; as executor of the natural, the peasant-writer dreams of Breton-Cornish and Iroquois alibis. The performative groping to light through the creative act is subsumed in the final fictions by origin worship, a source of cultural anxiety that goes beyond the maintenance of personal distinction in mass society to the confusion of individuality with identity. This gives nothing to aesthetic ordering, which, to quote Robert Hughes,

> is conscious and existential. . . . [I]dentity is an accident [which] guarantees absolutely nothing about the merits of the [artwork] made in it. What counts is the multicultural *person,* the individual who is more complex than his or her origins and who speaks to the complexities of others. (*American* 618–19)

The freedom asserted through wild acts documented in *Road, Cody,* and *Dharma Bums* ("I saw that my life was a vast glowing empty page, and I could do anything I wanted" [124]) disintegrates into dependency and nostalgia for the hegemonies of Church and State. As the romantic aspiration toward literary fame fades, Kerouac reverts to the folksy proletarianism of his parents and unleashes the latent hostility toward liberal values upon which the New Republicanism preys.[2] *The Dharma Bums'* Buddhist confidence in reconciliation to imperfection capitulates entirely to a belief in Original Sin—"[as named] in the theological Christian dogmatic sects but what I call 'Original Sacrifice'" (*VD* 263)—and to what Whitehead calls "an ultimate craving to infuse into the insistent particularity of emotion that non-temporal generality which primarily belongs to conceptual thought alone" (16). Deleuze and Guattari can now locate the former "figure of outward" as

> the artist possessing the soberest means who took revolutionary "flight," but who later finds himself immersed in dreams of a Great America, and then in search of his Breton ancestors of the superior race. Isn't the destiny of American literature that of crossing limits and frontiers, causing deterritorialized flows of desire to circulate, but also always making these flows transport fascisizing, moralizing, Puritan and familialist territorialities? (*Anti-Oedipus* 277–78)

The Spenglerian barbarian that haunted the generation of Yeats, Eliot, and Shaw with fascist allure and who enters the Legend through the revitalizing energies of Cassady, Snyder, and jazzmen makes his Second Coming as a "science fiction projection of human needs for eternal patterns of domination and submission" (Mottram, *Blood* 196), previously embodied in the Great World Snake of *Doctor Sax* with its flipside "IT" ("the horror, into the void" [201]). The writer's body incubates death, scrambling to reassume tame identities and newly terrified of mutability after two decades of limitless rampage. In the "tired middle age" of *Vanity of Duluoz*, Kerouac "slows down" into a negative epiphany of compulsive stasis:

> Yet I saw the cross just then when I closed my eyes after writing all this. I cant escape its mysterious penetration into all this brutality. I just simply SEE it all the time. . . . Madmen and suicidists see this. Also dying people and people in unbearable anguish. What SIN is there, but the sin of birth? (265)

Passions are evoked and clung to in a further sarcastic satori that craves sanctimony until, frustrated, it settles for immolation. Having written his life into autobiographical plurality and risk, Kerouac's rhetorical voice capitulates to a fully inhabited and narcissistic "I," one no longer concerned with the problems of representation and fixed historically as "the author of *On the Road* and other works." The reader's participatory space contracts accordingly. The protagonist conducts a final poisonous parody of communion—"Hic calix! . . . 'Here's the chalice,' and be sure there's wine in it"—and declares:

> I settled down to write, in solitude, in pain, writing hymns and prayers even at dawn, thinking, "When this book is finished, which is going to be the sum and substance and crap of everything I've been thru throughout this whole goddam life, I shall be redeemed." (*VD* 268)

The Legend's time gap between experience, memory, and the act of composition narrows and disappears altogether. In common with the "old writer" of Burroughs's *Western Lands,* who "couldn't write any more because he had reached the end of words, the end of what can be done with words. Shadow falling upon the mountain. Hurry up please, it's time" (215), the life of the "Memory Babe" synchronizes with a monologue referentially bound to earlier autobiographical territory. Moving inside the configuration he describes, Kerouac revises his story in a final narrative of overlay and self-comprehension that straddles parody and disgust:

> [A]s the Preacher sayeth: "Vanity of vanities . . . all is vanity." . . . For after all what is success? You kill yourself and a few others to get to

the top of your profession . . . so that when you reach middle age . . . you can stay home and cultivate your own garden in bliss; but by that time . . . mobs come rushing across your garden and trampling all your flowers. What's with that? (*VD* 23–29)

# 6

# Orality: "Mad to Talk"

Poetry Fetter'd Fetters the Human Race. Nations are Destroy'd
or Flourish in proportion as Their Poetry, Painting and Music
are Destroy'd or Flourish!
—William Blake, *Jerusalem*

The artist becomes a traitor to the human race. He scorns the
ordinary alphabet, which yields at most only a grammar of
thought, and adopts the symbol, the metaphor, the ideograph.
. . . He creates an impossible world out of an incomprehensible
language, a lie that enchants and enslaves men.
—Henry Miller, *The Wisdom of the Heart*

As Lipton observes in *The Holy Barbarians,* Beat writers, like
Whitman in the previous century, sought to restore poetry to
its ancient role as social function, a spell or ritualized drama
reintegrated with music and chanted by poet-prophet or shaman. Sparked by the electronic revolution in communications technology and
invigorated by the Dionysian persona adopted by Dylan Thomas during his
1950 recital tour—"the very image of poet as voice," according to Cid Corman (67)—the readings and poetry and jazz performances in San Francisco
that followed contribute to what McLuhan sees in *The Gutenberg Galaxy* as
a general reclamation of oral culture in America, reversing the dominance
of visual stress.

To Kerouac at this time, jazz signals a vital change in the literary use of
language, a new dedication of the word to an American orality. This aug-
ments the basis of his own first language, Joual, a patois variant on Québecois,
which underpins the Legend's emphasis on intuitive spoken transmission.

As the aspiring writer makes clear in a 1952 retort to Ginsberg, this is inextricably bound to a continual process of defamiliarization, the sensation of an object as perceived, not as recognized:

> Literature as you see it, using words like "verbal" & "images" etc. & things like that, well all the "paraphernalia of criticism" etc. is no longer my concern because the thing makes me say "shitty little beach in the reeds" is Pre-Literary, it happened to me to think that way before I learned the words the litterateurs use to describe what they're doing—At this moment I'm writing directly from the French in my head. (*SL, I* 101)

Ginsberg evidently learned fast. "By 1955," he notes, "I wrote poetry . . . arranged by phrasing or breath groups into little short line patterns . . . and long saxophone-like chorus lines I knew Kerouac would hear the *sound* of" ("Notes" 318). As Kerouac's ensuing manifestos demonstrate, the Beat focus of attention shifts to speaking the poem:

> The new American poetry as typified by the SF Renaissance (which means Ginsberg, me, Rexroth, Ferlinghetti, McClure, Corso, Gary Snyder, Philip Lamantia, Philip Whalen, I guess) is a kind of new-old Zen lunacy poetry, writing whatever comes into your head as it comes, poetry returned to its origin, in the bardic child, truly ORAL as Ferling said, instead of gray faced Academic quibbling. Poetry & prose had for long time fallen into the hands of the false. These new pure poets confess forth for the sheer joy of confession. They are CHILDREN. They are also childlike graybeard Homers singing in the street. They SING, they SWING. (*SP* vii)

Lifted from the realm of silent interpretation, the traditional bias of western academy, poetry returns to public performance, the Aristotelian sense of rhetorical address, where an audience participates in the recreation of sound and syntax to determine meaning. Renewing previous nineteenth- and twentieth-century drives—Rimbaud, Mallarmé, Dada, futurism—and paralleling Olson's emphasis on breath and syllable as the primary elements of verse, the Beat work is prepared on the page for bardic delivery and private reading, with sonic and visual components fused through controls of form and measure. Stressing musicality as much as notional architecture, this liberation of "the verse that print bred" is, according to Olson, flush with the struggle for personal freedom:

> What we have suffered from, is manuscript, press, the removal of verse from its producer and its reproducer, the voice, a removal by one, by

two removes from its place of origin and its destination. For the breath has a double meaning which latin had not yet lost. (*Collected* 245)

Embodying Kerouac's "pure masculine urge to freely sing" (*SP* vii), the phenomenal world experienced at multiple pitches is returned directly to consciousness. Moving far beyond representation, the spoken work undergoes a generative cycling between page and poet's body, reinstating literature's "muscular principle" and an appreciation of the pulse of vibrating air as the primary inner link with externality. "Language is a vehicle for feeling, language itself doesn't mean anything," contends Ginsberg. "I agree with Olson that language is an extension of physiology." Using Humphrey Osmond's terminology, Ginsberg expands further on his friend's method:

It wasn't that Kerouac couldn't do the same thing with regular meaning prose; it was that he was suddenly aware of the sound of the language, and got swimming in the seas of sound and guided his intellect on sound, rather than on dictionary associations with the meanings of the sounds. In other words, another kind of intelligence—still conscious, still reasonable, but another kind of reason, a reason founded on sounds rather than a reason founded on conceptual associations. If you can use the word reason for that. Or a "modality of consciousness." (*Mystery* 12)

Legislation by breath as opposed to inherited metrics emerges most obviously in the long adjectival measures of "October in the Railroad Earth," "intended to clack along all the way like a steam engine pulling a 100-car freight with a talky caboose at the end" (qtd. in Berrigan 101). The work's opening shows what "can still be done if the thinking during the swift writing is confessional and pure and all excited with the life of it" (101):

There was a little alley in San Francisco back of the Southern Pacific station at Third and Townsend in redbrick of drowsy lazy afternoons with everybody at work in offices in the air you feel the impending rush of their commuter frenzy as soon they'll be charging en masse from Market and Sansome buildings on foot and in buses and all well-dressed thru workingman Frisco of Walkup ? ? truck drivers and even the poor grime-bemarked Third Street of lost bums even Negroes so hopeless and long left East and meanings of responsibility and *try* that now all they do is stand there spitting in the broken glass sometimes fifty in one afternoon against one wall at Third and Howard and here's all these Millbrae and San Carlos neat-necktied producers and commuters of America and Steel civilization rushing by with San Francisco *Chronicles* and green *Call-Bulletins* not even enough time to be disdainful, they've got to catch 130, 132, 134, 136 all the way up to 146 till the time of evening supper in homes of the railroad earth when high in the sky the magic stars ride above the following hotshot freight trains. (*LT* 43)

Replicating the asymmetrical phrasing of his model, Charlie Parker, syllables are skipped and connectives and qualification phrases dumped, all to vary the pace of the meter. The density of what Kerouac calls "scatological buildup" transforms the semantics of a word-image derived from memory into malleable sonic material. This process is laid bare by metacommentary in *Old Angel Midnight*:

> The total turningabout & deep revival of world robe-flowing literature till it shd be something a man'd put his eyes on & continually read for the sake of reading & for the sake of the Tongue & not just these insipid stories writ in insipid aridities & paranoias bloomin & why yet the image—let's hear the Sound of the Universe, son. (4)

Like *Midnight* and "Railroad Earth," *Visions of Cody*'s elastic paragraphs, each a page or so long, collate disparate images in sequences that break open Kerouac's tendency in *On the Road* to hem expression within shorter, thematically bound cells ("I went to the cold water flat . . . I went away" [2–3]). Answering Twain's call for a new plain literary style with echoes of street prose, Kerouac trades on devices of onomatopoeia, his characteristic sound based in protracted vowels such as "whooping," "huge," and "brown doom gloom" and snapping consonants like "hotshot freight trains" and the Hopkinsesque

> Watching fat birds pomp
>   Noisefully in dry rackety
> Grovebottom leaves
>   and bamboo splitjoint
>   woodyards . . .
> to crash like a criminal
> thru bright brittle
> thickets (crrack).
>
> (*SD* 363)

Gerund is also a feature, augmented by nouns or adjectives jammed together: the German-style compounds of Dean's "loveproblems" (*OTR* 8), the "bookmovie" of the narrator's "dreambrain" (*BD* 21), the "muckchop rich as kincobs face" of the bestial Mr. Groscorp (*VG* 127), Lowell's "respectaburban wildhouses" (*DS* 9), and "those old tenements" where he had "fusskicked" as a baby (*SD* 296), intensifying Olson's "*kinetics* of the thing" (*Collected* 240). *The Subterraneans* enhances this management of pace by emphasizing present participle verbs within past tense prose. The cinematic observations of a San Francisco nightclub, for example, not only convey the frantic atmosphere of jazz, discussion, and gyrating bodies but also dramatize Kerouac's American ideal, straddling Bohemia, the West, and heroic proletarianism:

> So there we were at the Red Drum, a tableful of beers a few that is and all the gangs cutting in and out, paying a dollar quarter at the door, the little hip-pretending weazel there taking tickets, Paddy Cordavan floating in as prophesied (a big tall blond brakeman type subterranean from Eastern Washington cowboy-looking in jeans coming in to a wild generation party all smoky and mad and I yelled "Paddy Cordavan?" and "Yeah?" and he'd come over)—all sitting together, interesting groups at various tables, Julien, Roxanne (a woman of 25 prophesying the future style of America) . . . (13)

Kerouac introduces constant fluctuations of line-speed over pulse with repeated syllables and disjunctive punctuation, akin to the way that a jazz soloist trips himself up to defy prediction. As he tells Donald Allen in 1959, "The rhythm of how you decide to *rush your statement* determines the rhythm of the poem, whether it is a poem in verse-separated lines, or an endless one-line poem called prose" (*GB* 76). In an earlier letter, Kerouac cites a passage from *The Subterraneans* as an example of his "true beautiful urgent breathless rhythm":

> Extending the eye business, the time we closed our eyes (again not drinking, because of broke, poverty would have saved this romance) and I sent her messages, "Are you ready." and I see the first thing in my black eye world and ask her to describe it, amazing how we came to the same thing, it was some rapport, I saw crystal chandeliers and she saw white petals in a black bog just after some melding of images . . . my fear of communicating WHITE images to her in our telepathies for fear she'll be (in her fun) reminded of our racial difference, at that time making me feel guilty, now I realize it was love's gentility on my part—Lord. (*SL, I* 451)

Here Kerouac's sentences jettison frameworks of a distinct past, present, or future in order to embrace the dislocations of memory, perception, and vocabulary. The inconsistent tenses shuffle temporalities and stretch and

contract the action, giving the curious sensation of a narrator who is simultaneously in the past and the present. Even when the text pursues an ostensibly
linear course, the language is released from causal prescription into a new set
of conversational controls that Kerouac gleans from William Carlos Williams:
"measured pauses which are the essentials of our speech"—"divisions of the
*sounds* we hear"—"time and how to note it down" (*GB* 69).

Kerouac commentates on his struggle with the suffocating "formalism of
thought" in *Big Sur*'s coda ("Wroten Kerarc'h / in the labidalian / aristotelian
park / with slime a middle"), which is redressed with speed and fluency:
"Not overseas, be seas" (173). Elucidating further in his "Statement on Poetics," Kerouac gives a thematic function to the geological term "alluvial," the
solid mud, silt, and sand deposited by flowing water: "Add alluvials to the
end of your line when all is exhausted but something has to be said for some
specified irrational reason, since reason can never win out, because poetry
is NOT a science" (*GB* 76). He demonstrates this technique throughout *Book
of Dreams* and in his description of "Lester Young['s] chorus of 'You Can
Count On Me,' 1938," in *Cody*, its fragmentary cubist nature itself being part
of Kerouac's effort to register a barely communicable vision, with a line that
plunges into a barrage of clashing consonants and a swift metareference to
the saxophonist:

> [I]t was Lester started it all, the gloomy saintly serious goof who is
> behind the history of modern jazz . . . his drape, his drooping mel-
> ancholy disposition in the sidewalk, in the door, his porkpie hat. . . .
> [W]hat doorstanding influence has Cody gained from the master of his
> generation? what mysteries as well as masteries? . . . [T]he greatness
> of America in a single Negro musician—Lester is just like the river, the
> river starts in near Butte, Montana in frozen snow caps (Three Forks)
> and meanders on down across states and entire territorial areas of
> dun bleak land with hawthorn crackling in the sleet, picks up rivers at
> Bismarck, Omaha and St Louis just north, another at Kay-ro, another
> in Arkansas, Tennessee, comes deluging on New Orleans with muddy
> news from the land and a roar of subterranean excitement that is like
> the vibration of the entire land sucked of its gut in mad midnight,
> fevered, hot, the big mudhole rank clawpole old frogular pawed-soul
> titanic Mississippi from the North, full of wires, cold wood, and horn.
> (*VC* 455–56)

Learning from the expressive potential of long, unraveling sentences
deployed by Wolfe, Proust, and Joyce, such arrangements have little contact

with the directionless, rambling characteristic of Robert Lowell's claim for "open form." Rather, Kerouac shares much with Robert Duncan and his series *The Structure of Rime,* where rhyme is defined as any manner of organizing memory by repetition, similarity, echo, or mimetic effect in idea or cadence, an overall principle of arrangement as opposed to a clicking noise that marks a line's ending. Alluding specifically to *The Subterraneans,* Kerouac stresses that his prose builds with a disciplined use of imprecision learned from jazz ("blow as deep as you want to blow" [*GB* 69]) that precludes carelessness:

> [T]his whole paragraph was written in one breath as it were, and the "Lord" at the end of it is like its period, dot, more like the sometimes "Bop" at the end of Modern Music (Jazz) and intended as a release from the extent of the phrase, the rhythmic paragraph is one phrase. I don't use periods and semicolons, just dashes, which are interior little releases, as if a saxophonist drawing breath there. The effect is good prose, don't you think?—certainly not obtuse, opaque, heavy-handed or dull. Certainly not baroque. (*SL, I* 451)

Maintaining currency with Olson's "Projective Verse," Kerouac's alignment of punctuation and measure with breath favors the breaking of a phrase by dash instead of the conventional shudder of a full stop, as in the opening of chapter 15 of *Maggie Cassidy*:

> The sad traffic crunching in from winter, out to winter—The bleak blue raw feel of the wind from the woods citifying by the few sad lights—There I changed to the South Lowell bus—It would show up always catching at my throat—the mere name of it as the busdriver'd rolled it in the window enough to make my heart beat—I'd look at other people's faces to see if they saw the magic— (63)[1]

The methodology of writer as horn soloist qualifies his basis for reflecting and varying the emotional flow of a phrase, modifying syntax into new divisions of sound and cadence. Given subject-verb categories and standard punctuation are necessarily discarded:

> METHOD. No periods separating sentence-structures already arbitrarily riddled by false colons and timid usually needless commas—but the vigorous space dash separating rhetorical breathing (as jazz musician drawing breath between outblown phrases). (*GB* 69)

Influenced by his reading of the "Chinese Immortals" (*SL, II* 37), Kerouac through the 1950s strips down the flowery devices explored in *The Town and the City* (and retained in part for *The Subterraneans*) into a terse new style. By the time of *Cody,* meaning emerges wholly from precise rhythmic compression, an open-ended sonic and syntactic disconnection that never reveals its destination in advance—as, for example, in "Lester droopy porkpie hung his horn and blew bop lazy ideas inside jazz had everybody dreaming" (380) and in the built-in acceleration of pulse in "There and there alone we'll find our chops and smoky talk of the most important dinner time in Denver" (347).

Predictably, Kerouac's innovations faced institutional hostility beyond Truman Capote's flippant condemnation of *On the Road* as "typing, not writing" (qtd. in Winn 28) and Norman Podhoretz's attack on Spontaneous Prose as "an inept imitation of Faulkner and Joyce done by a man who thinks all you have to do . . . is sit back and pour out anything that pops into your head" ("Know-Nothing" 46). Having already told his agent that he "would rather die than betray my faith in my work which is inseparable from my life, without this faith any kind of money is mockery" (*SL, II* 11), and elsewhere boasted that "Hemingway has nothing over me when it comes to pernicketiness about craft" (*SL, II* 83), Kerouac's defense of his strategy as anything but artless, sloppy endeavor becomes increasingly pained as the career progresses:

> All my editors since Malcolm Cowley have had instructions to leave my prose exactly as I wrote it. In the days of Malcolm Cowley, with *On the Road* and *The Dharma Bums,* I had no power to stand by my style for better or for worse. . . . You simply give the reader the actual workings of your mind during the writing itself: you confess your thoughts about events in your own unchangeable way. . . . [D]id you ever hear a guy telling a long wild tale to a bunch of men in a bar and all are listening and smiling, did you ever hear that guy stop to revise himself, to go back to a previous sentence to improve it, to defray its rhythmic thought impact . . . he's passed over it like a part of the river flows over a rock once and for all and never returns and can never flow any other way in time? . . . I spent my entire youth rehashing, speculating and deleting and got so I was writing one sentence a day and the sentence had no FEELING. Goddamn it, FEELING is what I like in art, not CRAFTINESS and the hiding of feelings. (qtd. in Berrigan 101)

Invoking Heraclitus, Kerouac locates his phrasal basis as a once-only existential projection, distinct from mannered style. As Ginsberg corroborates:

> Kerouac told me that in the future literature would consist of what people actually wrote rather than what they tried to deceive other people into thinking they wrote, when they revised it later on. And I

saw opening up this whole universe where people wouldn't be able to lie anymore! They wouldn't be able to *correct* themselves any longer. They wouldn't be able to hide what they said. (*Deliberate* 263)

However, as the bowdlerized first editions of many of his texts, and *Cody* in particular, testify, Kerouac's publishers lacked the nerve to leave unsullied "the crude glad (if-you-wish-Carlylean) personal quavering sound of my own voice which took me so long (15 years of writing) to find and tap" (*SL, II* 15). His complaint to the editor of *The Subterraneans* draws on Whitman and Blake to unmask the accessibility motive as a common alibi for standardization and profit:

> I can't possibly go on as a responsible prose artist and also a believer in the impulses of my own heart and in the beauty of pure spontaneous language if I let editors take my sentences, which are my phrases that separate by dashes when "I draw a breath," each of which pours out to the tune of the whole story its rhythmic yawp of expostulation, & riddle them with commas, cut them in half, in three, in fours, ruin swing, making what was reasonably wordy prose even more wordy and unnaturally awkward (because castrated). In fact the manuscript of *Subterraneans,* I see by the photostats, is so (already) riddled and buckshot with commas and marks I can't see how you can restore the original out of it. The act of composition is wiser by far than the act of after-arrangement, "changes to help the reader" is a fallacious idea prejudging the lack of instinctual communication between avid scribbling narrator and avid reading reader, it is also a typically American business idea like removing the vitamins out of rice to make it white (popular). American publishing has no criteria for evaluating popular taste other than what it preconceiving feeds the populace. Who's to say what people like? (*SL, II* 15)[2]

The line's indentation and placement on a page and its horizontal and vertical white spaces as emphasized in *Some of the Dharma* actively score the works of the Legend for vocal performance. "Space means time," notes Gary Snyder in *The Real Work* (31), invoking Kerouac's translation of Cassady's speed into print discourse—a dance of the intellect within syntax that Pound calls *logopoeia*. In works such as the *Blues* series and *Old Angel Midnight* ("only the beginning of a lifelong work in multilingual sound representing the haddal-da-babra of babbling world tongues coming in thru my window at midnight [and] the only book I've ever written in which I allow myself the right to say anything I want" [*SL, II* 193]), this is illuminated via great improvised releases of sonic association, mindful of the need to avoid constraint within normative representations of self, as speech becomes narrative:

> Aw rust rust rust rust die die die pipe pipe ash ash die die ding dong ding ding ding rust cob die pipe ass rust die words—I'd as rather be permiganted in Rusty's moonlight Rork as be perdirated in this bile arta panataler where ack the orshy rosh crowshes my tired idiot hand O Lawd I is coming to you's soon's you's ready's as can readies be Mazatlan heroes point out Mexicos & all ye rhythmic bay fishermen don't hang fish eye soppy in my Ramadam give-cigarette Sop of Arab Squat—the Berber types that hang fardels on their woman back wd as lief Erick some son with blady matter I guess as whup a mule in sing-song pathetic mulejump field by quiet fluff smoke North Carolina (near Weldon) (Railroad Bridge) Roanoke Millionaire High-Ridge hi-party Hi-Fi million-dollar findriver skinfish Rod Tong Apple Finder John Sun Ford goodby Paw mule America Song— (OAM 59)

The use of dashes and recurring syllables assist both the eye and inner ear to accrue images at pace without loss of detail. Clauses pile up kinesthetically, accelerating the process of deciphering phonetic symbols into sound and breath gestalts in the reader. The gap between thought and notation narrows to capture an inclusive verticality, a motive Kerouac shares with Willem de Kooning: "It's never right, you know, because it doesn't have everything in it. So you keep going until you've put everything you can into it. Then you go onto the next one" (qtd. in Pepper). This surfaces with brilliant effect in the unpunctuated spatial catalog of *Old Angel Midnight*'s opening: "FRIDAY AFTERNOON IN THE UNIVERSE, in all directions in & out you got your men women dogs children horses pones tics perts parts pans pools palls pails parturiencies and petty Thieveries that turn into heavenly Buddha." Such a passage approximates "the actual movement of mind and voice in full vernacular," to call on Parkinson's early intuition of a Beat poetics:

> Accustomed to syllabic stress and foot verse, the normal audience for poetry is not prepared to take into consideration intensity (loudness), pitch, and duration, and the concept of breath pause is far from being ritualized. . . . The primary problem of poetry is notation, through the appearance of poem on page to indicate the reality of articulation. A poem is a score. . . . The Capital letters, the broken lines, the long long long lines, the shift from vernacular idiom to lofty rhetoric, these are attempts to shift from conventional idiom to actual, to increase the vocality of the verse. (287)

As Parkinson suggests, the experiments with jazz accompaniment are more dramatic instances of a contemporary stress on transliteration, coinciding not only with an impulse to transgress genre but with a reinstatement of performance traditions of lyric and instrument. Jazz antecedents for these readings range from the half-sung dialogues of Louis Armstrong's "That's When I'll Come Back to You" (1927), Duke Ellington's verse drama *A Drum Is a Woman* (1956), and Bessie Smith's blues poetry to the bop scatting of Dizzy Gillespie, Slim Gaillard, and Jon Hendricks—all "black talk" transformations of standard speech. In 1958, Langston Hughes read his poems on *Weary Blues* alongside Henry "Red" Allen and Charles Mingus, whose bass arco also underscores Hughes and Lonnie Elder's "Scenes in the City" on *Poetry and Jazz Symposium*. Of this union, Hughes suggests:

> The music should not only be a background to the poetry but should comment on it. I tell musicians . . . to improvise as much as they care to around what I read. . . . Then I listen to what they say in their playing, and that affects my own rhythms when I read. (notes for *Weary Blues*)

Further performances at the Cellar by Ferlinghetti and Rexroth—

> I didn't start this thing. Renegade monks were doing it in the Middle Ages. Charles Cros, a nineteenth century poet read his stuff . . . to *balmusette* bands. There have been countless talking-blues singers in the South. Maxwell Bodenheim did it in the 20s and Langston Hughes in the 30s, and even I did it in the late 20s, at the Green Mask in Chicago, with Frank Melrose, a K.C. pianist ("Disengagement" 188)[3]

—reinforce the Beat sense of this form as language-centered. After reading in public for the first time in 1957, albeit unsuccessfully (his residency opposite J. J. Johnson at the Village Vanguard closed a week prematurely), Kerouac produced a burst of recordings in 1959. While *Poetry for the Beat Generation* betrays little integration between the push of the voice and Steve Allen's urbane piano—the incongruity between the variable meters of the poetry and the rhythmic conservatism of the jazz plagued the form as a whole—*Blues and Haikus* attains empathy with "just the pure vibrating horn" blown by Zoot Sims and Al Cohn, the inflections of three-lined poems traded in call and response style with considerable verve. Kerouac is unaccompanied on *Readings on the Beat Generation,* the sensual, indeterminate nature of the voice given prominence by electronic amplification, "gear[ing] the human body into the energy of circuitry" (Mottram, *Blood* 183).

Giving an intensely physical basis for his work, the scores of the *Blues* series and *Midnight* are adapted on the recording for multiple performance, substantiating the dimension of sound into its inner movement, or what Frank

O'Hara calls the "shape of content" in his "Personism" manifesto. Organizing energy into what Paul Carroll terms the "skin, blood and organs" of form, the visual design of the page embodies "the living elements that animate the skeleton, offering that kind of total experience which a good poem affords" (33). Accordingly in *Big Sur,* Kerouac contemplates a monstrous urban pileup through typographic emphasis: "cityCityCITY" (53)—also the alternative title of "The Electrocution" (my "big science fiction phantasy preview" written "during Army McCarthy hearings and so it has wildly hip political flavor" [*SL, I* 494)]). This technique is again used in "AUDEN HAD NO ASS" from "Richmond Hill Blues," a poem redolent of Walter Abish's self-imposed constrictions in *Alphabetical Africa*:

> Auden had no ass
> Butler had no balls
> Carew had no crash
> . . .
> Quasi Quean had no Queasy
>        feelings
> R had no heart
> Studentio
>        had
>
>            no
>                    Stok
> . . .
>        X no Y or Z

(*BB* 86–87)

Fabulation extends in part 3 of *Visions of Cody* to simple line drawings and collages of imagined school essays and newspaper headlines, in the vein of the "Heart of the Hibernian Metropolis" chapter of *Ulysses.* The material form of the page admits contrary streams of marks, engendering a turbulence that deflects the narrative path from linearity. After inserting a song into his chronicle, Kerouac writes:

> Things have a deceiving look of peacefulness, the beast is actually ready to leap—lookout—yet what about those French dreams last spring?—what, sweet hype? can write?—find no machine to relabate your fond furlures; furloors, vleours, or velours, we know that in French, in print *à main* we cannot fail—
> O Telegraph Hill!
> Strange graces come to occupy this back seat, you mind, in (own) tides. (time?) Furbishoors, fruppery, nosootle, nonsootle, nonsottle,

sweattle, don't wrestle with this—trestle—(to prove I can go on effi-
ciently, otherwise I'll begin an abstract drawing) (*VC* 390–91)

Which indeed he does, an experiment in notation that takes its place
among the seminal designs in modernist literature, anticipated in 1895 by
the visual-verbal layout of Mallarmé's *Un Coup de dés jamais n'abolira le
hasard*—a progenitor of free-form measure beyond the vertical tabulations of
George Herbert's "Easter Wings," where shape guides meter in a Christian
crescendo; the disjunctive lineation of Samuel Richardson's *Clarissa,* which
signifies the disordered condition of the heroine's mind following rape;
and the marbling and blacking out of pages of Sterne's *Life and Opinions of
Tristram Shandy* to evoke mourning, all of which maintain the story's fixed
order. Drawing attention to the page as physical space for the organization
of signs, number 54 of *Old Angel Midnight* is exemplary in its typographi-
cal indications of speed and intensity without narrative. Patterned upon
isolated snap-units of meaning and dense word conjunctions, each line is
a pulse in itself:

> peep
> peep the
> bird tear the
> sad bird drop heart
> the dawn has slung
> her aw arrow drape
> to sissyfoo & made eastpink
> dink the dimple solstice men
> crut and so the birds go ttleep
> and now bird number two three four five
> sixen seven and seven million of em den
> dead bens barking now the birds are yakking
> & barking swinging Crack! Wow! Quiet! . . .

The effect brings to mind a Michael McClure poem, physically embodied
on the page with a spinal column to become a "spiritmeat" organism in its
own right. Like McClure, Kerouac directs performance by deploying irregular capitalization and organizing his verse around a shifting axis rather
than by sticking to conventional left-hand margins. Placing unevenly spaced
type within discrete sections, the emphasis is on the field as a whole: an accumulation of gestures that emerge as a single action. In the instance of texts
such as *Midnight* and *Some of the Dharma,* multidirectionality builds with the
contrasting lineation of adjacent passages. This fosters Mallarmé's sense of

[a] tremendous burst of greatness, of thought, or of emotion, contained in a sentence printed in large type, with one gradually descending line to a page, [which] should keep the reader breathless throughout the book and summon forth his powers of excitement. (83)

Page space, meaning, and environment work together to produce plasticity of thought and sound, the work's structure derived, as with *Un Coup de dés*, from syntactical discontinuity. As Mallarmé notes in the poem's preface:

[S]torytelling is avoided. . . . [F]rom its very design, there results for the person reading it aloud, a musical score. The difference in the printed characters between the preponderant, secondary, and adjacent motifs, dictates their importance for oral expression; the disposition of the characters: in the middle, on the top, or the bottom of the page, indicates the rise and fall in intonation. (105)

Disturbances of idea, meter, and margin break the authority conferred upon the surface lucidity of realism and its seduction of the reader into complicity. The spatial arrangement of language in *Desolation Angels* prolongs this drive while assuming a more familiar look with a playfulness gleaned from Joyce's great book of memory, *Finnegans Wake*:

I could go mad in this—O carryall menaya but the weel may track the rattle-burr, poniac the avoid devoidity runabout, minavoid the crail—Song of my all the vouring me the part de rail-ing carry all the pone—part you too may green and fly—welkin moon wrung salt upon the tides of come-on night, swing on the meadow shoulder, roll the boulder of Buddha over the pink partitioned west Pacific fog mow—O tiny tiny tiny human hope, O molded cracking thee mirror thee shook pa t n a watalaka—and more to go—
  Ping. (36)

Moving within a continuity of concerns that draws the found poetries of Kurt Schwitters and Tristan Tzara alongside the Northumbrian dialect verse of Basil Bunting, the "sound of the words spoken aloud is itself the meaning, just as the sound of the notes played on the proper instruments is the meaning of any piece of music" (Bunting, *Note* 211). While he may neglect to consider how the voice is also a product, as well as a vehicle, of the unitary ego in the West (Davidson 109), Kerouac courts a disembodied concrete poetry located by Bob Cobbing in "the physical structure of language—the sign made by the voice, and the symbol for that sign made on paper or in other material and visible form" (Cobbing and Griffiths 121). The ensuing overhaul of literature as a recreation of sound in line proceeds in free dissociative leaps, a further manifestation of the American thrust for rebirth through a language unimpeded by past significations.

The musical prose of Kerouac's favorite book, *Doctor Sax,* peppered with "'Joycean' invented-words [which] are really oral or aural sound-inventions, as in 'dreamblabbering'" (*SL, I* 451), is a case in point, weaving in and out of more formal syntax to recover the sensuous grasp of the child's unfettered mind and bind an entire novel:

> The thunderous husher of our sleep at night—
> I could hear it rise from the rocks in a groaning wush ululating with
> the water, sprawlsh, sprawlsh, oom, oom, zoooo, all night long the river
> says zooo, zooo, the stars are fixed in rooftops like ink. Merrimac, dark
> name, sported dark valleys: my Lowell had the great trees of antiquity
> in the rocky north waving over lost arrowhead and Indian scalps, the
> pebbles on the slatecliff beach are full of hidden beads and were stepped
> on barefoot by Indians. Merrimac comes swooping from a north of
> eternities, falls pissing over locks, cracks and froths on rocks, bloth,
> and rolls frawing to the kale, calmed in dewpile stones holes slaty sharp
> (we dove off, cut our feet, summer afternoon stinky hookies), rocks full
> of ugly old suckers not fit to eat, and crap from sewage, and dyes, and
> you swallowed mouthfuls of the chokeful water—By moonlight night
> I see the mighty Merrimac foaming in a thousand white horses upon
> the tragic plains below. Dream:—wooden sidewalk planks of Moody
> Street Bridge fall out, I hover on beams over rages of white horses in
> the roaring low,—moaning onward, armies and cavalries of charging
> Euplantus Eudronicus King Grays loop'd & curly like artists' work,
> and with clay souls' snow curlicue rooster togas in the fore front.
> I had a terror of those waves, those rocks— (12)

What magnificence! Despite the use of nonsemantic sounds and bebop's cadence and pace as paradigm, such passages remain language configurations. Notations of Cassady's performances in *Cody* and nongrammatical descriptions of Lowell in *Sax* and of the sea in *Big Sur* are in no way a substitution of musical score. Note signs do not tempt exegesis as word signs; these are literary forms in their own right with significant visual qualities, which alone justify their existence as printed poetries. They can be appreciated without knowledge of their sound-text dimensions, even though that information adds to them (Mottram, "Blackburn" 41–44).

Bypassing standard recognitions, Kerouac distills sound into pictorial signs, exploring the "tropisms" of consciousness, or "some perfecting of the sayless"

(*SL, I* 579) that vanishes upon transmutation into logical syntax. Kerouac makes it "on his own voice and mother tongue," to borrow Snyder's words, "while steering a course between crystal clouds of utterly incommunicable non-verbal states—and the gleaming daggers and glittering nets of language" (*Earth* 118). The resulting incantations testify not only to the Zen influence on Beat writing, in particular its emphasis on unmediated oral transmission honed from meditation on breath, but also to the contemporary impact of work by Pollock, Kline, and Rothko: a handling of paint freed from subordination to figurative shape, which charges the canvas with nondiscursive meanings.

Kerouac's pioneering understanding of these means separates sound and word from institutionalized usage and pilots the poem or novel as a container of energy, where oral autonomy breaches intellective rule to define shape and integrity. Entering what Samuel Beckett calls "the domain of the maker [which] is the domain of the feasible" (*Proust* 120), the gratuitous nature of the chosen contour becomes no less valid than the imposition of fourteenth-century protocols, such as the heroic couplet or Petrarchan sonnet. Kerouac effectively breaks, in Mottram's words,

> any simplistic surface of words, of syntax, into complex, more accurate articulations of the actual complexities of our lives, not to use the reductive simplifications of ironic versifiers, whose forms deliberately disturb nobody, except perhaps those who refuse to be dominated by sentences and mathematical metrics. Discovery and recognition of the discovered, freedom to explore and a will to new form. (qtd. in Skelt 35)

Far from making the ensuing work diaristic or baroque, Kerouac's syntax grows deeper roots and twists, recovers, and holds attention as no mere transmission of orthodox prose could. Learning honesty in ear and mouth, he notates the displacements of perception to provide a vivid transcription on the page with which to present that voice: a metatalk or *ta'wil* of revelation that anticipates "talk-poet" David Antin's bypassing of text in the creation of literary form. With a presence at the generative point of syllable and phrase, hearing becomes, to quote J. E. Orme,

> the main sense modality in the perception of change and time. Hearing only locates stimuli very vaguely in space, but it locates them with admirable precision in time. It is *par excellence* the sense which appreciates time, succession, rhythm and tempo. (9)

The act of writing is modified accordingly, the words of Paul Blackburn qualifying alongside Olson's definition of "field" as commentary on Kerouac's impetus:

I wouldn't even know whether a poem was finished or not unless my ear told me. . . . Now that forms are as open as they are, each poem has to find its own form. It has to do with the technique of juxtaposition and reading from the breath line and normal speech raised to its highest point. But that's abstracting a principle. . . . It's almost as though your technique is in your wrists and you're sitting at a typewriter instead of a piano. . . . [The writer has] got to hear his own voice saying it. ("Craft")

# The Field of Action

> The essential quality of poetry is that it makes a new effort of
> attention and discovers a new world within the known world.
> Man and the animals and the flowers all live within a strange
> and forever surging chaos. The chaos which we have got used
> to, we call a cosmos. The unspeakable inner chaos of which
> we are composed, we call consciousness. But man cannot live
> in chaos. The animals can. To the animal all is chaos, only
> there are a few recurring motions and aspects within the surge.
> The animal is content but man is not. Man must wrap himself
> in a vision, make a house of apparent form and stability, fixity.
> In his terror of chaos he begins by putting up an umbrella
> between himself and the everlasting world. Then he paints
> the underside of the umbrella like a firmament. Then comes
> a poet, enemy of convention, and makes a slit in the umbrella,
> and lo! the glimpse of chaos is a vision, a window to the sun.
> —D. H. Lawrence, *Chaos in Poetry*

Writing in 1974, Paul Blackburn records the possibilities open
to poets of his epoch, the foundations of which were laid
by Olson's pivotal essay "Projective Verse":

> We have had our gene-
> ration of innovators, 19
> 15 & the rest.
> What Pound and Williams & Moore have done
> is in the air, is, perhaps, the air.
> Let the species now give rise to a few
>         masters

(since the fields are open

and the air cleared)

("Shop" 27)

Blackburn alludes to Duncan's "Opening of the Field" and the clearing of the closed poem propagated by the New Critics, based on the security of tired metrics, smug irony, the self-regarding ego and its iambic thuds, and with it a cosmology long since eliminated by twentieth-century physics and geometries.[1] Sharing Olson's sense of "[projectile/[percussive/[prospective" form, Kerouac generates narratives that recognize the relative and indeterminate nature of the experienced world, validating the multiple and fluid over the singular and finite. Simultaneously invoking nonwestern praxis—"SUNYAVADA System: The monk-scholar Nagarjuna wrote a doctrine of relativity in 2nd Century AD 'The truth of no individual fact can be asserted because nothing is real apart from the whole'" (*SD* 20)—Kerouac's search moves within a literary continuum traceable to Ernest Fenollosa's critique of the claims of subject-predicate expression to embody the character of fact and his emulation of the ideogram as "shorthand pictures of actions or processes." "Like nature," suggests Fenollosa, "the Chinese words are alive and plastic, because *thing* and *action* are not formally separated" (22):

> A true noun, an isolated thing, does not exist in nature. Things are only the terminal points, or rather the meeting points, of actions, cross-sections cut through actions, snapshots. Neither can a pure verb, an abstract motion, be possible in nature. The eye sees noun and verb as one: things in motion, motion in things, and so the Chinese conception tends to represent them. . . . [I]n nature there is *no* completeness. . . . [N]o full sentence really completes a thought. . . . [A]cts are successive, even continuous; one causes or passes into another. And though we may string never so many clauses into a single compound sentence, motion leaks everywhere, like electricity from an exposed wire. All processes in nature are interrelated; and thus there could be no complete sentence (according to this definition) save one which it would take all time to pronounce. (17)

Or as Kerouac puts it in *Some of the Dharma*:

> These divisible multiple notes on
> the one indivisible simple Dharma!

The woodcutter

The woodcutting    } THIS TRIPLE WORLD

And the wood

The thinking, the thinker & the thought-of
—all 3 equally empty & same, in
reality indivisible.

(144)

Pound's complementary definition of image—"that which presents an intellectual and emotional complex in an instant of time" ("A Few Don'ts")—expands under Kerouac's hand into a compositional mobility based on extending phrases. Recasting the speech-text as a cell of energy, he takes on Alfred Korzybski's theories of General Semantics, which, reports Ginsberg, "cut Kerouac loose from that 'is of identity.' The theme was: don't confuse words and ideas with events. . . . This leaves the universe open" (*Deliberate* 369), and George Santayana's sense of the "tragedies" of "the little word *is*," which "marries and identifies different things with the greatest innocence; and yet no two are ever identical" (*Skepticism* 3). While the symbolic function of language implies a grid of equivalence, Spontaneous Prose suggests a self-referential force traveling through the occasion as recorded. "I saw the mush in over-symbolizations," Kerouac tells Cassady in 1949. "I even now see the reality of people as phantasy in itself [as you always did]" (*SL, I* 212).

As will be discussed in this chapter, Kerouac navigates a modernist wave, given bearings by Williams's mapping of the self in the process of interpretation, or as Gertrude Stein put it, "composition as explanation," and advanced by Duncan ("I inhabit my own poem" [*Fictive* 10]) and Olson's self-location as "part of the field of action" ("I would be an historian as Herodotus was, looking / for oneself for the evidence of / what is said" [*Maximus* 104–5]). The first person narrators in Kerouac's novels assume a temporary identity within the movements of language and perception as he dramatizes the mind incessantly conceiving itself. Acutely sensitive to the psycho-physiological process, his Legend stands as a graph of consciousness moving. "My greatest contribution to modern writing," he states in 1961, "is the idea of spontaneous notation of the mind actual while writing" (*SL, II* 302). Actions are arranged into manuscript fields of their own shape: the principle of "wild form," contingent upon experiences recollected and voices overheard and written into the configuration of thought as it flows. Philip Whalen's joyous portrayal of Kerouac at work lends a physical image to how memory is set off prior to launching full-tilt into the improvised act of writing:

> He would sit—at a typewriter, and he had all these pocket notebooks . . . open at his left-hand side on the typing table—and he'd be typing. He could type faster than any human being you ever saw. The most noise that you heard while he was typing was the carriage return, slamming back again and again. The little bell would bing-bang, bing-bang,

bing-bang! Just incredibly fast, faster than a teletype. And he'd laugh and say, Look at this! And he'd type and he'd laugh. Then he'd make a mistake, and this would lead him off into a possible part of a new paragraph, into a funny riff of some kind that he'd add while he was in the process of copying. Then, maybe he'd turn a page of the notebook and he'd look at that page and realize it was no good and he'd X it out. . . . And then he'd type a little bit and turn another page, and type the whole thing. . . . [A]gain, he would exclaim and laugh and carry on and have a big time doing it. (qtd. in Coolidge 389)

Rather than respecting divisions between the supposedly autonomous domains of writer, subject, and context, Kerouac responds by throwing the restless tensions between them into relief. This is in keeping with Alfred North Whitehead's concern with the coming into existence of the new. "The actual world is a process," he contends in *Process and Reality,*

the becoming of actual entities [called] creatures [or] creative produc-tions. . . . The misconception which has haunted philosophic literature throughout the centuries, is the notion of independent existence. . . . Every entity is only to be understood in terms of the way in which it is interwoven with the rest of the universe. (vi–viii)

The Legend becomes its own subject, each text emerging through the agency of the reflexive "I" and written into being as part of observation. In *Visions of Cody,* this allows Duluoz to melt into the consciousness of his numinous hero, embodying Gregory Bateson's Cybernetic-Zen "character-istics of immanence," where being and matter fold together in a dynamic and interdependent "ecology of mind" (*Steps* 19–24). The narrator, the corporeal world, and, by implication, the reader all inhabit the same field of mutually adjusting loops between body and environment. As a consequence, the per-ceiver becomes what is perceived within momentary changes of perspective, none of which is authoritative.

Here Jackson Pollock, responsible for the most striking innovations in pictorial space since Picasso and Braque, may be cited to shed further light on Kerouac's strategies. His vision of the relationship between the painter and the "all-over" canvas is concomitant with the principle of Spontaneous Prose, where the writer becomes the act of writing, which instantly comprises the page. In each instance, the changing stages of the self must be discovered and inscribed as a single action, unfettered by what Kerouac describes as "discriminate thinking." Harold Rosenberg's definition of "Action Paint-ing," a term coined in 1952 to clarify procedures introduced by Pollock and de Kooning, opens out this contemporary gesture:

A painting that is an act is inseparable from the biography of the artist. The painting itself is a "moment" in the adulterated mixture of
his life—whether "moment" means the actual minutes taken up with
spotting the canvas or the entire drama conducted in sign language.
The act-painting is of the same metaphysical substance as the artist's
existence. The new painting has broken down every distinction between art and life. (*Tradition* 25–26)

The classical dialectic of form and content, self and "other" (source of
eco-disconnection), and the distinctions between the act of making and the
product itself—the traditional means of assigning value in the West—dissolve. Grounded in "Essentials of Spontaneous Prose" and "Belief & Technique for Modern Prose," two statements of poetics that oppose predictive
rationalism, form must be charged with what Fielding Dawson calls "pure
intuition": the Black Mountain discipline of "total freedom in drawing and
writing that involved listening and seeing with such continuous intensity it
became my way of life" (7). Approximating Pollock's sense of performance,
Kerouac's narratives of "remembrance . . . written on the run" (*SL, I* 349)
overtake any fulfillment of a priori intention enforcing completion: a model
of literature that is a process, not a goal; a production, not an illustration.
By implication, organicism, that passive transaction between the mortal and
the nonhuman, implodes to be replaced by a study of how memory gathers
perceptions of the world. Action becomes the substance of what is expressed
rather than static denomination.

As previously noted, Kerouac enables this by frequently dispensing with
stock rhetorical connectives and blurring the given syntactical function
of words, transforming weakening adjectives into verbs; in part 1 of *Cody*,
for instance, "fried" becomes "frying" and "stormy" becomes "storming"
(32–33) to give images an evolving basis in the present. The disordered
results correspond, in Fenollosa's words, "to this universal form of action
in nature. This brings language close to *things*, and in its strong reliance
upon verbs it erects all speech into a kind of dramatic poetry. . . . Outside
grammar the word 'state' would hardly be regarded as scientific" (24). The
text's nonverbal inscriptions further emphasize slippage of denotation and
cadence generated by the voice, a deconditioning motivated by Joyce's
"fourworded wavespeech" in *Ulysses*: "seesoo, hrss, rsseeiss, ooos" (41). *Old
Angel Midnight*'s "sounds of the entire world . . . now swimming thru this
window" (1) channels this into an active critique of how the pattern of speech
affects meaning in a sentence, either diluting energy by "grammatizing" and
"categorizing" (Fenollosa 22) or by revealing "forgotten mental processes"
(Woolf, *Collected* 17):

I know boy what's I talkin about case I made the world & when I made
it I no lie & had Old Angel Midnight for my name and concocted up a
world so *nothing* you had forever thereafter make believe it's real—but
that's alright because now everything'll be alright & we'll soothe the
forever boys & girls & before we're thru we'll find a name for this God-
dam Golden Eternity & tell a story too—and but d y aver read a story as
vast as this that begins Friday Afternoon with workinmen on scaffolds
painting white paint & ants merlying in lil black dens & microbes war-
ring in yr kidney & mesaroolies microbing in the innards of mercery
& microbe microbes dreaming of the ultimate microbehood which
then ultimates outward to the endless vast empty atom which is this
imaginary universe, ending nowhere & ne'er e'en born . . . so that here
is all this infinite immaterial meadowlike golden ash swimswarmimg in
our enlighten brains & the silence Shh she-fallying in our endless ear
. . . & meanwhile it's timeless to the ends of the last lightyear . . . (1)

Kerouac learns from Williams ("No ideas but in things. . . . No ideas
but in the Facts" [*Autobiography* 390]), reports to Hal Chase in 1947 his
"new interest in things rather than ideas" (*SL, I* 107), and gives his exalted
fragments a direct basis in particulars, often a huge pileup, as the cluster of
substantives in the opening sections of *Cody* and the meditation paragraphs
of *Desolation Angels* demonstrate. Instead of reducing the incommunicable
multiplicity of a situation to self-contained units, Kerouac jams together
mobile images that, to quote Fenollosa, "bud . . . forth" from one another,
each given equality in weight, each given its own qualities (22). The world is
given to reconstruction, not representation: a test of writing as germination
of mind that builds on Edmund Husserl's directive to phenomenology as a
"descriptive psychology" or return to the "things themselves" (11–12). "The
only meaning the world has for me," Kerouac observes in his notebook, "is
how it unfolds to me" (qtd. in S. Turner 191).

Imagination becomes the cumulative power of the whole being focused
into understanding, a nonteleological set of effects or eternal middle, with
propositions begun without knowledge of an ending. "The mind-system
*cannot* stop," Kerouac announces to Ginsberg in 1955,

the Lankavatara admits it, the habit, the seed-energy of mind cannot
end, therefore there is no way to stop the mind-system as long as you
"live" and therefore no way to rid yourself, or obliterate, the "external"
world and therefore there is no reason for conceptions of enlightenment
and paths and Tathagatas or conceptions of any kind. (*SL, I* 483)

And as Ginsberg later notes in relation to *Cody*:

Here as distinct from his critic P., Kerouac is present in the world solitary musing, observing actual event, "mind clamped down on objects" completely anonymous, in a single universe of perception with no mental maneuvers of selfconscious manipulation of any reader's mind (he's writing for no reader but his own intelligent self)—completely *here,* watching the world—not generalizing in a study, but sketching solitude Mannahatta's cafeteria—"She just blew her nose daintily with a napkin; has private personal sad manners, at least externally, by which she makes her own formal existence known to herself . . ." (*Deliberate* 350)

Alongside this, Olson's distinction "between language as the act of the instant and language as the act of thought about the instant" (*Collected* 156) further realizes the crux of Spontaneous Prose: no separations between thinking, feeling, and the act of making. All three intersect in the Legend as a kinetic inscription of writing and an awareness of its process, combined with retreats into writing as an expression of rigidified thinking, usually related to stale ideological certainties prior to formation (*logos*). Praising *The Horn*'s dialogue passages to its author, John Clellon Holmes, in 1958, Kerouac revealingly adds that he'd just "met a bunch of college kids . . . who are really interested in you. And the reason is, they WANT analytical prose passages, they want certain things explained, which I don't satisfy in my narrative eagerness" (*SL, II* 141). In Stein's sense, Kerouac's mode of composition differs as "the thing seen by every one living in the living they are doing, they are the composing of the composition that at the time they are living is the composition of the time in which they are living" (*Writings* 516).

Kerouac then embodies the processual, allowing life and work to intertwine, to seek and find in the randomness of experience a new form made clear. In a 1949 letter to Ed White, he suggests that "the truth" exists not in formula but in the transition "from moment to moment incomprehensible, ungraspable, but terribly clear"—the Latin root of the word "moment" (*moveo*) conveying that swirl of movement within a satori of consciousness, shot through with the biographic occasion. Its untrappable rush across the brain forces the writer-hustler "to catch the fresh dream, the fresh thought" in a "dance on the edges of relative knowledge," as though he were "a fisherman of the deep, with old, partially useful nets." For the filter of "any formula would give a picture of false clearness, like glass reflecting a reflection only," as opposed to "the fire itself" (*SL, I* 186). This feeds directly into his fictions: "Man, wow, there's so many things to do, so many things to write!" yells the hero of *On the Road*:

"How to even *begin* to get it all down and without modified restraints and all hung-up on like literary inhibitions and grammatical fears . . ."

To which the narrator replies:

"That's right, man, now you're talking."

(10)

In the follow-up text, the westerner, Cody, identifies the requisite speed for this action:

I guess the reason I can't think of [the thought] and why I'm blocked is because I didn't formalize it or I didn't think about it long enough, soon as the thought hit me, why, I didn't think it out, because I was gonna blurt it out. Damn, if I'd have just spoken— (188)

Again, the fascination shared by the Legend's protagonists with the immediacy of jazz ("IT") comes into play on a thematic level through Kerouac's attempts to equalize the experience cited and its transformation into text. Sound and the creative act surge into being via a narrative that maintains the imminence of its own initiation. Stein's feeling for the writer's sense of the present resonates here:

The business of Art as I tried to explain in Composition as Explanation is to live in the actual present, that is the complete actual present, and to completely express that complete actual present. (*Lectures* 104)
. . .

Any of you when you write you try to remember what you are about to write and you will see immediately how lifeless the writing becomes that is why expository writing is so dull because it is all remembered, that is why illustration is so dull because you remember what somebody looked like and you make your illustration look like it. The minute your memory functions while you are doing anything it may be very popular but actually it is dull. And that is what a master-piece is not, it may be unwelcome but it is never dull. (*Masterpieces* 89)

Conversely, the knowledge of exactly what is to be written, how it will be completed, and what it will become renders the exercise pointless, since nothing outside the limits of official rhetoric can arise. Stein gives this a wider imperative:

The writer is to serve god or mammon by writing the way it has been written or by writing the way it is being written that is to say the way the writing is writing. That is for writing the difference between serving god and mammon. If you write the way it has already been written the way writing has already been written then you are serving mammon because you are living by something some one has already been earning or has earned. If you write as you are to be writing then you are serving as a writer god because you are not earning anything. If anything is to be earned you will not know what earning is therefore you are serving god. (*Lectures* 54)

Creativity becomes a course of learning for the artist, an adventurous breaking of the sets as opposed to further accounts of the known: "I do not want to begin again," Stein contends, "or go on with what was begun because after all I know I really do know that it can be done and if it can be done why do it" (*Lectures* 157). A non-imitative work like *Cody,* executed purely for the author's pleasure, shoots straight into this paradigm. Without prior definition, ideas and shapes emerge through the act of writing, the kind of open-form improvisation driving the American arts at midcentury. Whereas composer Earle Brown took his lead from "the creative function of 'non-control' in the art of Pollock and Alexander Calder," his contemporary Morton Feldman admired in their work "that complete independence from other art, that complete inner security to work with what was unknown to them" (Nyman 43). Robert Creeley similarly quotes Franz Kline: "I paint what I don't know" (Wagner and MacAdams 85), the obligation to preselect a technique subsumed by an aspiration to follow the unique dynamic of a situation. In the instance of Kerouac's work, this contributes to a confessional topography expressive of the self as part of a field of action. A new approach becomes necessary for each performance of writing, an act of profusion crucial to his treatment of memory, which stretches beyond the mere recall of Plato's "to invent is to discover, which is to remember" in *The Republic* (112) to questions of active fabulation.

With his ceremonial invocation of Henry Adams's "Adventurous Education" in the subtitle of *Vanity of Duluoz,* Kerouac registers the simultaneity of adventure and understanding as the body-mind collides with the social. As Mottram suggests with reference to Proust's *Remembrance of Things Past*:

> The unity is not constructed by exploring recollection or involuntary memory but by Search, and by Lost Time as time past, time wasted, time lost-track of—and Search for truth, research into memory and the retrieval of Lost Time, intersect and interact in a present structure, with various kinds of exuberant presentation. ("Preface" 53)

Mottram goes on to cite J. Z. Young's observation that conceptions of the "new" are always problematic, owing to the unavailability of scientific knowledge of memory processes: "There is some sort of physical trace embodying the past history of the individual," he writes. "As life proceeds, each new situation is compared with this representation of the past and a forecast is made of the action that is most likely to ensure homeostasis" (71). This is vital to considerations of Kerouac's serial discourse, where each event reconstitutes a vertical dynamism previously existent in another shape within the Legend. Deliberately redolent of "everpresent by-my-side Proust" (*SL, I* 475), *Visions of Cody* immerses the reader in gatherings of simultaneous impressions that cancel chronology. The ensuing liberation into a spatial continuum without beginning or end conjures a durational refrain named by Walter J. Ong as the "synchronic" present, which at midcentury "appears to have caught up into itself the entire past" (*Grain* 28). Kerouac renders this explicit in the "121st Chorus" of *Mexico City Blues*:

> Everything is in the same moment . . .
> I can taste the uneaten food
> > I'll find
> In the next city
> > in this dream . . .
> I cant tell the difference
> > between mental and real
>
> It's all happening
> It wont end
> It'll be good
> The money that was to have been spent
> > on the backward nations
> of the world, has already been
> > spent in Forward Time . . .

An architecture of the expanding present appears where boundaries fade, a sense of time neither inside nor outside perception, but one forming a series of divisions and foldings at its point of emergence. As with Joyce and "high-eternity-in-the-afternoon Proust" (*OTR* 288), the urge to create goes beyond the passivity of Wordsworthian recall in solitude of preknowledge and wells up from an intense need to "draw together" and "reweave" the "intermittent and opposite fragments" (Proust 468) rooted in memory, itself a metastructure. This "Running Proust," as Kerouac describes himself, advances the modernist prototype beyond the static unconscious triggers of Jacques Lacan's "signifying chains" (168) into an active compositional process. From *Cody*:

> I rolled my glasses for the first time on the jagged wood of the desk—it
> was when I got idea for racing, they meandered a race under my eyes—it

was a gray day—the whole idea of the *Turf* must have come to me like
(as just now and not since 1948) that so-seldom experience of seeing my
whole life's richness swimming in a palpable mothlike cloud, a cloud
I can really see and which I think is elfin and due really to my Celtic
blood—coming only in moments of *complete inspiration*. . . . In my life
I number them probably below five—at least on this level—

Followed by those first strips of race results, the *green ones*—the Turf
was inexpressibly connected with masturbation as Haunted Memories
like this must be. (45–46)

In *Doctor Sax* and *Visions of Gerard*, the placing of recurring images from
the Legend within new narratives means a complex evocation of the unaf-
fected mind of childhood—its Tom Sawyer–like "large-scale projections
of danger, magic, power, and innocence" (Davidson 67)—and prospects
for adulthood from the perspective of maturity. He defines this process as
a "TIC" in his "Editorial Explanation of Various Techniques of the Duluoz
Legend," which shapes the Legend's collage:

All my work to be written like BOOK OF DREAMS off Tics chronologically
appertaining in first person with fictionlike projections, bookmovies,
poems and subconscious universal railleries. . . . A Tic is a vision suddenly of memory. The ideal, formal Tic, as for a BOOK OF TICS is one
short and one longer sentence, generally about 50 words in all, the intro
sentence and the explaining sentence. (*SD* 321, 342)

Stressing the need to "write as deeply, fish as far down as you want, satisfy
yourself first, then reader cannot fail to receive telepathic shock and meaning-excitement by same laws operating in his own human mind" (*GB* 69),
Kerouac reworks Wordsworth's intention in *Lyrical Ballads* to re-create the
poet's experience of the "Influence of Natural Objects" in the reader's mind
by trancelike direct imagery. Whereas Ginsberg describes this as "initiation: Or this vision or this consciousness, of being alive unto myself, alive
myself unto the Creator" (qtd. in Clark 59), Kerouac conceives of it as the
creative act itself:

Begin not from preconceived idea of what to say about image but from
jewel center of interest in subject of image at *moment* of writing, and write
outwards swimming in a sea of language to peripheral release and exhaustion—Do not afterthink except for poetic or P.S. reasons. (*GB* 70)

His term "jewel center" fortifies a sense of luminosity within the initial
gathering of memories, activating sentences which emerge as a "FLASH" or
"Dreamflashes": "short sleepdreams or drowse daydreams of an enlightened

nature describable in a few words, BOOK OF FLASHES. Example: '*Bringing gray suitcases down from the attic of heaven I say "Me I'm not comin down any more!"*' (*SD* 342). The upshot is a gestural poetry that seeks to discover the recollected events of consciousness. "Memory and dream are intermixed in this mad universe," writes *Doctor Sax*'s narrator (8) on the visionary "paradise lost" of a Lowell infancy that can be regained only through exuberance. Michael McClure's words in paraphrase of Picasso offer Kerouac's position on this as much as his own:

> The kid standing in the vacant lot scratching magic marks in the dirt with a stick, directing the universe of spaceships and angel armies and huge caves and vast beings in their configurations, is the same as the gestural poet who imagines that with his new poem he can discover the origin of matter. We know there is a point where the body comes into being as the simultaneous expression of spirit and matter. In the language of a state of crisis, it is conceivably possible to discover the flaring of a sensory perception into universality, or to touch a point of consciousness where it joins an insight into reality.
>
> You can take the artist out of the child, but you can't take the child out of the artist. The artist is the one who maintains, in some guise or other, the bond of vision-play with his childhood. (*Simple* 20)

The resulting fictions, "telling eagerly the million things we know" (*SL, I* 274), are not exercises in displacement or therapy, endemic to the restoration of normative conditions and fixed identity. Experience is not "confessed" to the authority of a psychiatrist or priest for atonement or validation; rather, the goal is art. Kerouac's dream visions extend outward from their frames to give the reader a fertile understanding of "signs which mobilize . . . the involuntary and the unconscious: whence the Search as interpretation" (Deleuze, *Proust* 51). In so doing, Kerouac fields Stein's advice in *What Are Masterpieces*:

> At any moment when you are you you are without the memory of yourself because if you remember yourself while you are you you are not for the purposes of creating you. This is so important because it has so much to do with the question of a writer to his audience. . . . Think about how you create if you do create you do not remember yourself as you do create. (85–92)

Traveling through Legend time, Kerouac's depictions of self proliferate and disperse. The innumerable discourses that arise enable us to see "a hundred universes," as Proust says of Vinteuil or the painter Elstir, every mind a globe of unique, barely communicable knowledge employed in what physicist A. E. Eddington calls "World-building." The wonder of existence for Kerouac, too, is metamorphosis, the constant interplay between past and present through long bifurcating sentences that put Jean Piaget's location of "logic" and "autoregularity mechanisms" at the basis of memory to the test. As Piaget indicates in *Biology and Knowledge*:

> [C]ognitive schemata . . . imply no absolute beginning but are built up by a progression of equilibrations and autoregulations. Evocation is something of a much higher order than recognition and presupposes a symbolic function as well as the processes of inference and logical organization necessary for the mental reconstruction of the past. (37)

In common with bebop, Kerouac locates each repetition of events in the "now"—the word is furiously etched into the canvas of Pollock's *The White Bull* (1945), invoking the title of Parker's debut recording as leader, *Now's the Time,* from the same year—which accommodates the ahistorical urgency of "IT." Kerouac comprehends the generative spontaneity of jazz from the start in *The Town and the City,* registering the effect of the chord progressions of Billie Holiday's "She's Funny That Way" on jazzman Buddy Martin as a means of setting off recall: an intuition of the music's ability to breach official time anticipated by Miller in *The Colossus of Maroussi,* where swing band drums "give a feeling of something present" (141). New fictive possibilities arrive with the entrance of more experimentally inclined improvisers into jazz at the beginning of the 1940s, shaking it loose from singular measure and diatonic development. On Desolation Peak, Kerouac again contemplates these in terms of a memory device:

> Remembering, remembering, that sweet world so bitter to taste—the time I played Sarah Vaughan's "Our Father" on my little box in Rocky Mount and the colored maid Lula wept in the kitchen so I gave it to her so on Sunday mornings in the meadows and pine barrens of North Carolina now, emerging from her old man's bare house with the pickaninny porch, you hear the Divine Sarah—"for Thine is the Kingdom, and the Power, and the Glory, forever, a men"—the way her voice breaks into a bell on the "a" of amen, quivering, like a voice should—Bitter? because bugs thrash in mortal agony even on the table as you'd think, deathless fools that get up and walk off and are reborn, like us, "hooman beens"—like winged ants, the males, who are cast off by the females and go die, how utterly futile they are the way they climb windowpanes and just fall off when they get to the top, and do it again, till they exhausted die—And the one I saw one afternoon on my shack floor just thrashing and thrashing in the filthy dust from some

kind of fatal hopeless seizure—oi, the way we do, whether we can see it now or not— (62–63)

The recollected plasticity of the jazz phrase morphs into poetic line: a rhythmic pattern of varying length, speed, tone, and stress. Without breaching the text, the narrator goes on to register with Keatsian relish the kinesthetic interactions between images of food remembered, which soon become actual:

> Sweet? just as sweet, tho, as when dinner is bubbling in the pot and my mouth is watering, the marvelous pot of turnip greens, carrots, roastbeef, noodles and spices I made one night and ate barechested on the knoll, sitting crosslegged, in a little bowl, with chopsticks singing—Then the warm moonlit nights with still the red flare in the west—sweet enough, the breeze, the songs, the dense pine timber down in the valleys of the cracks—A cup of coffee and a cigarette, why zazen? and somewhere men are fighting with frighting carbines, their chests crisscrossed with ammo, their belts weighed down with grenades, thirsty, tired, hungry, scared, insaned—It must be that when the Lord thought forth the world he intended for it to include both me and my sad disciplined pain-heart A N D Bull Hubbard rolling on the floor in laughter at the foolishness of men— (63)

The prose admits nonverbal gestures, metanarrational comments, qualifications, and sudden memories to dart into the mind without breaking the flow: a vigorous act of self-comprehension. "Phenomena is what you see with your eyes open," notes Kerouac, "in my case the debris of one thousand hours of the living-conception in a mountain shack" (*DA* 60). As LeRoi Jones suggests in his 1959 letter to the *Evergreen Review* about Kerouac:

> [T]he spontaneous writer has to possess a particularly facile and amazingly impressionable mind, one that is able to collect and store not just snatches or episodic bits of events, but whole and elaborate associations: the whole impression *intact,* so that at the *trigger inference* the entire impression and association comes flooding through the writer's mind almost *in toto.* The resultant impression, of course, has been thoroughly incorporated and translated into the supraconsciousness or *writing voice* of the writer. The *external event* is now the internal or psychical event which is a combination of interpretation and pure reaction. (352)

Conversely, when the author's eyes are dulled by drunken stupor, the flaws rather than virtues of Spontaneous Prose become evident. Whereas William

James may claim with some justification that "the drunken consciousness is one bit of the mystic consciousness" (*Varieties* 408), the graph of sluggish mind degenerates into boorish tedium in *Satori in Paris* and some of the *Blues* poems. These are works that demand rigorous editing, if not disposal. Kerouac's candid analysis of the effects of psilocybin, given to him by Timothy Leary in January 1961 ("LSD or STP acid . . . stupefy the mind and hand for weeks on end," he writes in the *Chicago Tribune* [*GB* 184]), only fitfully extends to the consequences of alcoholism: "I am a hopeless paralyzed drunken mess and I don't know how long I'm going to live, if I keep on like this," he concedes in 1962. "It's my brain getting soft and paralyzed. Yet I have such a good time when I'm drunk, I feel such ecstasy for people, for books, for animals, for everything" (*SL, II* 333).

However, when younger and "feeling good" and "writing well, no tea and no wine and so my mind is sharper" (*SL, I* 536), his perception is tirelessly catalyzed, pursuing his own injunction to Holmes to

> write fast, get it all in, or out, up, down, everywhere, throw it, like Céline, like you yourself used to tell me to do, great god learn to type a thousand words a minute, buy two tape recorders, upset the silly laws, make the judges cream, instigate revolutions in the bottom of your attic, take it out, on, upward, cream, stars, Ah, revolvements, appendages, galaxies, time, tags, wild. (*SL, I* 521)

In the "Hector's Cafeteria" section of *Cody*, for example, the narrator is aroused by the rhythmic repetition of the preposition "of" in a cake litany and opens the planes of memory with a simple lateral shift to literary reference: "immense pans of cheesecake, of raspberry cream cake, of flaky rich Napoleons, of simple Boston cake, armies of éclairs, of enormously dark chocolate cake (gleaming scatological brown)—of deepish strudel, of time and the river." This transition is echoed at the end of the next paragraph:

> the whole counter gleaming with icy joy which is salty and nourishing—cold fish, herrings, onions—great loaves of rye bread sliced—so on—spreads of all kinds, egg salads big enough for a giant decorated and sprigged on a pan—in great sensuous shapes—salmon salads— (Poor Cody, in front of this in his scuffled-up beat Denver shoes, his literary "imitation" suit he had wanted to wear to be acceptable in New York cafeterias which he thought would be brown and plain like Denver cafeterias, with ordinary food)—(25–26)

Like Virginia Woolf, Kerouac uses parentheses not only to draw attention to his performative role in the text but also to counter linear restriction and lend "the sense of reading . . . two things at the same time" (Woolf, *Diary* 126). In contrast to the static food under examination, the seeing eye is in constant, simultaneous movement—a central feature, too, of the experiences described in *Book of Dreams*:

> I go thru a bustling golden cafeteria where a man rushes up to me and says a story about some blonde waitress somewhere who was so sloppy her sores ran while she served you—"Pimples," he said—I exhibit polite response but blankly he rushes off, so had I just stared at him gravely as I really wanted he would have persisted with something else (O the grief of the Lowell bridge over the canal, the old glassbroken walk for lovers on the canal lock wall, the nights I've jumped down dere per dream and in real life as a real boy prowled with Dicky and Who Else and the dream of the Flood Oersur-mounting it) (with raging whitesmash, river mouth grashin to show clash crash)—drash!—brash!—Aoooowayyy br—a—a— shh—I move on thru the kitchen and out the back . . . (113-14)

The effect of temporal coexistence approximates John Berger's pre-historic sense of living before language, "a seamless experience of wordlessness. Wordlessness means that everything is continuous. The later dream of an ideal language, a language which says all simultaneously, perhaps begins with the memory of this state without memories" (*And Our Faces* 51). In *Visions of Cody* and *Mexico City Blues,* this is initiated by sensual junctures of light and technology perceived at speed that serve as compositional sparks for expansions of both lived and potential experience. These include neon signs, gleaming auto fenders reflected in plate glass, "shiny food" glittering against electric cafeteria bulbs, "terrified" old ladies illuminated by floodlights on a movie set, chromed hubcaps, telegraph wires in the sun ("spindly tin-like crane towers of the trans-territorial electric power-lines standing in serried gloom" [*VC* 409]), and the pulsating American railroad, which in the "146th Chorus" of *Mexico City Blues* cuts into the speech planes of local switchmen:

> The blazing chickaball
>     Whap-by
> Extry special Super
>     High Job
> Ole 169 be
>     floundering
> Down to Kill Roy

"I love telephone poles all strung together and filing off into the distance . . . and giant steel power-line towers standing like aliens in ochre fields,"

Kerouac declares in 1951. "All the roads rushing, rushing, the burnt fields, lakes, farm buildings, fabulous cities. I like to write in the car because the process is so like the action—a stream of images unraveling like a ribbon (like a film)" (*SL, I* 271). The narrator's depiction of his "great immortal metropolitan in-the-city feeling that I first dug (and all of us) as an infant . . . smack in the heart of shiny glitters" in part 1 of *Cody* complicates these mind shifts but without the propagating basis in physical voyage:

> An immense plate glass window in this white cafeteria on a cold November evening in New York faces the street (Sixth Avenue) but with inside neon tubular lights reflected in the window and they in turn illuminating the Japanese garden walls which are therefore also reflected and hang in the street with the tubular neons (and with other things illuminated and reflected such as that enormous twenty-foot green door with its red and white exit sign reflected near the drapes to the left, a mirror pillar from deep inside, vaguely the white plumbing and at the top of things upper right hand side and the signs that are low in the window looking out, that say *Vegetarian Plate 60¢, Fish Cakes with Spaghetti, Bread and Butter* (no price) and are also reflected and hanging but only low on the sidewalk because also they're practically against it)—so that a great scene of New York at night with cars and cabs and people rushing by and *Amusement Center, Bookstore, Leo's Clothing, Printing,* and *Ward's Hamburger* and all of it November clear and dark is riddled by these diaphanous hanging neons, Japanese walls, door, exit signs— (32)

"But now let's examine it closer," he continues, announcing the book's fascination with the phenomenology of vision and notation, "[r]iddled and penetrated and obscured and rippled and haunted and of course like kaleidoscope over kaleidoscope" (32–33). In "all these confusions of reflected light," internal signs project onto "floating white faces" and cars that "flash by," dissolving the distinction between forms and external and enclosed space. As Davidson suggests, "Everything hangs in the air like a giant urban mobile," its "diaphanous" quality enhanced by Kerouac's tendency to intrude into his description with parenthetical remarks and qualifications: "[T]he people pass and you know what they are (two Texans I knew it! And two Negroes! I knew it!)" (*VC* 34). This "constant shifting of perspective" is endemic to "the larger problem of subjectivity in the novel itself as Duluoz seeks to gain a perspective on his main character while understanding his complicity in Cody's life [as both observer and object of observation]" (Davidson 72). What Kerouac terms the "mutual conditioning" of "the perceiving senses" and the "world of representations" in *Some of the Dharma* is tied into the ideal Buddhist apprehension of mind as "a mirror reflecting all forms and images instantaneously and without discrimination":

> What difference, whether I say my eye is inner sight looking at its outer projections, or whether I say the phenomena of the world is reflecting itself off its own eyeballs made for the purpose of sight,—it is all the domain of Sight, the Seeable (Darkness) Matter and the (Light) Seeing, and all illusion, and therefore that explains Buddha's sayin "The essential nature of the inner perception of sight is reflection of outer sights." . . . If emptiness was now and there was nothing to see, my eyeball would neither reflect outside objects, nor project its own inner light against the discriminating shadowiness of light-and-darkness in the outside universe, and it could only see fantastic blossoms (arising from its diseased sentient becloudment) hung in colorless emptiness appearing like the world's final phenomena. This is all you can say of "Reality." (21, 27)

Kerouac's investigation of these "laws of movement and reflection" as "memoried" continues in the "200th Chorus" of *Mexico City Blues*:

> White figures throughout
>     made of light,
> Like a truck becomes a square
>     mass of shifting light bars,
> Empty Apparitional secret
>     figure of the mind.
> More than that. Face
>     is mass of swarm-roe
>     starlight, insanity
>     itself personified
>     & taking up space
>     & penetrable throughout.

The effect is dazzling, a further commingling of disparate time-spaces without transition and ad infinitum sensual interplays between shape and surface, echoing both Pollock's "all-over" procedures and Olson's exploration of mind in "As the Dead Prey Upon Us," a poem Kerouac admired.[2] The relationship of Olson's speaker to domestic technologies (car, victrola, movie projector) as signs of transience is reconfigured by Kerouac as a spatial memory shift, approximating bop tendencies toward disjunctive quotations of tunes plucked from an improviser's wellspring. He deploys this technique again in *Desolation Angels*, another text that does not thematically stress mobility, recounting verbal signs for food in long lists with heightened attention to phrasal speed:

—Box of Chef Boyardee's Spaghetti Dinner, what a joyous name, I picture the Queen Mary docked in New York and Chefs going out to hit the town with little berets, towards the sparkling lights, or else I picture some sham chef with mustachio singin Italian arias in the kitchen on television cook shows—Pile of enveloped green pea powder soup, good with bacon, good as the Waldorf-Astoria and that Jarry Wagner first introduced me to that time we hiked and camped at Potrero Meadows and he dumped frying bacon into the whole soup pot and it was thick and rick in the smoky night air by the creek. . . . Canned whole boiled potatoes like shrunk heads and useless—(that only the deer eat)—the last two cans of Argentine roastbeef, of an original 15, very good, when I arrived in the lookout on that cold storming day with Andy and Marty on the horses I found 30¢ worth of canned meat and tuna, all good, which in my tightness I'd never have thought to buy. . . . Hozomeen, rock, never eats, never stores up debris, never sighs, never dreams of distant cities, never waits for Fall, never lies, maybe though he dies—Bah.

Every night I still ask the Lord, "Why?" and haven't heard a decent answer yet. (61–62)

Sitting in his shack, Dulouz's image in the mirror and the material form of his writing set off multiple layers of events, superimposed and refracting, which transgress boundaries of identity and chronological time and bear out Norbert Wiener's recognition that "to be alive is to participate in a continuous stream of influences from the outer world, in which we are merely the transitional stage" (49), before coming to rest in his by now characteristic desire for terminal surrender:

At night at my desk in the shack I see the reflection of myself in the black window, a rugged faced man in a dirty ragged shirt, need-a-shave, frowny, lipped, eyed, haired, nosed, eared, handed, necked, adamsappled, eyebrowed, a reflection just with all behind it the void of 7000000000000 light years of infinite darkness riddled by arbitrary limited-idea light, and yet there's a twinkle in me eye and I sing bawdy songs about the moon in the alleys of Dublin, about vodka hoy hoy, and then sad Mexico sundown-over-rocks songs about amor, corazón, and tequila—My desk is littered with papers, beautiful to look at thru half closed eyes the delicate milky litter of papers piled, like some old dream of a picture of papers, like papers piled on a desk in a cartoon, like a realistic scene from an old Russian film, and the oil lamp shadowing some in half. . . . It must be, it *is* the Golden Eternity enjoying itself with movies—Torture me in tanks, what else can I believe?—Cut me limbs

> off with a sword, what must I do, hate Kalinga to the bitter death and be-
> yond?—Pra, it's the mind. "Sleep in Heavenly Peace."—(*DA* 63–64)

Free of stable tenses and consecutive logic, the mental onrush fashions each phrase, continually changing the focus of attention and meeting Karl Jaspers's definition of process as interference or rupture. Again echoing Joyce, the detection of shifts between the speaker's immediate experience, recollection of the past, and projection of the future invites the reader to share the continuous present of the narrator's consciousness, an intimacy that dissolves the floors of memory within the praxis of Eliot, Pound, and Williams but with significantly enhanced levels of exuberance.

This intensifies through *Old Angel Midnight* and "October in the Railroad Earth," where the ownership of voice and memory is rendered ambiguous through a stream of consciousness prose, which enters and leaves many single viewpoints. Diverse thought and discourse patterns move through irregular first and third person channels, broken only by breath marks approximating the accelerando/deccelerando, crescendo/decrescendo tensions of a musical score before coming to rest in a cadence. The effect is of multipersonal subjectivity, a "world-mind" prose that fulfills Woolf's desire for fiction to

> resemble poetry in that it will give not only or mainly people's relations
> to each other and their activities together, as the novel has hitherto
> done, but it will give the relation of the mind to general ideas and its
> soliloquy in solitude. (*Collected* 19)

Woolf's detailed recording of the "moment," the crystallization of endlessly multiplied experiences, and Joyce's use of "epiphany," a retrieval of the past in order to register its effect on what follows, are remade into Kerouac's "telepathic-shock and meaning-excitement" (*GB* 69). In the Legend, this means no filtering: an act of confession that refuses repression. While Woolf handles this differently, isolating "moments of importance" rather than cinematically collapsing them together to make time bend, freeze, stretch, and reverse in a single paragraph as Kerouac does, her definition of fictive truth nonetheless stands as a prelude to the work of the Great Rememberer:

> Look within and life, it seems, is very far from being "like this."
> Examine for a moment an ordinary mind on an ordinary day. The
> mind receives a myriad impressions—trivial, fantastic, evanescent,
> or engraved with the sharpness of steel. From all sides they come, an
> incessant shower of innumerable atoms; and as they fall, as they shape
> themselves into the life of Monday or Tuesday, the accent falls differ-
> ently from of old; the moment of importance came not here but there;

so that, if a writer were a free man and not a slave, if he could write what he chose, not what he must, if he could base his work upon his own feeling and not upon convention, there would be no plot, no comedy, no tragedy, no love interest or catastrophe in the accepted style. . . . Life is not a series of gig lamps symmetrically arranged; life is a luminous halo, a semi-transparent envelope surrounding us from the beginning of consciousness to the end. Is it not the task of the novelist to convey this varying, this unknown and uncircumscribed spirit, whatever aberration or complexity it may display, with as little mixture of the alien and external as possible? (*Common* 189)

As with Woolf's memory books *Mrs. Dalloway, To the Lighthouse,* and *The Waves,* thinking and feeling in Kerouac's fictions generate recognizable patterns as they merge with events to become occasions in themselves, giving each work its shape. The coherence of "symmetrical" progressions is abandoned for disparate images engendered by intense experience. "The object," suggests Kerouac, "is set before the mind either in reality . . . or is set in the memory wherein it becomes the sketching from memory of a definite image-object" (*GB* 69). In *Cody* he provides a metacommentary on this, giving prominence to the hero's "whole frame of clothes capped by those terrible pants with six, seven holes in them and streaked with baby food, come, ice cream, ashes—I saw his whole life, I saw all the movies we'd ever been in, I saw for some reason he and his father on Larimer Street not caring in May." A further conjecture follows:

It's like when I'm looking through Wilson's bookshelf and start humming a tune while he's arguing with Marian—("Moonglow"). "What made you think of singing that?"
"I dunno."
"It'll forever be a mystery to me—"
No possible way of avoiding enigmas. (31)

Besides drawing on the biological bases of existence—food, sex, discharge—presented in emphatically sensual language, his techniques of activation include, in Mottram's words,

not only American figures of release, but European twentieth-century information. Memory is infused and intellected by cultural artifacts which he carries through the process of what he called "my own mind in my own real adventures" (*Vanity of Duluoz*), and which operate to break the sets of social enclosure from education, the Church, university in New York and war service. ("Preface" 57)

In *Old Angel Midnight,* and indeed throughout *Doctor Sax* and *Big Sur,* Kerouac takes on Woolf's symbol of waves—"them Einsteinian electromagnetic-gravitational waves, also words" (*SL, II* 254)—to describe the continuous interpenetrations of memory and the impersonal "abysses of time," gleaned from William James's definition of inner life:

> What is this universe
>     but a lot of waves
> And a craving desire
>     is a wave
> Belonging to a wave
>     in a world of waves
> So why put any down,
>     wave?
> Come on wave, WAVE!

(OAM 9)

Kerouac conceives of *Midnight* as

> my idea of how to make a try at a "spontaneous *Finnegans Wake*" with the Sounds of the Universe itself as the plot and all the neologisms, mental associations, puns, word-mixes from various languages and non-languages scribbled out in a strictly intuitional discipline at breakneck speed. (1)

As with Joyce, the memory "sketch" is discharged inside an improvisational field circling a choral refrain, in this case the word "Angel":

> The wush of trees on yonder eastern nabathaque Latin Walden axe-haiku of hill where woodsman Mahomet perceives will soon adown the morning drear to pail the bringup well suspender farmer trap moon so's cock go Bloody yurgle in the distance where Timmy hides, flat, looking with his eyes for purr me—O Angel, now is the time for all good men to come to the aid of their party, & ah Angel dont paperparty me, but make me honified in silken Honen honey-rubbed Oxen tongue of Cow Kiss, Ant Mat, silk girl ran, all the monkey-better-than secondary women of Sam Sarah the Sang of Blood this earth, this tool, this fool, look with your eyes, I'm tired of fooling O Angel bring it to me THE MAGIC SOUND OF SILENCE broken by first-bird's teepaleep— (55)

Sparked by happenstance, the narrative takes on a polymorphous quality without cause and effect sequence. "What I have written so far . . . has been what I saw with my own eyes," Kerouac later insists. "I'm writing about what happened. In life there is no plot. . . . You just take a spate of time" ("Jack Kerouac at Northport" 35). This chimes with Fenollosa's depiction of poetry in musical terms as "a time art, weaving its unities out of successive impressions of sound, [which] could with difficulty assimilate a verbal medium consisting largely of semi-pictorial appeals to the eye" (18), and informs Parkinson's consideration of the ongoing nature of Beat prose as "active revery"—one that not only confers a thematic function upon the typeroll manuscript of *On the Road* but also collides with the phenomenology of Kerouac's "wild form":

> Into this revery come past and present, but the revery is chiefly preoccupied with keeping up with the process unfolding outside and inside the narrator. Hence the long sentences, endlessly attempting to include the endless, the carelessness—even negligence—with the ordinary rules of grammatical function, so that noun, adjective, and verb interchange roles; after all, if the process is endlessly unpredictable and unfixed, grammatical categories are not relevant. It is a syntax of aimlessly continuing pleasure in which all elements are "like." Release, liberation from fixed categories, hilarity—it is an ongoing prose that cannot be concerned with its origins. There are no origins and no end, and the solid page of type without discriminations is the image of life solidly continuous without discriminations in value, and yet incomplete because it is literally one damned thing after another with no salvation or cease. There are no last things in this prose whereas the very division of experience into lines compels the discrimination of element from element. Even a poetic catalogue, which is by definition one thing after another, moves in blocks which have weight, and even if each unit weighs the same, the total weight increases with each succeeding integer. Not so in prose, the only limits coming from the size of the page. The ideal book by a writer of beat prose would be written on a single string of paper, printed on a roll, and moving endlessly from right to left, like a typewriter ribbon. (288)

However, Parkinson's claim for the omission of "discriminations in value" in the Beat text recedes alongside Kerouac's work. Shedding narrative plan and binding mythology (the scaffolding of *Finnegans Wake*), the projective composition of *Cody* is imbued with sheer risk and excitement through several hundred pages without flagging and precludes careless journalism. Given the titular stress, the act of writing itself becomes revelation, a discourse flush with Rosenberg's "Action" model—as Seymour Krim recognizes in using the term "Action Writing" in his introduction to *Desolation Angels*. In the

"Imitations of the Tape" section, for example, Kerouac brusquely interrupts his reveries over "bumkick denials of what at that time then [1950] I thought were undoubted truths" with an accumulating stream of thoughts, censuring himself over the mess of his domestic fuel arrangements and noting the price and nature of "caramels," followed by a further "[t]wo thoughts rush[ing] to the fore but I have to push them back again." These in turn proliferate without resolution or parenthesis closure before petering out with the insertion of a letter to Evelyn (301–2).

Like its Joycean source, *Midnight* also offers an inclusive pluralism of signs, where cycles of birth, death, perception, and sensuality are simultaneously made available to the mind through cubist juxtapositions of recurring phrases, images, and syntactical patterns. (Here Weinreich identifies three modes operating concurrently within Kerouac's rhetoric: synesthesia, the interaction of sense impressions; synchronicity, the effect of intertwining tropes; and syncopation, the result of long breath [62].) This panoramic appreciation of time and place is incarnated in Cassady's principle of non-selectivity within an environment that he calls "eyeballing" ("the knowledge of action") in *The First Third* (195–96), expressed in Dean's admiration for Rollo Greb, who "goes every direction, he lets it all out, he knows time . . . if you go like him all the time you'll finally get . . . 'IT! IT!'" (*OTR* 121). This is the very means of Spontaneous Prose: an unmediated way of seeing that collapses observation and interpretation together, a dismantling of automatic orders that schematize perception into habits of elucidation after the event. Henri Corbin's definition of the Sufi term *phainomenon* resonates at this point, an entry into the shifting, folding architecture of the imagination where the imposition of allegorical schemata on perception, or limit on the poetic text, serves only to mutilate ("Theory" 224–37). Kerouac explores this further in *Some of the Dharma*:

> Universal Mind free of all thought-conception is what recorded and registered the pure liquid seeing, since the eyeball itself has no perception of the sight it takes in or upon itself. Thought-perception is limited within the bounds of individuation, discrimination and conceptualization.
>
> But as perception exists everywhere purely
> permeating all space and "things" appearing
> dreamlike in space, it is infinite and not
> limited by sense-activity and its mental
> apparatus.
> The intellectual knowledge of this,
> and this writing of it,

depends on
thought-perception, not Intuitive Essence Perception,
and is therefore
limited,
impure,
truly unsatisfying.
What the disciple must
do is stare at things
till he sees perception
instead of things.
or,
". . . while looking
. . . what is it that reveals
the existence of yr. mind?"
SURANGAMA SUTRA (64–65)

Immersed in Eastern disciplines and disfavoring Aristotelian chains, Kerouac consistently reveals the ability to think in images, to place name against name, quality against quality, time-space against time-space, while retaining that passion for description inside the act of discovery that Stein saw as the basis of poetry. From *Book of Dreams*:

> [T]he ship's still in port, I run down to the stores and search frantically in dark lockers and funny little big-covered-but-small-insided iceboxes horizontally shaped (to the deck)—finally in a horrible burlap canvas bag prop icebox like the horror bag of the Kafka nightmare hero dragging his dragon green be-buttoned caterpillar machine burden bag across the gray strange stage of eternity racks and dust, I find plenty of milk . . . (103)

The perpetual reshuffling of disparate, even arbitrary scenes gives rise to the possibility of new tensions, or as Blake had it in "The Marriage of Heaven and Hell": "Without Contraries is no progression. Attraction and Repulsion, Reason and Energy, Love and Hate, all necessary to Human existence" (149).

Jerome Rothenberg's commentary on the *I Ching* as a manual of poetic techniques similarly holds for such examples of Kerouac's "free prose": each correspondence a chance hit acting on its subject and the entire field; every change a measurable burst of energy. Paraphrasing Jung's foreword to Wilhelm's translation, the matter of interest becomes the configuration of events in the moment of observation, not the hypothetical reasons that seemingly account for the coincidence. "Whatever falls within the same space determines the meaning of that space," notes Rothenberg:

What Jung called "synchronicity" (with the problems it raises of indeterminacy & the observer's part in structuring the real) becomes a principle of composition: common link between such otherwise different modes as chance poetry, automatic writing, "deep" image, collage, projective verse, etc., & between those & the whole world of non-sequential & non-causal thought. That modern physics at the same time moves closer to a situation in which anything-can-happen, is of interest too in any consideration of where we are. (*Pre-faces* 153–54)

The fascination for signs arising in persons, objects, and substances in *Cody* and *Desolation* thus sustains an experiential deciphering and expansion in the act of writing. The "jewel center" becomes an existential launch point for self-understanding, nourished by observation and conversation, a point from which information "radiates," to use Pound's term. This is implied by Kerouac in a letter to Ed White (1950), in which he speaks of his desire for a

> pen that spurts golden fire and winds shrouds around the man. I guess I want to be an angel of some kind. That is a fact. Not for immunity, but for the right to be near God. . . . Something is bound to happen. Some revelation is bound to appear to me soon, like light; like a scientific discovery, but not in a formula; so that in my work I will be able to reflect those mysteries in a glass—a glass not warped and dull like the glass of formulas—but a fiery glass. (qtd. in Morgan 32)

The groundwork for this is laid with the vorticism of Pound and Wyndham Lewis, defined as a sense of times, places, moments, and intensities of image, taken not as a static idea but as "a radiant node or cluster . . . a VORTEX, from which, and through which, and into which, ideas are constantly rushing" (Pound, *Gaudier-Brzeska* 92). The mind inside a culture seizes materials, "Constantly risking absurdity" (Ferlinghetti, *These* 96) in the hope that a composition can project new forms and therefore personal coherences. "If possible write 'without consciousness,'" recommends Kerouac,

> in semitrance (as Yeats' later "trance writing") allowing subconscious to admit in own uninhibited interesting necessary and so "modern" language what conscious art would censor, and write excitedly, swiftly, with writing-or-typing cramps, in accordance (as from center to periphery) with laws of orgasm, Reich's "beclouding of consciousness." *Come* from within, out—to relaxed and said. (*GB* 70–71)

Projecting a speeding process of intense physical and emotional change, Kerouac draws attention to a Dionysian presence within the etymology of creative vocabularies: the Hellenic root *exstasis,* agency of transformation, meaning both displacement and trance. The "ex-" prefix thus confers a desire for movement out of the security self ("ex-periment," "ex-pound," "ex-plode," "ex-plore," "ex-it"), the polar opposite to *stasis* and the notion of arrested force, which extends politically to the nation "State." Whereas John Ashbery speaks of the reckless beauty of the new in relation to currents in American painting, and de Kooning maintains that art "never seems to make me peaceful or pure. . . . I do not think . . . of art as a situation of comfort" (qtd. in Barr 14), Kerouac's pull toward the mad god's refusal of limit implies that to curb ecstasy would be to empty the creative act of meaning, the same exposure to risk outlined by McClure in *Hymns to St. Geryon*: "We are committed to an unqualified act . . . To clothe ourselves in the action, / to remove from the precious to the full swing . . . Not politics but ourselves—is the question" (23).

Kerouac then converges with Pollock and de Kooning in forging new configurations of energy with rational drives suspended, an accession to Sartre's sense of chance as a condition of life, whence the artist must make himself. "Only one way to write DULUOZ LEGEND," he declares in *Some of the Dharma,* "the way given to you as it comes, no need worrying about good or poor—" (350). Form emerges through inviting every observation, whether fortuitous or not, to enter the work, an unembodied momentum that demands a shape without prior existence, and makes of art, to paraphrase Lorca, a power, not a construction.[3] Taking off from Heidegger's belief that "[t]he artist must attune himself to that which wants to reveal itself and permit the process to happen through him," Creeley and Pollock give voice to a vital gestalt in midcentury American art:

> I'm *given* to write poems. I cannot anticipate their occasion. I have used all the intelligence that I can muster to follow the possibilities that the poem "underhand," as Olson would say, is declaring, but I cannot anticipate the necessary conclusions of the activity, nor can I judge in any sense, in moments of writing, the significance of that writing more than to recognize that it is being *permitted* to continue. I'm trying to say that, in writing, at least as I have experienced it, one is *in* the activity, and that fact itself is what I feel so deeply the significance of anything we call poetry. (Creeley, *Sense* 54)
>
> . . .
>
> My painting does not come from the easel. . . . On the floor I am more at ease. I feel nearer, more a part of the painting, since this way I can walk around it, work from the four sides and literally be *in* the painting. This is akin to the method of the Indian sand painters of the West.

... When I am *in* my painting, I'm not aware of what I'm doing. It is only after a sort of "get acquainted" period that I see what I have been about. I have no fears about making changes, destroying the image, etc., because the painting has a life of its own. I try to let it come through. It is only when I lose contact with the painting that the result is a mess. Otherwise there is pure harmony, an easy give and take, and the painting comes out well. (Pollock, "My Painting" 23)

Kerouac, too,

eschews "selectivity" and follow[s] free association of mind into limitless blow-on-subject seas of thought, swimming in seas of English with no discipline other than the story-line and the rhythm of rhetorical exhalation and expostulated statement, like a fist coming down on a table with each complete utterance, bang! (the spacedash). (*SL, II* 15)

This is what is meant by the adjective "wild" that peppers his work: self-propagating in accord with innate qualities, sustainable by natural exuberance rather than enforced by metropolitan legislation and custom, far-out, openly erotic, physical, spontaneous, and free. Running parallel to Kerouac, Snyder's "wildness" etiquette approximates the Chinese term *Dao,* the way of Great Nature, and further illuminates his friend's projective poetics:

eluding analysis, beyond categories, self-organizing, self-informing, playful, surprising, impermanent, insubstantial, independent, complete orderly, unmediated, freely manifesting, self-authenticating, self-willed, complex, quite simple. Both empty and real at the same time. In some cases we might call it sacred. It is not far from the Buddhist term *Dharma* with its original senses of forming and firming. . . . [F]rom another side, wilderness has implied chaos, eros, the unknown, realms of taboo, the habitat of both the ecstatic and the demonic. In both senses it is a place of archetypal power, teaching, and challenge. (*Practice* 10–11)

Aligning him with D. H. Lawrence, McClure credits Kerouac with "one of the finest, brightest sensoriums that has graced verse with intelligence and intellect" (*Scratching* 70). In *Mexico City Blues,* the poet identifies a principle of Dionysian myth-making beyond mere inscription of recollected event, consistent with a series honoring its author's spirit place ("Tea-High-Eternal-City-of-my-Imagination"). Written to reflect the city's slow pace, the work is built upon distinct acts of mind conceiving themselves:

The poem is like ourselves at our unchained moments when we are able to move from our established self-investments and stride on new stepping-stones to a point of risk, growth, change, or maturity. Kerouac was writing a mystical (in its hope), anarchist, epic-length, and open-ended poem. This great self-organizing act of verse-energy as it flows on and on, becoming more diverse, stronger in its self-supporting complexity . . . begins to create a fundament that never existed before. (McClure, *Scratching* 75)

Kerouac's "wild" impetus is further elucidated by Gaston Bachelard's sense of receptiveness to "the very ecstasy of the newness of image. The poetic image is a sudden salience on the surface of psyche" (xi), and by Deleuze's location of form at the

plane of immanence . . . within a given multiplicity: unifications, subjectifications, rationalizations, centralizations have no special status; they often amount to an impasse or closing off that prevents the multiplicity's growth, the extension and unfolding of its lines, the production of something new. (*Negotiations* 145–46)

In *Cody*, the hero's conversation is one of many elements that stimulate the book's form through which euphoria circulates to order itself, unobstructed by standardized devices. Kerouac's discussion of a jam session of "working-man tenors" stands as an analogue of his process:

[T]hey seemed to come on in their horns with a will, saying things, a lot to say, talkative horns, you could almost hear the words and better than that the harmony, made you hear the way to fill up blank spaces of time with the tune and the consequence of your hands and breath and soul. (407)

The creative act is patterned solely by its own integrity and converges with Nietzsche's notion of the Dionysian in *The Birth of Tragedy*, an energy lacking an image, which materializes upon fusion with its divergent stream:

I shall keep my eyes fixed on the two artistic deities of the Greeks, Apollo and Dionysus, and recognize in them the living and conspicuous representatives of two worlds of art differing in their intrinsic essence and in the highest aims. I see Apollo as the transfiguring genius of the principium individuationis through which alone the redemption in appearance is truly to be obtained; while by the mystical, triumphant cry of Dionysus the spell of individuation is broken, and the way lies open to the mothers of being, in the innermost heart of things. (3)

Reflecting their twinning in late Athenian society as reasoned creation, the improvised is brought into alignment with the planned as interdependent strains. Duncan's organization of forces in *Caesar's Gate* is useful here, not least in his summoning of Kerouac's own "con-man":

My music is not Apollo's but that of Mercury the Thief, the Dissembler, Lord of the Musical Comedy turn. But name me there, and I shall be offended Apollo. The two musics belong to one myth and mystery of the god of rapture and disease and of the other, his counterpart and instructor, magician-master of the lyre, the trickster god of what is too easy to believe. (iv)

The dialectic of the counterurges forges boundary, style, or field: a vocabulary of becoming, which is reworked by Lawrence in his essay "Poetry of the Present." Situated at the precise point where forms are provisional, he echoes Kurt Schwitters—"PRESENT Poetry aims at the relative life of untamed and non-classified functions, avoiding the false semblances" (*Poems* 190)—in speaking of the instant in nonteleological terms as a "surge." This is distinguished from the "poetry of the beginning," based on nostalgia, and the "poetry of the end," typified by Shelley's verse that rests upon the "ideal" of "exquisite finality." "There is another kind of poetry," Lawrence suggests,

> the poetry of that which is at hand, the immediate present. In the immediate present there is no perfection, no consummation, nothing finished. The strands are all flying, quivering, intermingling into the web, the waters are shaking the moon. There is no round, consummate moon on the face of running water, nor on the face of the unfinished tide. There are no gems of the living plasm. There is no plasmic finality, nothing crystal, permanent. (*Selected* 76)[4]

Lawrence's use of "plasm," a scientific term signifying permanent mutation as opposed to substance, could be a primer for Kerouac's fictions. His mobile act of writing is also spurred by a continuous creation/destruction dialogue, which flows beyond known territories and breaks apart their vertices. The emerging membrane of form resembles not a rigid shell but an active and responsive site, comprised of "its own *nature*," which decides the shape of what lies inside and out. To frame a position in advance of this would be to abstract experience into the anticipation/confirmation cycle of theory, a flight into what Bunting calls "the finality of definition" (*Three Essays* 4). Lawrence's "seething poetry of the incarnate Now" (*Selected* 77) recognizes no "antecedent unity of the Search" nor "ready-made criteria of organic totality," to call on Harold Bloom's disabling vocabularies of Aristotelian recession or "influence" (14–24). As Mottram points out, an activating form such as *Cody* resists the academic compulsion to impose technocratic mystique upon the text:

> Style and sound counter narrative as narrative presents time and therefore decay of youth, and of particular freedoms from the accepted

models of manhood and labor trained into working class men—in this
case of Cody and his processor—from childhood. These men know
that they create no privileged status for language out of a privileged
classification of some gentry who believes it owns both language and
criticism. ("Preface" 52)

The Legend's outline thus defies the crystallization drives behind New
Criticism, which in the postwar decade passes over the radical propositions
of Eliot's *Waste Land* in favor of his prescriptive notions of critical taste, pulling images out of a poem's network and ossifying meanings by classification.
The creative act becomes less an aperture to the energies of the unconscious
than a controlled means of institutionalizing thought into scholasticism, that
is, knowledge and taste organized as laws, affording decisive judgments on
history and verifying the reactionary *Stand* taken by Ransom, Young, Penn
Warren, Tate, and the others who made up the Twelve Southerners in 1930.
Conversely, to Kerouac,

> [t]he new American poetry as typified by the SF Renaissance . . . is
> diametrically opposed to the Eliot shot, who so dismally advises his
> dreary negative rules like the objective correlative, etc. which is just a
> lot of constipation and ultimately emasculation of the pure masculine
> urge to freely sing. . . . SF is the poetry of a new Holy Lunacy like that
> of ancient times (Li Po, Hanshan, Tom O Bedlam, Kit Smart, Blake)
> yet it also has that mental discipline typified by the haiku (Basho,
> Buson), that is, the discipline of pointing things out directly, purely,
> concretely, no abstractions or explanations, wham wham the true blue
> song of man. (*SP* 4)

By inference, overworked designated modes of language can desensitize and
paralyze the writer. Kerouac's attention to the energies of performance scorns
the neoclassical sense of precision upon which content is hung as a legitimation, a death-throw correlation of pre-Einsteinian science. The cinematic
stylization of slapstick in *Cody* provides a further critique:

> Supposing the Three Stooges were real? (and so I saw them spring
> into being at the side of Cody in the street right there) . . . goofing on
> the screen and in the streets that are the same streets as outside the
> theater only they are photographed in Hollywood by serious crews
> like Joan Rawshanks in the fog, and the Three Stooges were bopping
> one another . . . until, as Cody says, they've been at it for so many years
> in a thousand climactic efforts superclimbing and worked out every
> refinement of bopping one another so much that now, in the end, if it
> isn't already over, in the baroque period of the Three Stooges they are

finally bopping mechanically and sometimes so hard its impossible to bear (wince), but by now they've learned not only how to master the style of the blows but the symbol and acceptance of also, as though inured in their souls and of course long ago in their bodies, to buffetings and crashings in the rixy gloom of Thirties movies and B short subjects. . . . [T]he stooges don't feel the blows any more, Moe is iron, Curley's dead, Larry's gone, off the rocker. (352, 54)

Filmic simulacrum segues into lived experience without syntactical break. The grinding routines of mass culture become the "real," as actions submit to mimetic formulas and their intended audience. It takes the Dionysian "con-man" Cody to expose the link between aesthetic forms and the axis of consumer manipulation and blow them apart.

Kerouac thus works with ideas, forces, and people created in language itself, a configuration of life in Prosody—"the articulation of the total sound of a poem," according to Pound (*Literary Essays* 421)—through forms and meanings that move within and interpenetrate one another. The anti-authoritarian "new vision," pursued at length through the early 1940s by the "Young Prometheans" of Kerouac's Lowell circle, is given body in these narratives, where writing becomes an act of flexible epistemology. Amplifying Conrad's use of Marlow, the unreliable mediator of *Heart of Darkness* and *Lord Jim* who straddles the turning of the century, a novel such as *Visions of Cody* builds a hermeneutic enquiry into the fictive space of personal history, a movement away from documenting privileged moments in the lives of privileged men to testing the perceptual basis of knowledge itself. The text's metafictional treatment of friendship and loss in effect problematizes any tendency to frame doubt in vehicles of referentiality, dramatizing the limits of understanding and its enduring instability. With multiple impressions of a character's voice and actions over time made available at once, the layers of the past effectively become a sovereign speech-text of language.

However, by the time of *Big Sur* the experimental performance of writing itself becomes ancillary to writing *about* himself (reportage). To quote Williams:

[A] bad sign to me is always a religious or social tinge beginning to creep into a poet's work. You can put it down as a general rule that when a poet, in the broadest sense, begins to devote himself to the *subject matter* of his poems, *genre,* he has come to an end of his poetic means. (*Selected* 288)

Having devised a strategy to handle prose projections beyond the immediate into areas of myth and transcendence, critical vilification drives him instead into self-pleading. Poised like Hamlet against the call of the past, Kerouac retraces what Miller describes as "the paths to the earlier heroic life" and in so doing defeats

> the very element and quality of the heroic, for the hero never looks backward, nor does he ever doubt his powers. . . . Behind this process lies the idea not of "edifice" and "superstructure," which is culture and hence false, but of continuous birth, renewal, *life, life.* . . . In the myth there is no life for us. Only the myth lives in the myth. (*Hamlet* 124–29)

This theme is illuminated further by Barthes's analysis of how control rides upon habituation:

> For the very end of myths is to immobilize the world: they must suggest and mimic a universal order which has fixated once and for all the hierarchy of possession. Thus, every day and everywhere, man is stopped by myths, referred by them to this motionless prototype which lives in his place, stifles him in the manner of a huge internal parasite and assigns to his activity the narrow limits within which he is allowed to suffer without upsetting the world. (*Mythologies* 155)

As the temptations of dogma and repression beckon, Kerouac's ability to sustain "Reichian flows" against the erosions of accustomed civilization dissipates. "Came home full of exhilaration which became mental exhaustion," he tells Ginsberg after *The Dharma Bums*' publication party, effectively summarizing his life. "Like America I'm getting a nervous breakdown" (*SL, II* 154). The confidence of Kerouac's voluntary exile and deracination at the core of his writing, and indeed so much modernist writing, gives way to the sacramental rhetoric of incontestable harmony, which so enamored the New Critics: an "active conciliation," to cite the Jesuit Ong (*Barbarian* 284); no pain, no conflict, the neurotic's dream of a tranquilized existence that shadows his Mahayana studies from the start ("All yr. senses become purified and yr. mind returns to its primal, unborn, original state of perfection" [*SL, I* 498]).

The embryonic aspiration toward "[b]rothers living together and laughing their labors to fruition!" (*SL, I* 44) that buoys the fledgling man of letters modifies into the existential solution implicit in *On the Road* and *Visions of Cody* from a survivalist emergence into personal and social renewal ("I'm after knowledge, not salvation, or salvation thru knowledge anyhow" [*SL, I* 325]). This is superseded by the Buddhist discipline of *Dharma Bums* and *Desolation Angels,* where "nothing matters and we all know it" (108), which is, in turn, replaced by the tortuous fixity of *Big Sur, Satori in Paris,* and

*Vanity of Duluoz* ("I've seen the Cross again and again but there's a battle somewhere and the devils keep coming back" [*BS* 157]).

Viewed within the Legend as a whole, the fundamentalism of Kerouac's doctrinaire final position, based on literalist interpretations of sacred texts as pronouncements of immutable laws, serves only to throw his earlier antinomianism into relief. With nerve intact, Catholic and Buddhist scriptures are treated as generative access to an imaginal world, intensely personal calls for transformation that testify to Corbin's belief in alchemy as the sister of prophecy. "To incarnate" thus reads as a verb that renders creativity and embodied knowing a project for everyone. Countering the anxiety for authority and anticipating what would become known as "pro-noia" in 1960s America, Kerouac opens out a number of avant-garde literary propositions (the non-chronological territories of memory, composition by field) to relinquish control paradigms (the West, the University, Catholicism, Hollywood). "I feel that I have completely reached my peak maturity now," he affirms in 1952, "and am blowing such mad poetry and literature that I'll look back years later with amazement and chagrin that I can't do it any more" (*SL, I* 335).

Indeed, for a time autonomy is possible in mediating between the pull of a frontier mythology (boundless resources, perpetual material growth) and freedom in the Cold War State: the self-regulation of "wild form," or "self sustaining oasis," to use Burroughs's phrase for independence beyond "the land of the dead" (*Place* 188). It is this heretical impulse toward growth that assigns much of the Legend its visionary quality, a constellation—albeit temporary—of the imagination in its perpetual, magical emergence.

# 8

# Bop Prosody

[B]eware of changing to a new kind of music, for the change always involves far-reaching danger. Any alteration in the modes of music is always followed by alteration in the most fundamental laws of the state.
—Plato, *The Republic*

For all the inventive arts maintain, as it were, a sympathetic connection between each other, being no more than various expressions of one internal power, modified by different circumstances.
—Percy Bysshe Shelley, *A Defense of Poetry*

op began with jazz," notes Kerouac,

but one afternoon somewhere on a sidewalk maybe 1939, 1940, Dizzy Gillespie or Charley Parker or Thelonious Monk was walking down past a men's clothing store on 42nd Street or South Main in L.A. and from the loudspeaker they suddenly heard a wild impossible mistake in jazz that could only have been heard inside their own imaginary head, and that is a new art. Bop. The name derives from an accident. (*GB* 113)

Kerouac's playful commentary in "The Beginning of Bop" echoes his own poetics in affirming the value of chance in creativity, permitting freedoms that the careful execution of prior scheme may otherwise disallow. "*No revisions,*" he insists in "Essentials of Spontaneous Prose." "SCOPING. Not 'selectivity' of expression but following free deviation (association) of mind into limitless blow-on-subject seas of thought" (*GB* 69–70).

Whereas Seymour Krim notes a postwar agitation in American literature against the prevailing "cerebral-formalist" temper (*DA* 9), for writers such as Kerouac and Ginsberg, the one-off risk of jazz performance charges the act of making with new vitality. "First thought, best thought," advocates Ginsberg in paraphrase of Blake ("Notes" 318) and in thrall to Kerouac's uncompromising notation: "Time being of the essence in the purity of speech sketching language is undisturbed flow from the mind of personal secret idea words, *blowing* (as per jazz musician) on subject of image" (*GB* 69). "I want to be considered a jazz poet," Kerouac avows in the note to *Mexico City Blues*,

> blowing a long blues in an afternoon jam
> session on Sunday. I take 242 choruses;
> my ideas vary and sometimes roll from
> chorus to chorus or from halfway through
> a chorus to halfway into the next.

Kerouac records a process of discovery through imprecision, a libertarian attitude within the arts underpinning Beat attacks on neoclassicism and traceable to Charles Baudelaire's definition of completion in the paintings of Gustave Courbet.[1] "Improvisation releases you from old forms, stale thoughts," corroborates Ronald Sukenick.

> [I]t releases things that are released only with difficulty on a psychological basis. It allows in surprising things that are creeping around on the edges of consciousness. It prevents you from writing clichéd formulas. It's a release finally, a release of the imagination. (qtd. in LeClair and McCaffery 291)

As the achievements of scores of soloists working against the force of preconceived intention show, improvisation is not merely expediency in the absence of a clear plan. That failure within the format is detectable—as, for example, in the final studio dates of bop's ruined genius Charlie Parker—effectively upholds its validity.

Through the 1950s, the jazz vanguard thus catalyzes much activity across the arts, in particular the abstract expressionist strike against the European tradition of the "well-made" artifact, the jilting of high-finance Broadway values in the Living Theatre productions of Julian Beck and Judith Malina, and the repudiation of Hollywood's technical polish in the films of Jonas Mekas, Stan Brakhage, and John Cassavetes, an attempt to arrest the co-opting of art into social engineering with the loss of its archaic capacity for ritual healing and liberation.

The claim here is not that extemporization in literature, painting, and film is without precedent but that the conditions of postwar America heightened the relevance of its procedures. According to Kerouac, Shakespeare, too, "heard *sound* first then the words were there in his QUICK HEAD."

> [H]is handwritten manuscripts were hardly blotted, if at all, as he apparently flowed in his writing and wrote in an inspired hurry what he immediately heard sound-wise while his steel-trap brain kept shutting down on the exigencies of plot and character in that sea of ravening English that came out of him. (*GB* 88, 85)

As Kerouac's fictions imply, inclusive spontaneity may serve as a revolutionary gesture within an environment that relegates creativity to the utilitarian demands of industry. This is announced by Miller at the opening of *Tropic of Cancer*:

> I have been looking over my manuscripts, pages scrawled with revisions. Pages of *literature*. This frightens me a little. . . . I have made a silent compact with myself not to change a line of what I write. I am not interested in perfecting my thoughts, nor my actions. Beside the perfection of Turgenev I put the perfection of Dostoevski. . . . Here, then, in one and the same medium, we have two kinds of perfection. But in Van Gogh's letters there is a perfection beyond either of these. It is the triumph of the individual over art.
>
> There is only one thing which interests me vitally now, and that is the recording of all that is omitted in books. Nobody, so far as I can see, is making use of those elements in the air which give direction and motivation to our lives. (9, 11)

Such challenges to what Kerouac terms the "gray faced Academic quibbling" and "dry rules . . . set down" (*SP* 4) by Eliot and the New Critics complement an impromptu strain in the nation's poetics initiated by Whitman ("America is to be kept coarse and broad" [*Complete Poems* 774]) and further seeded by the populist thrust of Vachel Lindsay and Carl Sandburg. These actions transpose Nietzsche's late thinking in *The Anti-Christ* onto American modernity: a reenactment of archetypal conflicts between the primitivist drives of ecstasy and the unconscious, and the Apollonian tendency toward institutional culture and the socialized self. Spurred on by the new jazz, the ancient canons of art—unscripted, candid, moneyless—are reasserted in Beat times through a body of work that would radiate an irresistible power across US society.

In 1903, W. E. B. DuBois described African American music as "the singular spiritual heritage of the nation and the greatest gift of the negro people" (*Souls* 12). Since then hundreds of writers, painters, and composers have responded to jazz in all its cultural overtones however indirectly, its influence transgressing social and national boundaries. While many proclamations of enthusiasm were undoubtedly faddist, numerous artists of significance readily acknowledged an affinity with the music and its practitioners, some consciously adopting its formal procedures. By midcentury, the attraction to an earlier wave of jazz embodied in the work of Copland, Hindemith, Milhaud, Ravel, Satie, Shostakovich, Stravinsky, and Weill was commonly felt in the ever-increasing complexity of rhythm, instrumental technique, and expressive possibility across contemporary composition.

Having taken jazz into the realm of the avant-garde, where it would thrive in a refusal of generic conformity, bebop's speed of evolution accelerated its influence upon, and overlapped with, developments across disciplines. For Kerouac, bop provides a model for registering the prose rhythms of excited American life, much as New Orleans and swing styles had resonated for Sandburg, Langston Hughes, William Carlos Williams, and Stuart Davis. Whereas Davis claimed to be "particularly hep to the jive," to the extent where

> Earl Hines' hot piano and Negro jazz music . . . plays a role in determining the character of my paintings; not in the sense of describing them in graphic images, but by pre-determining an analogous dynamics in the design which becomes a new part of the American environment (qtd. in Hughes, *American* 430–35),

for LeRoi Jones jazz *is* American reality (*Reader* 242). Kerouac also confers recognition upon the music as central to the nation's culture, not merely through enumerating musicians' names and hipster expressions in his prose but by using it as a guide for writing: a fertile confluence between forms.

On an immediate level, Kerouac's attraction to jazz inherits its associations with the liberal revolt against Puritanism accompanying the music's spread across the North in the 1920s, a trigger for the founding of "anti-jazz" societies across religious denominations and Henry Ford's location of "degeneracy" at the crossroads of liquor, trade unionism, and the "abandoned sensuousness" of "bestial Jewish Jazz" (Ford 187). And while Bohemian leftists of the 1930s aligned themselves with boogie-woogie pianists such as Pine Top Smith and Meade Lux Lewis, the wartime united front sought bluesmen such as Leadbelly and Josh White for fund-raising parties in progressive Hollywood circles.

With confidence in national credibility in decline, a rebel identification with the tastes of a disenfranchised minority in the postwar era was inevitable. Although by no means a popular phenomenon, the new jazz of Charlie Parker and Dizzy Gillespie reflected unrest around black urban communities, and the word "bebop," which began as an onomatopoeic designation, soon came to denote dissent across US society, making an asset of alienation. Whereas Ferlinghetti saw "a natural affinity . . . between the 'protest poet' and the jazz musician who blows 'dissent on the horn'" (notes for *Poetry*), Lipton drew attention to the music's qualities of "ritual, healing or spiritual catharsis," which negate the sickness of mass conformity. Hitching up to its appeal to dissidence in the crew-cut world, Lipton even provided a prescriptive black jazz playlist for the beatnik, rounded off by Ginsberg's "Holy the groaning saxophone! Holy the bop apocalypse! Holy the jazzbands marijuana hipsters peace & junk & drums!" (*Howl* 27).

To Lipton, the sacred and ceremonial origins of music still lay close to the surface in jazz, giving voice to "the Dionysian, not the Apollonian, beat in music" (207). These concerns are anticipated by Miller in *The Colossus of Maroussi*, "praising God" for "the great Negro race which alone keeps America from falling apart" and describing the jazzman as a "barbarous" catalyst, "riffin' his way through the new land." Miller sanctifies contemporary swing transformers who breach "missionary culturization" to reinvoke a Golden Age:

Duke Ellington, that suave, super-civilized, double-jointed cobra with the steel-flanged wrists . . . Count Basie . . . long lost brother of Isidore Ducasse and last direct lineal descendant of the great and only Rimbaud. Joe [Jones] the chocolate cherub, Chick [Webb] who was already sprouting wings, Big Sid [Catlett], and Fats [Waller] and Ella [Fitzgerald] and sometimes Lionel [Hampton] the golden boy who carried everything in his hat.

Louis Armstrong then follows in the guise of "devolutionary" agent:

[T]he illustrious Agamemnon had told him once—to first get tight and quiet as a fiend, *and then blow!* Louis put his thick loving lips to the golden torque and blew. He blew one great big sour note like a rat bustin' open and the tears came to his eyes and the sweat rolled down his neck. Louis felt that he was bringing peace and joy to all the world. He filled his lungs again and blew a molten note that reached so far into the blue it froze and hung in the sky like a diamond-pointed star. Louis stood up and twisted the torque until it became a great shining bulge of ecstasy. The sweat was pouring down him like a river. Louis was so happy that his eyes began to sweat too and they made two golden pools of joy, one of which he named the King of Thebes in honor of Oedipus, his nearest of kin, who had lived to meet the Sphinx. . . . Louis's back in the land with a horse shoe round his neck. He's makin' ready to blow a fat rat-bustin' note that'll knock the blue and the grey into a twisted torque-mada. Why he wanna do that? To show he's satisfied. All them wars and civilizations ain't brought nobody no good. Just blood everywhere and people prayin' for peace. (140–45)

Although removed from the "blackface" slumming endemic to Jazz Age writing—an inverse aristocratism based upon proximity to extrovert sexuality—Miller's romanticism fails to reverse the common neglect of the music's performers and recoils from any critique of what Frank Kofsky calls the "cockroach capitalist" conditions of its production (15). Kerouac similarly assigns a function to the improviser that is purely instinctive rather than cultural-historical: an attribution reinforced by the etymology of the word "jass," a colloquialism for fornication across West African coastal dialects, subsequently ditched by the politicized improvisers of the 1960s.[2] "The drums were mad," notes Paradise of the frantic, delirious music of the Mexican night in *On the Road*:

The mambo beat is the conga beat from Congo, the river of Africa and the world; it's really the world beat. Oom-*ta*, ta-poo-*poom*—oom-*ta*, ta-poo-*poom*. The piano montunos showered down on us from the speaker. The cries of the leader were like great gasps in the air. The final trumpet choruses that came with drum climaxes on conga and bongo drums, on the great mad Chattanooga record, froze Dean in his tracks for a moment till he shuddered and sweated; then when the trumpets bit the drowsy air with their quivering echoes, like a cavern's or a cave's, his eyes grew large and round as though seeing the devil, and he closed them tight. I myself was shaken like a puppet by it; I heard the trumpets flail the light I had seen and trembled in my boots. (270)

The primitivist stress on the music of "the happy, true-hearted, ecstatic Negroes of America" (149) is alleviated to a degree by Kerouac's later tribute to its formal sophistication, before a characteristic return to Spenglerian trance:

Jazz is very complicated. It's just as complicated as Bach. The chords, the structures, the harmony and everything. And then it has a tremendous beat. You know, tremendous drummers. They can drive it. It has just a tremendous drive. It can drive you right out of yourself. (qtd. in Wallace)

Kerouac's confused envy of indigenous energies, whether black, tribal American, Japanese, Celtic, or Mexican, falls within Edward Said's definition of "Orientalism": an ideological construction from type opposed in every respect to the European and a mystique ascribed to the disaffiliated white man that accelerates beyond Beat. His admiration for the "Fellahin Indians of the world, the essential strain of the basic primitive, wailing humanity that stretches in a belt around the equatorial belly of the world," as he moves south of the border in *Road* is typical of an anthropological perspective that bespeaks the hegemonic norms of the era:

These people were unmistakably Indians and were not at all like the Pedros and Panchos of silly civilized American lore—they had high cheekbones, and slanted eyes, and soft ways; they were not fools, they were not clowns; they were great, grave Indians and they were the source of mankind and the fathers of it. The waves are Chinese, but the earth is an Indian thing. As essential as rocks in the desert are they in the desert of "history." And they knew this when we passed, ostensibly self-important moneybag Americans on a lark in their land; they knew who was the father and who was the son of antique life on earth, and made no comment. (264)

But while in the area of jazz he may fail to question the liberal stereotype of an untutored, non-individualistic "Negro folk-art" free from commercial taint, works such as *On the Road, Visions of Cody,* and *Mexico City Blues* nevertheless demonstrate a rare insight into the very structures of improvisation. Moreover, Kerouac's reception of the music and its atemporal initiations ("music alone . . . can take us right out of this world . . . and let us fondly imagine that we are on the verge of reaching the soul's final secret" [*OTR* 136]) is reiterated in the work of some contemporary African American writers. For instance, in his tale "The Screamers," LeRoi Jones draws out the feral consciousness ("the word Con-With/Scio-Know" [*Reader* 192]) of the new jazz, which can whip an audience into insurrection:

We screamed and screamed at the clear image of ourselves as we should always be. Ecstatic, completed, involved in a secret communal expression. It would be the form of the sweetest revolution, to huckle-buck into the fallen capital, and let the oppressors lindy-hop out. (176)

Henry Dumas's story "Will the Circle Be Unbroken?" which Jones praises in his essay, "The Changing Same," for its understanding of "music as an autonomous *judge* of civilizations, etc. Wow!" (*Reader* 191), also plugs into the terrifying ancestral violence of an occult "afro-horn," whose "shock-waves" can annihilate the white novice:

Inside the center of the gyrations is an atom stripped of time, black. The gathering of the hunters, deeper. Coming, laced in the energy of the sun. He is blowing. Magwa's hands. Reverence of skin. Under the single voices is the child of a woman, black. They are building back the wall, crumbling under the disturbance. (Dumas 90)

Amplifying his role in *The Colossus of Maroussi* and *On the Road*, both pieces politicize the jazz improviser as shamanic gatekeeper to the collective black psyche. Taking Nietzsche's definition of music in *The Birth of Tragedy* as the primal Dionysian manifestation and applying it to African American art, such texts unleash potent energies in a nation petrified by fear of the black man and flourishing civil rights and black nationalist movements, a concealed hostility underpinning the accusations of obscenity levied at Beat writing. (Ginsberg notes that the passage cited by the Boston court at *The Naked Lunch* obscenity trial as "grossly offensive," despite its innocuous language, was a satire of the "monstrous speech and thought processes" of the "anti-Negro . . . anti-Northern, anti-Semitic . . . Southern, white racist bureaucrat" [qtd. in Burroughs, *Naked* xxx–xxxi].)

Paradoxically, the force of such work comes not so much from the evocation of a primal energy released through archaic ceremony but from an imaginative poetics that amplifies the music's emotional intensity. As Jones concludes in 1965: "I have made theories, sought histories, tried to explain. But the music itself is not about any of those things. What do our words have to do with flowers? A rose is not sweet because we explain it so. We could say anything, and no one would answer" (*Black* 173). Having entered the Duluoz Legend as a magical resource, Kerouac similarly reflects in *Visions of Cody* upon the shortfall in the capacity of language to register the "rawest peak" of "Frisco jazz" during "the age of the wild tenorman," who blew with "honest frenzy" through "regular-course developments of bop," a vertical moment of release from the narrative of Cold War neurosis:

> [I]t wasn't jazz they were blowing, it was the frantic "It."
> "What's the IT, Cody?" I asked him that night.  ·
> "We'll all know when he hits it—there it is! he's got it!—hear—see everybody rock? It's the big moment of rapport all around that's making him rock; that's jazz; dig him, dig her, dig this place, dig these cats, this is all that's left, where else can you and go Jack?" It was absolutely true. We stood side by side sweating and jumpin in front of wild be-hatted tenormen blowing from their shoetops at the brown ceiling, . . . and wild women dancing, the ceiling roaring, people falling in from the street, from the door, no cops to bother anybody because it was summer, August 1949, and Frisco was blowing mad. (407)

Beyond the level of image, the harnessing of energy that creates the aural becomes a verbal action too, a principle informing poetries such as Jayne

Cortez's tribute to Charles Mingus, "Into This Time"; Frank O'Hara's elegy for Billie Holiday, "The Day Lady Died"; and Paul Blackburn's "Listening to Sonny Rollins at the Five Spot." Pursuing a related struggle for liberation from standardized metrics and notation and addressing shared concerns of performance, a poem's line mirrors the organization of a bop phrase into improvised sound patterns punctuated as unique events. In the case of Blackburn's homage to Rollins, this includes a motivic sense of syllable and breath that dazzlingly echoes the tenorman's signature style.

Such convergences are a source of formal exhilaration. In Blackburn's "How to Get Up Off It," Mottram recognizes the presence of

> Oscar Peterson playing Ellington, maybe a blues lineage, an extraordinary control of cadence and pace, length of measure, changes in rhythms, to which any poet discovering his own process could return. The poem is poised between sound and words, as Pound, having learned from the Provençal poets, advised: *motz el son*—and spaced for print and reading to guide an attentive skill to how the process should go. The eye picks up the poem, as the ear will in the oral performance. ("Blackburn" 42)

The prominence given by bop masters to chord substitutions over Tin Pan Alley song forms suggests a further analogy: Kerouac's reevaluation of a speech-discourse transgressing class and race in *Cody* and *Tristessa*, and merging with Williams's drive for an American idiom and concomitant new meter.

Works like these and choruses 239 to 241 of *Mexico City Blues* ("Charley Parker Looked like Buddha") testify to Kerouac's grasp of bop's complexity of energy. Poised against a common time oscillation, Parker's use of fluctuating tempos and placement of micro-accents and hiatuses prove revelatory for those working within the paradigm of Whitman's variable measure. Having recognized the possibilities opened for his own writing by the multiple speeds and four-bar shapes of "Chasin' the Bird," Creeley tells Olson: "I am more influenced by Charley Parker, in my acts, than by any other man, living or dead. . . . Bird makes Ez look like a school-boy, in point of rhythms" (Olson and Creeley, *Correspondence* 157). Miles Davis illustrates the saxophonist's freedom in this area by describing his offbeat solo entries:

> He could play so many different styles and never repeat the same musical idea. His creativity and musical ideas were endless. He used to turn the rhythm section around every night. Say we would be playing a blues. Bird would start on the eleventh bar. As the rhythm section stayed where they were, then Bird would play in such a way that it made the rhythm section sound like it was on 1 and 3 instead of 2 and

4. . . . Eventually Bird would come back to where the rhythm was, right on time. It was like he had planned it in his mind. (Davis and Troupe 91)

Born in 1920, disciplined by the free mobility, competitive pressure, and shared feeling of the Kansas City jam session, and styled in the emulation of its leading practitioners, Charlie "Yardbird" Parker arguably stands as the most influential jazz musician of the century, in spite of a studio career spanning only thirteen years. His playing transgresses all previous restrictions for extemporization within a tonal system, having, like pianist Art Tatum, the facility to turn a tune inside out and rebuild it architecturally without subordination to technical display. Advanced harmonic rules developed by Stravinsky and Schoenberg could be deployed at lightning speed with all the grace associated with Lester Young, who advised the fledgling Parker "to shape the air": it was not a matter of notes and pitches but "*sounds*" (Russell 68). The resulting conception is made all the more authoritative by a cutting tone, achieved by blowing on the thickest reed available.

With Parker at its core, bebop evolved through a series of experimental associations in the New York underground at the turn of the 1940s as "a reaction by young musicians against the sterility and formality of Swing as it moved to become a formal part of the mainstream American culture" (Jones, *Black* 16). As a stylized reflection of a feeble environment, swing had homogenized popular music across the nation in the late 1930s on the back of a surge in production of radios and gramophones. White bandleaders such as Artie Shaw, Benny Goodman, and the Dorsey Brothers assumed a social and financial status comparable to Hollywood screen actors, diverting attention from the music's ensemble scene to a radiating star as magic center. With arrangements often commissioned from outside writers, the need for improvisation was increasingly obviated, negating the risk in group expression characteristic of swing's antecedents—most notably the Chicago outfit led by Fletcher Henderson (reemployed in 1939 as Goodman's staff arranger)—and still found in bands led by Duke Ellington, Count Basie, and Jay McShann (with whom Parker first recorded in 1941) and in the work of surviving New Orleans musicians. Reduced to flattering a vocal refrain, solo lines gradually became integrated into ensemble passages, creating fixed forms with standardized effects. Consequently, a musician's technique was now confined to the interpretation of a score, characterized by "rhythmic regularity and melodic predictability" (Jones, *Black* 79).

Taking their cues from the Casa Loma Orchestra, arrangers such as Eddie Sauter and Boyd Raeburn channeled blues components into pastiche forms, a synthesized negritude for jazzing-up the American popular song. In vocal numbers this extended to a bowdlerized black street talk with titles like "Hut-Sut-Ralston," "Chicory-Chic," and "Marezy Doats": "a compromise," suggests LeRoi Jones, "whose most significant stance was finally catatonia and noncommunication" (*Blues* 171). The uniformity and commercialism of most groups rendered them incapable of serving as vehicles for serious expression, emptying jazz of revelation and demoting it to a variety turn. As Mottram notes, this was in keeping with the corporatist aesthetic of the 1930s northern city:

> The music of Earl Hines and his orchestra in Chicago in 1934 and New York in 1935 is the sound of *art deco,* of gangster-owned nightclubs. The size and density of the sound denotes value—a hard sophistication of earlier jazz inventions with dehumanized vocals—a musical commodity which comes across now almost as pure style, whose energy is tightly controlled surface fitted over elementary dance structure. It places itself at the disposal of patrons, so the emotion is never subtle or illuminating but modernistic and predictable. ("Living" 275)

Reverting to an open framework of rhythm section plus horns, bebop signaled the reemergence of individual and collective improvisation within a small group, the basis of jazz at its inception. Soloists such as Parker, Gillespie, Fats Navarro, Bud Powell, and Thelonious Monk released energies in celebration, violence, or anguish that were previously contained and neutralized within the over-organized big band (Cowley 195). Problematized by the American indifference to black practices unaligned with the parochialism of folk-form or show business, such gestures of cool defiance reconsigned bop performers to the social margins, provoking additional hostility among some older, established improvisers. This is swing drummer Dave Tough's account of a visit to a 52nd Street club in the mid-1940s:

> As we walked in, see, these cats snatched up their horns and blew crazy stuff. One would stop all of a sudden and another would start for no reason at all. We could never tell when a solo was supposed to begin or end. Then they quit all at once and walked off the stand. It scared us. (qtd. in Stearns 224–25)

To many of Tough's generation, bebop appeared an extremist music full of speeding tempos, shocking explosions, jagged accents, angular mixtures of consonance and dissonance, and manic switches between instrumental registers, requiring unsurpassed coordinations of nerve, muscle, and intellect. Challenge was central to the whole scene, musical complexity begetting pride in facility. Replacing swing's rigid demarcation of the ensemble, lines emerged from a dialogue between soloist and rhythm section. The balance of the band thus shifted, subsuming notions of accompaniment. Each member was given a front-line function with a duty to foment interaction, reappointing the music's tribal basis in ecstatic community.

No longer dependent upon unitary measure, jazz embraced multiplicity of time: each pulse a vertical instant in the music's progress through a succession of simultaneous signs. Bebop thus echoed directions in the music of Edgar Varèse, Charles Ives, John Cage, and Morton Feldman in undermining the rhythmically simplified, goal-directed force of organized sound allied by Spengler to the interchangeable, metronomic divisions of Newtonian mechanics (211)—a spur for the dominance of visual media, with music to be played as written. The ensuing "regular collective beat and rhythm of the machine" is endemic to the temporal and sonic patterns of the industrial State, according to Lewis Mumford, as it seeks to standardize experience:

> [F]or the clock is not merely a means of keeping track of the hours, but of synchronizing the actions of men. . . . [T]he new mechanical conception of time arose in part out of the routine of the monastery. . . . [I]t was, however, in the monasteries of the West that the desire for order and power, other than that expressed in the military domination of weaker men, first manifested itself. . . . [U]nder the rule of order, surprise and doubt and caprice and irregularity were put at bay. (*Technics* 280)

Displacing common-time, bop's fluency of measure conversely recalls Henri Bergson's open forms of "duration" that contrast to the classical homogenization of pulse (31). As the instrument providing controls for dance—the ultimate kinesthetic form demonized by the Puritan church—the drum was sped away by bebop from the backwaters of western music and its primary function as a military technology for hypnosis. In West Africa, from where more than 85 percent of New World slaves were seized, the drum had been put to varied uses in tribal communication and sacred ritual. Although banned during slavery for fear of inciting insurgency, its associated tradition of polyrhythm persisted in the hand-clapping and stomping of the Negro spiritual. By 1940, Kenny Clarke had assimilated this into a new style of drumming during his residency at Minton's Playhouse, forcing the beat's propulsion with greater urgency while giving greater attention to a soloist's needs. Whereas transitional swing drummers such as Sid Catlett and Jo Jones had started to move away from a prominent 2/4 offbeat, Clarke pioneered a more even stress with the ride cymbal, keeping the bass drum for sudden accents, or "dropping bombs." "In 1937 I'd gotten tired of playing like Jo Jones," he reports:

> It was time for jazz drummers to move ahead. I took the main beat away from the bass drum and up to the top cymbal. I found out I could get pitch and timbre variations up there, according to the way the stick struck the cymbal, and a pretty sound. The beat had a better flow. It was lighter and tastier. That left me free to use the bass drum, the tom-toms and snare for accents. I was trying to lay new rhythmic patterns over the regular beat. Solo lines were getting longer. Soloists needed more help from the drummer—kicks, accents, cues, all kinds of things like that. (qtd. in Russell 133)

The movement away from the limits of singular pulse that marked the music's origins in work songs and parades would accelerate over the next two decades through Max Roach and Art Blakey's use of polyrhythmic cross-measures and the "free" styles developed by Beaver Harris, Andrew Cyrille, Milford Graves, and Sonny Murray. "Bird was really responsible [for this]," contends Roach, "not just because his style called for a particular style of drumming, but because he set the tempos so fast it was impossible to play on a straight, Cozy Cole, four style. So we had to work out variations" (qtd. in Reisner 194). "We kept reading about rockets and jets and radar," Roach later adds, drawing a sense of total environment from his art, "and you can't play 4/4 music in times like that" (qtd. in McNally 82).

Building solos upon these sprinting exchanges, Parker disengages from, expands, or contracts the beat at will. Time suddenly doubles. "The beat in a Bop band is with the music, against it, behind it," explains the altoman. "It pushes it. It helps it. Help is the big thing. It has no continuity of beat, no steady chug-chug. [Swing] Jazz has, and that's why bop is more flexible" (qtd. in Levin and Wilson). The sheer speed of his phrasing within eighth-note values, a facet considered as mere decoration in earlier jazz, effectively fulfills John Cage's 1937 prophecy, "The Future of Music: Credo," with rhythmic agility integral to form:

> The composer (organizer of sound) will be faced not only with the entire field of sound but also with the entire field of time. The "frame" or fraction of a second, following established film technique, will probably be the basic unit in the measurement of time. No rhythm will be beyond the composer's reach. (*Silence* 5)

With percussion liberated, the bass now carried bop's time signature, giving the instrument its most important function yet. Above the steady cymbal legato, other instruments could vary their attack on the melodic line, adding to the polyrhythmic stress. This also emancipated the pianist. No longer anchored in left-hand "stride" patterns, complex punctuating chords could be fed to a soloist alongside darting right-hand runs.

The greatest beneficiary of such freedom was perhaps Thelonious Monk. Mythicized by Kerouac in "The Beginning of Bop" and lionized as "one of the greatest composers who ever lived, in music purely," in his *Escapade* column (*GB* 169), the pianist's contribution to the new jazz was as revolutionary as Parker's. His first recordings as leader, collected on *Genius of Modern Music* (1952), trade on the isolation and delay of notes and render space a new crux of rhythmic tension. Bop's undercurrent of unease is thus given a new context; pulse and melodic line separate, the midtempo consistency of Blakey's cymbal serving only to heighten the suspense.

Monk's fearlessness of silence thus contrasts with Parker's sense of pace, an alternative measure that is resolutely asymmetrical. Causal logic is devastated; surprise lines hang in the air, splintered beyond resolution—an obvious resource for poetry and prose. Moreover, his microtonal palate, achieved through simultaneous depression of adjacent black and white keys with finger, hand, or elbow, hints at the disturbance of equal temperament tuning in the work of Cage and Earle Brown. Overlays of arbitrarily pitched chords, at times clustering twelve notes, blur definitions of music and noise. "You can't shut the sound [of New York] out too easily; you always hear some kind of noise going on," Monk explains to Valerie Wilmer. "That's what I dig about it. You want to know what sounds I put into my music—well you have to go to New York to listen for yourself" (47). Melody is returned to sound itself, an infinite plasticity of vibrations that expose the relativity of terms such as consonance and dissonance and of the harmonic systems developed in eighteenth-century France and Germany and passed on as permanent and universal.

As with Parker, a Monk solo defies predictability as it switches between the lyrical and the fitful. Notions of musical personality as conveyed through vehicles of referentiality are ditched, bearing out Cage's claim that the "relation between sounds is more complex than can be prescribed" (*Silence* 49). While in the case of Parker and Bud Powell these assumptions are not wholly separable from the effects of chronic addiction and mental illness—the altoman was formally diagnosed as a schizophrenic with sociopathic tendencies, and several colleagues have testified to his ability to stretch the limits of human contradiction—bop lets rip new creative possibilities for self-dramatization that fracture the allusive routines of cliché and artifice.

To Beat writers, such virtuosity demonstrated how isolated fragments could be bound together at bewildering speed, within the three-minute constraints of 78-rpm playback technology. Identifying disjunction as a "positive feature" of Parker's solos, Max Harrison assigns the synthesis of march-like figures that make up "Klactoveedsedstene" (1947)—the title of which recalled not only Slim Gaillard's "Vout"-speak and Gillespie's scat singing but also Dada sound-text vocabularies without semantic reference (Cowley 198)[3]—as an example of the altoist's ability to realize a composition from apparently unrelated shards and pieces. Broken stop-start lines work in quotations from popular melodies, replacing the narrative linearity of a previous jazz generation—as exemplified by Lester Young's belief that a "solo should tell a story" (Litweiler 39)—with an intertextual barrage. The order of sounds placed within the chorus frame is collage, a principle of noncoherence, as suggested by the title of Parker's 1948 recording "Segments," rather than incoherence.

The track "Leap Frog," from the *Bird and Diz* sessions of 1950, intensifies these properties in a series of four-bar trade-offs between Parker and Gillespie. Despite drummer Buddy Rich's inflexible showmanship, their reflexes blaze to the antiphonal dropping of rhythmic and harmonic cues, aided by Monk and bassist Curly Russell. Throughout the four takes of the tune, repetition is circumvented, with risk courted at the manic tempo of crotchet = 330. Rows of fragments are seized from memory and fashioned into scores of shapes over the chord sequence: fierce, unpredictable, and colored by the vocalized timbres of the blues. Restatement of the outgoing theme, first deemed unnecessary by the overridden head-solo divisions of "Bird Gets the Worm" (1948), is now totally disregarded, the solos being complete statements in themselves. Abandonment is informal, announced only by scruffy drum roll.

Having predicted bebop's eventual progression into atonality, such feats testify to Parker's intuition that he would soon need new modes to meet his expressive potential. Notwithstanding temporary incursions into different keys via a language of "blue notes" and raised or flattened intervals, his radicalism is contained by the diatonic thirty-two-bar "standard" and twelve-bar blues: a projective act inside a given superstructure. While Parker tells Robert Reisner, "They teach you there's a boundary line to music. But, man, there's no boundary line to art" (27), in practice, he resisted confinement to jazz materials alone, a principle of cultural collision endemic to a form that thrives on ignoring distinctions between popular and learned, black and European. To this end, he expressed an interest in recording with Moondog, the blind street performer of Hell's Kitchen who, with his battery of homemade instruments and "Snaketime" music, became something of an adjunct to the 52nd Street world, and also sought a meeting with Stravinsky and consulted Varèse, whose explorations in urban sounds he found thrilling. Varèse relays Parker's final approach in 1955:

> He said, "Take me as you would a baby and teach me music. I only write in one voice. I want to have structure. I want to write orchestral scores. I'll give you any amount you wish. I make a lot of money. I'm a good cook; I'll cook for you." . . . I left for Europe and told him to call me up after Easter when I would be back. Charlie died before Easter. He spoke of being tired of the environment his work relegated him to, "I'm so steeped in this and can't get out," he said. (qtd. in Reisner 229–30)

In refusing to appease commentators who demanded the comfort of category, the altoman took on Thomas Kuhn's idea of the changing "paradigm" of scientific revolutions, overturning logical positivist versions of history as steady progression within fixed parameters. As Julian Cowley suggests, herein lies the source of the hostility accorded to bebop in the 1940s, leading to accusations of its practitioners as "mad" or "anti-jazz," which in turn recalled the 1939 reception of *Finnegans Wake* as an "anti-novel" (196). The reactions of critics in *Downbeat* and *Metronome* who dismissed early recordings by Young, Parker, Powell, and Navarro (before uselessly reversing their opinions a decade later by re-reviewing them to great acclaim) displayed not only a slavish conservatism but also a debilitating view of the way art is made: a failure to grasp that rather than consigning received styles to an unusable past (the consumer trajectory), the vanguard in each field assimilates them in order to determine the contemporary relevance of their lessons; or as Robert Duncan has it: "a new order is a contention in the heart of existing orders" (*Fictive* 111).

LeRoi Jones's essay "Hunting Is Not Those Heads on the Wall" uses bop to clarify this issue, his point being that a series of polished mannerisms emulating the technical facility of an artist does not extend his or her innovative spirit, regardless of how revelatory or disruptive the original model may have been. "A saxophonist who continues to 'play like' Charlie Parker," writes Jones, "cannot understand that Parker wasn't certain that what happened had to sound like that" (qtd. in Allen and Tallman 380). As the alternate takes of "Parker's Mood," "Mohawk," and "Leap Frog" affirm, Parker's genius resides in his spirit of restless inquiry, a ceaseless investigation of the forms an improvisation might take (Cowley 195). Manipulating rhythmic cells in a highly personal way, he stands as an archetype of revolt, cast into a condition of perpetual emergence with only his integrity for refuge, refusing to hole himself up in an archive and craft for commerce.

This is the prerogative that excites Kerouac, an application of procedures that do not forecast guaranteed results. "For what is indeed odder to a creator than the end product of his work?" asks Paul Valéry.

> He has known nothing of it beyond his sketches for parts, fragments, steps to be taken, and his impression of what he has done is quite other than that of the whole and accomplished thing; he has known nothing of its perfection but only of trials, attempts. (45)

As Kerouac advises Philip Whalen in August 1958, "[D]on't pre-think what critics or readers might think of your 'awkwardness,' since your 'awkwardness' you'll see will turn out in the end to be the true meat of your style & story. . . . It means you're really art-ing it . . . not hack-ing" (*SL, II* 146). Reiterating Parker's own insistence at the music's height in 1949 that bop "could barely label its present trends, much less make prognostications about the future" (qtd. in Levin and Wilson), Ralph Ellison detects within Parker's sound itself the same error of framing the "new" retrospectively as conscious fulfillment of style:

> For all its velocity, brilliance and imagination there is in it a great deal of loneliness, self-deprecation and self-pity. With this there is a quality which seems to issue from its vibratoless tone: a sound of amateurish ineffectuality, as though he could never quite make it. . . . [H]e captured something of the discordances, the yearning, romance and cunning of the age and ordered it into a haunting art. He was not the god they see in him but for once the beatniks are correct. Bird lives—perhaps because his tradition and his art blew him to the meaningful center of things. (230–31)

However, by the mid-1950s, as Jones recognizes and A. B. Spellman corroborates,

> [t]he discovery had gone out of Bebop—it had become as formalistic as any movement does once it has solved its original problem. . . . [I]t was that indefiniteness of not knowing how the music was going to sound before it is played that enhanced its emotional expression. (12)

Retreating from its regenerative basis in musical intermarriage and new symbiotic relationships, jazz largely submitted once again to charm rather than to risk, to the demands of entertainment and contrived arrangements executed with conscientious precision (Cowley 195). Some truly innovative music was created, notably by Miles Davis in collaboration with Gil Evans; by Lennie Tristano, who experimented with multi-track recording and collective free improvisation; by Art Blakey and Horace Silver's Jazz Messengers; and by the Modern Jazz Quartet, who infused baroque forms with blues and swing inflections. But in the hands of the copyists, jazz returned to the standards of derivative technique witnessed in the 1930s, resuming the conceptual orientation that Parker's Dionysian breakthroughs so explosively defied.

However, stagnation was only temporary. As John Litweiler notes in *The Freedom Principle,* a progressive quest for freedom marks every point of renewal in jazz, a crusade to increase the capacity for expression. Whereas the earliest jazz musicians asserted the independence of rhythm and phrase from neighboring turn-of-the-century sounds, Louis Armstrong symbolized the liberated soloist in the late 1920s, Count Basie's band offered rhythmic expansion in the next decade, and Parker, Gillespie, and Monk mapped a new ensemble basis in the 1940s. In the late 1950s, a new generation of black improvisers led by Sonny Rollins, Charles Mingus, Cecil Taylor, John Coltrane, and, most significantly, Ornette Coleman surfaced to consolidate the music's vanguard position and Parker's demand for rejuvenation.

Three years after the bop founder's death in 1955 from a spiraling financial and biological pact, Coleman emerges on *Something Else!!!! The Music of Ornette Coleman* with a white plastic alto and a new principle: "[T]he pattern for the tune will be forgotten, and the tune itself will be the pattern, and won't have to be forced into conventional patterns" (notes). Relinquishing standard song-forms and piano harmonies, his prophecy would become musical fact within two years. "I know exactly what I am doing," he later reiterates. "I'm beginning where Charlie Parker stopped" (qtd. in Mellers 345–46).

The saxophonist had arrived in New York in 1957, and in an eruption of controversy one year later opened at the Five Spot, the East Village club patronized by painters, filmmakers, and writers drawn to jazz as a self-consciously American art form. Coleman proceeded to dismantle boundaries for individual and collective extemporization, courting surprise and constantly reevaluating "a musical syntax which though necessarily derived from Parker, was a copy of no one" (Spellman 79). Gunther Schuller, an early supporter, identifies the "utter and complete freedom" of his conception and the evolution of his materials from bop:

> His musical inspiration operates in a world uncluttered by conventional bar lines, conventional chord changes, and conventional ways of blowing or fingering a saxophone. Such practical "limitations" did not even have to be overcome in his music; they somehow never existed for him. Despite this—or more accurately, *because* of this—his playing has a deep inner logic. Not an obvious surface logic, it is based on subtleties of reaction, subtleties of timing and color that are, I think, quite new to jazz. . . . [A]ll these qualities are the more startling because they are not only imbued with a profound love and knowledge of jazz tradition,

but are the first realization of all that is implicit in the music of Charlie Parker. (notes for Coleman, *Shape*)

Befriended by John Lewis, Coleman obtained his first record contract with Contemporary in 1958 before securing a longer-term deal the following year with Atlantic, an eminent documenter of black music in this period. Reflecting the practice of his working quartet featuring trumpeter Don Cherry, bassist Charlie Haden, and either Ed Blackwell or Billy Higgins on drums, studio dates such as *Tomorrow Is the Question!* and *The Shape of Jazz to Come* advocate atonal self-regulation without limitation of strict pulse. Coleman's disposal of regimented chorus and chordal mass, sources of reference and security that direct a soloist into running acrobatically through scales within a harmonic maze, serves only to enhance communication. "Music is for our feelings," affirms the saxophonist. "I think jazz should try to express more kinds of feeling than it has up to now" (notes for *Shape*). Moving beyond the modal innovations of Evans, Davis, and Coltrane, Coleman seeks to restore plasticity to jazz above claims of style. "My melodic approach is based on phrasing," he contends,

> and my phrasing is an extension of how I hear the intervals and pitch of the tune I play. There is no end to pitch. You can play flat in tune and sharp in tune. It's a question of vibration. My phrasing is spontaneous, not a style. A style happens when your phrasing hardens. Jazz is the only music in which the same note can be played night after night but differently each time. It's the hidden things, the subconscious that lies in your body and lets you know: you feel this, you play this. (qtd. in Mellers 346)

Broadening the scope of performance, Coleman and Cherry are free to "relate to the emotion, the pitch, the rhythm, the melody of a theme without relating to chords or bar divisions" (notes for *Shape*). With customary drum press-rolls on the turnaround between choruses erased, Haden, too, forsakes conventional positions on his instrument. Rather than placing preconceived chords under a soloist and harmonically limiting the choice of notes, the bassist is empowered to investigate pitches for each group moment: "I don't know how it's going to sound before I play it any more than anybody else does," argues Haden, "so how can we talk about it before I play it? . . . [I]f I am just going to use the changes themselves, I might as well write out what I am going to play" (notes for *Shape*).

Melody thus creates its own structure as it moves, taking Olson's sense of "proprioception" into an ensemble environment. The ensuing shapes are often unusual and asymmetrical, enhanced by the fluency of Coleman's lines, which always breathe beautifully. Although distanced from the aharmonic blues of Big Bill Broonzy or Sonny Terry, the results are not random but mix chance with determinacy. As Haden suggests, "From realizing that I can make mistakes, I have come to realize there is an order to what I do" (notes for *Shape*). The effect combines a new formality with freedom of measure in sound, the significance of which stands peer to Stravinsky's elimination of unitary time signature and bar lines in *The Rite of Spring*.

Whereas these 1959 LPs reveal few signs of traditional organization other than those derived from the musical events themselves, jazz assumes unprecedented freedom and risk with Coleman's double quartet recording, *Free Jazz*. Likening his compositional process to that employed by Jackson Pollock—the painter gave the title *Free Form* to a 1946 canvas, while the saxophonist reproduced *White Light* on his LP sleeve—Coleman forges an art that gains meaning through the action of its creation. The unique content of a series of sounds alone now qualifies possibilities of form, with inherited programs jettisoned, a modernist insistence from the time of Pound, Stein, and Williams that resonates across genres.[4]

Recovering multiple voicing from the dead hand of West Coast classicism, Coleman fully comprehends the interactive potential of the jazz ensemble. With each player situated inside his own harmonic and temporal cycle, the constraints of standard roles (soloist, accompanist, timekeeper) give way to fluid conversational interchange. Individual participation thus energizes a disciplined group democracy, suggesting a metaphorical critique of power relations in a society that subjugates active community to the demands of passive spectatorism.

Following the example of George Antheil's "Treatise on Harmony," which plots harmony as a function of rhythm within the time-space of cubist geometries, Coleman pursues the closer integration of sound elements in order to realize form dynamically. Dispensing with the tripartite abstractions of melody, harmony, and rhythm into exclusive elements, Coleman implicitly applies Buckminster Fuller's concept of "synergy" in design,

> which means the behavior of whole systems unpredicted by the behavior of any of its parts taken separately, requir[ing] the reversal of our present system of compartmentalization of knowledge and of going from the particular toward the ever more special. (*Earth* 176)

As Cowley notes, such a correlation is more than coincidence. Coleman expressed profound admiration for Fuller, attending lectures through the 1960s and 1970s and dedicating compositions to the theoretician of comprehensive anticipatory design science. Coleman's idiosyncratic "harmolodic" system can be seen as a musical translation of Fuller's vision of the global

ordering of utilities, a realization of techno-anarchistic society that maxi-
mizes individual freedom, with patterns of private ownership adjusted to
specialization discarded. In his essay "The Music of the New Life," Fuller
contends that "in the world of music and in the world of art, human beings
have attained much spontaneous and realistic coordination" (*Utopia* 95),
his point being that the benign, liberatory potential of technology may be
realized only after the collective adoption of new modes of understanding
and behavior, to which artists, and especially musicians, are most closely
attuned (Cowley 196–97).

In this respect, Coleman's music exemplifies Fuller's "spontaneous and
realistic coordination," with the uniformity of parts cast into disarray through
open-ended heterophony. As the saxophonist suggests, harmolodics

> can be used in almost any kind of expression. You can think harmo-
> lodically. You can write fiction and poetry in harmolodic. Harmolodic
> allows a person to use a multiplicity of elements to express more than
> one direction at one time. . . . It's better to eliminate the styles and past
> categories and be you. ("Harmolodic" 47)

Answering Cage's call for jazz musicians to quit the reiteration of singular
measures and apply the lessons of Ives's Fourth Symphony, where "everything is happening at the same time" (*Anthology* 163), the improvisers of *Free
Jazz* connect to several different lines simultaneously, without obligation to
take their place within, or oppose, ascendant group meters. With permuta-
tions shifting and sliding in response to ever-new situations, the variety of
exchanges characterizing bebop expands greatly. Non-cadential disjunctions
counteract the linear unfolding of sound, subsuming the western emphasis
on progression toward a peak. Performer and listener alike are immersed in
a tide of immediacy, an effect analogous to the ceremonial ecstasy of West
African "spirit possession" that is never far from the surface of jazz—as
acknowledged by the title of Coltrane's collective improvisation *Ascension,*
which takes its stimulus from *Free Jazz.*

In his individual sound, too, Coleman amplifies Parker's self-dramatization into plurality, quoting, often within the same phrase, from a glossary
of saxophone styles that recall the musical personalities of predecessors.
Romantic associations of style with organic procedure are junked as moods
alternate erratically between austere experiment and pure circus, disrupting
expectation-deviation-completion cycles. Taking on Lester Young's plea to
extend creative responsibility beyond the bandstand—"the only worthwhile
audience is an audience of active participants" (qtd. in Russell 204)—*Free
Jazz* invites the listener to build a personal elucidation of the fragmented
character of events. The audience remains autonomous, denied the luxury

of passive empathy with a narrative deriving from a fixed point of view that overlooks the mechanics of performance. Interpretation is guided by the diverse voices of Coleman, Cherry, Freddie Hubbard, and Eric Dolphy, who intensify bebop's assimilation of black American urban tensions to generate a group sound transgressing cultural frontiers.

Against their solo measures, the double rhythm section initiates a variable sixteenth-note pulse, traced as part of its collective memory. Trumpeter Hubbard, in particular, adheres to blues licks, contending not only with Coleman's characteristically American ambition to liberate the "new" from inheritance, as implied by the album title, but also with applications of the term "abstract" to sound and the more general misnomer of "free" anything in art. To call on Williams: "There is no such thing as free verse! Verse is measure of some sort, [unless it is to] run down and become formally non-extant" (*Autobiography* 264). And while Dolphy plays "notes that would not ordinarily be said to be in a given key," he would "hear them as proper. I don't think I 'leave the changes' as the expression goes; every note I play has some reference to the chords of a piece" (Carr, Fairweather, and Priestley 140).

Laying bare the inventive process, the assimilative and reproductive functions of art are declared in what Alfred Willener calls "the dialectical synthesis created by a group or an individual, redefining known elements, elements that have just been played and experienced, while inventing new elements in the course of the activity itself" (230). The crashing emplacements of gospel, blues, swing, and contemporary European propositions converge in *Free Jazz* at a volatile juncture, orchestrated as an equilibrium of fluid lines, each its own trajectory.

Recognizing Coleman's desire for communication, Spellman echoes Andre Breton's credo that nothing but "the Marvelous" is beautiful and remarks that "the new musician has been primarily involved in the cultivation of the Marvelous. And he judges his work more by the frequency with which the Marvelous occurs than by compositional values" (83). Encouraging his collaborators to act without external control, Coleman's approach proved equally liberating for other noted contemporaries. Litweiler observes that for saxophonist Albert Ayler, music began "with sound itself, and from there you can create what relationships you wish without the baggage of theory" (170). And as soprano player Steve Lacy recalls,

> when Ornette hit the scene, that was the end of the theories. He destroyed the theories. I remember that at that time he said, very carefully, "Well, you just have a certain amount of space and you put what you want in it." And that was a revelation. (qtd. in Bailey 73)

Any gesture becomes acceptable in exploring what Cage describes as "the academically forbidden 'non-musical' field of sound insofar as is manually possible," a widening of methods, which he notes had "already taken place in Oriental cultures and in hot jazz":

WHEREAS, IN THE PAST, THE POINT OF DISAGREEMENT HAS BEEN BETWEEN DISSONANCE AND CONSONANCE, IT WILL BE, IN THE IMMEDIATE FUTURE, BETWEEN NOISE AND SO-CALLED MUSICAL SOUNDS. THE PRESENT METHODS OF WRITING MUSIC, PRINCIPALLY THOSE WHICH EMPLOY HARMONY AND ITS REFERENCE TO PARTICULAR STEPS IN THE FIELD OF SOUND, WILL BE INADEQUATE FOR THE COMPOSER, WHO WILL BE FACED WITH THE ENTIRE FIELD OF SOUND. (*Silence* 4)

While the Dionysian embrace of extramusical values—chance, noise, amplified volume, dance, and the visuals of performance—in the work of Jimi Hendrix and Jim Morrison signaled exceptions to the kitsch dilution of blues into rock and roll, Coleman's working bands continued through the 1960s to transgress barriers between the soloist and the group, and the new and the recognizable, to set an example to artists across disciplines. Moving within a protest tradition, his music emerged at the cusp of a new black consciousness period in the United States to assume an overtly political impetus, the de facto censorship of jazz throughout the century testifying to the affront caused to the authoritarian sense of order when faced with the metaphor of a flexible collaboration of individuals dedicated to reappraising materials drawn from multiple cultures (Cowley 198).

While jazzmen had always taken intractable European instruments and "Africanized" them through vocalized inflections, blue notes, and bent pitches, Coleman reengineers Euro-American frameworks at the deepest level of form. The saxophonist, who was raised in Fort Worth, Texas, one of the nation's more racist environments, thus perpetuates a practice extending back to slavery times, when sacred music and "sorrow songs" were vehicles used by a disenfranchised people to articulate their desires, carrying resistance in coded form. However, by 1960 such secrecy had become unnecessary. Reflecting the militant mood of black society, Coleman flouts the middlebrow consumption ethic of the official jazz scene to symbolize the improviser's refusal of constraints imposed by "a concern for maintaining tonalism, the primacy of melody, a distrust of new languages, codes or instruments, a refusal of the abnormal"—characteristics cited by Jacques Attali as common to all totalitarian regimes (8).[5]

In the late 1950s, Kerouac met many of the emerging improvisers in Coleman's circle, including Don Cherry and Cecil Taylor, who congregated alongside poets at the West 20th Street apartment of Hettie and LeRoi Jones. Writing in *Escapade* in December 1960, Kerouac names over one hundred "great solo-ists" in his "parade of great wailers who will make the New Wave Jazz pop" and "implement the new phrase and harmony." "The first breakthrough since Charlie Parker," he notes, "has been accomplished by Ornette Coleman and Donald Cherry with his little cornet and . . . it will lead the way, like Parker's way into a whole new era of jazz" (*GB* 169). Others credited for the "great jazz resurgence" here and elsewhere include "Charley Haden (of Ornette's group) (a bassplayer of the future)," "Billy Higgins (original thinker)" (169), Cecil Taylor—"the great new bop pianist now playing nightly at the Five Spot on 3rd Avenue and 4th Street with Dennis Charles on drums" (*SL, I* 593), and "John 'Train' Coltrane"—"a veritable 'saint' of music" (*GB* 170), who "show-ers his rough notes from his big tenor horn all over [the club]" (*LT* 111).

Beyond his obvious enthusiasm for the new generation of post-boppers, the tracing of correspondences between jazz developments and his fiction serves not only to illuminate his "*Lingual Spontaneity* . . . a kind of challenge Jazz Ses-sion for letters—(about time)" (*SL, I* 510), but also to bring out the radicalism of *Visions of Cody,* his own multiphasic improvisation. By 1939, Kerouac was sufficiently aware of the swing scene to have interviewed Count Basie, Lester Young, and Glenn Miller for the *Horace Mann Record.* Kerouac befriended jazz journalist Seymour Wise and producer George Avakian during his first year in New York and regularly frequented the 52nd Street clubs. Throughout this period, Kerouac was registered at Columbia University and lived in proximity to the new music as it was developing in Harlem. In "The Origins of the Beat Generation," Kerouac recalls visiting "the old Minton's Playhouse" in 1940 when "Young, Ben Webster, Joey Guy, [and] Charlie Christian" (*GB* 60) were experimenting with bebop motifs alongside their then unknown younger col-leagues. With the February 1945 release of Parker and Gillespie's "Groovin' High," underpinned by Slam Stewart and Cozy Cole's anachronistic pulse, followed in November by the frenetic "Ko-Ko," with an authentic bop rhythm section, the new jazz mutated into recognizable style, allowing Kerouac to assimilate its lessons into his theory of Spontaneous Prose.

As witness to the instantaneous realization of form on the bandstand, Kerouac discerns new possibilities from what novelist Steve Katz speaks of as "that thrilling tension between the freedom of blowing and the imperatives of order" (qtd. in LeClair and McCaffery 223). The ethic of improvisation defeating imitation and repetition fulfills his idea of an oral prose, called "spontaneous bop prosody and original classic literature" in the dedication of *Howl.* Garnering this from Kerouac, Ginsberg notes that the "discipline comes in learning how to improvise freely, how to use rules to walk on rather than imitate from" (*Mystery* 14). Combining the demands of impulse with rigorous inquiry, bebop's high-speed registration of nuance becomes the primary Beat model, transposing the immediacy of a group art that takes place in public over an appointed duration into an individual literary act by renewing its convention of personal time controls.

In a 1951 letter to Cassady, Kerouac reports that he has begun to "re-write" *On the Road* in "my-finally-at-last-found style and hope," one that allows him to "come up with even greater complicated sentences & VISIONS." Comparing his new technique to that employed by a major bop innovator ("So from now on just call me Lee Konitz"), Kerouac emphasizes the spoken basis of his new poetics by recommending that Cassady "try reading" the enclosed "three now-typed up-revised pages" of the book "on your tape, slowly," adding that "I already made a tape of jazz writing at Newman's back room" (*SL, I* 326–27). As Kerouac tells Alfred Kazin, his New School teacher and "leading American critic in the middle of my energy and delight in American literature," three years later, the stress is on bodily response without need for correction: "I've invented a new prose, Modern Prose, jazzlike, breathlessly swift spontaneous and unrevised floods. . . . [I]t comes out wild, at least it comes out pure, it comes out and reads like butter" (*SL, I* 449).

The pressure on bop improvisers to turn it on at call is also echoed within Kerouac's proposals. "As for my regular English verse, I knocked it off fast like the prose," he indicates to Ted Berrigan, "just as a . . . jazz musician has to get out . . . his statement within a certain number of bars, within one chorus, which spills over into the next, but he has to stop where the chorus page *stops*" (Berrigan 116). Bop structures translate into "blowing phrases," the length of breath comprising the measure to link with Olson's emphasis on "the HEAD, by way of the EAR, to the SYLLABLE / the HEART, by way of the BREATH, to the LINE" as energy in language (*Collected* 242). Kerouac is asked about this in the same interview:

> Yes, jazz and bop, in the sense of say, a tenor man drawing a breath and blowing a phrase on his saxophone, till he runs out of breath, and when he does, his sentence, his statement's been made. . . . [T]hat's how I therefore separate my sentences, as breath separations of the mind. . . . I formulated the theory of breath as measure, in prose and verse, never mind what Olson, Charles Olson says, I formulated that theory in 1953 at the request of Burroughs and Ginsberg. Then there's the raciness and freedom and humor of jazz instead of all that dreary analysis. (Berrigan 116)

Such an analogy clarifies the relationship between language and the unconscious in his writing, a predetermined arrangement rendered by choice balanced against the free play of imagination, which admits the possibility of noncoherence. Kerouac's recourse to nonverbal signs deliberately problematizes the dominance over selection of materials traditionally enjoyed by writers. "[I]n describing the stormy sea in *Desolation Angels*," he maintains, "I heard the sound 'Peligroso' for 'Peligroso Roar' without knowing what it meant, wrote it down involuntarily, later found out it means 'dangerous' in Spanish" (*GB* 177). Rather than straining to assert precise correlations of sound and meaning, such gestures permit vague descriptions of experience merely in terms of probability.

As with any genuinely investigative confession, the chance occurrences of mind and the conversations sustained through *Visions of Cody* include exposure to vulnerability ("What a man most wishes to hide, revise and un-say, is precisely what Literature is waiting and bleeding for" [*GB* 49]). Byronesque uses of humor, in addition, serve not only to undermine the causal binding of conventional narratives but also to work as a survival technique beyond tactics of diversion. Transcending Kerouac's later bouts of alcoholic self-pity and the constraint of identity by custom, parody features to identify and transgress limits. Forms are invented to coincide with given values, blurring or eliminating evaluative parameters in a spirit of Blakean excess and shattering orthodox continuities. As the admiring and playful nods to bop heroes such as Charlie Parker (with his "Irish St Patrick patootle stick" [*MCB* 242]), Lester Young ("droopy porkpied hung his horn"), Billie Holiday ("had rocks in her heart"), and Lionel Hampton ("would jump in the audience and whale his saxophone at everybody with sweat, claps, jumping fools in the aisles" [*GB* 113–18]) suggest, Kerouac's use of comic description displays a further debt to jazz.

A defining element of the music from its ragtime evolution, the parodic tendency is especially pronounced in bebop, most notably in Dizzy Gillespie's persona of scornful superiority removed from the "mugging" of Armstrong's generation, and in Parker's practice of inserting unlikely quotations in solos. The countless performances that conclude with four-bar recitations of Percy Grainger's "English Country Garden," the most incongruous of all tagged onto his poignant 1951 reading of "Lover Man," have little to do with traditional patterns of rhetoric but serve to enforce duplicity and disjunction—a trait of traditional Buddhist musical styles, too. During a growth period in the struggle for civil rights, such mockeries of expectation blast away the gratification of what was inevitably a mainly white audience, the effectiveness of which, like a Lenny Bruce routine, depends upon familiarity with the subject under attack.

Reflecting the content of Robert Frank's film *Pull My Daisy*, with screenplay and narration by Kerouac, the verbal "goof" play in *Cody* draws the characters into a related sense of chaos and liberation, an ecstatic tomfoolery that in this case carries no evident ideological message. This would be taken further in 1964 by the novelist Ken Kesey, who, inspired by *On the Road,* set out to explore the potential of consciousness-altering psychedelics in order to create a community of ecstasy, revolt, and social change. With Cassady again deployed as Dionysian protagonist, Kesey assumed that the practical joking of his followers, the "Merry Pranksters"—the medieval connotation in itself invoked the Lord of Misrule—would work toward mystic mobility and vigor rather than repetition and stasis (Mottram, *Blood* 214).

However, as Bruce's act and such novels as *One Flew over the Cuckoo's Nest* demonstrate, the comic effect of the absurd and gratuitous takes on a simultaneous function as a critique of the role of language in American mass society, in the service of such genocidal atrocities as war in the Far East and the dropping of atomic bombs. A parallel can be drawn to Dada activity, which countered the official propaganda of World War I by dismantling received codes, engaging in free play with existing signs, and creating new ones without anterior meaning in order to reveal the political basis of commonsense reasoning (Cowley 197–98). Taking ideology as the total function of language and meaning in a cultural context, Kerouac's conscious or tacit use of bop, Dada, and Zen strategies throughout the Legend renders the concept of truth through language elusive.

Taking his cues from jazz, Kerouac thus moves within a range of mid-century transgressions of certainty or fixed performance in art, embracing abstract expressionism, Burroughs and Gysin's hacking and splicing of sonic and visual materials, and Cage's use of the prepared piano alongside composition by *I Ching,* Taoist patterning, or coin tossing. "We are merely facilitating processes," declares Cage of his collaboration with choreographer Merce Cunningham, "so that anything can happen" (*Writer* 92). Kerouac similarly chooses procedures of indeterminacy to release the self from conscious identity and style via linguistic play. "Anything goes," he learns from Rabelais. "One point of reference (as in relativity science) is as true as another, and go to it. *Take liberties* with your art" (*SL, I* 205). In the case of his *Blues* poems, linear sense is disrupted by the given strictures of the writing act itself, which, corresponding to the ongoing nature of the twelve-bar form, shapes the statement:

> In my system, the form of blues choruses is limited by the small page of the breastpocket notebook in which they are written, like the form of a set number of bars in a jazz blues chorus, and so sometimes the word-meaning can carry from one chorus into another, or not, just like the phrase-meaning can carry harmonically from one chorus to the other, or not, in jazz, so that, in these blues as in jazz, the form is determined by time, and by the musician's spontaneous phrasing &

harmonizing with the beat of the time as it waves & waves on by in measured choruses.

It's all gotta be non stop ad libbing within each chorus, or the gig is shot. (*BB* 1)

In *Desolation Angels,* a dictionary is selected as a program external to personality as a means of fracturing habit in composition—a variant of the lipogram used in avant-garde literature both ancient (from sixth century BC, according to George Perec) and modern. Having slowed and then dissolved the linear processes binding the self within an oral-visual sign pattern, before moving into triangulated shapes and handwritten notation ("come, now, children, wake up—come, now is the time, wake up—. . . WHO WRITES WRONG ON THE WHO THE WHY THE WHAT WAIT O THING I I I I I I I I I I I I I O MODIIGRAGA NA PA RA TO MA NI CO SA PA RI MA TO MA NA PA SHOOOOOOO BIZA RIIII————" [79]), Kerouac works alphabetically between the words "black" and "bleed," applying given semantic definitions as "jewel centers" for improvisation prior to casting them adrift and rerouting them inwardly over the nodes of memory, "blowing (as per jazz musician) on subject of image" (*GB* 69):

Sword etc., flat part of an oar or calamity, sudden vio-dashing young fellow, lent gust of wind; forcible stream of leaf, air, blare of a trumpet or horn, blamable deserving of Explosion as of gunpowder, blame, find fault with Blight; censure, Imputation of a blatant Brawling noisy, Speak ill, blaze, Burn with a blameful meriting flame, send forth a flaming light, less, without blame innocent, torch, firebrand, stream of blame-lessly blameless flame of light, bursting out, actless . . . (*DA* 80)

Even a breakdown in the recall of memory can serve as a spur to the act of writing, as *Old Angel Midnight*'s metacommentary testifies:

Ah Angel Midnightmare—
Ah Crack Jabberwack, play piano, paint, pop your pile anum coitus semenized olium o hell what's his biblical name, the pot that spilt in the room ere Sarad had hers, ad her share, the name, the word, for mastur-bators, the Neptune o YA you know the name, the Bible Keen Mexican yowl that old tree still hangs in the same moonlight—Ilium, Anum, Ard Bar, Arnum, Odium, Odious, *ONAN!* ONAN KERAQUACK go heal yr own toiletbowl, stop dropping shavings in mine, & leave my grave unsung, my death unlearn, my qualities you can have, but onanist no quarter given you Angel Midnight by in that holy gallows of the moon! (29)

Such an exercise fulfills the opening injunction of *Doctor Sax*:

The other night I had a dream that I was sitting on the sidewalk on Moody Street, Pawtucketville, Lowell, Mass., with a pencil in my hand saying to myself "Describe the wrinkly tar of this sidewalk, also the iron pickets of Textile Institute, or the doorway where Lousy and you and G. J.'s always sittin and dont stop to think of words when you do stop, just stop to think of the picture better—and let your mind off yourself in this work." (7)

Of course, Kerouac's generation of text through leitmotif, dreams, and the nonrational has many significant precursors. At the end of the nineteenth century, William James and Gertrude Stein both experimented with automatic writing as a means of working out the act of composition prior to the senses, with minimum conscious intercession. Emerson's essay "Self-Reliance" also located the "American Sublime" within a section entitled "Spontaneity or Instinct," which he described as "the essence of genius, of virtue, and of life . . . that deep force, the last fact behind which analysts cannot go" (185). And in the 1920s, Breton's surrealist manifestos and his sense of "total revolt" prefigured many of Kerouac's imperatives and even his use of symbolism, directly associating the surreal with the spontaneous. If its restriction of creativity to a taxonomy common to schools or movements is discarded, then Breton's "Secrets of the Magical Surrealist Art: written Surrealist composition or first and last draft" anticipates Kerouac's recommendations in "Essentials of Spontaneous Prose" for maximizing the "receptive" condition of mind for the written undertaking:

> Forget about your genius, your talents, and the talents of everyone else. Keep reminding yourself that literature is one of the saddest roads that leads to everything. Write quickly, without any preconceived subject, fast enough so that you will not remember what you're writing and be tempted to reread what you have written. The first sentence will come spontaneously, so compelling is the truth that with every passing second there is a sentence unknown to our consciousness which is only crying out to be heard. . . . The fact still remains that punctuation no doubt resists the absolute continuity of the flow with which we are concerned, although it may seem as necessary to the arrangement of knots in a vibrating cord. Go on as long as you like. Put your trust in the inexhaustible nature of the murmur. (29–30)

This can be placed against Kerouac's painterly sense of "sketching language" in "Essentials of Spontaneous Prose" and a 1952 letter to Ginsberg where he credits further significant predecessors:

Sketching (Ed White casually mentioned it in 124th Chinese Restaurant near Columbia, "Why don't you just sketch in the streets like a painter but with words") which I did. . . . everything activates in front of you in myriad profusion, you just have to purify your mind and let it pour the words (which effortless angels of the vision fly when you stand in front of reality) and write with 100% personal honesty both psychic and social etc. and slap it all down shameless, willynilly, rapidly until sometimes I got so inspired I lost consciousness I was writing. Traditional source: Yeats' trance writing, of course. It's the *only way to write.* I haven't sketched in a long time now and have to start again because you get better with practice. . . . I think the greatest line in *On the Road* . . . is "The charging restless mute unvoiced road keening in a seizure of tarpaulin power." . . . It will take 50 years for people to realize that that's a road. In fact I distinctly remember hovering over the word "tarpaulin." . . . Do you understand Blake? Dickinson? and Shakespeare when he wants to mouth the general sound of doom, "peaked, like John a Dreams" . . . simply does what he hears . . . "greasy Joan doth keel the pot (and birds sit brooding in the snow)." (*SL, I* 356–57)

Kerouac later adds: "In another sense spontaneous, or ad lib, artistic writing imitates as best it can the flow of the mind as it moves in spacetime continuum. . . . To break through the barrier of language with WORDS, you have to be in orbit around your mind" (*GB* 176–77). Echoing Breton's belief in primitive revelation through automatist expressions of "the Marvelous," as found in the dream transcripts of *Les Champs Magnétiques Littérature,* Kerouac's prose is redolent not of untutored self-promotion but of a desire to free observation and orality from the limitations of logic. From "Essentials of Spontaneous Prose":

Shakespearian stress of dramatic need to speak now in own unalterable way or forever hold tongue . . . (*GB* 70)

And "Belief & Technique for Modern Prose":

12. In tranced fixation dreaming upon object before you
13. Remove literary, grammatical and syntactical inhibition
14. Like Proust be an old teahead of time
15. Telling the true story of the world in interior monolog
16. The jewel center of interest is the eye within the eye
17. Write in recollection and amazement for yourself
18. Work from pithy middle eye out, swimming in language sea
19. Accept loss forever (*GB* 72)

However, Breton's cultivation of celerity through juxtaposition differs from Kerouac's version of speed-writing: an American space of complex processes, reflecting the abstract expressionist abandonment of mythic narrative and profligate lyricism. As Kerouac asserts: "The main thing, I feel, is that urgency of explaining something has its own words and rhythm, and time is of the essence—Modern Prose" (*SL, I* 450). This steady focus enters the Legend in *On the Road,* where the term "parking lot" serves as a primer for the memory of Dean's sheer velocity, which translates into compositional technique:

> [H]e only worked like a dog in parking lots. The most fantastic park-ing-lot attendant in the world, he can back a car forty miles an hour into a tight squeeze and stop at the wall, jump out, race among fenders, leap into another car, circle it fifty miles an hour in a narrow space, back swiftly into a tight spot, *hump,* snap the car with the emergency so you see it bounce as he flies out; then clear to the ticket shack, sprinting like a track star, hand a ticket, leap into a newly arrived car before the owner's half out, leap literally under him as he steps out, start the car with the door flapping, and roar off to the next available spot, arc, pop in, brake, out, run; working like that without pause eight hours a night, evening rush hours and after-theater rush hours, in greasy wino pants with a frayed fur-lined jacket and beat shoes that flap. (12)

The passage draws its impact from the onomatopoeic use of fertile staccato words ("back," "leap," "stop"), repeated to convey Dean's erratic changes of direction. The pulse of the prose then drives a rapid succession of image-statements as they shoot, collide, and amass vertically in the mind. This is witnessed again in the kinesthetic descriptions of the bakery and Hector's Cafeteria in *Visions of Cody* and in the pastoral memory flash of *Old Angel Midnight*:

> The Mill Valley trees, the pines with green mint look and there's a tangled eucalyptus hulk stick fallen thru the late sunlight tangle of those needles, hanging from it like a live wire connecting it to the ground—just below, the notches where little Fred sought to fell sad pine—not bleeding much—just a lot of crystal sap the ants are mining in, motionless like cows on the grass . . . (8)

As distinct from surrealism, what Kerouac variously describes as "sketch-ing," "bop prosody," "free prose," and "wild form" through "infantile pileup of scatological buildup" implies neither allegiance to Freudian programme nor surrender of creative controls but a willingness to experiment beyond the rationalist drives of socialization. What emerges is an American diction receptive to the flow of indomitable involuntary thoughts, flush with the actual movement of things awaiting release: an act of attention to the dynamic "self-existence" of events without impediments of hierarchy, classification, or comparison. Whereas Cassady thinks of this as "eyeballing," Olson defines it as "unselectedness" in "Human Universe": "For any of us, at any instant, are juxtaposed to any experience, even an overwhelming single one, on several more planes than the arbitrary and discursive which we inherit can declare" (*Collected* 160).

In the "176th Chorus" of *Mexico City Blues,* Kerouac identifies "my clever brain" as the primary threat to observation: "The reason why there are so many things / Is because the mind breaks it up." His "struggle to sketch the flow that already exists intact in mind" and confer "the [Bookmovie] in words, the visual American form" (*GB* 72–73), is resolved by the methodology devised for *On the Road* of a single paragraph engineered from memory. Crucially, this discovery coincides with his reading of Dwight Goddard's anthology, *A Buddhist Bible,* and his attendance of Daisetz Suzuki's lectures at the New School in 1953. Initially finding support in Christ's counsel to his disciples in Mark 13:11 to "[t]ake no thought beforehand what ye shall speak, neither do ye premeditate; but whatsoever shall be given you in that hour, that speak ye: for it is not ye that speak, but the Holy Ghost" (qtd. in *GB* 176), Kerouac gleans the imperative of unselfconsciousness as preparation for writing, a means of breaking what Williams calls the "complicated ritualistic forms designed to separate the work from reality" (*Imaginations* 102).

Suzuki's description of the receptive, flexible mind cultivated by the archer in *Zen and Japanese Culture* complements bop's embodiment of immediacy, an active attentiveness from great facility leading to mind before language. The sensuality of *On the Road* merges with Buddhist discipline, compared in Kerouac's poem "How to Meditate" to "instantaneous / ecstasy like a shot of heroin or morphine" (*SP* 27). Situated within a place of nonconceptualization, the skilled improviser aims for the existential fault line or white-heat point, a prosthetics of the body-mind inside an occasion that, as Kerouac understands it, applies as much to writing, painting, and bop as to football, erotics, and comedy. Kerouac's quotation of the *Surangama Sutra* in "The First Word" draws a definitive analogy:

> Gotama Buddha says, "If you are now desirous of more perfectly understanding Supreme Enlightenment, you must learn to answer spontaneously and with no recourse to discriminate thinking. For the Tathagatas (the passers-through) in the ten quarters of the universes, because of the straight-forwardness of their minds and the spontaneity of their mentations, have ever remained, from beginning time to end-

less time, of one pure Suchness with the enlightening nature of pure Mind Essence." (*GB* 175–76)

Only when, as LeRoi Jones notes, Kerouac

> encounters lags in his insight or spontaneity . . . he is duped, when he tries painstakingly and often painfully to conjure intellectually . . . and writes these conjurings down (instead of what they are supposed to conjure) . . . his prose becomes stiff, awkward and *untrue*. Intellectual conjuring has nothing to do with the creative act as such, though it may certainly be concomitant with it. ("Letter about Kerouac's Spontaneous Prose" 349)

This illuminates Kerouac's rejection of "craftiness" as neoclassical falsification and his demand for a projective act of nerve concomitant with the "now" that leaves conscious validation behind: "[T]ap from yourself the song of yourself, *blow!—now!—your* way is your only way—'good'—or 'bad'—always honest. ('ludicrous') spontaneous, 'confessional' interesting, because not 'crafted.' Craft *is* craft" (*GB* 70). As he tells Robert Giroux:

> [C]ritics have failed to realize that spontaneous writing of narrative prose is infinitely more difficult than careful slow painstaking writing with opportunities to revise—Because spontaneous writing is an ordeal requiring immediate discipline—They seem to think there's no discipline involved— (*SL, II* 325).

This, too, is the great lesson of jazz, outlined by pianist Bill Evans on the notes for Miles Davis's *Kind of Blue*:

> There is a Japanese visual art in which the artist is forced to be spontaneous. He must paint on a thin stretched parchment with a special brush and black water paint in such a way that an unnatural or interrupted stroke will destroy the line or break through the parchment. Erasures or changes are impossible. These artists must practice a particular discipline, that of allowing the idea to express itself in communication with their hands in such a direct way that deliberation cannot interfere. The resulting pictures lack the complex composition and textures of ordinary painting, but it is said that those who see will find something captured that escapes explanation. This conviction that direct deed is the most meaningful reflection, I believe, has prompted the evolution of the extremely severe and unique disciplines of the jazz or improvising musician.

Echoing Whitman's old-age ambitions at Camden ("I don't want beautiful results—I want results: honest results: expression, expression" [*Complete Poems*

784]), a gap closes between the discovery of experience, the impromptu movement from within, and the description of meaning or retrospective definition
from without. To Creeley, the duration taken to compose a poem becomes

> literally the time it takes to type or otherwise write it—because I *do* work
> in this fashion of simply sitting down and writing, usually without any
> process of revision. So that if it goes—or, rather, comes—in an opening
> way, it continues till it closes, and that's usually when I stop. (qtd. in
> Wagner and MacAdams 88)

And as Kerouac affirms: "By not revising what you've already written you
simply give the reader the actual workings of your mind during the writing
itself: you confess your thoughts about events in your own unchangeable
way" (qtd. in Berrigan 100–101).

Struggling to sustain the adaptive reflex within the more conventional
narratives of *On the Road, The Subterraneans,* and *The Dharma Bums,*
Kerouac retains low-pitched "passing" paragraphs, giving an uneven vacil-
lation that alongside the discovery of *Visions of Cody*'s extended "wild form"
is resolved most convincingly in the novella or excerpt structures of "October
in the Railroad Earth" and *Old Angel Midnight.* Jones cites the passage in
*Road* where the narrator, Dean, and their friends depart for the West from
Old Bull's house in Louisiana as an example of Kerouac's recourse to "intellectual conjuring": "What is that feeling when you're driving away from
people and they recede on the plain till you see their specks dispersing?—it's
the too-huge world vaulting us, and it's good-bye. But we lean forward to the
next crazy venture beneath the skies" (148)—the point of transition to "true"
poetry, contends Jones: "After the first *primer* sentence ('the scatological
build up'), he reaches the key word and jewel center of this association and
he is off and 'unconscious'" ("Letter about Kerouac's Spontaneous Prose"
350). The ground for "trance" writing "without consciousness" has been
prepared, and the journey can begin:

> We wheeled through the sultry old light of Algiers, back on the ferry,
> back toward the mud-splashed, crabbed old ships across the river, back
> on Canal, and out; on a two-lane highway to Baton Rouge in purple
> darkness; swung west there, crossed the Mississippi at a place called
> Port Allen. Port Allen—where the river's all rain and roses in a misty
> pinpoint darkness and where we swung around a circular drive in
> yellow foglight and suddenly saw the great black body below a bridge
> and crossed eternity again. (*OTR* 148)

Here the "riff" or obligato device in jazz, a rhythmic trigger repeated
with subtle variations over a chord sequence and used in call and response

exchanges between improviser and ensemble, is analogous to Kerouac's sense of "jewel center." Tailored for the jam session and formalized by Count Basie, riff-based improvisation was the definitive element of 1930s Kansas style, stimulating the kind of heated tenor sax trade-off that drives Dean frantic in *On the Road*. In the passage cited, the reiteration of "back" creates a momentum analogous to a soloist's rhetorical evocation of tension prior to slowing down into a cadence: "the great black body below a bridge and crossed eternity again"—a mark of Kerouac's desire for a vocabulary of security that accelerates through the Legend. Recalling Lester Young's signature use of "false fingering" to vary pitch quality over a single note with each repetition, this approach is sustained through a percussive phrase ("Port Allen") in counterpoint to the dominant pulse before releasing pent-up energies upon rejoining the ascendant line. Kerouac's prose admits Young's exhilaration of pace with sound reinforcing sense by alliteration and assonance, forcing the mind back to the key word "wheeled."

This is equally suggestive of what Deleuze and Guattari call a "refrain" or *ritournelle* ("little return"), defined as a rhythmic pattern that fixes stability in the heart of chaos (a child in the dark humming a tune for comfort) (*Thousand* 310). The refrain is an adventure with a playful "catalytic function," a temporary architecture enabling the emergence of the new from existing circumstances. The repetitive "pull" of the refrain does more than reinforce the dominant tempo; it invites other perspectives by inventive flourishes and improvisations and also by silent reference to the developments that are blocked off by the need to return to the "round"—or movements that one is "refrained from" by the refrain.

Crucially, the refrain lies not at a point of musical origin but rather at its middle. It is a place of established patterns, which nevertheless give an opening to surprising encounters, as with Lester Young's courting of the unexpected, the unusual, the enchanting. In Kerouac's prose, the riff or refrain inspires a similar meeting of energies as phrases rush together, transgressing full-stop cut-off points. The effect is sonata-like, with cells moved around and repeated under skilled handling of pressure.

The next section employs variations in timbre and the obligato ("down along") with even greater dramatic effect, regathering the forward propulsion with breath commas. Amplifying the litanous rhetoric of Whitman and Twain, the question "What is the Mississippi River?" is used as "jewel center" to provoke exalted discharge:

> a washed clod in the rainy night, a soft plopping from drooping Missouri banks, a dissolving, a riding of the tide down the eternal waterbed, a contribution to brown foams, a voyaging past endless vales and

trees and levees, down along, down along, by Memphis, Greenville, Eudora, Vicksburg, Natchez, Port Allen, and Port Orleans and Port of the Deltas, by Potash, Venice, and the Night's Great Gulf, and out. (*OTR* 148)

Precisely because Kerouac sheds consensus orders of syntax, his "free prose," like Coleman's *Free Jazz,* demands attention to compositional planning beyond meeting the burdens of standard paragraphed form or, in Coleman's case, the given frameworks for extemporization. The condition of surprise supplants an orthodox language geared toward habitual responses, the recognition of which, according to Litweiler, is embodied in the saxophonist's late-1950s playing:

> The organization of these Coleman solos makes clear that uncertainty is the content of life, and even things that we take for certainties (such as his cell motives) are ever altering shape and character. By turns he fears or embraces this ambiguity; but he constantly faces it, and by his example, he condemns those who seek resolution or finality as timid. (39)

The suggestion here is that the skills of the post-bop musician reflect the need for flexibility and immediacy in the survival strategies adopted by African Americans, given the part played by the unknown and extreme in their lives. The narratives of jazz are not deterministic structures but a state of mind, preparations for dealing with constant change. Similarly, as Sukenick points out, the Bohemian tradition stemming from responses to industrialism in 1830s Paris, to which Kerouac ambivalently subscribes,

> endures its changes precisely because it is not the result of a willed strategy, but responds to an unchanging antagonism between the way of life imposed by our pragmatic business society and the humanistic values by which our culture has taught us to experience and judge the quality of our individual and collective lives. (5–6)

In *Visions of Cody,* Kerouac adopts the vanguard jazz soloist's attitude that anything can happen, the Dionysian flux of Pomeroy energizing the text into any shape necessary. The novel thus presents a kind of coherence that exists by virtue of its unpredictability, obliterating tendencies to solidify into identifiable styles and concerns. Recalling the orientation of *Free Jazz* and Pollock's "all-over" paintings, its "structure [is] possessed of its own organisation [which] in turn derives from the circumstances of its making"—Creeley's sense of the twentieth-century imperative of form following function (qtd. in Olson, *Selected Writings* 7). With given coordinates of presentation rejected, along with preemptive scaffolding and obligatory lineation, the appearance of the writing is necessarily unfinished, or even ragged with inconsistencies. As with Coleman's work, the ongoing process of construction remains omnipresent. Kerouac reports his intentions:

> I got sick and tired of the conventional English sentence which seemed to me to be so ironbound in its rules, so inadmissible with reference to the actual format of my mind as I had learned to probe it in the modern spirit of Freud and Jung, that I couldn't express myself through that form any more. . . . Shame seems to be the key to repression in writing as well as in psychological malady. If you don't stick to what you first thought, and to the words the thought brought, what's the sense of bothering with it anyway, what's the sense of foisting your little lies on others? What I find to be really "stupefying in its unreadability" is this laborious and dreary lying called craft and revision by writers, and certainly recognized by sharpest psychologists as sheer blockage of the mental spontaneous process known 2,500 years ago as "The Seven Streams of Swiftness." (*GB* 145)

In *Desolation Angels,* Kerouac writes of an alternative set of regulations for arranging his materials: "There's a certain amount of control going on [in my writing] like a man telling a story in a bar without interruptions or even one pause" (280). However, as the alternative takes of Parker's studio recordings illustrate, improvisation need not discount revision, which, in defiance of the standardization drives of the book trade, retrieves essential control over authorship. In the case of *Cody,* published posthumously in 1973 after Kerouac's own amendments, re-composition becomes the means of redressing commercial intrusion by *Road*'s editors. And while his prose reads with an impromptu sense consistent with his aesthetic claims, there is much evidence of alteration in Kerouac's manuscripts. As he tells Charles Sampas, *The Scripture of the Golden Eternity* was written "[i]n pencil, carefully revised and everything, because it was a scripture. I had no right to be spontaneous" (*SL, II* 19).

As already suggested, a principle of revision and overlay makes up the axis of the Legend as a whole—as in *Desolation Angels*' "[d]reams of a kid and this whole world is nothing but a big sleep made of reawakened material (soon to reawake)" (65)—with each novel a reconstruction at a new pitch of autobiographical material previously documented. The proximity to jazz is reiterated in this process of telling and retelling, which surges out of the emotion carried in familiar phrase shapes, such as *Cody*'s melancholy repetitions of "enormity of my soul," "earth of labor and sorrow," "heady dark," "rainy night," and "unutterably sad." These converge with the hoisting of bop lines above familiar chord progressions, vehicles for the regeneration of the new, subjected to perpetual reassessment and reforged in many directions over several years. As Ralph Ellison explains:

> Each true jazz moment (as distinct from the uninspired commercial performance) springs from a contest in which each artist challenges all the rest; each solo flight, or improvisation, represents (like the successive canvases of a painter) a definition of his identity: as individual, as member of the collectivity and as a link in the chain of tradition. Thus, because jazz finds its very life in an endless improvisation upon traditional materials, the jazz-man must lose his identity even as he finds it— (234)

The methodology of Spontaneous Prose similarly denotes what Weinreich calls a "double movement in the act of composition" (118), a serial multiplication of self that synchronizes advancement and reiteration of past experience in the process of being recorded. At the provisional end of *Pic*, for instance (removed at the behest of Kerouac's mother), the two black brothers stand by the road with their thumbs out, attracting the attentions of two older travelers named Dean Moriarty and Sal Paradise who give them a ride—a convolution worthy of *Don Quixote*. Revision also becomes a thematic issue in part 3 of *On the Road*, where the third transcontinental car journey consists only of revisits except, significantly, for the automobile town of Detroit (Ellis 42). The narrative stands as both commentary on the modus operandi of the Legend and prophecy for the refreshment of authorial strategy, as Sal discerns "flashing by outside several scenes that I remembered from 1947":

> All that old road of the past unreeling dizzily as if the cup of life had been overturned and everything gone mad. My eyes ached in nightmare day. . . . Great horrors that we were going to crash . . . took hold of me. . . . [N]ow I could feel the road some twenty inches beneath me, unfurling and flying and hissing at incredible speeds across the groaning continent. (220–21)

Kerouac renders this metaphor explicit in *Desolation Angels*, through saxophonist Brue Moore's discovery in music of "that pure message to give to the world" and Moore's need "to carry the message along for several chorus-chapters, his ideas get tireder than at first, he does give up at the right time—besides he wants to play a new tune—I do just that, tap him on the shoe-top to acknowledge he's right" (226–27). The result in both fields is a parallel structure of circular or vertical recapitulation and horizontal progression, a mandala pattern that Kerouac calls "Eternal Recurrence": "a story / not a philosophy, / & stories last forever" (*SL, II* 245). By implication, performance possibilities are multiple. Analogous to Charles Mingus's commitment to his Jazz Workshop, a group in perpetual rehearsal, the anguished search for perfectibility in completion evaporates with no single interpretation designated authoritative. The Legend's tiered approach to recall extends beyond previous points of abandonment in a tireless process of rewriting, a conscious echo of Joyce's attempt to render antiquity contemporaneous with the present and the essence of Kerouac's definition of "Beat":

> It's *béat,* it's the beat to keep, it's the beat of the heart, it's being beat and down in the world and like oldtime lowdown and like in ancient civilizations the slave boatmen rowing galleys to a beat and servants spinning pottery to a beat. (*DA* 151)

The revelation from Kerouac's letters that *On the Road* and *Visions of Cody* are the same book only reinforces the significance of his desire to advance multiple techniques simultaneously, a practice mirrored in the visual arts by Picasso's interwar portraiture and by de Kooning's *Women,* where subjects are continually reworked in many styles to explore the possibilities of presentation. The emergence of jazz as a resource for fictive memory in *Road* presents yet further potentials that are fully realized in *Cody* and *Desolation Angels.* Warren Tallman identifies the function of Kerouac's musical correspondences in his essay "Kerouac's Sound," aligning *The Town and the City*'s narrative with the sentimental linearity of 1930s swing, as compared to *On the Road*'s incursion into bebop, "where the sounds become BIFF, BOFF, BLIP, BLEEP, BOP, BEEP, CLINCK, ZOWIE! Sounds break up, and are replaced by other sounds. The journey is NOW. The narrative is a Humpty Dumpty heap. Such is the condition of NOW" (Tallman 70).

Tallman invokes a bebop impetus, which permits longer and more rhythmically complex lines than the rigid "stride" accents of earlier styles, a facet reflected in the extended measures of Parker and Kerouac. The latter's observation of the treatment of a standard in "The Beginning of Bop" runs close to Parker's own explanation of his breakthrough in phrasing the higher intervals of a chord over the changes of "Cherokee" and gives further insight into the processes of his own writing:

> The tune they were playing was *All the Things You Are* . . . they slowed it down and dragged behind it at half tempo dinosaur proportions— changed the placing of the note in the middle of the harmony to an outer more precarious position where also its sense of not belonging was enhanced by the general atonality produced with everyone exteriorizing the tune's harmony. (*GB* 115–16)

Considered in the light of Kerouac's own spoken-voice recordings, phrases such as "Lee, who wouldn't talk to me even if he knew me" from *Cody* (40) and "The rooftop of the beatup / tenement" from the "4th Chorus" of "San Francisco Blues" jettison the monotonous sense of foot associated with the iambic pentameter—Cleanth Brooks's closed "pattern of resolved stresses" (203) and the first test of conservativism in English poetry—and advocate a choppy, refractive bebop measure. As drummer-poet Clark Coolidge suggests, the tendency of percussionists such as Roy Porter and Max Roach to shut down a phrase with a hard crack-stop across surprise beats on tracks such as "Ko-Ko" and "Ornithology" also contributes to Kerouac's notations, as described in *Book of Dreams*: "Robert Whitmore my buddy on the SS Carruth is showing me how he describes an apartment building when he writes, 'the wander wada rada rall a gonna gay, *Zack*!' the flow of words and the releasing bop-sound of at the end of a prose rhythm paragraph" (101).

The onomatopoeic bop gesture surfaces again in *Old Angel Midnight* to end a section of unwinding disconnected syntax with characteristic suddenness: "He thinks I'm competitive in a long pleasant souse of Wishing all of ye bleed stay meditation everybody martini destroy my black" (6). The nonstop, unrevised feel of the prose in *The Subterraneans,* written in three Benzedrine-assisted nights in October 1953, also renders the bop influence conscious and paramount. The evocation of a San Francisco nightclub with Parker radiating at its center builds, as John Tytell suggests, "on improvised digressions as jazz does, using what blues players call 'landmarks,' repeated images that help to unify, and 'scat calling,' using the voice as an instrument" (199):

> . . . and up on the stand Bird Parker with solemn eyes who'd been busted fairly recently and had now returned to a kind of bop dead Frisco but had just discovered or been told about the Red Drum, the great new generation gang wailing and gathering there, so here he was on the stand, examining them with his eyes as he blew his now-settled-down-into-regulated-design "crazy" notes—the booming drums, the high ceiling. . . . I saw [Bird] distinctly digging Mardou several times also myself directly into my eye looking to search if really I was that great writer I thought myself to be as if he knew my thoughts and ambitions or remembered me from other night clubs and other coasts, other Chicagos—not a challenging look but the king and founder of the bop generation at least the sound of it in digging his audience digging the eyes, the secret eyes him-watching, as he just pursed his lips and let great lungs and immortal fingers work, his eyes separate and interested and humane, the kindest jazz musician there could be while being and therefore naturally the greatest— (*SU* 13–14)

"Whistling [everybody] onto the brink of eternity" in *Mexico City Blues* and a chief progenitor of "IT" throughout the Legend, Parker is perceived by Kerouac in terms of mutual fascination, the jazzman reflecting the writer in an imagined correspondence of mind. Complementing his own writing process, from "'crazy' notes" to a narrative "now-settled-down-into-regulated-design," Kerouac gleans transferable techniques from Parker for mapping mental fluctuations over time in minute detail. In particular, his erratic changes of direction mid-solo, re-starts, and variations of impetus suggest an elliptical "plateau," an eternal middle forgoing the expenditure of ecstasy in singular climax and dissipation. The ability to combine circumstances and bring group activity to an intense fabric that flares for an instant inspires Kerouac's disconnection from systematized chronology ("Time stops") and his subsequent awareness that "[n]othing is muddy that *runs in time* and to laws of *time*" (*GB* 70). From *On the Road*:

> "Now, man, that alto man last night had IT—he held it once he found it; I've never seen a guy who could hold so long." I wanted to know what "IT" meant. "Ah well"—Dean laughed—"now you're asking me impon-de-rables—ahem! Here's a guy and everybody's there, right? Up to him to put down what's on everybody's mind . . . and then he rises to his fate and has to blow equal to it. All of a sudden somewhere in the middle of the chorus he *gets it*—everybody looks up and knows; they listen; he picks it up and carries. Time stops. . . ." Dean could go no further; he was sweating telling about it. (194)

Taking this logic further, the transition from bop to free improvisation could be seen to parallel Kerouac's progression from *Road* to *Cody,* the bowdlerized publication of which coincided with the release of *Free Jazz* in 1961. In his analysis of early Coleman recordings, Litweiler maintains that "as the faint, lingering shadow of chorus structures disappears, classic narrative form . . . becomes irrelevant. That's because music with a beginning, middle, and end imposes the structure of fiction on the passage of life, says Coleman implicitly" (39). Assuming that Litweiler's prototype of fiction refers exclusively to realist models, this observation doubles as commentary on Kerouac's adventurous reinvigoration of form and recalls Pollock's assertion over his control of the flow of paint: "[T]here is no accident, just as there is no beginning and no end" (Robertson 194).

In addition to Olson's sense of "composition by field" determined by content alone, "as opposed to inherited line, stanza, over-all form, what is the 'old' base of the non-projective" (*Collected* 239), the switching pulse pursued by Coleman's groups at this time defies any regulation of strong and weak beats to permit, in effect, the same plasticity of line marking *Visions of Cody* and *Mexico City Blues*. Noting in 1960 that "alto players are phrasing faster and better than ever: Ornette Coleman can play exactly like Bird if he wants to but he's forged ahead to a new vision," Kerouac credits Lee Konitz, whose 1949 recordings with the Lennie Tristano Sextet were the first to be made without preset limits of key, rhythm, or duration, for having "inspired me in 1951 'to write the way he plays'" (*GB* 179), and in *Cody* suggests that "[h]e can take care of himself even though he goofs and does 'April in Paris' from inside out as if the tune was the room he lived in and was going out at midnight with his coat on" (40).[6] Konitz's comments regarding standards also reverberate against Kerouac's attitude toward his source materials:

> I feel that in improvisation, the tune should serve as a vehicle for musi-
> cal variations—and that the ultimate goal is to have as much freedom
> from the harmonic, melodic, and rhythmical restrictions of the tune
> as possible—but the tune must serve to hold the chords and variations
> together. For this reason, I have never been concerned with finding
> new tunes to play. I often feel that I could play and record the same
> tunes over and over and still come up with fresh variations. (notes for
> *Real Lee*)

Moreover, Kerouac's ability to hold divergent voices and approaches in tension mirrors a post-bop impulse rooted in the New Orleans band styles of Jelly Roll Morton, Kid Ory, and King Oliver. Here too, the heterophony of *Free Jazz* is illuminating, the effects of tonal and rhythmic freedom and the dissolution of fixed roles assisting the creation of sonic designs that John Coltrane terms "multi-directional" (notes for *Live*). Kerouac's jazz prose also "deliberately scrambles all the codes," to apply Deleuze and Guattari's terminology, "by quickly shifting from one to another, according to the questions asked him, never invoking the same genealogy, never recording the same event in the same way" (*Anti-Oedipus* 67). In so doing, his narratives initiate an extensional thrust that LeRoi Jones identifies in trumpeter Cherry's noncadential contributions to Coleman's quartet: namely that "the completion of one statement simply reintroduces the possibility of more" (*Black* 170).

Volatile new material constantly surfaces as imagination and change secure the creative act from the void of stasis and predictability. The mind is dramatized in a generative condition of permanent emergence: the "eternal return" of Nietzsche's *Will to Power,* or what Mercea Eliade calls the "architectonic spiritual center" (110)—a topography of poetic space for the endless proliferation of forms unbounded by stable "truth." Maintaining currency with the canvases of Pollock and de Kooning, where "each stroke had to be a decision, and was answered by a new question" (Rosenberg, *Tradition* 33), Kerouac accomplishes a feat of writing that activates leaps of memory in dissociative combinations across time-space, repelling any fall in phrasal pitch that may indicate closure. From *Old Angel Midnight*:

> Lou Little explaining to the newsreel audience how this football player went mad & shows how on a Columbia Practice Hillside it started with father & son, the gray reaches of the Eternity Library beyond—I go visit my sweet Alene in her subterranean pad near the 3rd Avenue El & Henry St of old Mike Mike milkcan Ashcan Lower Eastside Dreams & pink murders & there she wont ope the door because I cant get the job I tried so hard to get & the woman said my form wasnt right but Neal made it but regretfully it is he's shipping out & I'm on the ship with with him telling him "If you wash dishes dont say a word, if you're a yeoman do yr work all well"—I can see he hates to go without me to this other Grayshore—Sitting before my stove on a cold gray Saturday morning with my coffee & my pipe, eating jello—remembering the little jello cartoon that filled me with such joy as a kid on Sarah Avenue, the little prince wouldnt take pheasant or delicate birds or celestial puddings or even Mominuan Icecream but when the little bird brought him jello inverted in a rill mold cup he went wild & saved the kingdom, red jello like mine, in the little dear lovable pages—of long ago—My form is delight delight delight. (12)

Again Parker's late performances and those of the early Coleman Quartet shed light in their tendency to dispense with "head" announcements in the rush to enter explorative action, thematic fragments and chords being accorded only the briefest acknowledgment. Kerouac's practices correspond in using given structures merely as a basis or armature, significations to be broken up and rearranged with all sorts of techniques of omission and augmentation in compositional play. The Legend then offers a collage in perpetual transition, violating expectations of cadence and measure while permitting glimpses of past forms. Like the post-bop improviser, Kerouac may choose or be forced to retreat into the arena of inherited responses (blues "licks," dance figures) "so long as he can stuff it full of all the disjunctions that this code was designed to eliminate" (Deleuze and Guattari, *Anti-Oedipus* 15). The use of self-referentiality celebrates the jazz-bricoleur's joy in artifice, absorbing the memory of episodes and forms within the Legend as well as of exterior literary resources, which are then reworked masterfully from within as a test of formal possibility.

The convergence with jazz in Kerouac's work thus extends beyond literary homage to inform the possibilities of the act of writing itself, a characteristically American rejection of prior norms and constraints made to enter the present with contemporary techniques of expression. This is wholly in keeping with comparisons of the influence of surrealist automatic writing and Dada collage on abstract expressionism and Beat writing respectively: cross-formal resources informed by the entire range of liberation concerns.

Fed by the sensory experience of the music, Kerouac calls on bop not merely as metaphor but as unmediated access to an all-encompassing euphoria, which dissolves subject and environment. Planned and spontaneous procedures are reconciled in what Robert Motherwell describes as "a dialectic between the conscious (straight lines, designed shapes, weighted colors, abstract language) and the unconscious (soft lines, obscured shapes, *automatism*)." The resolution? "A synthesis which differs as a whole from either" (qtd. in Janis 90). Under Kerouac's hand, this agency seeks transgression of civic control in form itself, a drive that brooks no refusal in giving rise to involuntary orders of energy, which range forth and spread across the Legend.

# Beyond Beat

> I hope that it is true, as Marshall McLuhan says, that the power of the arts to anticipate future social and technological developments, by a generation or more, has long been recognized; and that this concept of the arts as prophetic contrasts with the popular idea of them as mere self-expression.
> —Earle Brown, *Form in New Music*

> World needs new tendencies in poeting and paintry.
> —Kurt Schwitters

> And everybody in NY so involved in IMPOSSIBLE multiplicity
> . . .
> —Jack Kerouac, letter to Allen Ginsberg, December 1956

By the beginning of the new century, much critical comment had accumulated on the New York school of painters, a relative paucity on the city's loose alliance of composers, and less still on the poets banded together as the Black Mountain School in the seminal *New American Poetry* anthology. And while post-bop developments in jazz are seldom aired on radio, histories of the music occasionally surface but without the acknowledgment of connections to other artistic fields, part of an ongoing denigration of black art that cannot be assimilated within a generic ghetto and a sign of the cultural priorities assigned to respective forms in general.

Kerouac's fiction has fared differently, though little better. The media onslaught began with the publication of *On the Road* and continued with the 1959 Hollywood treatment of *The Subterraneans,* cleansed of the central couple's psychological ruin and miscegenation (then a crime in many southern states), and numerous cover blurbs of mass-market reprints of his books that willfully misrepresented their author: *On the Road*'s "riotous odyssey of two American drop-outs, by the drop-out who started it all" (1966), who is also depicted on the back of *The Dharma Bums* as "the man who launched the hippie world, the daddy of the swinging psychedelic generation" (1967), to cite but two examples.

This has since been intensified by a flood of biographies, fetishizing Kerouac's death by endlessly rehearsing the details of his decline into an alcoholic redneck, his sexual encounters with men, and the disgraceful neglect of his daughter, Jan. Hashed in journalistic styles that his work implicitly negates, these have been augmented by a string of hagiographies uncritically absorbed in Beat's own self-representations that recycle Kerouac's work "by reducing it to the know-nothing relaxations of a hyped body" (Mottram, "Preface" 50).

Because of the disconcerting imbalance in the pattern of Kerouac's life, not to mention his complicity in events that often he alone chronicled, consideration given to his twenty-year spell of creativity tends to be outweighed by the more salable coverage of his final decade of bitter aimlessness, a reduction of an author to a case and his work to an adjunct. Beyond the scholarship informing Ann Charters's edition of his letters and a dozen or so invaluable monographs and essays that this present book draws upon, comparatively few attempts have been made to engage critically with Kerouac's fictions.

Pitched between cult adoration and snobbish dismissal, his marginal status persists, isolated from the attention necessary to illuminate a writer outside the official focus. For as Kerouac realized by 1960, "[I]t's the Academic recognition that will really take care of me in my old age . . . NOT the temporary admiration for the wrong reasons coming from the wrong thinkers" (*SL, II* 274).[1] However, while the time-warp nostalgia of market-style now generated in his name means that Kerouac's currency has never been higher—Herbert Gold believes that the Beat filtering of Bohemia in the late 1950s effectively released lifestyle consumerism into the United States (*Bohemia* 248)—the Duluoz Legend continues to be denied the literary prestige and cultural framing that it deserves.

Kerouac sought publication in vain after the low-key response to *The Town and the City*—"I've been through every conceivable disgrace now," he complained to his agent in October 1956, "and no rejection or acceptance by publishers can alter that awful final feeling of death—of life-which-is-death" (*SL, I* 589)—but his breakthrough arrived the following September with Gilbert Millstein's designation of *On the Road* in the *New York Times* as a "historic occasion," meriting "exegesis and detailing of background." However, appreciation was far from unanimous, and the hostile die that still guides the reception of his work was rapidly cast. The refusal to entertain American literature within Lionel Trilling's canon at Columbia, or Chicago University's "Great Books" course, had long since prejudiced readers against emerging native writers. In the case of Norman Podhoretz's *Making It,* Beat styles were complacently misinterpreted in a bid to stabilize academic definitions of culture. "The plain truth," he declared in the *Partisan Review,* "is that the primitivism of the Beat Generation serves first of all as a cover for an anti-intellectualism so bitter that it makes the ordinary American's hatred of eggheads seem positively benign" (306).

By the end of the 1950s, Beat writers would be routinely subjected to the middlebrow abuse more recently reserved for painters, having followed hoods, communists, pot smokers (courtesy of the Hearst Corporation's need to protect its lumber monopolies by demonizing hemp), sexualized extraterrestrials—including Nathan Juran's *Brain from Planet Arous* ("the incredible space brain invades a human body with its destructive evil power") and *Attack of the 50 Ft. Woman* ("see a female colossus, her mountainous torso, skyscraper limbs, giant desires")—and even grasshoppers, which justified the use of lethal crop pesticides in a 1956 TV broadcast, as alien forces plotting to disrupt American life.

Vilifying Bob Kaufman, *San Francisco Chronicle* columnist Herb Caen meshed a number of national paranoias to coin the term "beatnik," the pejorative of the era, soon to be superseded by "hippie" and "student" as media symbols for juvenile delinquency and target terms for a parent generation. Whereas by 1960, Burroughs, Ferlinghetti, and Ginsberg had been prosecuted for obscenity, Elias Wilentz identified "Beat" and "Generation" as appropriations by a "commercial, predatory and murderous society," which was geared up for an assault on disaffiliation in all its manifestations:

> Ironically, the attachment of this vivid label is largely due to the double-handed efforts of *Life* and *Time* who, early in the game, picked up the "beats" as the great American rebellion of youth and our times. This they lampooned in their stylish language of rhetorical deceits. . . . The term lost any significant meanings, assuming it ever had a specific one, and broke down to a physical type—a kid with beard, rumpled clothes, sandals, bongo drum, jazz records and a copy of *Howl.* Hints of sexual immoralities and use of drugs added a perverted glamour. The "beats"—whether in Venice, California or Greenwich Village, New York—were lumped together [and] assumed mythic proportions and the Beat Generation had arrived . . . typical

for America which would rather catalogue people than attempt to understand them. (8)

Whereas Walter Ong framed Beat as the self-delusion of a "professional outsider"—the "barbarian in reverse, for he insists that he, the outsider as outsider, is the real Greek who has the integrity which the insiders or squares have sacrificed to cheap security" (*Barbarian* 283)—Podhoretz attacked Kerouac as a "barbarian," "spiritually underprivileged," and "crippled of the soul" and accused Beat writers of leading a "conspiracy to overthrow civilization and replace it with "the world of the adolescent street gang" ("Know-Nothing" 308–18). And while *Life* magazine insulted Kerouac as "the only avant-garde writer ever hatched by the athletic department at Columbia University,"[2] Herbert Gold denigrated *On the Road* in *The Nation* as "proof of an illness rather than creation of art, a novel."

Out of many such examples, Carolyn Cassady cites Art Cohn's *Chronicle* review, "Sick Little Bums," as typical of the pernicious reactions, which "fed [Kerouac's] paranoia" ("I'm afraid to close my eyes for all the turmoiled universes I see tilting and expanding suddenly exploding suddenly clawing in to my center, faces, yelling mouths, long-haired yellers, sudden evil confidences, sudden rat-tat-tats of cerebral committees arguing about 'Jack' and talking about him as if he wasn't there—" [*BS* 156]) and hastened his alcoholic immolation:

> This, then is the new religion, the Jehovah of the Beaten handed down from his Mount: Thou shalt kill for the sake of killing. Thou shalt defile all flesh, including your own. Thou shalt deny thy birthright and resign from the human race. Thou shalt contribute nothing to the world except scorn. Thou shalt destroy the innocent. Thou shalt make a mockery of morality, justice, law, common fairness and, most of all, love. Thou shalt dishonor thy father and mother and curse them for giving thee birth.
>
> Amen, you pathetic, self-pitying, degenerate bums, amen! (290–91)

This deluge is, of course, highly invidious, part of a lingering distrust of popular movements on the part of those who might otherwise have claimed to rejoice in America's democratic identity but who recoiled in panic from mobile challenges to hypocrisy and repression. William Carlos Williams sums this up beautifully in *Paterson*:

> Moveless
> he envies the men that ran
> and could run off
> toward the peripheries—

```
to other centers, direct—
for clarity (if
they found it)
          loveliness and
authority in the world—

a sort of springtime
toward which their minds aspired
but which he saw,
within himself—ice bound . . .
```

(35)

Although positioned outside the literary establishment, all the significant Beat writers were conversant with developments across the arts over several centuries, Kerouac and Ginsberg's time spent under such accomplished teachers as Trilling, Mark Van Doren, Alfred Kazin, and Daisetz Suzuki qualifying their more obvious distaste for institutional burdens. And while Burroughs consciously sought an underworld of violent risk to cultivate what Creeley calls an observation of despair and degradation and a "commitment to sensation, as an alternative logic to organizational 'goodness' and 'purpose'" (*Quick Graph* 327), his stint at Harvard with T. S. Eliot and attendance of Korzybski's lectures at the Institute of General Semantics added to friendships with many stateless exiles of note in Tangier. As opposed to the "beatnik" status-seeker, "the beat writer is serious and ambitious," confirms Thomas Parkinson. "He is usually well-educated and always a student of his craft. Sometimes, as is the case with Gary Snyder, he is a very learned man, and his knowledge of literature and its history is dense and extensive" (280).

Moreover, like precursor and supporter Henry Miller—"[A]nd so my dear compatriots? How will you label me now? Un-American? It won't fit, I'm afraid. I'm even more American than you, only against the grain" (*Tropic of Capricorn* 159)—neither Kerouac nor Ginsberg were anti-American: another focus of conservative vitriol. Whereas the latter's faith in the soiled nation is maintained in poems such as "America" and "Waking in New York," Kerouac avidly takes up Whitman's dream of antinomian society in *Desolation Angels*:

And I know that America is too vast with people too vast to ever be degraded to the low level of a slave nation, and I can go hitch hiking down that road and on into the remaining years of my life knowing that outside of a couple fights in bars started by drunks I'll have not a hair on my head (and I need a haircut) harmed by Totalitarian cruelty. (46)

Taking their place inside "the second great eruption of a century-long poetics of resistance" (Rothenberg and Joris, *Two* 362), Beat motives break from leftist traditions of formulating revolt in terms of utopian models of social organization (Ginsberg: "I am a rebel, not a revolutionist" [qtd. in Parkinson 277]). With prewar socialist aspirations for an energized proletariat that could "break the ideological fetters of the old order" (Tipple 273) liquidated by the capitalist recovery of the New Deal itself, any response to the WASP message of permanent racism and inequality had to cut loose from dialectical materialism, a discourse more appropriate to the manufacturing masses and Henry Ford's vision of human products than to an America gearing up for a lifestyle economy. As Lipton suggests, the "disaffiliate has no blueprint for the future . . . joins no political parties," and refuses engagement with his or her well-paid spokesmen "with all the mass media at their command and all the laws and the police on their side" (149–50).

While it was clear from voting patterns and the absence of protest against military interventions in Korea that much of organized labor supported Cold War foreign policy, knowledge of the Hitler-Stalin pact, the release of transcripts from the Moscow Trials, and the 1948 coup in Czechoslovakia, followed in 1956 by the Kremlin's bloody suppression of the Budapest uprising, effectively dissolved whatever residual faith had remained in Marxist-Leninism. Domestically, the defeat of Wallace in 1948, the curtailment of union power by Taft-Hartley legislation, the execution of Julius and Ethel Rosenberg, the House Un-American Activities Committee witch hunts, and the agitation against wealth redistribution by groups such as the John Birch Society and the Christian Anti-Communist Crusade resurrected prewar "red scare" tactics and further undermined class activism.

Through the 1950s, a new pluralistic Left would gradually take shape in America that rejected the economic fatalism of the Third International and the "end of ideology" functionalism endorsed by sociologists such as Daniel Bell, Daniel Boorstin, and Paul Lazarsfeld. Their "consensus" liberalism, as C. Wright Mills pointed out, masked a pragmatic conservatism in keeping with the values of a vast new suburban middle class, fashioned around Madison Avenue's batch of image-types and satisfied by an evasive market bureaucracy.

True to its Bay Area legacy of anarcho-pacifism, Beat writing unquestionably contributed to the New Left's reinterpretation of political engagement as cultural change at all social levels. However, Beat's often unfocused attitude toward protest, resistance, and diagnosis arguably reduced its impetus to an insurrectionary beginning, one that could bypass anarchism and slip into guru worship, as seen in Kerouac's search for Maharishi carriers of ancestry and Ginsberg's defense of Chögyam Trungpa's ludicrous "experiment in monarchy" at Naropa. While Kerouac inherited D. H. Lawrence's contempt for locating the individual within the parameters of an industrial aggregate—what Edward Dahlberg in the 1930s called "living mythically"—his drift into right-wing reaction shows the dangers of political naïveté ("Myself I'm only an ex-sailor, I have no politics, I don't even vote" [*GB* 91]).

Asserting in 1957 that "[t]he Beat Generation has no interest in politics, only in mysticism, that's their religion. It's kids standing on the street and talking about the end of the world" (qtd. in Beatty 6), Kerouac claims the next year that "the political apathy of the Beat Generation is in itself a 'political' movement: i.e., will influence political decisions in the future and possibly transfer politics to their rightful aims, i.e., sense" (qtd. in "On the Road Back"). And while he accuses "all the old timers" in Greenwich Village of "turning politicians, getting up petitions for civil rights and all that kind of stuff. It's politics, not art anymore" (qtd. in V. Duncan, "Kerouac"), Kerouac's response to Ferlinghetti's invitation to join the Fair Play for Cuba Committee reflects his reading of such propagandist bilge as *The God That Failed* on Desolation Peak and typifies his increasing entrenchment: "I've got my own revolution right here in Northport—the American revolution" (*SL, II* 290).

However, as is proven by Ferlinghetti, who rallied to libertarian causes with broadsides such as *One Thousand Fearful Words for Fidel Castro, Where Is Vietnam?* and *Tyrannus Nix?* and by Ginsberg, who recovered the poet's old informational role with *Planet News* and *The Fall of America*, political exertion need not signify doctrinal sclerosis. Their dissolving of the personal into the political boosted the vigorous opposition to US foreign policy in Asia and Latin America in their work, a perspective echoed through the 1960s and beyond in the poetry of Robert Duncan, Denise Levertov, and William Everson and refracted through the biosphere activism of Michael McClure and Gary Snyder. In each case, revolution ceases to be the exclusive concern of the State in favor of what Snyder calls "a spiritual ascesis for the whole community" (*Earth* 121). This is a stance that, in Eric Mottram's words, resists "both the dispersal of energy and its relegation to energy-defeating art forms. It demonstrates possibilities in challenging war and post-war decadence and stasis, while engaging no replacement ideology" ("Preface" 54).

Nevertheless, by 1959 Seymour Krim notes that the experimental nature of Kerouac's fiction and his implicit critique of hegemonic norms was barely noticed by readers "because the life he seemed to glorify—promiscuity, pot-smoking, the hot pursuit of speed, kicks, excitement—was so much more tangible than art" ("King" 358). As Kerouac concedes, "What is called the 'Beat Generation,' is really a revolution in manners" (*Safe* 25). Admittedly as the 1960s wore on, his refuge in public postures of self-abuse supplied plenty of ammunition for misinterpretation. Referring to an incident in which Kerouac urinated into a Cedar Bar ashtray following his heckling of Frank O'Hara at a Living Theater reading, Sukenick contends that "the artistic license of unappreciated genius is one of the bonuses of cultural alienation, which was still the going pose, but it also helps to infantilize and, therefore, neutralize that genius as well" (56).

Walking into the voyeuristic gaze conventionally directed at the jazz hero as stylized failure, Kerouac reinforces the cliché of artist as perennial child and reproduces its pattern of dependence and submission. As Kenneth Rexroth observes with regard to Charlie Parker and Dylan Thomas, such torrential bursts of self-destruction in fact "communicate one central theme: Against the ruin of the world, there is only one defense—the creative act" ("Disengagement" 181). Having initially spurned profit and Henri Michaux's sense of "[a]dult-finished-dead; nuances of the same state" (76), Kerouac is paralyzed by the encroachment of business predators, a rapacious media, the recurrences of childhood conditioning, and sheer fatigue—as corroborated by Norman Mailer's perception of a man who "was tired, as indeed why should he not be, for he has traveled in a world where adrenalin devours the blood" (qtd. in Wakefield 167).

Alongside the blurring of life and fiction—a consequence of the Legend's intricate combination of autobiography and invention—the reception of Kerouac's work has tended to overlook its relationship to an American avant-garde where formal cross-fertilization is almost customary. An early bid to map comparative impulses was made by Rexroth, who sought to identify "the one technical development in the first wave" of postwar art. "Thomas and Parker have more in common than theme, attitude, life pattern," he writes in 1957.

> Ornament is confabulation in the interstices of structure. A poem by Dylan Thomas, a saxophone solo by Charles Parker, a painting by Jackson Pollock—these are pure confabulations as ends in themselves. Confabulation has come to determine structure. ("Disengagement" 181–83)

However, beyond this and the pioneering example of Mottram's "Area Studies," few attempts have been made to evaluate what Harold Rosenberg terms "trans-formal effort," which, in the case of the Beat Bohemian formation, is as much social as aesthetic (Davidson 6). This is in keeping with an academic orthodoxy that, to quote Allan Janik and Stephen Toulmin,

> treat[s] the developments in question as episodes in a more or less self-contained history of, say, painting or legal theory, architectural

design or epistemology. Any suggestion that their cross-interactions might have been as significant as their own internal evolutions will be considered only grudgingly, after all internal factors have been demonstrably exhausted. (15)

By the 1950s, interdisciplinary exchange becomes an open motive with jazz musicians, poets, painters, choreographers, and political dissenters, such as those involved in the Berkeley Free Speech Movement, interacting on the level of process itself, each, as Alfred Willener observes, expressing "a revolutionary desire for social emancipation . . . the emancipation of the non-formal . . . the desire to avoid being confined within a particular school, within existing rhythmic patterns" (230). In such instances, the use of genre or style as definitive precludes the diverse interests held by an artist beyond the contiguous demands of the era and restricts the prerogative of freedom; for Willem de Kooning, speaking to his painters' community at Studio 35 in 1950, it is therefore "disastrous to name ourselves" (qtd. in Motherwell and Reinhardt 88).[3]

Such thinking animates Cage's "Theatre Piece No. 1" (1952) at Black Mountain College—the first "Happening" synthesizing the visual designs of Robert Rauschenberg, Merce Cunningham's dance, the poetries of Olson and M. C. Richards recited from ladders, and the pianism of David Tudor, among films, slides, records, and radios—and 1960s successors such as Greenwich Village "intermedia" performance art, the "total environment" Electric Circus Discotheque in the East Village, and Ken Kesey's three-day Acid Test of 1965: mobile dramas of imagination, space, and time, in which one medium is never wholly ascendant over another. Without division of auditorium from performance area, the liberating disorder of such events recalled, in Mottram's words, that of the "Revivalist sessions in 18th and 19th century America . . . the awakening of emotions in forms contrary to established modes of assumed rationality, and the promotion of an expanding experience from ecstasy to new community" (*Blood* 186–87).

Disregarding convenience tags, not to mention the inevitable sectarian rivalries among participants and subgroups, Kerouac's fictions contributes to, and are nourished by, this wider range of actions within a triangulated arc of New York, San Francisco, and Black Mountain, civic areas that intensify creative developments beyond class and race. However, "[n]o one has brought this to the foreground," argues Fielding Dawson:

[T]he school and what was going on in New York was a distinct, even obvious, harmony, drawing as they did on each other. . . . In April of 1953 . . . in New York . . . [Franz Kline] took me to meet DeKooning,

and having just shaken hands and Franz mentioning I was visiting
on spring break from Black Mountain DeKooning said he had been
there in 1948 and of a sudden we were talking about the school, and
DeKooning talking about Olson. Had I read that book on Melville, no
not yet but I would, DeKooning's yes yes hint of impatience, hit, I say,
in his eagerness to express how it interested him, in no detail save tone
of voice and that was PLENTY! because it was reflective because it was
touching an intuitive area DeKooning was familiar with.

 The energetic atemporal. (47–48)

Downplayed by Kerouac as "a fad . . . no more than four or five friends
around Columbia University in the late 1940s" who shared a "serious" brief
to reinvent the techniques of writing (qtd. in Aronowitz, "Beat"), the self-
imposed generational banding, like Dada before it, signals no shared goal,
nor rupture with preceding groups. If anything, Beat serves to Americanize
and democratize modernist currents, a denial of received connections in
favor of "prophesying a new style for American culture . . . completely free
from European influences (unlike the Lost Generation), a new incantation,"
reports Kerouac. "The same thing was going on in the postwar France of
Sartre and Genet and what's more we knew about it" (*GB* 47).

 As the heterogeneous nature of such writing demonstrates, disciplin-
ary borders and cliques shatter in the push to access the widest range of
experience possible. The enclosure of generic movement is replaced by an
existential coincidence of interests and techniques, questions of competitive
origin or influence being subsumed by gut devotion to the necessity of art.
Clement Greenberg's grasp of the motivation behind New York painting is
transferable across the contemporary scene:

> [V]ery little in "abstract expressionism" is, or ever was, program-
> matic; individual artists may have made "statements" but there were no
> manifestoes; nor have there been "spokesmen." What happened, rather,
> was that a certain cluster of challenges was encountered, separately
> yet almost simultaneously, by six or seven painters who had their first
> one-man shows at Peggy Guggenheim's Art of the Century gallery in
> New York between 1943 and 1946. (211)

Convivial interaction, a common anti-Statist point of view, and a commitment to open form give frameworks for individual energy. As Sukenick
suggests, "Once discovered, the underground became an education in survival—emotional, creative, and intellectual survival—that schools did not
offer. And it provided a supporting community of like-minded hold-outs
from an imposed way of life" (6).

"Survival" here means the gathering of limitless experience beyond the parochial and anecdotal concerns of the self. Attention is directed outward, and unprejudiced adventures ensue. These include Beat incursions into Buddhism; Olson's Mayan studies; Jerome Rothenberg and Dennis Tedlock's Ethnopoetics; translated world poetries by Ferlinghetti, Rexroth, and Paul Blackburn; African percussion techniques explored by Art Blakey, Max Roach, John Coltrane, and Yusef Lateef; international myths deployed in New York painting; Henry Miller's subjective histories of ancient Greece; and Ed Sanders's reworking of Egyptian hieroglyphs—attempts to reappraise the "primitive" and "sacred" through art and to address man's relation to man and ecology alike. Rather than advocate the reinstatement of a particular archaic system, the desire in each case is to learn from vanishing models of small, classless societies, complementing subterranean traditions of resistance to the twin authorities of State and organized religion.

This shared disregard of boundaries—personal and national, social and aesthetic—reflects Kerouac's own deviation from literary precursors. Taking Richard Ellmann's proposition that artworks are not objects of "autotelic purity" but the results of momentary convergences of forces in which past and present deeds, pressures, and fascinations play a determining role (*along* 114), Kerouac shows that the notional adjuncts of criticism (biography, context, background) are less relevant to prosody than the charting of wider changes of perception within a period: an opening of the Aristotelian definition of "poetics" to include the whole range of knowledge that makes social intervention possible. This is, of course, inimical to the New Critical quarantine of art from life, which reduces the creative act to a subordinate consolidation of theory. "They all think writing is a 'profession' that's their trouble," Kerouac tells Philip Whalen. "To me it's the day" (*SL, II* 177).

To counter that "profession" means to reverse the academic dependency on classification that Pound attacks in *Guide to Kulchur* ("Does any really good mind ever 'get a kick' out of stuff that has been put into water-tight compartments and hermetically sealed?" [32]) and the Platonic definition of knowledge as activation of prior universal forms in the mind, which converts into bourgeois "intellectual capital." Rigged by a professional caste who know "more and more about less and less," this, in Mumford's words, "finally turns into secret knowledge—accessible only to an inner priesthood, whose sense of power is in turn inflated by their privileged command of 'trade' or official secrets" (*Pentagon* 24).

The thrill of admitting no guaranteed outcome in the act of writing that marks the Legend's phenomenological opposition between discovery and recognition invites a radically different approach to interpretation, one that liberates the creative forces from the tutelage of the advocates of power described by Richard Huelsenbeck in the days of the Cabaret Voltaire. Polarized against Emerson's model of the "American scholar" immersed in the reinvigoration of beginnings, the autonomous zone of academic criticism is "something different from the talk of poets & artists," contends Rothenberg,

> & such talk about poetry & life—coming generously from my contemporaries—has fed me from the start of my own work. . . . [P]oetry & life aren't separate (whatever that might mean). . . . [T]he poetic discourse is a discourse, always, on the life from which the poem springs. (*Pre-faces* 3–4)

For de Kooning, too, it follows that theories of art remained

> always in a state of development parallel to the development of painting itself. They influenced each other and vice versa. But all of a sudden, in that famous turn of a century, a few people thought they could take the bull by the horns and invent an aesthetic beforehand. After immediately disagreeing with each other, they began to form all kinds of groups, each with the idea of freeing art, and each demanding that you should obey them. Most of these theories have finally dwindled away into politics or strange forms of spiritualism. ("Abstract Art")

Moving within the same period, Fielding Dawson draws a similar distinction between creative production and its retrospective taxonomy:

> The one thing we did not have in the 50s was the words to speak, to tell what we were doing. But we did *all* the rest, except—again—be able to answer Harold Rosenberg's repeated question:
> "Does anybody have any ideas?"
> In the crowded Cedar Tavern. Nobody could answer because we were doing, and not thinking, and Harold's astute query predicted from that point on that critics would speak for the artists, and in magazines and books circulate (and establish) labels that define over and over just who was doing what in their newest work, while along the way, ever resentful, and jealous, happy happy to empty their intellectual bladders and bowels on . . . things that got in their way, like Black Mountain . . . all that blather to compensate for personal creative ignorance in terms of drawing or painting, or even how to see, and sense the space and free release on a piece of paper, in tar splashed on a sidewalk, or torn posters on long cement, wood, or stone, or brick walls there in the city, or outside the city, of any city, anywhere in the world, and I hope these words bring alive the verve, the fresh vitality in space, in our composing atemporal images, finding a new, vivid, rewarding—great doors opened—freedom. (51)

For all his incursions into peasant Catholicism and ancestral mysticism, Kerouac shares that same urge to make instead of to describe the transformations of experience without "trick[ing] them to conform to any formula"—Hemingway's expression in *A Movable Feast* (136) for a referential world of mirrors that projects a symbol rather than the thing itself. Kerouac's fictions come from the body-mind intelligence urging its cares and making decisions as the possible narrative emerges, prior to any incorporation into familiar correspondence or critical analogy. Like *Ulysses,* works such as *Visions of Cody, Old Angel Midnight, Doctor Sax* and the *Blues* series spring from no prototype and are unrepeatable. Each text is a complete presentation, an enactment or sutra that stands for nothing and withers if codified into separable datum.

The working out of relationships between thought, speech, and action through the Legend is therefore less concerned with dialectical discourses and the retreat into representation that, to Foucault, "Western thought has so long held sacred as a form of power and an access to reality" (qtd. in Deleuze and Guattari, *Anti-Oedipus* xiii) than with the reconnection of art to desire in the face of the "pernicious *industrialization of vision*" (Virilio 89). Or as Kerouac has it:

> If you were not here
> To see the world
> With your special
> Conditioned eyes
> What makes you think
> It would look like that?
>
> (*SD* 7)

This fuses with a frontier impulse embedded in American life and art, which sloughs off the predetermining weight of the past, be it immigrant identity or ideological authority. "Why should we not also enjoy an original relation to the universe?" asks Emerson in 1836. "The sun shines today also. . . . There are new lands, new men, new thoughts" (35). The self-reliant, self-sculpting strain is also proclaimed by Whitman in *Leaves of Grass* ("Walking freely out from the old traditions, as our politics has walked out, American poets and literats recognize nothing behind them superior to what is present with them" [*Complete Poems* 770]), endorsed by Olson as "the American advantage" ("At all costs. Clear the air. Clear our equity" [qtd. in Malanga 141]), and applied by Robert Goldwater to the abstract expressionist position "of being ahead rather than behind, of having absolutely no models however immediate and illustrious, of being entirely and completely on one's own—this was a new heady atmosphere" (26).

Echoing Pollock's discovery of new techniques—sculptor Harry Jackson relates "that he started dripping paint because he became so excited while painting the mural for Peggy Guggenheim, that he lost hope of keeping up with his excitement using a brush" (qtd. in Potter 98)—Kerouac's forms emerge ecstatically, paralleling Duncan's intuition in *Groundwork* of "elemental sparks, outpouring vitalities" that give the gesture

> its own "organic decorum, the complete
> loyalty of a work of art to a shaping
>      principle
>           within itself—"
>
> (71)

His hermeneutic visions of what flash into mind share this sense of morphology: of making experience into form.

However, without such receptive bearings, Kerouac's achievement remains consigned to the market subgenre of "cult fiction"—a safe and useless place—or condemned as "elitist" and "obscure," which raises questions of who legitimates taste. Moreover, to filter the Legend's narratives through an academic apparatus designed to gauge nineteenth-century form is to brand its creator inarticulate. As Kerouac himself complains to Carl Solomon over his rejection of *Visions of Cody* in 1952:

> When something is incomprehensible to me ("Finnegans Wake,"
> Lowry's "Under the Volcano," "Delilah" by Marcus Goodrich) I try
> to understand it, the author's intellect, and passion, and mystery. To
> label it incoherent is not only a semantic mistake but an act of cowardice
> and intellectual death.

"Rough[ing] against the grain of established ideas" (*SL, I* 376), Kerouac's fictions adhere to no prescriptive tradition: a concept that not only implies that the risk has been taken long before a writer embarks upon a book but also obscures the nonlinear origins and role of accident in creativity and the tensions—personal, sociological, and technical—from which such approaches evolve.

Voyaging through a test of language that, to quote Rothenberg, "must in all events resist rigidity & closure" (*Pre-faces* 3), Spontaneous Prose becomes one more transdisciplinary action of "outward" in Beat times. As noted previously, Coleman was highly aware of the analogies between his music and the "all-over" work of Pollock, who in the 1940s learned much from jazz and linguistic collage. According to Rosenberg, Pollock identified himself more eagerly with Hart Crane, Dylan Thomas, and James Joyce than with previous painters. "In throwing, dribbling, and blotting his pigments," he contends, "he brought paint into closer approximation of the resiliencies of verbal utterance":

> The essential form of drip painting is calligraphy. In tying to the picture surface color layers of different depths, Pollock produced the visual equivalent of a play on words—a standard feature of oracular pronouncements. Masterworks like *Full Fathom Five* and *Lavender Mist* transform themselves from sheer sensuous revels in paint into visionary landscapes, then back again into contentless agitations of materials. Their immediate derivation is not the work of any painter but Pollock's favorite readings, from *Rimbaud* to *Finnegans Wake*. ("Art World")

Pollock's explorations of optical depth beyond finite definition that thrilled Kerouac—he feted him as a "genius" in 1962 for creating "immense Samapattis of color" from "splashing and throwing and dancing around" (*GB* 77)—in turn bear relation to Kerouac's prosody, both of which fuse indeterminacy and precision within spatial fields. Ferlinghetti confirms this common strain in speaking of "a continuous line from the beginning of the poem to the end, like a Jackson Pollock painting . . . so you have what I call 'open form' composition, whereas Robert Duncan uses the term 'Open Field'" (qtd. in Smith 92). Michael McClure similarly identifies a "gestalt across the arts," indicating a variety of analogous procedures that need not imply a synchronized program (qtd. in Chassman 16–18). And while Creeley writes of the effect of Charlie Parker on his writing—as indeed does Ishmael Reed, whose "Neo HooDoo" aesthetic takes the altoman as its paragon—Kerouac, Ginsberg, and Holmes followed the example of Hemingway and Williams by studying impressionism, enrolling for Meyer Schapiro's classes at the New School in 1949.

Kerouac would embark on his own amateur painting career in Mexico City in 1956, visiting the Louvre the following year and confirming his passion for the entire

> HISTORY OF ART: from Egyptians & wall carvers to . . . DeHootch, Treck, Van Velsen, Kalf and all the Dutchmen and Italians . . . back to Van Gogh and Renoir and Degas and Cézanne . . . via Goya, Greco, Velázquez and Tintoretto this movement back, to exact *painting* (not imitating) of nature. . . . So I will paint what I see, color and line, exactly FAST. (*SL, II* 29)

Reflecting Ginsberg's attempt to translate Cézanne's tonal juxtaposition or "petites sensations" into poetic word clusters and multiple perspectives, Kerouac sees possibilities in Van Gogh's "crazy blue Chinese church" for his own prose method, beyond the more general appearance of words on the page:

> [T]he hurrying woman, the spontaneous brush stroke, the secret of it is Japanese, is what for instance makes the woman's back, white, because her back is unpainted canvas with a few black thick script strokes (so that I wasn't wrong when I started painting God last Fall in doing everything fast like I write and that's it). (*SL, II* 29)

Regularly accompanying Kerouac to the Friday night discussions between painters at the Eighth Street Club in the early 1950s, Ginsberg fortifies the sense of compatibility between contemporary literature and painting by situating the Beat "attention to the happening" within the "time of De Kooning, Kline & gesture painting, Abstract Expressionism" (*Deliberate* 351). As Dore Ashton corroborates:

> Kerouac particularly, and to a lesser degree Ginsberg, sought out the painters. It was not unusual to see Kerouac and Kline with a group of younger artists drinking at the Cedar and finishing up the night at Kline's studio. Whenever there was a party at the Club the Beats turned up, sometimes high on marijuana, sitting in the rear of the loft while the artists—still faithful to liquor—danced and bellowed loudly. Ginsberg was the more influential poet to fraternize with the New York School. . . . His very presence reinforced the instinctive rebellion of the painters. His admiration for those alienated and magically inclined precursors—Rimbaud, Yeats, Céline, and of course Whitman—paralleled the Artists' predilections. (277)

Aiming to inspire cross-fertilization, the Club inherited the connections made in Alfred Stieglitz's circle between painters and poets such as Hart Crane, Muriel Rukheyser, and Gertrude Stein. Williams writes of a complementary bias within objectivism in the 1920s: "What were we seeking? No one knew consistently enough to formulate a 'movement.' We were restless and constrained, closely allied with the painters. Impressionism, dadasim, surrealism applied to both painting and the poem" (*Autobiography* 148).

Throughout the 1950s, the availability of centers of exchange, extending from the institutional setting of Black Mountain College to the informality of the Cedar Bar, provided a milieu that rendered the consideration of formal interactions unavoidable. Like his fellow poet Kenneth Koch, Frank O'Hara was steeped in the traditions of Apollinaire and Jacob: prepared for a range of roles, including curator at the Museum of Modern Art and assistant editor of *Art News*. In the notes for Morton Feldman's *Works, 1951–57*, O'Hara writes:

The last ten years have seen American composers, painters and poets assuming leading roles in the world of international art to a degree hitherto unexpected. Led by the painters, our whole cultural milieu has changed and is still changing. . . . The influence of aesthetic ideas has also been mutual: the very extremity of the differences between the arts has thrown their technical analogies into sharp relief. . . . [I]t is in the framework of these mutual influences that Morton Feldman could cite, along with the playing of Fournier, Rachmaninoff and Tudor and the friendship of John Cage, the paintings of Philip Guston as important influences on his work. He adds, "Guston made me aware of the 'metaphysical place' which we all have but which so many of us are not sensitive to by previous conviction." . . . Like the artists involved in the new American painting, [Feldman] was pursuing a personal search for expression which could not be limited by any system.

Cage's achievements in music are similarly augmented by his poetry, lectures, and paintings, and both his and Feldman's graphic scores can be contemplated as visual works in their own right. Feldman's *Projections* of 1951 is exemplary: a series of drawn signs for the "high middle or low register of the instrument . . . within a given time structure. Entrances within this structure, as well as actual pitches and dynamics, [are] freely chosen by the performer" (notes). Deprived of an economy of restriction and metaphor, speeds are very slow, paralleling the effect of dominant single tones in the paintings of Elseworth Kelly, Barnett Newman, Mark Rothko, and Ad Reinhardt. This serves, in the composer's words, "to project sounds in time, free from compositional rhetoric," the aim being "not to involve the performer in memory (or) relationships" or in sounds that "had an inherent symbolic shape" (notes).

Feldman's remarks from a 1966 interview complement his "environmental" works dedicated to poets and painters such as O'Hara, Beckett, Rothko, and Guston and further illuminate his tendency to think about "sonic adventure" in the language of visual art: "My compositions are really not 'compositions' at all. One might call them time canvases in which I more or less prime the canvas with an overall hue of music" (Mottram, "Notes for Feldman Lecture" 32).

The example of Feldman's friend Merce Cunningham, who in 1945 broke with Martha Graham's company to design a choreography that liberated the body from musical representation and narrative continuity, is also worth citing. To quote Cage, his collaborator over five decades:

As in abstract painting, it is assumed that an element (a movement, a sound, a change of light) is in and of itself expressive; what it communicates is in large part determined by the observer himself. It is assumed that the dance supports itself and does not need support from the music. The two arts take place in common place and time, but each art expresses this Space-Time in its own way. The result is an activity of interpenetrations in time and space, not counterpoints, nor controlled relationships, but flexibilities as are known from the mobiles of Alexander Calder. (*Writer* 91)

Elements within each performance are no longer conceived with the intention of provoking psychological recognitions in an audience. As Cage suggests, "Whereas other music and dance generally attempt to 'say' something, this theatre is one that 'presents' activity. This can be said to affirm life" (92). Spontaneous Prose thus takes its place within a more general shift in attention across the American scene, from finished artifact to inventive process. After the bop 1940s, principles of imprecision, inconclusiveness, and multiplicity became possibilities across forms, Coleman's 1958 prophecy of a "free" music converging with the aims of much contemporary art. Referring to John Chamberlain and Franz Kline, for instance, Creeley realized that abstract expressionism augmented jazz in providing a "way of thinking of the process of writing that made both the thing said and the way of saying it an integral event" (qtd. in Chassman 60). "I hadn't realized as yet that a number of American painters had made the shift I was myself so anxious to accomplish," he later recalls,

that they had, in fact, already begun to move away from the insistently *pictorial* . . . to a manifest directly of the *energy* inherent in the materials. . . . [P]ossibly the attraction the artist had for people like myself—think of O'Hara, Ashbery, Koch, Duncan, McClure, Ginsberg; or Kerouac's wistful claim that he could probably paint better than Kline—was that lovely uncluttered directness of perception and act we found in so many of them. . . . It may also have been the *energy* these people generated, which so attracted us. (*Essays* 369–71)

As McClure, who seized upon Pollock's heroic engagement and dynamic open rhythms, also discovered, the rejection of causal and discursive procedures had consequences for a poetic language with a Whiteheadian emphasis on "Field." Admitting that he "totally bought Abstract Expressionism as spiritual autobiography," McClure found that the permission in Pollock's canvases became "so integral . . . that his work began immersing my way of thinking in such a subtle way so early I can't tell you when" (qtd. in Chassman 16, 58).

Although as many similarities and differences exist among the New York painters as between painters and writers, common processes within their work are highly significant. Naming Pollock as the figure who "broke the ice," de Kooning identified the historical importance of Pollock's first "all-over" webs of poured paint (*Cathedral, Full Fathom Five,* and *Lucifer*) from 1947: a celebration of art as performance beyond immediate genre that spurred his own all-over abstracts of flat, open, inter-sliding forms (*Asheville* and *Attic*) in 1948.[4] As Rosenberg explains:

> At a certain moment the canvas began to appear to one American painter after another as an arena in which to act—rather than as a space in which to reproduce, re-design, analyze, or "express" an object, actual or imagined. What was to go on the canvas was not a picture but an event. The painter no longer approached his easel with an image in his mind; he went up to it with material in his hand to do something to that other piece of material in front of him. The image would be the result of this encounter. (*Tradition* 25)

The elimination of the subject marking associated phases of abstraction or expressionism is done not for aesthetic "purification," as in the "perfect" relations of space and color advocated by Kandinsky, Klee, and Mondrian, but to remove any impediment to the act of painting. "Form, color, composition, drawing are auxiliaries—[all] can be dispensed with," argues Rosenberg. "What matters always is the revelation contained in the act. It is to be taken for granted that in the final effect, the image, whatever be or not be in it, will be a *tension*." As Ad Reinhardt demonstrates, the unpainted canvas is now also a legitimate prospect, preventing the relegation of image into epistemology by foreclosing the "confusi[on of] painting with everything that is not painting" (*Tradition* 26–28).

However, while Pollock devotes his chief statement about his work in *Possibilities* entirely to method, he also acknowledges that a composition must be judged on the success of its formal qualities: "Naturally, the result is the thing," he affirms. "[I]t doesn't make much difference how the paint is put on as long as something has been said. Technique is just a means of arriving at a statement." In his mature canvases, and in those of Kline, de Kooning, and Robert Motherwell, cartoons function not as steps in the ascent toward a finished product but as separate actions. "I don't work from drawings, I don't make sketches . . . into a final painting," Pollock corroborates. "I approach painting in the same sense as one approaches drawing; that is, it's direct. . . . [T]he more immediate, the more direct—the greater the possibilities of making a . . . statement" ("Excerpts"). The work therefore does not antedate the process of painting. The creative gesture alone blazes the trail; calligraphic signature becomes fact. "Anything is relevant to it," adds Rosenberg. "Anything that has to do with action—psychology, philosophy, history, mythology, hero worship, anything but art criticism" (*Tradition* 25). The image emerges from this electrifying dialogue between elements as an act of existential responsibility, the basis of which is laid by Sartre:

> It is clearly understood that there is no definite painting to be made, that the artist is engaged in the making of his painting, and that the painting to be made is precisely the painting he will have made. It is precisely understood that there are no *a priori* aesthetic values, but that there are values which appear subsequently in the coherence of the painting, in the correspondence between what the artist intended and the result. Nobody can tell what the painting of tomorrow will be like. Painting can be judged only after it has once been made. . . . We can never say that a work of art is arbitrary. . . . What art and ethics have in common is that we have creation and invention in both cases. (*Existentialism* 42–43)

As LeRoi Jones observes with regard to Charlie Parker, whose recordings often provided a working soundtrack for Pollock, such results are provisional and do not necessarily have to happen that way (Allen and Tallman 378). Enacted in physical movement, the canvas is its own occasion, overcoming the execution of fixed purpose within what Kline calls "a complete situation" (qtd. in Rosenberg, "Hans Hofmann"). Philip Guston's thoughts on the subject lend further clarity:

> [E]very idea [follows] from the daily work: from an in-fighting in painting itself—in the confusion of painting. . . . As you paint, changing and destroying, nothing can be assumed. . . . The only morality in painting revolves around the moment when you are permitted to "see" and the painting takes over. . . . [U]nless you work up until that point—when you don't even know what you're "seeing" but suddenly make a vault and "see"—you are not finished, no matter how great and reasonable your intentions are. . . . When you do not paint from things or ideas—when there is no model, in other words—certainly something else is happening and that is the constant question, "What is happening?" ("Statement")

The Beat page thus follows the transformation of canvas from a site where information is re-presented to a phenomenological dramatization of mind through which the artist travels via surface alterations. (Pollock: "I want to express my feelings rather than illustrate them" ["Excerpts"].) Verbal art as kinesis replaces mimetic subject—as Mailer quickly realized in judging Kerouac not as a novelist but "instead as an action painter or a bard" (*Advertisements* 310). Having been told by Pound in 1931 that "I have allus held that sometime somehow god damn etc something ought to git started ON THE BLOODY SPOT," Williams in his entreaty from "A Beginning on the Short Story (Notes)" reiterates this major American impetus in the arts:

> Now go ahead and do it. Name the actions and perform them—yourself. . . . You are in the creative process—a function in nature—relegated to the deity. You have now entered what is referred to as the divine function of the artist. Let's keep away from frightening words and say you are nature—in action. It is an action, a moving process—the verb dominates; you are to *make*. (*Essays* 305–6)

With referential conventions now invidious, language must become newly accustomed to what Rosenberg terms "a situation in which the act itself is the 'object.'" The call is for an intimate

> vocabulary of action: its inception, duration, direction—psychic state, concentration and relaxation of the will, passivity, alert waiting. [The critic] must become a connoisseur of the gradations between the automatic, the spontaneous, the evoked. (*Tradition* 29)

In common with Kline, for whom structure emerges "through the painting of it . . . plastically. . . . What I try to do is to create the painting so that the overall thing has that particular emotion; not particularly just the forms in it" (qtd. in Sylvester), Kerouac no longer chases down preconceived trajectories but seeks to make of writing an action itself, one that incarnates the latent energies uncovered by Duncan in *Fictive Certainties*:

> I do not believe in a Creation by Chance or by Predestined Form but in a Creation by Creative Will that realizes Itself in Form evolving in the play of primordial patterns. And in my work I evolve the form for a poem by an insistent attention to what happens in inattentions, a care for inaccuracies; for I strive in the poem not to make some imitation of a model experience but to go deeper into the experience of the process of the poem itself. (88)

Kerouac's Spontaneous Prose also surges existentially forward by an accumulation of decisions: knowledge of form and therefore meaning being contingent upon its appearance. In the case of *Visions of Cody,* improvisation extends to a series of marks or pre-signs that the author moves through and tries out as he reflects upon the practice of writing. The rhetorical sense of line, which embraces verbal and visual syntax and musical cell, now signifies bodily motion, too: a poetics of pulse and gesture as opposed to outline or cadence. Echoing Duncan's rejection of catharsis in favor of self-perpetuating spatial forms in *Groundwork Before the War*—itself a product of his 1952 collage collaboration with Jess Collins—Kerouac's goal is the invention of surprise ideas that can energize and sustain proposals for multiple shapes within a field, one that comprises neither exhaustive belief (totalism) nor architecture of fixed proposition (system).

Crucially in Cold War America, such openness and eclecticism in the arts occur simultaneously with an increase in governmental tyranny. While developments in his work yield no expressly causal relationship to political machinations, Kerouac's investigation of ways to remove boundary at the generative point of language proposes a fertile opposition to Marcuse's "total administration state"; for as Ludwig Wittgenstein observes in *Philosophical Investigations*, a contradiction always has a civil status (125). Emerging in the same period as Sartre's *What Is Literature?*, with its repositioning of the "committed" writer, a text such as *Visions of Cody* provides the "invitation," to quote Mottram, "to participate in a kind of play of the most important kind, [a] creative organization of emotion and knowledge for personal and social bearings" without the need for "dogma and ignorance as a refuge from responsibility" (qtd. in Skelt 29–30).

Kerouac's notations broach the screened artifice of the expressive tools afforded by the State to undermine the policing of what Ginsberg in "Wichita Vortex Sutra" terms "formulas of reality" and what Burroughs in *Electronic Revolution* calls "Reality Studios." As both Burroughs's *Naked Lunch* and the Living Theater production of Jack Gelber's *The Connection* reveal, the degradation in awareness of how language generates perception through time depends upon the principle of addiction, enclosing "a man in a required role that requisitions his liberty" and subjecting him to the constant recycling of "old forms of power, old ideas, old technology; insane recoveries of exhausting and exhausted actions and ideologies" (Mottram, *Blood* 30–32). As McLuhan discerns in 1951:

> Ours is the first age in which thousands of the best-trained individual minds have made it a full-time business to get inside the collective public mind. To get inside in order to manipulate, exploit, control is the object now. And to generate heat not light is the intention. To keep everybody in the helpless state engendered by prolonged mental rutting is the effect of many ads and much entertainment alike. . . . It is observable that the more illusion and falsehood needed to maintain any given state of affairs, the more tyranny is needed to maintain the illusion and falsehood. Today the tyrant rules not by club or fist, but, disguised as a market researcher, he shepherds his flocks in the ways of utility and comfort. (*Mechanical* v–vi)

Rather than assure that correspondences meet proper obligations for "truth" within endlessly reproduced mass images, the perpetual shifts within Kerouac's fictions court only risk, an ongoing test of the First Amendment to the Constitution. Working on *Visions of Cody* most intensively in 1951, Kerouac devises his multidirectional form at the time that McCarthy surfaces with his allegations over un-American activities, alongside Hoover's framing of Alger Hiss. A diagnosis ensues of the nation's linguistic pathologies, what Ginsberg terms its "habit-image-reaction of fear/violence" (*Deliberate* 10), or the constitutive fables of American authority, which the book scrambles, dissolves, and re-orders.

Kerouac thus implicitly comprehends the dangers of a frontier mythology commissioned by the domestic realm on the verge of collapse into market ideology. As Ginsberg confirms, *Cody*

> is also an analysis & Disillusionment with all the heroic Imagery of US—The personal experience and discovery from raw materials at private Hand, not from the general Concept . . . from Jack's experience on the street with Nationalist Imagery of previous generations, & his familiarity, sympathy & Disillusionment with the American myth, even unto its hero, his Hero King, Neal. (*Deliberate* 355)

With its foreground in neurotic swings of cultural mood, lurches in the economy, and national professions of righteousness accompanied by foreign policies of mass murder, Kerouac's ambivalence toward narrative representation dramatizes a positive and necessary crisis of identity in what he calls the "Abstract war" years (*VC* 381), a text bearing witness to bewilderment over the nature of American experience.

Whereas in *On the Road* the challenge to boundary is partially disabled by a didactic mode of storytelling internalized within American power (Ellis 52–53), the search for euphoric plateaus in *Visions of Cody* is revitalized by refusing aggressive conformity to the singular. Self-conscious techniques of narration intervene to circumvent any compromise of the speech-text's immediacy into official syntax, Duluoz no longer "making the mistake of following a bum story line already written" (*VC* 402)—that is, the self written into prescriptive formula. Echoing Olson's entreaty in "La Preface" to "[p]ut war away with time, come into space" (*Collected* xiv), and Duncan's pursuit of "vast extensions of meaning, trance, and fantasy, alchemistries of language . . . the depths of the immediate" (qtd. in Olson, *Collected* xiv), the novel pretends neither truth nor accuracy but intensifies experience as a multiplier for invention.

Taking Williams's belief that a "work of art is important only as evidence, in its structure, of a new world which it has been created to affirm. Poetry is a rival government always in opposition to its cruder replicas" (*Essays* 196) and Duncan's sense of the "choreographies" of every poem that "[s]urely . . . extend into actual space" (*Bending* 6), Kerouac's Legend offers a new cosmology: a social rhetoric that marries the Dionysian with the rigor of writing as performance. This is what he implies when describing jazz as a "new world philosophy" or Charlie Parker as a "great / creator of forms / That ultimately find expression / In mores and what have you" (*MCB* 239). Works such as *Visions of Cody, Old Angel Midnight,* and "October in the Railroad Earth" posit desire as an exploration of unlimited connections, resonating beyond each single work into a wider heightening of energies ready for activation.

In this respect, the need to avoid parameters, hierarchies, and sky-gods gathered by Deleuze and Guattari into a series of axioms and matrices—Nomadology, War Machine, Deterritorialization, Rhizome—is preempted, to quote Jeff Nuttall, "in art before philosophy stumbled on the question— / Blake before Freud, Shakespeare before Kierkegaard, Koch and Ashbery before Baudrillard, Dos Passos before McLuhan" (96). In each instance the traditional securities are challenged by what Mottram describes as "a boundary crossing and ecstatic program which immediately takes on both a social and political implication" (*Blood* 200). Kerouac's arrangement of signs and techniques explodes an incalculable number of effects as it moves within the cultural terrain and emerges, having left a mark on all contemporary forms of expression against which a period can be read. The map of society is consequently redrawn. To call on Deleuze:

> The world revealed by art reacts on all the others, as new sensuous signs colored with aesthetic meaning are integrated. But without art we should not have understood this, nor transcended the law of interpretation which corresponds to the analysis of [the sign]. . . . All signs converge upon art; all apprenticeships, by the most diverse paths, are already unconscious apprenticeships to art itself. At the deepest level, the essential is in the signs of art. (*Proust* 25)

Absolving the self from its relations to ideological centers, the Legend shakes off what Ginsberg calls the "Syndrome of Shutdown" (*Mystery* 21) and answers Foucault's call for a mode of "living counter to fascism": a serial test of the possibilities of discourse and identity through "proliferation, juxtaposition, and disjunction, and not by subdivision and pyramidal hierarchization" (Deleuze and Guattari, *Anti-Oedipus* xiii). *Cody*'s translation of Cassady's "fever of excitement attuned only to flushed joy of exploration" (N. Cassady 79), in particular, loosens language from the unitary and totalizing paranoia embodied by J. Edgar Hoover, disastrous prototype of the industrial bureaucrat and willful dominator of man through surveillance.

Placed alongside Williams's endorsement, also in 1951, of Dallam Simpson's claim that "the whole aim of the gang that runs Russia, USA, Britain and France is to destroy the contemplative life altogether, to its last vestige, and to create 'WORK' until no one shall be left with time to think about anything" (*Autobiography* 307), the sense of Beat under Kerouac's hand testifies to the exuberant life of the body-mind. In the face of ambitions to induce what Marcuse calls "a totalitarian, routinized, value-free equilibrium beloved of behaviorists" (151), Kerouac draws on the Bohemian communities of New York and San Francisco as late centers of variety and energy in America, reconciling heretical drives for open society, ecological balance, and classlessness with national incarnations of a Great Subculture.

Sheer ebullience—"a swinging group of new American men bent on joy" (*GB* 57)—wards off the negative State (law, lack, limit), honoring what Blake and Reich identify as the necessity of volition over duty. "Desire becomes a positive force rather than one to struggle with," contends Sukenick, attesting to Rexroth's belief that "a natural society" is bound by "an all-pervading Eros" (qtd. in Lipton 304). "For all of its negations of the status quo," Sukenick continues, "the underground is firmly based on affirmation." Citing Emerson—"Poets are free and they make free . . . whether in an ode, or in an action, or in looks and behavior"—Sukenick maintains that the Dionysian discharge built into the Beat struggle is the axis of feasible community itself:

> I question the very possibility of moral power without this affirmative emotional dimension. Ought is not a positive number. Ought is neutral, neutered, nothing. No feeling. Ought requires enforcement and generates resentment. Even conceding the rule of law, ultimately a democracy can be based only on people doing what they want to do. . . . Unlocking the chains of thought and expressing that liberation draws out the whole of our intelligence, which does not consist merely of the rational and analytic faculties. . . . Keats's Mermaid Tavern is a sacred place, where talking, drinking, and carousing unleash the chained gods, obscene and holy, dangerous and creative, that can destroy us or lead us to a greater depth and scope of thought. Or both. (Sukenick 6–7)

Kerouac's stress on the social euphoria of art ("The Beat Generation's goal is ecstasy" [qtd. in "Roadster"]) offers release from the internalized condition of obedience, defined by Freud in *Group Psychology and the Analysis of Ego* in 1921 as the psychic penetration of mass desire and given the contemporary definition of "adjustment" in Reisman's *Lonely Crowd* and Whyte's *Organization Man*. "But there was a wisdom in it all," writes *The Dharma Bums'* narrator of his withdrawal from Mumford's "megamachine,"

as you'll see if you take a walk some night on a suburban street and pass
house after house on both sides of the street each with the lamplight
of the living room, shining golden, and inside the little blue square of
the television, each living family riveting its attention on probably one
show; nobody talking; silence in the yards; dogs barking at you because
you pass on human feet instead of on wheels. You'll see what I mean,
when it begins to appear like everybody in the world is soon going to
be thinking the same way and the Zen Lunatics have long joined dust,
laughter on their dust lips. (104)

Williams's prewar diagnosis of "the trouble with us all. We're not half used
up. And that unused portion drives us crazy" (qtd. in Mottram, "Living"
285) is updated in *Cody*'s tableaux of "a very successful young American . . .
executive," an archetype of cautious conformity and ultimately a mercenary
official of the Affluent Society rewarded for his allegiance: "just . . . bored
. . . nothing to do in his soul but flounce around and yawn and wait, always
wait, wait; the dullness of the heart gone dead" (119). "This is the story
of America," adds the narrator of *On the Road* at its conclusion, his status
relegated to that of security guard: "Everybody's doing what they are supposed to do" (384).

The challenge in each case is whether the private citizen can resist a
commodified identity from the onslaught of total social styling, as initiated
by Edward Bernays's Democracity theme of the 1939 World's Fair: an authoritarian model of a frictionless polity closed to change in which all places
are assigned and a spectator-control prototype for Disneyland ("factory for
the manufacture of one-level meaning and the repression of imagination"
[Hughes, *American* 461]). As Kerouac reports in 1958:

In actuality there was only a handful of real hip swinging cats and what
there was vanished mighty swiftly during the Korean War when (and
after) a sinister new kind of efficiency appeared in America; maybe
it was the result of the universalization of television and nothing else
(the Polite Total Police Control of Dragnet's "peace" officers), but the
beat characters after 1950 vanished into jails and madhouses, or were
shamed into silent conformity. (*GB* 48)

It is here that Kerouac's invitation to intervene creatively without surrender
to mass programming seems most potent, in the face of a contrary training
threatening reassertion (Sukenick: "[T]he tension Twain sees in America
between stability and freedom is not something peculiar to an individual or
an era, but still conditions the moment" [237]). The Duluoz Legend asserts
the restorative value of mobility and transformation at a time when the nation's

controllers are tightening the deadly yoke of prejudice for unity: impoverishing, paranoid, and sacrificial. In the context of "TOO MANY COPS AND TOO MANY LAWS and general killjoy culture . . . spreading Cancer of Americanism" (*SL, II* 44, 58), Kerouac's expansive "hunger for voyages . . . that haunts Americans, who are a nomad race," recorded by Wolfe (452) occurs inside a western compulsion, which, as Mottram observes,

> is increased once the speed of political and industrial change accelerates beyond what conventional, almost static, rates of change can carry. An intoxication with language frees itself from the body's panics (which could so easily shift back into stasis, and did in Kerouac's last days) and those tendencies towards which Russell Jacoby calls "social amnesia"—"memory driven out of mind by the social and economic dynamic of society." That the created text will hold even if the socio-economic dynamic cannot is the hope and the praxis. An autobiographical discourse becomes a true possible history, the really social rather than what sociologists and historians conceptualize as truth. ("Preface" 59)

Reconfiguring the entire language of past and present away from Market State consignments to instant redundancy, the Legend invades the prescriptive historiography of the traditional novel with a notion of experience charged with perpetual change. Kerouac thus shares that quality identified by Duncan, quoting Olson, as the urge

> to re-establish us in the ideal, to redeem all idealism from the commitments that claim prior authority there. "Otherwise the present will lose what America is the inheritor of: a secularization which not only loses nothing of the divine but by seeing process in reality redeems all idealism from theocracy or mobocracy, whether it is rational or superstitious, whether it is democratic or socialism." (qtd. in Olson, *Collected* xiv)

Countering the deadening transmission of official "news information"— "this is what you hear in New York all the time," writes Kerouac in *Cody,* "this week's *Life,* last week's *Time,* their concepts are all brought up . . . well, that was pretty neat I *must say*" (306)—the Legend bears testimony to an otherwise unacknowledged or "buried life" (Wolfe's subtitle for *Look Homeward, Angel*). Kerouac's wild form promotes a form of gnosis, which takes the experienced world as primary, disregards the habit of categories— commercial, academic, aesthetic—discovers its own measure, and maps an environment as initial act.

Transcending the pull of available grids inviting superimposition, he forges a literary confession of the self as witness to an occasion, something unique to what is recorded (Stein: "[T]he composition in which we live makes the art which we see and hear" [*Lectures* 165]). As Kerouac maintains, this is

> the only sure thing you can remember when you look back to see what people were doing during an important historical moment ... the poor souls actually sitting in that mysterious godlike stuff that later makes them say, "Listen, I was there . . ."
>
> (*VC* 341)

# 10

## *Liberation Visions*

Dylan Thomas died in 1954 in a room at the Chelsea, hotel to
Bohemia, after years of suicidal drinking. Parker went in '55
and Jackson Pollock drove his car into a tree in the Hamptons
in '56 after he'd fallen off the wagon for the last time. Three
lives without second acts. Charlie Parker, the saint of Bop
Kerouac admired, died on Kerouac's thirty-third birthday,
as Kerouac himself would go, also to an early grave, on Dizzy
Gillespie's birthday. When they hear Bird had died, Ted
Joans and three friends in the Village set off in four different
directions by subway and on foot with chalk and charcoal
to resurrect his spirit in the underground that revered him.
Soon the graffiti began appearing chalked all through the
New York subways and then in the johns of underground bars
and then in hip places all across the country: BIRD LIVES. The
Kilroy sign of another generation. KILROY WAS HERE, the killer
king projection of US GI's blasting their way across Europe.
BIRD LIVES, the flight of imagination toward freedom and
incandescent life.
— Ronald Sukenick, *Down and In*

While his jaundiced condition no doubt affected his judgment, Kerouac recognized that his "permissible dream"
of the regenerative nation had gone by the time of *Vanity
of Duluoz.* "America, the word, the sound is the sound of
my unhappiness, the pronunciation of my beat and stupid grief—" he had
previously lamented in *Cody.* "My happiness has no such name as America,
it has a more personal smaller more tittering secret name—" (118). Charles

Olson's indictment in *Maximus* adds to this and to dozens of other mid-century requiems for the defeat of New Eden, including Robert and Helen Lynd's *Middletown,* David Reisman's *The Lonely Crowd,* and C. Wright Mills's *White Collar*:

> desperate
> ugly
> cruel
> Land this Nation
> which never
> lets anyone
> come to
> shore . . .
> What is the heart, turning
> beating itself out leftward
> in hell to know heaven
> in this filthy land
> in this foul country where
> human lives are so much trash
> It is the dirty restlessness
> of fear and shame—human shame which doesn't even know how right
> it is to hate   what ignorance
> pervades
> the social climbing of this
> Ararat

(Olson, *Maximus* 497–98)

Paralyzed by vested interests and incapable of addressing its catastrophic levels of urban poverty, racism, and ecological attrition on an institutional level, the United States had lost touch with the vitality that had formerly made it so compelling. By the mid-1960s, the candid, colloquial style of the nation's art, so often the engine of cultural renewal, had been largely enervated by a combination of media overload and endlessly replayed Duchampian irony, a formula sponsoring cozy dialogue with the corporate class and its cultural programmers.

Again, the New York visual arts vanguard led the charge. Whereas Jasper Johns and Robert Rauschenberg continued to resist neat limitation by using junk and mythic American symbols in provisional gestures, which declared the body's presence and retained Dada's policy of indifference toward audience-seeking and salability, pop conceptualists such as Andy Warhol, Robert Morris, James Rosenquist, and Claes Oldenburg favored an attitude of easy assimilation. "These artists made good press," pointed out Jack Flam, "and good press is one of the backbones of commerce. Since the most cohesive force in American society is commerce, what started out as a cultural apostasy quickly became an acceptable part of American 'high culture'" (qtd. in Motherwell xiii).[1]

Signaling a commitment to the impersonal and reproducible consistent with their market orientation, the new arts leadership capitulated to a fascination with the controlled execution of fixed intention. Having isolated and codified the notion of sincerity as style, pop became the common coin of art, undermining the assumption uniting the postwar writing, painting, and music avant-gardes that direct expression was both possible and desirable. For Kerouac, the "new distaste in the culture since 1960" meant

> a trend towards the Ian Fleming type of sadistic facetiousness and "sickjoke" grisliness about human affairs, a grotesque hatred for the humble and the suffering heart, an admiration for the mechanistic smoothy *killer of sincerity,* a new infernal mockery sniggering down the alleys of the earth. (*SL, II* 408)

This change of temper would spur the post-structuralist fascination with theory and the purely self-referential release of meaning—in itself a perpetuation of the New Critical insistence on the authority of the text—a habit of enclosing discourse in a frame of quotation marks that denoted, to Robert Hughes, "a glumly mistrustful, fin-de-siècle period style that seems at least as fixed and repetitive as the mannerisms of late Abstract Expressionism" ("Effusiveness"). The discharge of energy on canvas or page was thus superseded by a decreasingly ironic celebration of mass production, commercializing futurist and constructivist preoccupations with the mechanical. This chimed with an "inverse millenarianism" and its language of exhaustion and endings (of history, of ideology, of democracy) that, to Fredric Jameson, characterized the new era of globalization and its digital systems of surveillance, mediating any "creative" impulse—if indeed, one could still entertain so speculative a fancy (Davidson 200).

Whereas the crisis in confidence in collective progression after the war had made the values of industrial technology distasteful, the role of the artist now became analogous to that of the mercantile designer. "I want to be a machine," boasted Warhol in 1962 (qtd. in Hughes, *Shock* 349), before trumpeting his belief that "Business art is the step that comes after Art. I started as a commercial artist, and I want to finish as a business artist. . . . [M]aking money is art and working is art and good business is the best art" (*Philosophy* 56). Accordingly, his silk-screen reproductions of consumer icons and the deadpan realism of Rosenquist's billboard-style pictures guaranteed orders of the homogeneous and the contrived, physical manifestations of a fixed and deterministic reality. Aping the manufacturing field where principles of scientific management were universally enforced—Ray Kroc, the milkshake machine salesman who bought out the McDonald brothers in 1961, declared that his company would not "trust some people who are non-conformists. We will make conformists out of them in a hurry. . . . The organization cannot trust the individual; the individual must trust the organization" (qtd. in Schlosser 5)—such laboratory-aura art-products served to "immerse the spectator in a sheath of prophylaxis," to quote Rosenberg,

> and reassure him of the operation in art of a rationale of conception, practice, and utility. . . . The art of the sixties is not *worked*—it is *done* according to plan. The aesthetic of cleanliness has a political dimension; the fuss about banning thick paint or "painterliness" from [the Museum of Modern Art exhibition] "The 1960s," derives from the wish to affirm middle-class tidiness and security. (*Artworks* 109–11)

The incorporation of Dada's anti-art gestures into the business mainstream thus accompanied the transference of Beat dissidence into the boutique hippyism of the later 1960s: style as "boundary and uniform," as Mottram saw it; "attitudes congealed into an aggressive conformity which could be assumed and purchased like any other consumer-spectator product. Hippie capitalists and rock millionaires inevitably moved into control" (*Blood* 91). Unsurprisingly, for many the shorthand posture of self-advertisement through alienation would become increasingly hysterical and impotent. As Kerouac recalls:

> [S]uddenly the Korean postwar youth emerged cool and beat, had picked up the gestures and the style; soon it was everywhere, the new look, the "twisted" slouchy look; finally it began to appear even in movies (James Dean) and on television; bop arrangements that were once the secret ecstasy music of beat contemplatives began to appear in every pit in every square orchestra book (cf. the works of Neal Hefti and not meaning Basie's book), the bop visions became common property of the commercial, popular cultural world; the use of expressions like "crazy," "hungup," "hassle," "make it," "like" ("like make it over sometime, like"), "go," became familiar and common usage; the ingestion of drugs became official (tranquilizers and the rest); and even the clothes style of the beat hipsters carried over to the new rock 'n' roll youth via Montgomery Clift (leather jacket), Marlon Brando (T-shirt) and Elvis Presley (long sideburns), and the Beat Generation, though dead, was resurrected and justified. (*GB* 48–49)

A rush of articles typified by the 1959 "Squaresville U.S.A. vs. Beatsville" feature in *Life*, designed, as McClure observes, "to cajole the public into some tarring and feathering" ("Painting" 37), prompted many to dissociate from public display. Within months of his favorable *New York Times* notice, Kerouac had the measure of a fashion epidemic trading wrongly in his name:

> Do you know what a beatnik is? Usually some guy who says "I hate my father. I hate my mother." So they leave home in Indiana and they come to New York. They write a line of poetry, type it up in a great big expensive five dollar binding book, put it under their arm, put on sandals, grow a little goatee, walk down the street and say they're poets. It's just kind of a fad. It was invented by the press. Listen, I'm a railroad brakeman, merchant marine deck-hand in war time. Beatniks don't do those things. They don't work. They don't get jobs. (qtd. in "Roadster")

Preparing a biographical note in 1954, Kerouac tells Ginsberg: "I really mean it, I would like to be anonymous like W. [Burroughs] and go around secretly enjoying world. Like my Orestes prince in disguise striding across the land" (*SL, I* 431). Six years later and "driven mad . . . by endless telegrams, phonecalls, requests, mail, visitors, reporters, snoopers," Kerouac experiences firsthand "the horror of literary notoriety" (*BS* 4). "You'll find me jaded, compared to last time," he warns Carolyn Cassady after Millstein's "discovery":

> Too much adulation is worse than non-reception, I see now, except on the economic level. "Too much adulation" means also the disgusting abuse from critics, which has caused my family in Lowell to announce, for instance, that I have disgraced the name of Kerouac, when all the time the disgrace emanates from critics and press. (*SL, II* 195)

And again in October 1962: "I'm so sick and tired of being insulted by critics I've just decided not to publish any more, except for already-written *Visions of Gerard* and *Desolation Angels*" (qtd. in C. Cassady 368).

This experience is fictionalized in *Big Sur,* where Duluoz is traumatized by drunken fans "puking in my study, stealing books and even pencils," who expect him to act like a "beatnik." Realizing he is "surrounded and outnumbered and ha[s] to get away to solitude again or die" (8), Kerouac hitchhikes to California in "[o]ne fast move or I'm gone" (qtd. in C. Cassady 12), withdraws, and reconfigures "The Crack-Up" of a Catholic drunk from a previous generation. Having fled New York for Burroughs's hotel room in Tangier after making the revisions demanded by Viking for *On the Road,* Kerouac further laments the cult of his accidental making in *Desolation Angels:*

And just like in New York or Frisco or anywhere there they are all hunching around in marijuana smoke, talking, the cool girls with long thin legs in slacks, the men with goatees, all an enormous drag after all and at the time (1957) not even started yet officially with the name of "Beat Generation." To think that I had so much to do with it, too, in fact at that very moment the manuscript of *Road* was being linotyped for imminent publication and I was already sick of the whole subject. . . . But all I could do was sit on the edge of the bed in despair like Lazarus listening to their awful "likes" and "like you know" and "wow crazy" and "a wig, man" "a real gas"—All this was about to sprout out all over America even down to High School level and be attributed in part to my doing! (351–52)[2]

Set against market confusions of understanding with publicity, and the mass impatience with anything beyond easy identification with the routine ego, Kerouac follows Melville—"So far as I am individually concerned and independent of my pocket, it is my earnest desire to write those sorts of books which are said to fail" (*Letters* 267)—and declares in *Visions of Cody* that on these terms, "[n]ot even success in America . . . matters" (410).

However, such wishes count for little in the rapacious midcentury nation. As the biographical circumstances of Kerouac and scores of fellow travelers across the arts testify, to maintain a belief in "order, tenderness and piety," as he movingly avowed in a late interview, when "[o]ur lives are no longer ours" (*SL, II* 203) would prove too great a long-term challenge for body and mind.

Whereas Ginsberg retained inspiration by navigating around an iconic status made available by the loosening of class attitudes, the vulnerability of many intensified with the huckster-merchandising of "youth" fashions, slang, and sounds. Among the first to cut Kerouac adrift from writers who were "saleable, and therefore viable in our society" ("It is of the greatest social significance that the novelists who say, 'I am proud to be delinquent' are nevertheless sold in editions of hundreds of thousands" ["Disengagement" 187–88]), Rexroth was quick to intercept the rituals of what Kerouac called "Bourgeois-Bohemian Materialism" (*GB* 49), soon to dominate every facet of US commodity culture. "The hipster is the furious square," Rexroth wrote the following year (1958), the target of his censure modified by the fact of his wife's temporary decampment with Robert Creeley. "The Beat novelists and poets and their camp followers are debauched Puritans. In their utter ignorance they embrace the false image which their enemies the squares have painted" (Rexroth, *Bird* 40). As he had previously noted:

The disengagement of the creator, who, as creator, is necessarily judge, is one thing, but the utter nihilism of the emptied-out hipster is another.

What is going to come of an attitude like this? It is impossible to go on indefinitely saying: "I am proud to be a delinquent," without destroying all civilized values. Between such persons no true enduring interpersonal relationships can be built, and of course, nothing resembling a true "culture"—an at-homeness of men with each other, their work, their loves, their environment. ("Disengagement" 193)

Whereas the New Left at the turn of the 1960s ignited such decisive social actions as the lunch counter sit-ins, the freedom rides, the draft resistance, and the free speech movement, Timothy Leary's rhetoric of hedonistic nonintervention by contrast recoiled into intellectual flabbiness. Bypassing the urban eco-utopianism of the Diggers, the gadget mantra "Turn on, tune in, drop out" trashed discrimination between energy and wastage, insurgence and fugitiveness, personal love and public posturing, and getting high and financing narcotic syndicates. In so doing, it arguably provoked the nation's lurch to the authoritarian right, the breakdowns at Haight-Ashbury achieving prominence soon after voters sanctioned Reagan, Wallace, and Maddox and an escalation of the Vietnam War.

Business drives to protract adolescence and champion apolitical outsiderdom beyond that decade, not to mention the army's use of psilocybin in Vietnam, have continued to demonstrate that the traditional shamanic context for the Dionysian breakthrough is crucial if desires are not "to diminish into mere rebelliousness, licensed orgy or ritual which re-energizes the reactionary and lethal status quo" (Mottram, *Blood* 193). Indeed, by 1972, Abbie Hoffman, Jerry Rubin, and Ed Sanders, co-writers of *Vote!*, would claim that "to glorify youth is to hate yourself." While the yippies, initiated upon Paul Goodman's dissenting intelligence, may have been "responsible for the excesses of youth culture," it was now clear that they "had been lured into a Madison Avenue trap: the bourgeois romancing of youth." What mattered now, they argued, was not "do-your-own-thing anarchy" but the organization of "a more humanistic society along socialist principles" (8–10).

However, unlike the hippie generation that he partly inspired, Kerouac leaves us a creative resource that resists market accelerations into the closure of "heritage" and the anesthetizing of radicalism. His experimental impulse draws attention to unstated political dimensions in the knowledge that art must always escape enlistment for partisan ends; even his late work refuses to bear the tired ideological message that it is loosely intended to convey. Given a just appraisal, the Duluoz Legend stands for the recovery of vitality in the face of university and media commodifications of the arts and of business appropriations of the word "creative" to legitimize internalized consumerism.

To take on this major body of work as it moves through the "dead air" of the conformist 1950s (Mailer, *Advertisements* 19) is to unleash what Duncan calls the "answering intensity of the imagination to hold its own values," for the "threshold" of "Pound, Lawrence, Joyce, H. D., Eliot" and their "black voice" revealing "the deep-going falsehood and evil of the modern state . . . remain . . . ours. The time of war and exploitation, the infamy and lies of the new capitalist war-state, continue" ("Rites" 17). This means a frontal assault on the vocabularies of industrial bureaucracy that can reverse the pattern of relations between individuals and machines and, in Ivan Illich's words,

> permit the evolution of a life-style and of a political system which give priority to the protection, the maximum use, and the enjoyment of the one resource that is almost equally distributed among all people: personal energy under personal control. (12–13)

Gambling on an assembly of propositions drawn from deliberate and implied intersections between literature, painting, and subterranean oral traditions (including jazz), Kerouac posits nothing less than a liberatory counterpoetics, which opposes privileged institutional authority over what fiction and poetry "are": namely, a fascination with the coherent self of the Protestant ethic (the bourgeois individual) and the entrenched middle-brow "confessionalism" of the Auden-Larkin axis, with its pathetic tone of defensiveness, cynicism, and limited irony glorified by Delmore Schwartz as "a failure of nerve" (qtd. in Rothenberg and Joris, *Two* 4). Writing becomes the work of unleashing perception with a view to constant realignment; while man is "bound by skin, ego, society, and species boundaries," to quote Snyder, "consciousness has boundaries of a different order, the mind is free" (*Earth* 127).

Asserting the responsibility of form as vision, Kerouac dramatizes Wittgenstein's sense of philosophy as "a struggle with the fascination that forms of expression have upon us. . . . [T]he limits of my language mean the limits of my world" (*Tractatus* 5.6). His Dionysian insistence on creativity as "raw, unfinished, and ineluctably in process" assumes a fast current of play or goofing in the "excitedness of pure being . . . to get back that intensity into the language" (Stein, *Four* vi) and a reassertion of the Blake-Whitman lineage of poet as seer and chronicler, where language itself becomes the instrument of revelation (Rothenberg and Joris, *Two* 11–12).

This transmission extends into the relationships between history and memory and their notations in the face of the Amnesia State's construction of a conglomerate "reality" (Kerouac: "Of what consequence a forgotten child's fear a quarter of a century ago in this Twentieth Century of recorded man?" [*SL, I* 258]). This is a recurrent theme in a nation where, as *Time* magazine suggests, "history without memory confines Americans to a sort of eternal present" (P. Smith). Such drives are consistent with the historic role of capitalism, which, being dependent upon the promise of eventual fulfillment, must sever links with the past in order to continually reproduce itself. Unforeseen even by Karl Marx and Adam Smith, this is borne out in the targeting of "global realization" toward the social group with the weakest attachment to yesterday: children. This, as John Berger notes, is the metaphysic of capital. Publicity, its language, is situated in a permanently deferred future excluding even the present and so "eliminates all becoming, all development. Experience is impossible within it" (*Ways* 153).

Kerouac's attempt to discover the sacred, embodied voice of the imagination recognizes the danger of complicity in the mind-forged manacles of a "[c]ivilization [that] takes us one more step removed from intuitive realization of what has been made manifest in this we call our life—" (*SD* 54). In the face of intensified mass-mediation, the poet's task is to prize language away from State plutocracy ("Our Friend the Atom"), to make a white magic in the form of Ginsberg's "absolute contrary field" (qtd. in Carroll 101) against the black magic of transnational surveillance. Life must be explored and widened and its rejuvenating expression invented; otherwise the mind itself will be composed from without, branded by the corporate monarchy, gridded within Burroughs's mythology of conditioned behavior. This is a political intervention at the profoundest level, the heroic search for humane language in an Imperial America self-actualizing into world cop, sex hero, and moral terminus (Ginsberg: "[A]lmost all our language has been taxed by war" [*Planet* 126]).

Oriented against the entropy of what Dean Moriarty calls "our holy American slop-jaws in Washington . . . planning fur-ther inconveniences" (*OTR* 110), the legacy of Jack Kerouac's work propels us into renewal, advancing what Eric Mottram terms "the enterprise of risk with intelligence and form, the passion and precision available in inventive language, and the pleasures of encountering such a field of energetic creativity" ("Treacherous" 133).

Notes

Works Cited

Index

# Notes

## 2. Dionysus Descends

1. Ironically Wolfe told his editor that *Of Time and the River* was flawed by his mode of working, which consisted of writing as frenetically as possible for extended periods and then assembling the results into narrative form (Donald 217–20).

2. Burroughs, whose fictions turn on the social uses of ecstasy, was entranced by the rural Marabout orders of Moroccan Sufism and their ritual celebrations of the goat god, Bou Jaloud, a survival of the Persian Dionysus cults and Pan himself, according to Brion Gysin. "Musicians are magicians in Morocco," writes Burroughs of his experience in 1973, when Ornette Coleman journeyed to the Riff foothills to record with the Master Musicians of the Jajouka ("Face to Face"). Visiting Burroughs in Tangier in spring 1957, Kerouac writes excitedly of this "strange wild Arab town—old as Time" and of Berber mountain herdsman and "nighted drums" at Ramadan: "All the Arabs play flutes from 3 AM till 7 PM the next day, and feast in between. . . . I've really absorbed all there is in Morocco" (*SL, II* 10–22).

3. Whereas Céline proposed that "reason died in 1914 . . . after that everybody began to rave" (*North* 25), Mina Loy's record of a "crisis in consciousness" the same year (6) preempted Lawrence's dating of western implosion in *Kangaroo*:

> It was in 1915 the old world ended. In the winter 1915–16 the spirit of old London collapsed; the city, in some way, perished, perished from being the heart of the world, and became a vortex of broken passions, lusts, hopes, fears, and horrors. The integrity of London collapsed and the genuine debasement began, the unspeakable baseness of the press and the public voice. (18)

4. See Gary Snyder:

> Class-structured civilized society is a kind of mass-ego. To transcend the ego is to go beyond society as well. "Beyond" there lies, inwardly, the unconscious. Outwardly, the equivalent of the unconscious is the wilderness: both

of these terms meet, one step even farther on, as one. . . . [I]t is necessary to look exhaustively into the negative and demonic potentials of the unconscious, and by recognizing these powers—symbolically acting them out—one releases himself from these forces. By this profound exorcism and ritual drama, the Great Subculture destroys the one credible claim of Church and State to a necessary function. (*Earth* 115)

5. Mottram draws attention to Nicholas Ray's *Rebel Without a Cause,* which presents the emblems of domestic settlement—parents, law, local police, wives—and turns on the familiar instruments of American middle-class life: telephones, guns, alcohol, and, most vitally, cars, which are used by the teenage protagonists in a twentieth-century jousting tournament (*Blood* 8).

6. Whereas Mussolini prided himself on his sunlit, shirtless skiing and posed for photographers in the saddles of motorbikes and horses and in airplane cockpits, Malcolm Campbell's "Bluebird" broke the world land-speed record sporting fascist colors. The cult of speed also animated Henry Williamson's self-projection as fascist and literary man of action. His *Goodbye West Country* echoes the spirit of *On the Road,* packed with tales of racing through England and Germany in his open roadster, "The Silver Eagle." To Valentine Cunningham this is "the classic fascist passage: the heroic union of speed-merchants and tough guys craved by all fascist leaders and actually achieved by Moseley—who made much of the jockey, the (woman) speedway star, the boxer, in his Union" (87).

## 3. "The Too Huge World"

1. "The book's flood of language," Kerouac continues,

is like *Ulysses* and should be treated with the same gravity. If Wyn or Carl insist on cutting it up to make the "story" more intelligible I'll refuse; and offer them another book which I'll commence writing at once, because now I know where I'm headed. . . . If necessary, change title to Visions of Neal or somethin, and I write new Road for Wyn. (*SL, I* 355–7)

The issue of textual interweaving emerges during Kerouac's TV debut on the *Steve Allen Show* in 1957, in which he reads from a manuscript concealed behind a copy of *Road* and combines its conclusion with the unpublished *Cody*'s.

## 4. Fabulous Artifice

1. Playful references to *Finnegans Wake* also appear throughout *Book of Blues,* as, for example, in the "WIFE & 3" section of "Richmond Hill Blues":

> Little Cathy gladdy
> with sun cheeks
> beeted
> Jamie hiding hugging
> her knees
> Mother Earwicker solemn,

lovely, flesh legs
white.

(84)

2. See Barry Miles:

Kerouac resolutely and somewhat petulantly remained in a hermetic little literary corner of his own making. . . . [W]riting his slightly fictionalized journals . . . he attempts no heroic or adult themes. There is no story. . . . As memoirs, his books are also unsatisfactory because the names of his friends and associates have been changed. . . . [W]ithout knowing who the characters are—Ginsberg, Burroughs, Corso, Snyder, Holmes, etc.—some of the books, such as *Desolation Angels* or *Vanity of Duluoz,* lose much of their interest. . . . [T]he myth that Kerouac himself perpetuated [is] that the books tell the true honest story of his life. (xiv–xvi)

3. This applies equally to the fine arts. Offsetting the postwar invasion of financial controls, Washington sponsored a European touring exhibition, "Advancing American Art," which included work by Rothko, Motherwell, and Pollock and projected an image of the United States as a model of democratic freedom, hitching onto the reputation of the Federal Art Project. However, following Republican charges of elitism, political deviance, and immorality directed toward the government, Secretary of State Marshall rescinded the exhibition in 1947, followed in 1951 by the Board of Trustees' removal of two paintings by Picasso and Pollock from display at the Los Angeles County Museum of Art for "political and aesthetic unorthodoxy." The leitmotif of this era is Congressman Dondero's speech to the House of Representatives in 1949. Trading on shadowy references to the 1930s' immigration of European artists who catalyzed American developments away from realism ("Expressionism aims to destroy by aping the primitive and insane. . . . Abstraction aims to destroy by the creation of brainstorms"), Dondero played on recurring national fears of invasion, invoking the Senate's offensive on the 1913 Armory Show ("Léger and Duchamp are now in the United States to aid in the destruction of our standards and traditions. . . . The question is, what have we, the plain American people, done to deserve this sore affliction that has been visited upon us so direly; who has brought down this curse upon us; who has let into our homeland this horde of germ-carrying art vermin?"). Stalin, who appointed social realism mandatory in 1932 on pain of judicial murder, and Hitler, who exiled modernism from Germany, would have concurred. It would be left to CIA goons in psychological warfare, in tandem with venture capitalists such as the Rockefellers, to ideologically launder an art commensurate with American greatness.

## 5. Beatitude and Sacrifice

1. See Robert Creeley:

To begin with, I was shy of the word "poet" and all its associations in a world I was then intimate with. It was not, in short, a fit attention for a young man raised in the New England manner, compact of Puritanically derived sense of speech and sensuality. Life was real and earnest, and one had best get on with it. (*Measure* 54)

2. Charters draws attention to the lifelong right-wing persona adopted by Kerouac when corresponding with his family. For instance, a 1948 letter to his sister and brother-in-law observes that

a war against Communism, if and when it comes, is a war against the *real* enemy of American life: the psychology of neurotic malcontent. The only trouble is, fighting Russia alone is not fighting the Communism in England and France and China and India and—America. . . . [That last fiasco] was just Communist-inspired on one hand, and uselessly directed against the German race on the other. (*SL, I* 144–5)

## 6. Orality

1. Kerouac:

I mean to use my dashes as definite separation of definite whole statements— [others] try to use dashes to separate clauses WITHIN a sentence which is not what I mean at all—For the separation of clauses and statements WITHIN a sentence I use parentheses, as you know. (*SL, II* 324–5)

2. Kerouac: "Clearly, publishing is now in a flux of commercialism that began during World War II; for instance I wonder if Thomas Wolfe's wild huge books would be published today if he were just coming up, like me" (*SL, I* 466).

3. See David Meltzer:

As a 20 year old poet, I thought all the [Beat poets,] with the exception of Kerouac, identified more with the jazz prior to Bebop. It's the difference between someone shaped by the Beatles or bent out of shape by Capt. Beefheart & His Magic Band. When I read my poetry at the Cellar I consciously attempted to improvise words. . . . I would scribble out an outline of a poem—a "head" arrangement using key phrases, images—a general direction of where I wanted the work to go. There would also be written verses as anchors for areas when I improvised, created lyric or poem on the spot—in context with the music and the idea of a poem. This way there was more real exchange between musicians and poet. For me the other poets read outside the music, reading poems against the background of jazz. (notes for *Howls, Raps and Roars*)

## 7. The Field of Action

1. See R. D. Carmichael:

Neither the authority of man alone nor the authority of fact alone is sufficient. The universe, as known to us, is a joint phenomenon of the observer and observed; and every process of discovery in natural science or in other branches of human knowledge will acquire its best when it is in accordance with this fundamental principle. (7)

And Max Born: "For, beyond the bounds of science, too, objective and relative reflection is a gain, a release from prejudice, a liberation of the spirit from standards whose claim to absolute validity melts away before the critical judgement of the relativist" (12).

2. Olson wrote to Kerouac in September 1957 to express admiration for "Neal and the Three Stooges" in *New Editions* and "Old Lucien Midnight" in *Combustion*, "claiming [him] as a poet" to Don Allen: "It's a tight form—and delicious" (qtd. in *SL, II* 67).

3. See Schoenberg on composing: "an unnamable sense of a sounding & moving space, of a form with characteristic relationships; of moving masses whose shape is unnamable & not amenable to comparison" (*Self-Portrait* 74).

4. This essay prefaced the first US impression of Lawrence's poems, edited by Rexroth in 1946.

## 8. Bop Prosody

1. See Juan Gris, writing in 1917:

I hope that ultimately I shall be able to express very precisely, and by means of pure intellectual elements, an imaginary reality. This really amounts to a sort of painting which is inaccurate but precise, just the opposite of bad painting which is accurate but not precise. (*Letters* 53)

2. Ornette Coleman:

Once I heard Eubie Blake say that when he was playing in black bands for white audiences, during the time when segregation was strong, that the musicians had to go on stage without any written music. The musicians would go backstage, look at the music, then leave the music there and go out and play it. He was saying that they had a more saleable appeal if they pretended not to know what they were doing. The white audience felt safer. ("Harmolodic" 47)

3. As Cowley notes, Tristran Tzara's Dada approach to language interested many postwar American writers and provides further connections with jazz. This occurs most obviously in the collage of swing, showmanship, free jazz, astrology, and Egyptian mythological tract and electronics deployed by Sun Ra's Arkestra. In *The Freedom Principle,* John Litweiler also remarks upon the "Dada atmosphere" of a 1967 gig by the Roscoe Mitchell Quartet (177), whose members maintained links with Ra's organization through the Association for the Advancement of Creative Music. An offshoot of this, the Art Ensemble of Chicago, echoed the Arkestra in performances that resembled a sermon, drama, and stand-up comedy routine all at once. With its tribal makeup and idiosyncratic couture, the ensemble generated a rolling slide-show of aural and visual images—forests seething with life, village

fiestas, traffic jams, arguments, stampedes—built upon references from every jazz era. Central to the AEC and Mitchell's quartet was Lester Bowie, a trumpeter who had worked in carnival ensembles as well as bop bands. His playful combinations of the incongruous recall the freedom claimed for the novel in Ishmael Reed's *Yellow Back Radio Broke-Down*, a book whose hero is called "crazy dada nigger" by a social realist commentator (35). In the same vein, LeRoi Jones, author of the poem "Black Dada Nihilismus," brands the rhythm and blues "barwalkin'" saxophonist Big Jay McNeeley "the first Dada coon of the age" in *The Screamers*. Lying on his back and producing an animalistic wail through his horn, he is compared to Marcel Duchamp's "L.H.O.O.Q."—"the Mona Lisa with the moustache" (Cowley 197–99). And in *Down and In*, Sukenick refers to a party thrown by Ted Joans and attended by Charlie Parker, "dedicated to Surrealism, Dada, and the Mau Mau" (50). Designated "the only Afro-American surrealist" by Andre Breton, Joans in *Afrodisia* prescribes a 1960s fusion of black nationalism, jazz, and dated eroticism. A related ambience informs the description of a street fight in Chester Himes's story *A Rage in Harlem* (1957), where slash wounds yield not blood but "old clothes" and "dried printer's ink from the layers of old newspapers" (*Collected* 89). "I thought I was writing realism," Himes declares. "It never occurred to me that I was writing absurdity. Realism and absurdity are so similar in the lives of American blacks that one cannot tell the difference" (*My Life* 109).

4. See also Samuel Taylor Coleridge, writing in 1818:

> The organic form . . . is innate; it shapes as it develops itself from within, and the fulness of its development is one and the same with the perfection of its outward form . . . for it is even this that constitutes its genius—the power of acting creatively under laws of its own origination. (239)

5. Goebbels drew up performance instructions in Nazi Germany, which restricted syncopated rhythms to a maximum of eight bars and forbade the playing of saxophones in higher registers and trumpets with mutes, lest they should reduce their "noble" sound into a "Jewish or Negroid whine." Lord Reith, the first chairman of the BBC, was delighted by this and lamented that Britain "should be behind in dealing with this filthy product of modernity." Soviet propaganda of the early 1950s used similar tactics to demonize American culture, identifying the playing of saxophones with murder and treason. An allegiance to jazz through the next three decades continued to qualify as a gesture of resistance; in September 1986, five Czechoslovakian free improvisers were indicted in Prague on trumped up charges of engaging in "unauthorised business enterprises" and subsequently imprisoned (Hrebeniak 4).

6. Kerouac in 1948:

> I really am tremendously prophetic about jazz. . . . [W]hen I went to see Tristano I overheard some of the cats discussing him in the john. . . . They agreed that Tristano was more profound than Stravinsky, which I think is a gross understatement. He is very close to Beethoven, as all the musicians agree. . . . The guy is standing the music world on its ear. (*SL, I* 141)

## 9. Beyond Beat

1. In the same letter, Kerouac thanks Granville H. Jones for sending his MA thesis on his work, telling him that this was

the only thing too that has made me happy in three years, since the publication of On the Road and the subsequent sickeningness of "being famous" (being used by everybody and his uncle) and of course the nausea of phoney criticisms and even worse the nausea of false enthusiasms based on the wrong reasons (as for instance those who "admire" me for being so "wild & irresponsible" etc.) What you've written about me has restored my faith in my own writing. What you say, I knew (not being vain), always knew. But no one ever said it out loud, or cared to say it. And I was being terribly discouraged by the scandalous lack of critical fairness. (*SL, II* 274)

2. The typical position of the article's writer, Paul O'Neil, is established by his excruciating adventure in the beatnik idiom. Describing the United States as "the biggest, sweetest and most succulent casaba ever produced by the melon patch of civilization," O'Neil likened "the improbable rebels of the Beat Generation" to "the hairiest, scrawniest and most discontented specimens [of fruit flies] . . . who not only refuse to sample the seeping juices of American plenty and American social advance but scrape their feelers in discordant scorn of any and all who do."

3. See Richard Pousette-Dart:

[B]eware of all schools, isms, creeds, or entanglements which would tend to make [the artist] other than himself. He must stand alone, free and open in all directions for exits and entrances, and yet with all freedom, he must be solid and real in the substance of his form. (qtd. in Tuchman 126)

And see Bradley Walker Tomlin:

Formulation of belief has a way of losing its brightness and of fencing one in. The artist having found, and publicly declared, what seem to be the answers, will then in all likelihood swear to protect them, as if upon oath, since stated beliefs, like certificates in the anterooms of practitioners, imply the authority to pursue a predictable course of action. (qtd. in Barr 80)

4. Mark Rothko's transition from biomorphic surrealist forms to progressively simplified color spots floating in delimited fields (*No. 26, No. 48,* and *No. 49*) took place in 1947. Within two years, Barnett Newman also started to work in color fields articulated in bands (*Abraham* and *Covenant*).

## 10. Liberation Visions

1. Flam quotes Marcel Duchamp in 1962:

This Neo-Dada which they call New Realism, Pop Art, Assemblage, etc., is an easy way out and lives on what Dada did. When I discovered ready-mades I thought to discourage aesthetics. . . . I threw the bottle-rack and the urinal into their faces as a challenge and now they admire them for their aesthetic beauty (qtd. in Motherwell xiii).

2. This should be read against Kerouac's earlier suggestion to his agent that in "Rock n Roll Hooligan England . . . it would double the sales to change [*On the Road*'s] title to ROCK AND ROLL ROAD" (*SL, II* 22–27); his later boast to Lucien Carr that he'd "got big intellectual (classic) letter from big producer who wants big socko ending where Dean crashes & dies, utilizing myth of James Dean on ROAD story, I dunt care" (*SL, II* 109); and his subsequent "absolute refus[al] to let any cruelty be injected into a movie version of ROAD. . . . Fuck these killers of the world's heart" (*SL, II* 120).

# Works Cited

## Works by Jack Kerouac

*The Town and the City.* New York: Harcourt, 1950.
*On the Road.* New York: Viking, 1957. London: Penguin, 1988.
*The Subterraneans.* New York: Grove, 1958, 1981.
*The Dharma Bums.* New York: Viking, 1958. London: Paladin, 1992.
*Doctor Sax.* New York: Grove 1959. London: Paladin, 1992.
*Maggie Cassidy.* New York: Avon, 1959. London: Paladin, 1991.
*Mexico City Blues.* New York: Grove, 1959, 1990.
*Visions of Cody.* Abridged ed. New York: New Directions, 1960.
*The Scripture of the Golden Eternity.* New York: Totem/Corinth, 1960. San Francisco: City Lights, 1994.
*Tristessa.* New York: Avon, 1960. London: Paladin, 1992.
*Lonesome Traveler.* New York: McGraw-Hill, 1960. London: Grafton, 1972.
*Rimbaud.* San Francisco: City Lights, 1960.
*Book of Dreams.* San Francisco: City Lights, 1961.
*Pull My Daisy.* New York: Grove, 1961.
*Big Sur.* New York: Farrar, 1962. London: Paladin, 1992.
*Visions of Gerard.* New York: Farrar, 1963. London: Paladin, 1992.
*Desolation Angels.* New York: Coward-McCann, 1965. London: Paladin, 1990.
*Satori in Paris.* New York: Grove, 1966. London: Paladin, 1991.
*Vanity of Duluoz.* New York: Coward-McCann, 1968. London: Paladin, 1990.
*Scattered Poems.* Ed. Ann Charters. San Francisco: City Lights, 1971.
*Pic.* New York: Grove, 1971.
"Jack Kerouac at Northport, Part One." *Athanor* (Winter/Spring 1971).
*Visions of Cody.* New York: McGraw-Hill, 1973. London: Flamingo, 1992.
*Trip Trap: Haiku along the Road from San Francisco to New York 1959,* with Albert Saijo and Lew Welch. Bolinas, CA: Grey Fox, 1973.

*Two Early Stories.* New York: Aloe, 1973.

*Heaven and Other Poems.* Ed. Donald Allen. Bolinas, CA: Grey Fox, 1977.

*Take Care of My Ghost, Ghost,* with Allen Ginsberg. New York: Ghost, 1977.

*Old Angel Midnight.* London: Midnight, 1985. San Francisco: Grey Fox, 1993.

*Safe in Heaven Dead: Interviews with Jack Kerouac.* Ed. Michael White. Madras: Hanuman, 1990.

*The Jack Kerouac Collection.* Rhino CD set, 1990. Reissue of Jack Kerouac and Steve Allen, *Poetry for the Beat Generation,* Hanover LP, 1959; Jack Kerouac, *Blues and Haikus,* with Al Cohn and Zoot Sims, Hanover LP, 1959; and Jack Kerouac, *Readings by Jack Kerouac on the Beat Generation,* Verve LP, 1960.

*Pomes All Sizes.* San Francisco: City Lights, 1992.

*Good Blonde & Others.* San Francisco: Grey Fox, 1993.

*Book of Blues.* New York: Penguin, 1995.

*The Portable Jack Kerouac.* Ed. Ann Charters. New York: Viking, 1995.

*San Francisco Blues.* New York: Penguin, 1995.

*Selected Letters: 1940–1956.* Ed. Ann Charters. New York: Viking, 1995.

*Some of the Dharma.* New York: Viking, 1997.

*Selected Letters, 1957–1969.* Ed. Ann Charters. New York: Viking, 1999.

*Atop an Underwood.* Ed. Paul Marion. New York: Penguin, 2000.

*Orpheus Emerged.* New York: ibooks, 2000.

## Other Works

Adams, Henry. *The Education of Henry Adams.* 1918. London: Penguin, 1995.

Allen, Donald, and Robert Creeley, eds. *New American Story.* New York: Grove, 1965.

Allen, Donald, and Warren Tallman, eds. *The Poetics of the New American Poetry.* New York: Grove, 1973.

Anderson, Sherwood. *Winesburg, Ohio.* 1919. London: Penguin, 1991.

Aronowitz, Alfred G. "The Beat Generation, Part II." *New York Post,* Mar. 10, 1959.

———. "The Yen for Zen." *Escapade,* Oct. 6, 1960.

Ashbery, John. *Reported Sightings: Art Chronicles, 1957–1987.* Cambridge: Harvard UP, 1991.

Ashton, Dore. *The New York School: A Cultural Reckoning.* Berkeley: U of California P, 1972.

Attali, Jacques. *Noise: The Political Economy of Music.* Trans. Brian Massumi. Theory and History of Literature, Vol. 16. Minneapolis: U of Minnesota P, 1985.

Bachelard, Gaston. *The Poetics of Space.* Trans. Maria Jolas, Boston: Beacon, 1964.

Bailey, Derek. *Improvisation: Its Nature and Practice in Music.* Ashbourne: Moorland, 1980.

Barr, Alfred H., ed. *The New American Painting.* New York: Museum of Modern Art, 1959.

Barthes, Roland. *Mythologies.* Trans. Annette Lavers. New York: Noonday, 1972.

———. *Writing Degree Zero.* Trans. Annette Lavers and Colin Smith. New York: Hill and Wang, 1967.

Bataille, Georges. "The Pineal Eye." *Visions of Excess: Selected Writings, 1927–1939.* Trans and ed. Allan Stoekl. Minneapolis: U of Minnesota P, 1985.

Bateson, Gregory. *Naven: A Survey of the Problems Suggested by a Composite Picture of the Culture of a New Guinea Tribe Drawn from Three Points of View.* Oxford: Oxford UP, 1958.

———. *Steps to an Ecology of Mind: Collected Essays in Anthropology, Psychiatry, Evolution, and Epistemology.* Chicago: U of Chicago P, 2000.

Baudelaire, Charles. *Art in Paris, 1845–1862: Salons and Other Exhibitions.* Ed. and trans. Jonathan Mayne. London: Phaidon, 1965.

Baudrillard, Jean. *Selected Writings.* Trans. Mark Poster. Cambridge, England: Polity, 1988.

Beatty, Jerome. "Trade Winds." *Saturday Review,* Sept. 28, 1957.

Beckett, Samuel. *Proust and Three Dialogues with Georges Duthuit.* London: Calder, 1987.

Beiles, Sinclair, William S. Burroughs, Gregory Corso, and Brion Gysin. *Minutes to Go.* San Francisco: Beach, 1968.

Benjamin, Walter. *Illuminations.* Trans. Harry Zohn. New York: Schocken, 1969.

Berger, John. *And Our Faces, My Heart, Brief as Photos.* London: Penguin, 1978.

———. *Ways of Seeing.* London: BBC and Penguin, 1972.

Bergson, Henri. *Duration and Simultaneity, with Reference to Einstein's Theory.* Trans. Leon Jacobson. Indianapolis: Bobbs-Merrill, 1965.

Bernal, J. D. *The Extension of Man: A History of Physics before 1900.* London: Weidenfeld, 1972.

Bernays, Edward L. *Propaganda.* New York: Liveright, 1928.

Berrigan, Ted. "The Art of Fiction XLI: Jack Kerouac." *Paris Review* 43 (Summer 1968). Reprinted in *Beat Writers at Work: The Paris Review.* Ed. George Plimpton. New York: Modern, 1999.

Black, Jack. *You Can't Win: The Autobiography of Jack Black.* New York: Macmillan, 1926.

Blackburn, Paul. "Craft Interview." *New York Quarterly,* Spring 1970.

———. *The Selected Poems.* Ed. Edith Jarolim. New York: Persea, 1989.

———. "Shop Talk." *Sixpack* 7/8 (Spring/Summer 1974).

Blake, William. *Complete Writings.* Ed. Geoffrey Keynes. Oxford and New York: Oxford UP, 1972.

Blanchot, Maurice. *L'entrietien infini.* Paris: Gallimard, 1969.

Bloom, Harold. *The Anxiety of Influence: A Theory of Poetry.* New York and Oxford: Oxford UP, 1963.

"Books News from Publicity Department." Farrar, Straus, and Cudahy, Spring 1963.

Born, Max. *Einstein's Theory of Relativity.* New York: Dover, 1962.

Boulez, Pierre. *Orientations: Collected Writings.* Ed. Jean-Jacques Nattiez. Trans. Martin Cooper. London: Faber, 1986.

Breton, André. *Manifestoes of Surrealism.* Trans. Richard Seaver and Helen R. Lane. Ann Arbor: U of Michigan P, 1972.

Brooks, Cleanth. *The Well Wrought Urn.* New York: Harcourt, 1947.

Brown, Earle. "Form in New Music." *Darmstädter Beiträge zur Neuen Musik* 10 (1965).

Brown, Norman O. *Closing Time.* New York: Random, 1973.

———. *Life Against Death: The Psychoanalytical Meaning of History.* New York: Vintage, 1959.

———. *Love's Body.* New York: Vintage, 1966.

Buckley, Will, Jr. "The Hippies." *Firing Line,* TV program, WOR, New York City. Sept. 1968.

Bunting, Basil. *A Note on Briggflatts.* Durham: Basil Bunting Poetry Archive, 1994.

———. *Three Essays.* Ed. Richard Caddel. Durham: Basil Bunting Poetry Archive, 1994.

Burroughs, William S. *The Adding Machine: Collected Essays.* London: Calder, 1985.

———. *Electronic Revolution.* Bonn: Expanded Media Editions, 1976.

———. "Face to Face with the Goat God." *Oui,* Aug. 1973.

———. *The Naked Lunch.* New York: Grove, 1959.

———. *The Place of the Dead Roads.* New York: Holt, 1983.

———. *The Western Lands.* New York: Viking, 1987.

Butterick, George. *A Guide to The Maximus Poems of Charles Olson.* Berkeley: U of California P, 1978.

Cage, John. *John Cage: An Anthology.* Ed. Richard Kostelanetz. New York: Da Capo, 1991.

———. *Silence: Lectures and Writings.* Hanover, NH: Wesleyan UP, 1961.

———. *Writer: Previously Uncollected Pieces.* Ed. Richard Kostelanetz. New York: Limelight, 1993.

Calloway, Cab. *Minnie the Moocher.* RCA LP, 1981.

Carmichael, R. D. *The Theory of Relativity.* New York: Wiley, 1913.

Carr, Ian, Digby Fairweather, and Brian Priestley. *Jazz: The Essential Companion.* London: Paladin, 1988.

Carroll, Paul. *The Poem in Its Skin.* Chicago: Big Table, 1968.

Cassady, Carolyn. *Off the Road: My Years with Cassady, Kerouac, and Ginsberg.* New York: Morrow, 1990.

Cassady, Neal. *The First Third.* San Francisco: City Lights, 1981.

Cassavetes, John, dir. *Shadows.* Castle Hill Productions, 1959.

Cawley, A. C., and J. J. Anderson, eds. *Pearl, Cleanness, Patience, Sir Gawain and the Green Knight.* London: Everyman, 1962.

Céline, Louis-Ferdinand. *Journey to the End of the Night.* Trans. Ralph Manheim. New York: New Directions, 1983.

——. *North.* Trans. Ralph Manheim. London: Bodley Head, 1972.

Cervantes Saavedra, Miguel de. *Don Quixote.* Trans. J. M. Cohen. London: Penguin, 1950.

Charters, Ann, ed. *The Beats: Literary Bohemians in Postwar America.* Detroit: Gale, 1984. Vols. 16 and 17 of *Dictionary of Literary Biography.* Ed. Matthew J. Bruccoli and Richard Layman. 328 vols. to date. 1978–2006.

——, ed. *Kerouac: A Biography.* New York: St. Martin's, 1973.

——, ed. *The Penguin Book of the Beats.* London: Penguin, 1992.

Chassman, Neil. *Poets of the Cities: New York and San Francisco, 1950–1965.* Dallas: Museum of Fine Arts, 1974.

Chipp, Herschel B., ed. *Theories of Modern Art: A Source Book by Artists and Critics.* Berkeley: U of California P, 1968.

Chomsky, Noam. *The Chomsky Reader.* Ed. James Peck. London: Serpent's Tail, 1988.

Clark, Thomas. "The Art of Poetry: Allen Ginsberg." *Paris Review* 35 (Summer 1966). Reprinted in *Beat Writers at Work: The Paris Review.* Ed. George Plimpton. New York: Modern, 1999.

Cobbing, Bob, and Bill Griffiths, eds. *Verbi Visi Voco.* London: Writers Forum, 1992.

Coleman, Ornette. *Free Jazz.* Atlantic LP, 1960.

——. "Harmolodic = Highest Instinct: Something to Think About." *City Lights Review* 3 (1991).

——. *The Shape of Jazz To Come.* Atlantic LP, 1959.

——. *Something Else!!!! The Music of Ornette Coleman.* Contemporary LP, 1958.

——. *Tomorrow Is the Question! The New Music of Ornette Coleman.* Contemporary LP, 1959.

Coleridge, Samuel Taylor. *Selected Poetry and Prose.* Ed. Kathleen Raine. London: Penguin, 1957.

Coltrane, John. *Ascension.* Impulse! LP, 1965.

——. *Live at the Village Vanguard Again!* Impulse! LP, 1966.

Conrad, Joseph. *The Complete Short Fiction of Joseph Conrad, Volume Two: The Stories.* London: Pickering, 1992.

——. *Heart of Darkness.* 1902. London: Penguin, 1985.

——. *Lord Jim.* 1900. Oxford: Oxford UP, 1983.

Cook, Bruce. *The Beat Generation: The Tumultuous '50's Movement and Its Impact on Today.* New York: Scribner's, 1971.

Coolidge, Clark. "Kerouac." *Disembodied Poetics: Annals of the Jack Kerouac School.* Ed. Anne Waldman and Andrew Schelling. Albuquerque: U of New Mexico P, 1995.

Corbin, Henri. *Spiritual Body and Celestial Earth: From Mazdean Iran to Shi'ite Iran.* Trans. Nancy Pearson. Princeton, NJ: Princeton UP, 1977.

——. "The Theory of Visionary Knowledge in Islamic Philosophy." *Temenos* 8 (1987).

Corman, Cid. *At Their Word: Essays on the Arts of Language, Volume Two.* Santa Barbara: Black Sparrow, 1978.

Cowley, Julian. "Jazz and Fiction in Post-Bebop America." *Review of Contemporary Fiction* 34 (1987).

Crane, Hart. *Complete Poems.* Newcastle, England: Bloodaxe, 1984.

Creeley, Robert. *The Collected Essays.* Berkeley: U of California P, 1989.

——. *The Collected Poems, 1945–1975.* Berkeley: U of California P, 1982.

——. *The Collected Prose.* Berkeley: U of California P, 1988.

——. *A Quick Graph: Collected Notes and Essays.* San Francisco: Four Seasons, 1970.

——. *A Sense of Measure.* London: Calder, 1972.

Cunningham, Valentine. *British Writers of the Thirties.* Oxford: Oxford UP, 1988.

Davidson, Michael. *The San Francisco Renaissance.* Cambridge: Cambridge UP, 1989.

Davis, Miles. *Kind of Blue.* Columbia LP, 1959.

Davis, Miles, and Quincy Troupe. *Miles: The Autobiography.* New York: Simon, 1989.

Dawson, Fielding. *The Black Mountain Book.* Rocky Mount: North Carolina Wesleyan College P, 1991.

Debord, Guy. *The Society of the Spectacle.* Trans. Donald Nicholson-Smith. New York: Zone, 1995.

de Crèvecoeur, J. Hector St. John. *Letters from an American Farmer.* 1782. Oxford: Oxford UP, 1997.

De Hirsch, Storm. "A Talk with de Kooning." *Intro Bulletin* 1.1 (Oct. 1955).

de Kooning, Willem. *Collected Writings.* Madras: Hanuman, 1988.

——. "The Renaissance and Order." *trans/formation* 1.2 (1951).

——. "What Abstract Art Means to Me." *The Museum of Modern Art Bulletin* 18.3 (Spring 1951).

Deleuze, Gilles. *Negotiations.* Trans. Martin Joughin. New York: Columbia UP, 1995.

——. *Proust and Signs.* Trans. Richard Howard. London: Athlone, 1999.

Deleuze, Gilles, and Félix Guattari. *Anti-Oedipus: Capitalism and Schizophrenia, Volume One.* Trans. Robert Hurley, Mark Seem, and Helen R. Lane. London: Athlone, 1984.

——. *A Thousand Plateaus: Capitalism and Schizophrenia, Volume Two.* Trans. Brian Massumi. London: Athlone, 1987.

Derrida, Jacques. *Writing and Difference.* Trans. Alan Bass. London: Routledge and Kegan Paul, 1978.

de Tocqueville, Alexis. *Democracy in America, 1835–40.* Ed. J. P. Mayer. Trans. George Lawrence. London: Fontana, 1994.

Diderot, Denis. *Jacques the Fatalist and His Master.* Trans. J. Robert Loy. New York: Norton, 1978.

Dodds, E. R. *The Greeks and the Irrational.* Boston: Beacon, 1951.

Donald, David Herbert. *Look Homeward: A Life of Thomas Wolfe*. Boston: Little, 1987.

Dos Passos, John. *U.S.A.* Boston: Houghton, 1938.

Dostoevsky, Fyodor. *The Idiot*. Trans. Alan Myers. Oxford: Oxford UP, 1992.

———. *The Possessed*. Trans. Constance Garnett. London: Heinemann, 1914.

DuBois, W. E. B. *The Souls of Black Folk*. 1903. Millwood, NY: Kraus-Thompson, 1973.

Dumas, Henry. *Goodbye, Sweetwater: New and Selected Stories*. Ed. Eugene B. Redmond. New York: Thunder's Mouth, 1988.

Duncan, Robert. *Bending the Bow*. New York: New Directions, 1968.

———. *Caesar's Gate: Poems, 1949–1950*. Palma de Mallorca, Spain: Divers, 1955.

———. *Fictive Certainties*. New York: New Directions, 1985.

———. *Groundwork: Before the War*. New York: New Directions, 1984.

———. *The Opening of the Field*. New York: New Directions, 1960.

———. "Rites of Participation: Parts I and II." *A Caterpillar Anthology*. Ed. Clayton Eshleman. New York: Anchor, 1971.

Duncan, Val. "Kerouac Revisited." *Newsday*, July 18, 1964.

Eddington, Arthur. *Science and the Unseen World*. London: Allen, 1929.

Eliade, Mercea. *The Sacred and the Profane: The Nature of Religion*. Trans. Willard R. Trask. New York: Harcourt, 1959.

Eliot, T. S. *Selected Poems*. London: Faber, 1954.

———. *Selected Prose*. Ed. Frank Kermode. London: Faber, 1975.

Ellis, R. J. "'I Am Only a Jolly Storyteller': Jack Kerouac's *On the Road* and *Visions of Cody*." *The Beat Generation Writers*. Ed. A. Robert Lee. London: Pluto, 1996.

Ellison, Ralph. *Shadow and Act*. New York: Vintage, 1964.

Ellmann, Richard. *along the riverrun: Selected Essays*. London: Penguin, 1989.

———. *James Joyce*. Oxford: Oxford UP, 1982.

Emerson, Ralph Waldo. *Selected Works*. Ed. Larzer Ziff. London: Penguin, 1982.

Engels, Friedrich. *The Origins of the Family, Private Property and the State*. 1884. London: Lawrence, 1972.

Eshleman, Clayton, ed. *A Caterpillar Anthology*. New York: Anchor, 1971.

Euripides. *The Bacchae and Other Plays*. Trans. Philip Vellacott. London: Penguin, 1973.

Everson, William. "Dionysus and the Beat—Four Letters on the Archetype." *Sparrow* 63 (1977).

Ewen, Stuart. *PR! A Social History of Spin*. New York: Basic, 1998.

Fariña, Richard. *Been Down So Long It Looks Like Up to Me*. 1966. London: Penguin, 1983.

Federman, Raymond, ed. *Surfiction: Fiction Now and Tomorrow*. Chicago: Swallow, 1975.

Feldman, Morton. *Projections*. New York: Peters, 1951.

———. *Works, 1951–57*. Columbia LP, 1959.

Fenollosa, Ernest. "The Chinese Written Character as Resource for Modern Poetry." *The Poetics of the New American Poetry*. Ed. Donald Allen and Warren Tallman. New York: Grove, 1973.

Ferlinghetti, Lawrence. *Poetry in the Cellar*. Fantasy LP, 1958.

———. *These are My Rivers: New and Selected Poems, 1955–1993*. New York: New Directions, 1993.

———. *Tyrannus Nix*. New York: New Directions, 1969.

Feyerabend, Paul. *Against Method*. London: New Left, 1975.

Fitzgerald, F. Scott. *The Great Gatsby*. 1926. London: Penguin, 1990.

———. *Tender Is the Night*. 1934. London: Penguin, 1997.

Flaubert, Gustave. *Selected Letters*. Trans. Geoffrey Wall. London: Penguin, 1997.

Foner, Philip S., ed. *Jack London: American Rebel—A Collection of His Social Writings Together with an Extensive Study of the Man and His Times*. New York: Citadel, 1947.

Ford, Henry. *The International Jew*. Dearborn, MI: Dearborn, 1922.

Foucault, Michel. *The History of Sexuality, Volume One: An Introduction*. 1976. Trans. Robert Hurley. London: Penguin, 1979.

Frank, Robert, dir. *Pull My Daisy*. G-String Enterprises, 1959.

Freud, Sigmund. *Beyond the Pleasure Principle*. Trans. James Strachey. 1920. New York: Norton, 1961.

———. *Group Psychology and the Analysis of the Ego*. Trans. James Strachey. London: International Psychoanalytical, 1922.

Fuller, Richard Buckminster. *Earth Inc.* New York: Doubleday/Anchor, 1973.

———. *Utopia or Oblivion: The Prospects for Humanity*. London: Allen Lane, 1970.

Fuller, Richard Buckminster, Jerome Agel, and Quentin Fiore. *I Seem to Be a Verb*. New York: Bantam, 1970.

Gelber, Jack. *The Connection*. New York: Evergreen/Grove, 1960.

Genet, Jean, dir. *Chant d'Amour*. BFI, 1950.

———. *The Thief's Journal*. Trans. Bernard Frechtman. London: Penguin, 1967.

Giamo, Ben. *Kerouac, the Word and the Way: Prose Artist as Spiritual Quester*. Carbondale: Southern Illinois UP, 2000.

Gide, Andrè. *The Immoralist*. Trans. Dorothy Bussy. London: Penguin, 1960.

Gifford, Barry, and Lawrence Lee. *Jack's Book: An Oral Biography of Jack Kerouac*. New York: St. Martin's, 1978.

Ginsberg, Allen. *Allen Verbatim: Lectures on Poetry, Politics, Consciousness*. Ed. Gordon Ball. New York: McGraw-Hill, 1975.

———. *Deliberate Prose: Selected Essays, 1952–1995*. Ed. Bill Morgan. New York: Harper, 2000.

———. *The Fall of America: Poems of These States, 1965–1971*. San Francisco: City Lights, 1972.

———. *Howl and Other Poems*. San Francisco: City Lights, 1956.

———. *Journals: Early Fifties, Early Sixties*. New York: Grove, 1977.

———. *Kaddish and Other Poems, 1958–1960*. San Francisco: City Lights, 1961.

———. *Mystery in the Universe*. New York: Privately printed, 1965.

————. "Notes for *Howl and Other Poems*." 1957. *The Poetics of the New American Poetry*. Ed. Donald Allen and Warren Tallman. New York: Grove, 1973.

————. *Planet News, 1961–1967.* San Francisco: City Lights, 1968.

Godard, Jean-Luc, dir. *Vivre sa vie.* BFI, 1962.

Gold, Herbert. *Bohemia: Where Art, Angst, Love, and Strong Coffee Meet.* New York: Simon, 1993.

————. "Hip, Cool, Beat—and Frantic." *Nation* 184 (Nov. 16, 1957).

Goldman, Albert. *Ladies and Gentlemen, Lenny Bruce!* London: Penguin, 1991.

Goldthorpe, J. E. *Family Life in Western Societies: A Historical Sociology of Family Relationships in Britain and North America.* Cambridge: Cambridge UP, 1987.

Goldwater, Robert. "Reflections on the New York School." *Quadrum* 8 (1960).

Greenberg, Clement. *Art and Culture: Critical Essays.* Boston: Beacon, 1961.

Gris, Juan. *Letters.* Ed. and trans. Douglas Cooper. London: Privately printed, 1956.

Guston, Philip. "Statement." *It Is* 5 (Spring 1960).

Hemingway, Ernest. *A Movable Feast.* 1960. London: Arrow, 1994.

————. *To Have and Have Not.* London: Penguin, 1955.

Hess, Thomas B., and Harold Rosenberg. *Action Painting . . . 1958.* Dallas: Dallas Museum for Contemporary Arts, 1958.

Himes, Chester. *The Collected Stories.* New York: Thunder's Mouth, 1991.

————. *My Life of Absurdity: The Autobiography of Chester Himes, Volume Two.* New York: Doubleday, 1976.

Hoffman, Abbie, Jerry Rubin, and Ed Sanders. *Vote!* New York: Warner, 1972.

Hollander, John. Rev. of *Howl and Other Poems*, by Allen Ginsberg. *Partisan Review* 28 (Summer 1957).

Holmes, John Clellon. *Go!* 1952. New York: New American Library, 1980.

————. "The Philosophy of the Beat Generation." *Esquire*, Feb. 1958.

————. "This Is the Beat Generation." *New York Times Magazine*, Nov. 16, 1952.

*Howls, Raps and Roars: Recordings from the San Francisco Poetry Renaissance.* Fantasy CD set, 1993.

Hrebeniak, Michael. Introduction to *Arts Council of England Review of Jazz Funding.* Unpublished HM Government document, 1995.

Hughes, Langston. *Selected Poems.* New York: Knopf, 1959.

Hughes, Langston, Charles Mingus, and Leonard Feather. *Weary Blues.* Verve LP, 1958.

Hughes, Robert. *American Visions: The Epic History of Art in America.* London: Harvill, 1997.

————. "Effusiveness and Immersion: Review of 'Hand-Painted Pop: American Art in Transition, 1955–1962,' Whitney Museum of American Art." *Time*, Aug. 23, 1993.

————. *The Shock of the New.* London: Thames, 1981.

Huncke, Herbert. *The Evening Sun Turned Crimson.* Amsterdam: Neptune, 1980.

Hunt, Timothy. *Kerouac's Crooked Road: Development of a Fiction.* Hamden, CT: Archon, 1981.

Husserl, Edmund. *The Idea of Phenomenology.* Trans. Lee Hardy. Dordrecht/ Boston: Kluwer Academic, 1999.

Illich, Ivan. *Tools for Conviviality.* New York: Harper, 1973.

James, William. *The Principles of Psychology.* 1890. Cambridge: Harvard UP, 1981.

———. *The Varieties of Religious Experience.* 1902. London: Penguin, 1985.

Janik, Allan, and Stephen Toulmin. *Wittgenstein's Vienna.* New York: Simon, 1973.

Janis, Sidney. *Abstract and Surrealist Art in America.* New York: Reynal, 1944.

Joans, Ted. *Afrodisia.* London: Boyars, 1970.

Johnson, Joyce. "Outlaw Days." *The Beats*: Literary Bohemians in Postwar America. Detroit: Gale, 1984. Vol. 17 of *Dictionary of Literary Biography.* Ed. Matthew J. Bruccoli and Richard Layman. 328 vols. to date. 1978–2006.

Jones, James T. *Jack Kerouac's Duluoz Legend: The Mythic Form of an Autobiographical Fiction.* Carbondale: Southern Illinois UP, 1999.

Jones, LeRoi/Amiri Baraka. *Black Music.* New York: Morrow, 1968.

———. *Blues People: Negro Music in White America.* New York: Morrow, 1963.

———. "Letter about Kerouac's Spontaneous Prose." *Evergreen Review* 8 (1959). Reprinted in *The Penguin Book of the Beats.* Ed. Ann Charters. London: Penguin, 1992.

———. "Letter to the Editors." *Partisan Review* 32 (Summer 1958).

———, ed. *The Moderns: An Anthology of New Writing in America.* New York: Corinth, 1963.

———. *The Reader.* Ed. William J. Harris. New York: Thunder's Mouth, 1991.

Joyce, James. *Finnegans Wake.* London: Faber, 1939.

———. *A Portrait of the Artist as a Young Man.* 1916. London: Grafton, 1977.

———. *Selected Letters.* Ed. Richard Ellman. London: Faber, 1975.

———. *Ulysses.* 1922. London: Penguin, 1986.

Juran, Nathan, dir. *The Attack of the 50 Ft. Woman.* Warner, 1958.

———. *The Brain from Planet Arous.* Image Entertainment, 1958.

Keats, John. *The Complete Poems.* Ed. John Barnard. London: Penguin, 1986.

———. *Letters—A Selection.* Ed. Robert Gittings. Oxford: Oxford UP, 1970.

Kesey, Ken. *One Flew over the Cuckoo's Nest.* New York: Viking, 1962.

Kinsey, Alfred C., Wardell B. Pomeroy, and Clyde E. Martin. *Sexual Behavior in the Human Male.* Philadelphia: Saunders, 1948.

Knickerbocker, Conrad. "The Art of Fiction: William Seward Burroughs II." *Paris Review* 31 (Summer 1965). Reprinted in *Beat Writers at Work: The Paris Review.* Ed. George Plimpton. New York: Modern, 1999.

Kofsky, Frank. *Black Nationalism and the Revolution in Music.* New York: Pathfinder, 1970.

Konitz, Lee. *The Real Lee Konitz.* Atlantic LP, 1959.

Korzybski, Alfred. *Science and Sanity: An Introduction to Non-Aristotelian*

*Systems and General Semantics.* 1933. Englewood, NJ: International Non-Aristotelian Library, 1954.

Krim, Seymour, ed. "King of the Beats." *Commonweal* 69 (Jan. 2, 1959).

——. *Views of a Nearsighted Cannoneer.* New York: Excelsior, 1968.

Kuhn, Thomas. *The Structure of Scientific Revolutions.* Chicago: U of Chicago P, 1962.

Lacan, Jacques. *Écrits: A Selection.* Trans. Alan Sheridan. 1977. London: Routledge, 1989.

Laing, R. D. *The Self and Others: Further Studies in Sanity and Madness.* London: Tavistock, 1961.

Lawrence, D. H. *Aaron's Rod.* 1922. New York: Penguin, 1976.

——. *Kangaroo.* 1923. London: Penguin, 1989.

——. *Selected Critical Writings.* Oxford: Oxford UP, 1998.

——. *Studies in Classic American Literature.* 1924. London: Penguin, 1971.

——. *Women in Love.* 1920. London: Penguin, 1986.

Leary, Timothy. *Flashbacks: An Autobiography.* Los Angeles: Tarcher, 1983.

LeClair, Tom, and Larry McCaffery, eds. *Anything Can Happen: Interviews with Contemporary American Novelists.* Urbana: U of Illinois P, 1983.

Lee, A. Robert, ed. *The Beat Generation Writers.* London: Pluto, 1996.

Levin, Michael, and John S. Wilson. "No Bop Roots in Jazz: Parker." *Down Beat,* Sept. 9, 1949.

Lévi-Strauss, Claude. *The Savage Mind.* Chicago: U of Chicago P, 1966.

Lewis, Wyndham, ed. *Blast 1,* 1914. Santa Rosa: Black Sparrow, 1989.

Lifton, Robert Jay. *Boundaries: Psychological Man in Revolution.* New York: Vintage, 1970.

Lipset, Seymour Martin, and Reinhard Bendix. *Social Mobility in Industrial Society.* Berkeley: U of California P, 1959.

Lipton, Lawrence. *The Holy Barbarians.* New York: Messner, 1959.

Litweiler, John. *The Freedom Principle: Jazz after 1958.* New York: Morrow, 1984.

London, Jack. *"The Call of the Wild," "White Fang" and Other Stories.* London: Penguin, 1981.

——. *On the Road: The Tramp Diary, and Other Hobo Writings.* Ed. Richard W. Etulain. Logan: Utah State UP, 1979.

Loy, Mina. *Lunar Baedeker and Time-Tables: Selected Poems.* Highlands, NC: Williams, 1958.

Lynd, Robert, and Helen Lynd. *Middletown.* New York: Dutton, 1929.

MacDonald, Dwight. *Against the American Grain.* New York: Random, 1963.

MacDougall, Ranald, dir. *The Subterraneans.* MGM, 1960.

Madden, Andrew P. "The Art of Poetry: Lawrence Ferlinghetti." *Paris Review* 147 (Summer 1998). Reprinted in *Beat Writers at Work: The Paris Review.* Ed. George Plimpton. New York: Modern, 1999.

Mailer, Norman. *Advertisements for Myself.* 1959. Cambridge: Harvard UP, 1992.

——. "Gaining an Empire, Losing Democracy?" *International Herald Tribune,* Feb. 25, 2003.

Malanga, Gerard. "The Art of Poetry: Charles Olson." *Paris Review* 50 (Spring 1970). Reprinted in *Beat Writers at Work*: The Paris Review. Ed. George Plimpton. New York: Modern, 1999.

Mallarmé, Stephané. *Selected Poetry and Prose.* Ed. Mary Ann Caws. New York: New Directions, 1982.

Malraux, Andre. *The Voices of Silence.* Trans. Stuart Gilbert. New York: Doubleday, 1953.

Marcuse, Herbert. *One Dimensional Man.* London: Routledge, 1964.

Mascaro, Juan, trans. *The Dhammapada.* London: Penguin, 1973.

Maynard, John A. *Venice West: The Beat Generation in Southern California.* New Brunswick: Rutgers UP, 1993.

McClure, Michael. *The Beard.* San Francisco: Coyote, 1967.

———. *Ghost Tantras.* San Francisco: Four Seasons Foundation, 1964.

———. *Hymns to St. Geryon.* San Francisco: Auerhahn, 1959.

———. "Painting Beat by Numbers." *The Rolling Stone Book of the Beats.* Ed. Holly George Warren. London: Bloomsbury, 1999.

———. *Scratching the Beat Surface.* San Francisco: North Point, 1992.

———. *Simple Eyes & Other Poems.* New York: New Directions, 1994.

———. "Wolf Net." *Io* 20 (1974).

McGann, Jerome J. *The Romantic Ideology.* Chicago: U of Chicago P, 1983.

McLintock, Jack. "This Is How the Ride Ends." *Esquire,* Mar. 1970.

McLuhan, Marshall. *The Gutenberg Galaxy.* London: Routledge, 1962.

———. *The Mechanical Bride.* 1951. London: Routledge, 1967.

McNally, Dennis. *Desolate Angel: Jack Kerouac, The Beat Generation and America.* New York: Delta, 1990.

Mellers, Wilfred. *Music in a New Found Land: Themes and Developments in the History of American Music.* 1965. London: Faber, 1987.

Melville, Herman. *The Confidence Man: His Masquerade.* 1857. New York: Airmont, 1966.

———. *The Letters of Herman Melville.* New Haven: Yale UP, 1960.

———. *Moby Dick; Or, The Whale.* 1851. New York: Norton, 1967.

Mezzrow, Mezz, and Bernard Wolfe. *Really the Blues.* 1946. London: Harper, 1993.

Michaux, Henri. *Darkness Moves: An Henri Michaux Anthology, 1927–1984.* Ed. and trans. David Ball. Berkeley: U of California P, 1994.

Miles, Barry. *Jack Kerouac, King of the Beats: A Portrait.* London: Virgin, 1998.

Miller, Alan, dir. *John Cage: I Have Nothing to Say and I Am Saying It.* WNET-New York, 1990.

Miller, Arthur. *Timebends: An Autobiography.* New York: Grove, 1987.

———. *A View from the Bridge/All My Sons.* London: Penguin, 1961.

Miller, Henry. *The Air Conditioned Nightmare.* New York: New Directions, 1945.

———. *Big Sur and the Oranges of Hieronymous Bosch.* New York: New Directions, 1957.

———. *The Colossus of Maroussi.* 1941. London: Penguin, 1950.

———. *Hamlet, Volume One.* Puerto Rico: Carrefour, 1939.

———. *Stand Still Like the Hummingbird.* New York: New Directions, 1962.

———. *Tropic of Cancer.* 1934. New York: Grove, 1961.

———. *Tropic of Capricorn.* 1939. London: Calder, 1964.

———. *The Wisdom of the Heart.* New York: New Directions, 1960.

Millstein, Gilbert. Rev. of *On the Road,* by Jack Kerouac. *New York Times,* Sept. 5, 1957.

Monk, Thelonious. *Genius of Modern Music, Volumes One and Two, 1947–1952.* Blue Note CD, 1989.

Morgan, Speer, ed. "Living on the Fringe: The Jack Kerouac Letters." *Missouri Review* 17.3 (1994).

Motherwell, Robert, ed. *The Dada Painters and Poets: An Anthology.* 1951. Boston: Belknap/Harvard, 1981.

Motherwell, Robert, and Adolph Reinhardt, eds. *Modern Artists in America.* New York: Henborn, Schultz, 1951.

Motte, Warren F., Jr. *Oulipo: A Primer of Potential Literature.* Lincoln: U of Nebraska P, 1986.

Mottram, Eric. *Blood on the Nash Ambassador: Investigations in American Culture.* London: Hutchinson Radius, 1989.

———. "Living Mythically: The Thirties." *Journal of American Studies* 6.3 (Dec. 1972).

———. "Notes for Feldman Lecture, Tate Gallery: Feldman—Rothko—O'Hara." *Spanner* 3.9 (1973).

———. "Notes on Poetics." *Journal of Comparative Poïetics* 1.1 (Spring 1989).

———. "Paul Blackburn: Writing, Inscription and Performance." *Ninth Decade* 10 (1989).

———. "A Preface to *Visions of Cody.*" *The Review of Contemporary Fiction* 3.2 (Summer 1983).

———. *Selected Poems.* Twickenham: North and South, 1989.

———. "A Treacherous Assault on British Poetry." *The New British Poetry.* Ed. Gillian Allnut, Fred D'Aguiar, Ken Edwards, and Eric Mottram. London: Paladin, 1988.

———. *William Burroughs: The Algebra of Need.* London: Boyars, 1977.

Mumford, Lewis. *The Pentagon of Power: The Myth of the Machine.* New York: Harcourt, 1970.

———. *Technics and Civilisation.* London: Routledge, 1934.

Murray, Albert. *Stomping the Blues.* New York: McGraw-Hill, 1976.

Nicosia, Gerald. *Memory Babe: A Critical Biography of Jack Kerouac.* 1983. Berkeley: U of California P, 1994.

Nietzsche, Friedrich. *The Anti-Christ.* Trans. R. J. Hollingdale. London: Penguin, 1969.

———. *The Birth of Tragedy.* Trans. Clifton P. Fadiman. New York: Modern, 1927.

Nuttall, Jeff. "In Memory of Eric Mottram." *Radical Poetics* 1 (1997).

Nyman, Michael. *Experimental Music: Cage and Beyond.* New York: Schirmer, 1974.

O'Hara, Frank. *The Collected Poems.* Ed. Donald Allen. New York: Knopf, 1972.

Olson, Charles. *Additional Prose.* Ed. George Butterick. Bolinas: Four Seasons, 1974.

———. *Collected Prose.* Ed. Donald Allen and Benjamin Friedlander. Berkeley: U of California P, 1997.

———. *The Maximus Poems.* Berkeley: U of California P, 1983.

———. *Selected Poems.* Ed. Robert Creeley. Berkeley: U of California P, 1993.

———. *Selected Writings.* Ed. Robert Creeley. New York: New Directions, 1966.

———. *The Special View of History.* Ed. Ann Charters. Berkeley: Oyez, 1970,.

Olson, Charles, and Robert Creeley. *The Complete Correspondence, Volume IV.* Ed. George Butterick. Santa Barbara: Black Sparrow, 1980.

O'Neil, Paul. "Beats: Sad but Noisy Rebels." *Life,* Nov. 30, 1959.

Ong, Walter J. *The Barbarian Within, and Other Fugitive Essays and Studies.* New York: Macmillan, 1962.

———. *In the Human Grain: Further Explorations of Contemporary Culture.* New York: Macmillan, 1967.

———. *Orality and Literacy: The Technologizing of the Word.* London: Methuen, 1982.

"On the Road Back: How the Beat Generation Got That Way, According to Its Seer." *San Francisco Examiner,* Oct. 5, 1958.

Orme, J. E. *Time, Experience and Behaviour.* London: Iliffe, 1969.

Orwell, George. "W. B. Yeats." *Horizon,* Jan. 1943.

Parker, Charlie. *Bird and Diz.* Verve LP, 1950.

———. *The Dial Masters: Original Choice Takes.* Spotlight CD, 1995.

Parkinson, Thomas, ed. *A Casebook on the Beat.* New York: Crowell, 1961.

Partch, Harry. *The Music of Harry Partch.* CRI CD, 1989.

Pell, Richard. *The Liberal Mind in a Conservative Age: American Intellectuals in the 1940s and 1950s.* Middletown, CT: Wesleyan UP, 1989.

Pepper, Curtis. "The Indomitable de Kooning." *New York Times Magazine,* Nov. 20, 1983.

Phillips, Lisa, ed. *Beat Culture and the New America: 1950–1965.* Paris: Whitney Museum of American Art/Flammarion, 1995.

Piaget, Jean. *Biology and Knowledge: An Essay on the Relations Between Organic Regulations and Cognitive Processes.* Trans. B. Walsh Chicago: U of Chicago P, 1971.

Pilger, John. *Hidden Agendas.* London: Vintage, 1998.

Plato. *The Republic.* Ed. and trans. James Adam. Cambridge: Cambridge UP, 1963.

Plimpton, George, ed. *Beat Writers at Work: The Paris Review.* New York: Modern, 1999.

———, ed. *Writers at Work: The Paris Review Interviews, Fourth Series.* New York: Penguin, 1976.

Podhoretz, Norman. "The Know-Nothing Bohemians." *Partisan Review* 25 (Spring 1958).

——. *Making It.* New York: Random, 1959.

Pollock, Jackson. "Excerpts from an Interview Taped by William Wright." *Art in America* 53.4 (Aug.–Sept. 1965).

——. "My Painting." *Possibilities* 1 (Winter 1947–48).

Potter, Jeffrey. *To a Violent Grave: An Oral Biography of Jackson Pollock.* New York: Pushcart, 1985.

Pound, Ezra. *Antheil and the Treatise on Harmony.* Paris: Three Mountains, 1924.

——. *The Cantos.* London: Faber, 1954.

——. "A Few Don'ts by an Imagiste." *Poetry* 1.6 (Mar. 1913).

——. *Gaudier-Brzeska: A Memoir.* New York: New Directions, 1974.

——. *Guide to Kulchur.* 1938. London: Owen, 1952.

——. *The Literary Essays of Ezra Pound.* Ed. T. S. Eliot. London: Faber, 1960.

——. *Personae.* New York: New Directions, 1949.

Proust, Marcel. *Remembrance of Things Past, Volumes One to Three.* Trans. C. K. Scott Moncrieff and Terence Kilmartin. London: Penguin, 1983.

Pulver, Max. "Jesus' Round Dance and Crucifixion According to the Acts of St. John." *The Mysteries: Papers from the Eranos Yearbooks.* Ed. Joseph Campbell. Princeton, NJ: Princeton UP, 1978.

Pynchon, Thomas. *The Crying of Lot 49.* 1966. London: Picador, 1979.

——. *Gravity's Rainbow.* 1973. London: Picador, 1974.

Ray, Nicholas, dir. *Rebel Without a Cause.* Warner, 1955.

Reed, Ishmael. *Yellow Back Radio Broke-Down.* New York: Doubleday, 1969.

Reich, Wilhelm. *The Mass Psychology of Fascism.* Trans. Vincent R. Carfagno. 1946. London: Souvenir, 1972.

Reisner, Robert, ed. *Bird: The Legend of Charlie Parker.* 1962. New York: Da Capo, 1977.

Rexroth, Kenneth. "The Beat Generation." BBC radio broadcast, 1966.

——. *Bird in the Bush: Obvious Essays.* New York: New Directions, 1959.

——. "Disengagement: The Art of the Beat Generation." *New World Writing,* no. 11. New York: New American Library, 1957. Reprinted in *A Casebook on the Beat.* Ed. Thomas Parkinson. New York: Crowell, 1961.

Riefenstahl, Leni, dir. *Olympia.* Homevision, 1938.

——. *Triumph of the Will.* Timeless, 1935.

Riesman, David, Nathan Glazer, and Reuel Denney. *The Lonely Crowd: A Study of the Changing American Character.* New Haven: Yale UP, 1950.

Rimbaud, Arthur. *Complete Works and Selected Letters.* Trans. Wallace Fowlie. Chicago: U of Chicago P, 1966.

"Roadster." *New York Herald Tribune,* Books and Authors sec., Sept. 22, 1957.

Robbe-Grillet, Alain. *Snapshots and For a New Novel.* Trans. Barbara Wright. London: Calder, 1965.

Robertson, Bryan. *Jackson Pollock.* London: Thames and Hudson, 1960.

Rosenberg, Harold. *Art on the Edge.* Chicago: U of Chicago P, 1975.

———. *Artworks and Packages.* 1969. Chicago: U of Chicago P, 1982.

———. "The Art World: The Mythic Art." *New Yorker* 43.11 (May 1967).

———. "Hans Hofmann: Nature into Action." *Art News* 56.2 (May 1957).

———. *The Tradition of the New.* New York: Horizon, 1960.

Rothenberg, Jerome. *Pre-faces and Other Writings.* New York: New Directions, 1981.

Rothenberg, Jerome, and Diane Rothenberg, eds. *Symposium of the Whole: A Range of Discourse Toward an Ethnopoetics.* Berkeley: U of California P, 1983.

Rothenberg, Jerome, and Pierre Joris, eds. *Poems for the Millennium: The University of California Book of Modern and Postmodern Poetry, Volume One, From Fin-de-Siècle to Negritude.* Berkeley: U of California P, 1995.

———. *Poems for the Millennium: The University of California Book of Modern and Postmodern Poetry, Volume Two, From Postwar to Millennium.* Berkeley: U of California P, 1998.

Russell, Ross. *Bird Lives!* 1972. London: Quartet, 1976.

Said, Edward. *Orientalism.* London: Routledge, 1978.

Sanders, Ed. *Tales of Beatnik Glory.* New York: Citadel, 1990.

Santayana, George. *Skepticism and Animal Faith: Introduction to a System of Philosophy.* New York: Dover, 1955.

Saroyan, William. *The Reader.* New York: Braziller, 1958.

Sartre, Jean-Paul. *Existentialism and Humanism.* Trans. Bernard Frechtman. London: Methuen, 1948.

———. *What Is Literature?* Trans. Bernard Frechtman. London: Methuen, 1950.

Schlosser, Eric. *Fast Food Nation.* London: Penguin, 2002.

Schoenberg, Arnold. *Self-Portrait: A Collection of Articles, Programme Notes, and Letters by the Composer about His Own Works.* Ed. Nuria Schoenberg. Pacific Palisades: Belmont Music, 1988.

Scholes, Robert. *Fabulation and Metafiction.* Urbana: U of Illinois P, 1979.

Schwitters, Kurt. *Poems Performances Pieces Proses Plays Poetics.* Ed. Jerome Rothenberg and Pierre Joris. Philadelphia: Temple UP, 1983.

Seelye, Catherine, ed. *Charles Olson and Ezra Pound: An Encounter at St. Elizabeth's.* New York: Grossman, 1975.

Seitz, William C. *The Art of Assemblage.* New York: Museum of Modern Art, 1961.

Shelley, Percy Bysshe. *Shelley's Prose.* Ed. David Lee Clark. London: Fourth Estate, 1988.

Skelt, Peterjohn. *Prospect into Breath: Interviews with North and South Writers.* Twickenham: North and South, 1991.

Smith, Larry. *Lawrence Ferlinghetti: Poet at Large.* Carbondale: Southern Illinois UP, 1983.

Smith, Patrick. "Remembering the Past." *Time,* Apr. 28, 1997.

Snyder, Gary. *Earth House Hold.* New York: New Directions, 1969.

———. *A Place in Space.* Washington, DC: Counterpoint, 1995.

———. *The Practice of the Wild.* New York: North Point, 1990.

————. *The Real Work: Interviews and Talks, 1964–1979*. New York: New Directions, 1980.

Spellman, A. B. *Four Lives in the Bebop Business*. 1966. New York: Limelight, 1985.

Spengler, Oswald. *The Decline of the West*. Ed. Helmut Werner. Trans. Charles Francis Atkinson. 1932. Oxford: Oxford UP, 1991.

"Squaresville U.S.A. vs. Beatsville." *Life*, Sept. 21, 1959.

Stearns, Marshall W. *The Story of Jazz*. London: Oxford UP, 1972.

Stein, Gertrude. *Four in America*. 1934. New Haven: Yale UP, 1947.

————. *Lectures in America*. 1935. London: Virago, 1988.

————. *What Are Masterpieces*. Los Angeles: Conference, 1940.

————. *Writings 1903–1932*. Ed. Catherine Stimpson. New York: Library of America, 1998.

Stephenson, Gregory. *The Daybreak Boys: Essays on the Literature of the Beat Generation*. Carbondale: Southern Illinois UP, 1990.

Sterne, Laurence. *The Life and Opinions of Tristram Shandy*. 1767. London: Penguin, 1985.

Sukenick, Ronald. *Down and In: Life in the Underground*. New York: Beech Tree, 1987.

Suzuki, Daisetz T. *Zen and Japanese Culture*. Princeton, NJ: Princeton UP/ Bollingen, 1959.

Swartz, Omar. *The View from "On the Road": The Rhetorical Vision of Jack Kerouac*. Carbondale: Southern Illinois UP, 1999.

Sylvester, David. "An Interview with Franz Kline." *Living Arts* 1.1 (Spring 1963).

Tallman, Warren. "Kerouac's Sound." *Tamarack Review* Spring 1959.

Tanner, Tony. *The American Mystery: American Literature from Emerson to DeLillo*. Cambridge: Cambridge UP, 2000.

Thoreau, Henry David. *Excursions: The Writings of Henry David Thoreau*, Volume IX. New York: Riverside, 1894.

————. *Walden; or, Life in the Woods*. 1854. New York: Dover, 1985.

Tipple, John. *Crisis of the American Dream: A History of American Social Thought, 1920–1940*. New York: Pegasus, 1968.

Townsend, Benjamin. "An Interview with Clyfford Still." *Gallery Notes*, Albright-Knox Art Gallery, 24.2 (Summer 1961).

Tristano, Lennie. *Digression*. Capitol 78', 1949.

————. *Yesterdays/Intuition*. Capitol 78', 1949.

Tuchman, Maurice, ed. *New York School: The First Generation*. New York: New York Graphic Society, 1965.

Turner, Frederick Jackson. *Frontier and Section*. Ed. R. A. Billington. Englewood Cliffs, NJ: Prentice Hall, 1961.

Turner, Steve. *Angelheaded Hipster: A Life of Jack Kerouac*. New York: Viking, 1996.

Twain, Mark. *The Adventures of Huckleberry Finn*. 1884. London: Bloomsbury, 1996.

Twelve Southerners. *I'll Take My Stand: The South and the Agrarian Tradition.* New York: Harper, 1930.

Tytell, John. *Naked Angels: The Life and Literature of the Beat Generation.* New York: McGraw-Hill, 1976.

Unger, Irwin. *A History of the American New Left, 1959–72.* New York: Harper, 1974.

Valéry, Paul. *Collected Works, Volume Two: Poems in the Rough.* Ed. Jackson Mathews. Trans. Hilary Corke. Princeton, NJ: Princeton UP, 1969.

Virilio, Paul. *Open Sky.* Trans. Julie Rose. London: Verso, 1997.

Wagner, Linda, and Lewis MacAdams, Jr. "The Art of Poetry: Robert White Creeley." *Paris Review* 44 (Winter 1968). Reprinted in *Beat Writers at Work: The Paris Review.* Ed. George Plimpton. New York: Modern, 1999.

Wakefield, Dan. *New York in the Fifties.* Boston and New York: Houghton/Seymour Lawrence, 1992.

Waldman, Anne, and Andrew Schelling, eds. *Disembodied Poetics: Annals of the Jack Kerouac School.* Albuquerque: U of New Mexico P, 1995.

Wallace, Mike. "Mike Wallace Asks Jack Kerouac, 'What Is the Beat Generation?'" *New York Post,* Jan. 21, 1958.

Warhol, Andy, dir. *The Chelsea Girls.* Raro, 1966.

———. *The Philosophy of Andy Warhol: From A to B and Back Again.* London: Cassell, 1975.

———, dir. *Sleep.* Andy Warhol Museum, 1963.

Watts, Alan. *Beat Zen, Square Zen, Zen.* San Francisco: City Lights, 1959.

Weinreich, Regina. *The Spontaneous Poetics of Jack Kerouac: A Study of the Fiction.* Carbondale: Southern Illinois UP, 1987.

Whitehead, Alfred North. *Process and Reality.* New York: Free, 1979.

Whitman, Walt. *The Complete Poems.* Ed. Francis Murphy. London: Penguin, 1986.

———. *Democratic Vistas: 1860–1880.* Ed. Alan Trachtenberg. New York: Braziller, 1970.

Whyte, William H. *The Organization Man.* New York: Simon, 1956.

Wiener, Norbert. *The Human Use of Human Beings.* Boston: Houghton, 1950.

Wilentz, Elias, ed. *The Beat Scene.* New York: Corinth, 1960.

Wilhelm, Hellmut. *Heaven, Earth and Man in the Book of Changes.* Seattle: U of Washington P, 1917.

Willener, Alfred. *The Action-Image of Society.* Trans. A. M. Sheridan-Smith. London: Tavistock, 1970.

Williams, William Carlos. *The Autobiography.* New York: New Directions, 1948.

———. *The Collected Shorter Poems.* New York: New Directions, 1951.

———. *Imaginations.* New York: New Directions, 1972.

———. *In the American Grain.* 1925. New York: New Directions, 1956.

———. *Paterson.* 1963. New York: New Directions, 1995.

———. *Selected Essays.* New York: New Directions, 1954.

Williamson, Henry. *Goodbye West Country.* London: Putnam, 1937.

Williamson, Kevin, ed. *Rebel Yell.* Edinburgh: Rebel, 1998.

Wilmer, Valerie. *Jazz People.* 1970. London: Allison, 1977.

Wilson, Sloan. *The Man in the Gray Flannel Suit.* New York: Simon, 1955.

Winn, Janet. "Capote, Mailer and Miss Parker." *New Republic,* Feb. 9, 1959.

Wittgenstein, Ludwig. *Philosophical Investigations.* Trans. G. E. M. Anscombe. Oxford: Blackwell, 1967.

———. *Tractatus Logico-Philosophicus.* Trans. D. F. Pears and B. F. McGuiness. London: Routledge, 1961.

Wolf, Daniel, and Edwin Fancher, eds. *The Village Voice Reader: A Mixed Bag from the Greenwich Village Newspaper.* New York: Doubleday, 1962.

Wolfe, Thomas. *Look Homeward, Angel.* 1929. London: Penguin, 1984.

Woolf, Virginia. *Collected Essays, Volume Two.* Ed. Leonard Woolf. London: Hogarth, 1966.

———. *The Common Reader.* London: Hogarth, 1925.

———. *The Diary of Virginia Woolf, Volume Three: 1925–1930.* Ed. Annie Olivier Bell. London: Hogarth, 1980.

———. *Mrs. Dalloway.* 1925. London: Grafton, 1989.

———. *To the Lighthouse.* 1927. London: Grafton, 1987.

———. *The Waves.* 1931. Oxford: Blackwell, 1993.

Wordsworth, William. *The Poetical Works.* London: Oxford UP, 1917.

Wright Mills, C. *The Power Elite.* New York: Oxford UP, 1956.

———. *White Collar: The American Middle Classes.* New York: Oxford UP, 1951.

Yeats, W. B. *Essays.* London: Macmillan, 1924.

———. *Poems: A New Selection.* Ed. A. Norman Jeffares. London: Macmillan, 1984.

Young, J. Z. *An Introduction to the Study of Man.* Oxford: Clarendon, 1971.

Zukofsky, Louis. *All: The Collected Shorter Poems, 1956–64.* New York: Norton, 1966

# Index

**Michael Hrebeniak** teaches at Cambridge and Cranfield universities, having previously been Lecturer in Humanities at the Royal Academy of Music. He has produced CD recordings and documentaries on poetry for Channel 4 TV, and his arts journalism has appeared in the *Guardian* and the *Observer* and on BBC Radio. He is the editor of *Radical Poetics*.